Greek Satyr Play

CALIFORNIA CLASSICAL STUDIES

NUMBER 3

Editorial Board Chair: Donald Mastronarde

Editorial Board: Alessandro Barchiesi, Todd Hickey, Emily Mackil, Richard Martin, Robert Morstein-Marx, J. Theodore Peña, Kim Shelton

California Classical Studies publishes peer-reviewed long-form scholarship with online open access and print-on-demand availability. The primary aim of the series is to disseminate basic research (editing and analysis of primary materials both textual and physical), data-heavy research, and highly specialized research of the kind that is either hard to place with the leading publishers in Classics or extremely expensive for libraries and individuals when produced by a leading academic publisher. In addition to promoting archaeological publications, papyrological and epigraphic studies, technical textual studies, and the like, the series will also produce selected titles of a more general profile.

The startup phase of this project (2013–2015) is supported by a grant from the Andrew W. Mellon Foundation.

Also in the series:

Number 1: Leslie Kurke, *The Traffic in Praise: Pindar and the Poetics of Social Economy*, 2013

Number 2: Edward Courtney, *A Commentary on the Satires of Juvenal*, 2013

GREEK SATYR PLAY

Five Studies

Mark Griffith

CALIFORNIA
CLASSICAL
STUDIES

Berkeley, California

New material (Preface, Introduction) © 2015 by Mark Griffith.

Chapter 1: "Slaves of Dionysos: Satyrs, Audience, and the Ends of the *Oresteia.*" *Classical Antiquity* 22 (2002) 195-258. © 2002 The University of California Press. By permission of University of California Press.

Chapter 2: "Satyrs, Citizens, and Self-Presentation," *Satyr Drama: Tragedy at Play*, ed. G. W. M. Harrison (Swansea 2005) 161-99. © 2005 Mark Griffith. By permission of Anton Powell and the Classical Press of Wales.

Chapter 3: "Sophocles' Satyr-plays and the Language of Romance," *Sophocles and the Greek Language: Aspects of Diction, Syntax and Pragmatics*, eds I. J. F. de Jong and A. Rijksbaron (*Mnemosyne Supplement* 269, Leiden 2006) 51-72. © 2008 Koninklijke Brill NV, Leiden. By permission of Koninklijke Brill NV. http://www.brill.com/publications/mnemosyne-supplements

Chapter 4: "Satyr Play and Tragedy, Face to Face," *The Pronomos Vase and its Context*, eds. O. Taplin and R. Wyles (Oxford 2010) 47-63. © 2010 Oliver Taplin and Rosie Wyles. By permission of Oxford University Press. www.oup.com

Chapter 5: "Greek Middlebrow Drama (Something to Do with Aphrodite?)," *Performance, Iconography, Reception: Studies in Honour of Oliver Taplin*, eds. M. Revermann and P. Wilson (Oxford 2008) 59-87. © 2008 Oxford University Press. By permission of Oxford University Press. www.oup.com

California Classical Studies
c/o Department of Classics
University of California
Berkeley, California 94720–2520
USA
http://calclassicalstudies.org
email: ccseditorial@berkeley.edu

ISBN 9781939926043

Library of Congress Control Number: 2015935048

CONTENTS

Preface vii
Abbreviations x
List of Figures xii

    Introduction 1
1. Slaves of Dionysos: Satyrs, Audience, and the Ends of the *Oresteia* 14
    FIGURES *appear after page* 74
2. Satyrs, Citizens, and Self-Presentation 75
3. Sophocles' Satyr Plays and the Language of Romance 109
4. Satyr Play and Tragedy, Face to Face (and East to West?): The Pronomos Vase 129
5. Greek Middlebrow Drama (Something to Do with Aphrodite?) 146

Bibliography 170
Index of Authors and Works Discussed 183
General Index 185

PREFACE

This collection of "Five Studies" is intended to make more readily available, and to a wider audience, the journal articles and chapters in conference volumes or Festschrifts that I published on the subject of Greek satyr drama between 2002 and 2010. The five chapters are fairly coherent and coordinated between one another, and develop a broadly consistent account of this major performance genre within fifth-century Athenian culture; but I did not write them originally with an eye to their becoming a single monograph, and they do not claim in any sense to be comprehensive in their coverage of this whole topic. These are still just "five studies"; and each of them still bears the marks of its original context of publication. In particular, there is some overlap here and there (especially between Chapters 1 and 2), and some inevitable repetition in the introductory material to each Chapter, as I outline (originally, to quite different audiences/readerships) my overall approach to the study of Greek tragedy and satyr play in their original social context.

In preparing these five contributions for re-publication in this volume, I have not attempted any large-scale revisions or updates. Each Chapter is presented essentially as it was originally published, with just a few minor corrections and some cross-references. Thus, for example, the spelling and citation conventions differ in some cases from one chapter to another. I hope this is not found to be too distracting. Occasionally I have indicated within square brackets the existence of more recent work on a particular topic that has been published since the first appearance of my article. For ease of citation and reference back to the original publications, their page numbers are included (likewise in square brackets) within the text throughout. The Introduction has been newly composed for this volume, and there I make note of some of the most important contributions relating to Greek satyr drama that have appeared over the last ten years or so, while also attempting to contextualize my own work within the scholarly currents of the 1990s and 2000s.

I am very grateful to several individuals and institutions for generously allowing me to reproduce in this volume materials (text and/or images) that were originally published elsewhere: the University of California Press and the Editors of *Classical Antiquity* (Chapter 1); George W. M. Harrison, along with Anton Powell and the Classical Press of Wales (Chapter 2); Albert Rijksbaron and Irene De Jong, along with Brill Publishers (Chapter 3); Martin Revermann and Peter Wilson, Oliver Taplin and Rosie Wyles, along with the Oxford University Press (Chapters 4 and 5).

For permission to reproduce particular images I warmly thank the following: Staatliche Antikensammlungen und Glyptothek, Munich (Fig. 4); Thomas Mannack (Beazley Archive) and the Oxford University Press (Fig. 5c); Kunsthistorisches Museum, Vienna (Fig. 8a); The Martin von Wagner Museum, Universität Würzburg (Fig. 8b); The Trustees of the British Museum, London (Fig. 10); The Houghton Library, Harvard University (Figs. 11 and 12).

In three cases (Figs 1, 2, 7), I have used for this volume drawings of vase-images, rather than the photographs reproduced in the original publications. I am especially indebted and grateful to Elizabeth Wahle (Fig. 2) and François Lissarrague (Fig. 7) for their drawings and for their gracious permission to publish them in this volume. I also thank Eric Csapo for his permission to include E. R. Malyon's drawing of the Pronomos Vase (Fig. 5b).

I would like to take this occasion to thank once again those who, by inviting me to participate in conferences or commemorative volumes, originally spurred me to think more seriously and specifically about various aspects of Greek satyr play, and subsequently to write up the results: in particular, the Ohio State University's Classics Department (for Chapter 1), George W. M. Harrison and Jane E. Francis (Chapter 2); Albert Rijskbaron and Irene De Jong (Chapter 3); Martin Revermann and Peter Wilson (Chapter 4); Oliver Taplin, Edith Hall, Amanda Wrigley, and Rosie Wyles (Chapter 5). Further acknowledgments to individual scholars whose expertise and advice were helpful to me are appended to particular Chapters, in the form in which these appeared in the original publications.

Several of the ideas that made their way into these chapters—especially ideas formulated in the early stages (i.e., during the late 1990s), when I was focusing mainly on tragedy but beginning to notice elements of satyr play that seemed suggestively relevant—eventually emerged and became more coherent and better articulated thanks to the critiques, advice, and example of several of my Berkeley colleagues and graduate students: in particular, I owe large debts of various kinds to the late Janet Adelman; to Carol Clover, Kathleen McCarthy, and the late Crawford Greenewalt; and to Erik Gunderson, Peter Mostkoff, David Jacobson, Roger Travis, and Victoria Wohl. My good fortune in holding a joint position within two different departments at Berkeley, i.e. Classics and TDPS (Theater, Dance, and Performance Studies), was also crucial, and I am grateful for opportunities given me to present informally some portions of this work at various times to both constituencies.

For the practical preparation of this volume for the series California Classical Studies I acknowledge an enormous debt of gratitude to two individuals above all: Anna Pisarello and Donald Mastronarde.

I wish to express my thanks and appreciation to five friends and colleagues who have helped me over the years, perhaps more than they each realize, to keep seeking to expand my horizons in the exploration of ancient Greek culture, literature, and mentalities—while also, each of them in different ways, always being willing to offer particular advice, inspiration, and acute, patient correction, as well as their own exemplary scholarly practice: Leslie Kurke, Donald Mastronarde, Bernd Seidensticker, Victoria Wohl, and Froma Zeitlin. These "Five Studies" could never have come into existence without the distinctive input, example, and encouragement of each of them. Above all, I am grateful to two of these, my long-time Berkeley colleagues Leslie Kurke and Donald Mastronarde, for their unfailing support, advice, and unmatched expertise. I dedicate this book to them.

Mark Griffith
Berkeley, July 2015

ABBREVIATIONS

ARV^2 = Beazley, J. D., ed. *Athenian Red-Figure Vasepainters*. 2nd ed. Oxford, 1963.
CHCL = *Cambridge History of Classical Literature*
CPG = von Leutsche, E. L., and F. G. Schneidewin, *Corpus Paroemiographorum Graecorum*. 2 vols. Göttingen, 1839–1851.
KPS = Krumeich, R., N. Pechstein, and B. Seidensticker, eds. *Das griechische Satyrspiel*. Darmstadt, 1999.
LIMC = *Lexicon Iconographicum Mythologiae Classicae*. 8 vols. Zurich, 1981–1997.
PMG = Page, D. L., ed. *Poetae Melici Graeci*. Oxford, 1959.
PMGF = Davies, M., ed. *Poetarum Melicorum Graecorum Fragmenta*. Vol. 1, Oxford, 1991.
RE = Pauly, A., and G. Wissowa, *Realencyclopädie der classischen Altertumswissenschaft*, ed. W. Kranz et al. 1894–1978.
TLG = Thesaurus Linguae Graecae (http://stephanus.tlg.uci.edu)
TrGF = Snell, B., S. Radt, and R. Kannicht, eds. *Tragicorum Graecorum Fragmenta*. 5 vols. Göttingen, 1971–2005.

Journal Abbreviations

AJA	*American Journal of Archaeology*
AJP	*American Journal of Philology*
BCH	*Bulletin de correspondance hellénique*
BICS	*Bulletin of the Institute of Classical Studies* (London)
C&M	*Classica et Mediaevalia*
CA	*Classical Antiquity*
CJ	*Classical Journal*
CP	*Classical Philology*
CQ	*Classical Quarterly*
CR	*Classical Review*
CSCA	*California Studies in Classical Antiquity*
G&R	*Greece & Rome*
GRBS	*Greek, Roman, and Byzantine Studies*
HSCP	*Harvard Studies in Classical Philology*

ICS	Illinois Classical Studies
JDAI	Jahrbuch des Deutschen Archäologischen Instituts
JHS	Journal of Hellenic Studies
LCM	Liverpool Classical Monthly
MDAI(A)	Mitteilungen des Deutschen Archäologischen Instituts (Athenische Abteilung)
MH	Museum Helveticum
PCPS	Proceedings of the Cambridge Philological Society
QUCC	Quaderni Urbinati di Cultura Classica
RhM	Rheinisches Museum
RFIC	Rivista di filologia e di instruzione classica
RCS	Rivista di Studi Classici
SBAW	Sitzungsberichte der Bayerischen Akademie der Wissenschaften
SIFC	Studi italiani di filologia classica

LIST OF FIGURES

Figure 1: Return of Hephaestus with satyrs. Detail of Attic Black-Figure volute-krater by Kleitias and Ergotimos ("François Vase"; sixth century BCE). Museo Archeologico, Florence 4209.
Facsimile from A. Furtwängler and K. Reichhold, *Griechische Vasenmalerei: Auswahl hervorragender Vasenbilder*, vol. 1 (Munich 1904).
Figure 2: Costumed aulos-player with two comic choreuts or actors dressed as fighting cocks. Athenian Red-Figure calyx-krater (late fifth century BCE). Formerly in The J. Paul Getty Museum (82.AE.83); now the property of the Superintendency of Naples.
Drawing by Elizabeth Wahle.
Figure 3: Comic scene of Birth of Helen. South Italian Red-Figure vase from Bari (fourth century BCE).
From M. Bieber, *Die Denkmäler zum Theaterwesen im Altertum* (Berlin 1920).
Figure 4: Theater-satyr standing by a mixing-bowl. Athenian Red-Figure cup by Makron (ARV^2 475, 267; early fifth century BCE). Munich Antikensammlungen # 2657.
Courtesy of the Staatliche Antikensammlungen und Glyptothek, Munich. Photograph by Krueger-Moessner.
Figure 5: Aulos-player, poet, actors, and satyr-chorus. Athenian Red-Figure volute-krater (ARV^2 1336,1; "Pronomos Vase," late fifth century BCE). Museo Archeologico Nazionale, Naples 81673, H3240.
Fig. 5a: Pronomos Vase: facsimile of obverse of vase, from Furtwängler-Reichhold vol. 3. 143/144.
Photograph by Jerry Kapler.
Fig. 5b: Pronomos Vase: drawing of same scene as 5a, by E. R. Malyon. Reproduced courtesy of Eric Csapo.
Fig. 5c: Pronomos Vase: composite facsimile from Furtwängler-Reichhold, combining obverse and reverse scenes.
Merged photograph by Ian Cartwright; number-key supplied by

Thomas Mannack.
Courtesy of T. Mannack (Beazley Archive) and the Oxford University Press.

Figure 6: Theater-satyr helping Dionysus in war against the Giants. Attic Red-Figure cup by Apollodorus (ARV^2 121, 23; early fifth century BCE). Lost; formerly in Rome.
From Brommer 1959.

Figure 7: Three youthful satyr-choreuts, rehearsing. Apulian Red-Figure bell-krater attributed to the Tarporley Painter (early fourth century BCE). Sydney, Nicholson Museum NM 47.05.
Drawing by François Lissarrague.

Figure 8a: Amymone surrounded by satyrs. Attic Red-Figure bell-krater (ARV^2 1155.6; mid-fifth century BCE). Kunsthistorisches Museum Inv. # IV 1011.
Courtesy of the Kunsthistorisches Museum, Vienna.

Figure 8b: Amymone and Poseidon, surrounded by satyrs. Athenian Red-Figure bell-krater by the Painter of the Würzburg Amymone (ARV^2 1440,1; mid-fifth century BCE). Martin von Wagner Museum # L 634.
Courtesy of the Martin von Wagner Museum, Universität Würzburg. Photograph by K. Oehrlein.

Figure 9: Sacrifice of Iphigenia. Pompeiian wall-painting, from the House of the Tragic Poet (first century CE). National Museum, Naples.
Image from WikiCommons.

Figure 10: Sacrifice and transformation of Iphigenia. Tarentine Red-Figure volute-krater (fourth century BCE). British Museum 1865.1-3.21 (F159).
Courtesy of the Trustees of the British Museum.

Figure 11: The Virginia Serenaders, 1844.
Courtesy of the Houghton Library, Harvard University.

Figure 12: William Henry Lane ("Juba") dancing at Vauxhall Gardens, London. (Woodcut from the *Illustrated London News*, August 5, 1848.)
Courtesy of the Houghton Library, Harvard University.

Greek Satyr Play

INTRODUCTION

The five essays collected together in this volume were written during the years 2000–2009, for a variety of different contexts. Their main focus is the satyr plays that were composed and produced by Aeschylus, Sophocles, and their contemporaries during the fifth century BCE in Athens; and they seek to open up and explore further a genre of dramatic performance that was, I argue, a vibrant and important component of the annual dramatic festival there. Although this genre is much less well preserved than either the tragedy or comedy of that period (only one complete satyr drama survives, i.e. Euripides' *Cyclops*), numerous fragments do exist of the satyr plays of Pratinas, Aeschylus, Sophocles, Achaeus, and other playwrights of that period; and we also possess more than a dozen fifth-century vase paintings that depict satyr play chorus-members rehearsing or performing—a far greater number, curiously, than we possess for tragic or comic choruses.[1] In these essays I argue that the formal and aesthetic characteristics of these plays, and hence their psycho-social dynamics and function, can be to some extent recovered and assessed, and that these operated in a distinctively complementary mode to those of the tragedies that accompanied them. Specifically, my readings of the textual and visual evidence suggest that fifth-century satyr drama functioned not simply as low farce and buffoonery, nor for the most part as burlesque or parody, nor yet as primitivistic fertility ritual (though all of these elements were present to some degree), but rather as a kind of "romantic" middle genre between tragedy and comedy, possessed of a special flavor and charm of its own.

Up until the 1990s, Greek satyr drama had been for decades a neglected field of study visited by only a handful of specialists—theater historians, text critics, and scholars of Athenian vase-painting.[2] Few books and articles written on Aeschy-

---

[1] Brommer 1959; Hedreen 1992: 105–24; KPS 1999: 41–73 (Krumeich).

[2] The most thoughtful and useful contributions were mostly German: in particular, Guggisberg 1947, Brommer 1959, Steffen 1935, 1979, Seidensticker 1979, 1989; also Rossi 1972/1989 (originally in Italian) and Chourmouziades 1974 (in Modern Greek). In English, people often relied on Pickard-Cambridge 1927/1962, Sutton 1980. See further Chapter 1, n. 1 below.

lus, Sophocles, or Euripides made any mention at all of their satyr plays. When scholars did mention them, it was usually in a perfunctory way, acknowledging the historical fact that the tragedians competed with tetralogies at the annual City Dionysia but treating the satyr plays as nothing more than a minor, light-hearted coda to the preceding trilogies,[3] a gaudy, naughty, but inconsequential/extraneous cherry, as it were, perched on top of the more complex and gastronomically rich tragic sundae;[4] or else discussion was focused on Euripides' *Alcestis*, a tragedy which was listed in the performance records (*didaskaliae*) as the fourth play of the tetralogy of 438 BCE, that is, in the position of a satyr play.[5] In a critical climate that tended to emphasize above all the literary complexities and moral or theological aspects of Greek drama, satyr plays were not regarded as relevant to the "worldview" of an Aeschylus or Sophocles. *Cyclops* and *Alcestis* did sometimes provide springboards from which critics could explore what they took to be Euripides' ironic, or parodic, or decadently un-tragic vision; but in general few attempts were made to include the satyric component of the three great tragedians' work in assessing their overall theatrical or artistic achievement.[6]

Accounts of the origins of tragedy, of course, have always included some discussion of satyr drama, though this discussion has often been fairly desultory and dismissive. Aristotle mentions *to saturikon* in his *Poetics* (4.1449a18-20) as an early, and apparently "small and ridiculous" performance genre or style (*mikroi muthoi, lexis geloia*) out of which a more elevated and "solemn, serious" (*semnos, spoudaios*) tragic diction and plot-type evolved; and the Augustan Roman poet Horace includes an extended discussion of satyr drama in his *Ars Poetica* (220-39), though in his case there is no indication that he regards this as in any sense a precursor to tragedy.[7] The fact that satyrs are intrinsically connected to Dionysus, however, whereas the characters, plots, and choruses of most surviving Greek tragedies do "not [contain] anything [much that is overtly] to do with

---

[3] It is generally agreed as probable, though not absolutely certain, that fifth-century satyr plays were performed as the fourth and final drama, following three tragedies, in a tetralogy composed by one playwright at the annual City Dionysia. This certainly is how we find them listed in the didascalic records. The arrangement in later centuries was different. For full—and skeptical—discussion of the evidence for the placement of satyr plays (before, within, or after their tragic trilogy; or as a separate item), see Sansone (forthcoming).

[4] The current Wikipedia article on "Satyr Play" (accessed May 2015) begins: "Satyr plays were an ancient Greek form of tragicomedy, similar in spirit to the bawdy satire of burlesque. They featured choruses of satyrs, were based on Greek mythology, and were rife with mock drunkenness, brazen sexuality (including phallic props), pranks, sight gags, and general merriment."

[5] Second *hypoth*. to Eur. *Alcestis*. See Seidensticker 1982: 129–52, Conacher 1988: 35–37, Parker 2007: xix–xxiii, lv–lvi, with further references.; also now the interesting suggestions of Shaw 2014: 78–105.

[6] Even as recently as 2008, the Fondation Hardt volume devoted to Aeschylus (*Entretiens* 54) included no discussion at all of his satyr plays: Jouanna and Montanari 2009.

[7] Brink 1971: 273–77.

Dionysus...,"⁸ has always posed challenging questions to modern scholars. So, whereas theories of a ritual origin for Greek drama have usually involved various notions of rustic—perhaps Peloponnesian—Dionysian choral performances,⁹ scholars have generally found it difficult to reconcile what we are told about dithyramb as a starting-point/source for early tragedy with what we are told about satyrs: dithyramb and satyr play seem in fact always to have been quite different and distinct genres.¹⁰ In any case, even those critics who have seen satyr drama as contributing significantly to the origins of tragedy have mostly treated it as essentially a precursor, rather than a coeval, to tragedy, regarding its fifth-century survival/revival as no more than an old-fashioned, rustic sop to lower-class tastes among the Athenians, rather than as a vital and vibrant element in the tragedians' performance repertoire.¹¹ It may be added that among Classicists, interest in the ritual origins and/or ritual function of Greek drama, which had loomed large in the early decades of the twentieth century,¹² had dwindled and fallen somewhat out of fashion by the 1950s, even while theater-makers and theater historians and critics outside Classics continued to hold on more tenaciously and imaginatively to such theories.¹³

---

⁸The proverbial remark *ouden pros ton Dionuson* is found in several ancient sources, from the Hellenistic period on, including Plutarch (*Symp.* 1.1.5, 615a) and the *Suda* (o 806 Adler); and is discussed with relation to satyr drama by Zenobius (5.40 = *CPG* 1.137); see e.g. Scullion 2005: 33. It is not clear whether this complaint was directed originally against tragedy or dithyramb or both, for having abandoned their original focus on Dionysus and his rituals.

⁹See esp. Pickard-Cambridge 1968/1989; Csapo and Miller 2007, *passim*; Shaw 2014: 30–55.

¹⁰Griffith 2013b, and other essays in Kowalzig and Wilson 2013.

¹¹This tendency still persists, alas, in some quarters: so, e.g., Silk 2014: 35, "It is hard to get a theoretical handle on satyr-play and its relation to the canonical genre of tragedy. Satyr-play is not only contextually dependent on tragedy, and textually derivative on tragedy [sic], but also, on all the extant evidence, hugely inferior to tragedy.... Satyric drama as we know it offers no hint of any stylistic, formal, imaginative breakthroughs, no 'satyric' vision of life comparable to the comic or tragic visions, and yet no 'entertainment value' comparable to that offered by Old Comedy either. Satyr-play is quaint, limited, effectively parasitic on tragedy: in evaluative terms, entirely marginal. What is the synchronic rationale of its *persisting* contextual attachment to tragedy—a low value text [sic] embedded in a high-value context?" (emphasis in the original). Silk proceeds to argue (ignoring the visual and papyrological evidence completely) that in fact hardly anybody really paid much attention to these satyr plays: e.g. (36), "For the fifth century, actually, it is not clear in what sense satyr-play *was* valued... Any evidence for fifth- or fourth-century responses to satyr-play is extraordinarily... limited." I hope the present volume will persuade at least some readers otherwise concerning most of these claims.

¹²Notably Gilbert Murray, Jane Harrison, Francis Cornford, William Ridgeway. Influentially negative/critical of this "myth and ritual" approach were U. von Wilamowitz, A. Pickard-Cambridge, G. F. Else, and plenty of others, esp. those educated at Oxbridge. On the partial return into critical favor among Classicists of the so-called "Cambridge Ritualists" in recent years, see Calder 1991; also M. Griffith "Gilbert Murray and Greek Literature," in C. Stray (ed.) *Gilbert Murray Reassessed* (Oxford 2007) 51–80.

¹³Cf. esp. Theodore Gaster's *Thespis* (1961), which contained a Forward by Gilbert Murray and relied heavily on his and Cornford's arguments about the ritual origins of drama, while adding fur-

Of course, one main reason for that persistent critical neglect of satyr drama is obvious enough: the relative paucity and fragmented, confusing nature of the surviving material. Only one satyr play survives complete: Euripides' *Cyclops*;[14] and while papyrus discoveries of the twentieth century have gradually—and significantly—enhanced the body of satyric texts,[15] the standard editions of the surviving tragedies of Aeschylus, Sophocles, and Euripides, whether in the original Greek or in translation, have usually omitted all of these fragmentary remains, with the result that casual readers often would be completely unaware that Aeschylus and Sophocles even wrote satyr plays at all, while more serious students had to go looking in specialist editions of the fragments or else in monographs devoted specifically to the history of satyr drama, to get any first-hand acquaintance with these materials.[16] Not surprisingly, few did so.

In more recent years, however, the genre has attracted a remarkable—and fully-deserved—revival of interest. From being a "niche" field and a scholarly backwater it has evolved into quite a strong current—if not quite a mainstream—of critical commentary, both as a component of the larger Classical and Hellenistic Greek performance scene and as a specific phenomenon in its own right. The reasons for this revival are numerous, and I shall mention just some of them briefly here.

First and foremost, new editions and guides to study have radically improved the landscape for researchers and students. The completion of Snell-Radt-Kannicht's monumental *Tragicorum Graecorum Fragmenta* provided at last a full-

---

ther Near Eastern material as well. Also highly influential were Northrop Frye's *Anatomy of Criticism* (1957), René Girard's *Violence and the Sacred* (1972/1977)—both of which, in their different but overlapping ways, promoted notions of "tragedy" as a symbolic system built on mimetic violence involving an individual's fall/death and a community's resulting health and benefit—and Victor Turner's *The Ritual Process* (1969; cf. too Turner 1982, Schechner 1976). Another important, and not always sufficiently recognized, contributor to these debates was George Thomson, whose Marxist, anthropologically-oriented *Aeschylus and Athens: A Study in the Social Origins of Drama* (first ed. 1941) went through four editions and grew eventually into an ambitious and far-reaching two-volume set of *Studies in Ancient Greek Society* (1954, 1961). Thomson's work (which included a valuable commentary on *The Oresteia*), along with that of E. R. Dodds, made a strong impression on me in my early years as a student of Greek culture and drama.

[14]The text of *Cyclops* [*Kuklôps*] is preserved in the two medieval manuscripts (L and P) that contain the so-called "alphabetic" plays of Euripides (i.e. those whose titles begin with the letters epsilon, êta, iota, and kappa).

[15]Most significantly, the large Oxyrhynchus papyrus of Sophocles' *Ichneutai* (*Trackers*, or *Searchers*), first published in 1912 (P. Oxy. 1174 + 2081[a] = Sophocles F 314 Radt), containing over 350 lines—perhaps about half the play; also additional papyri from Oxyrhynchus, much smaller but still containing quite substantial fragments of several Aeschylean satyr dramas (including *Theôroi/Isthmiastai*, *Diktyoulkoi*, *Prometheus Purkaeus*).

[16]The only readily-available English translation of Sophocles' *Trackers* was for many years the Penguin version by R. L. Green, which was published along with E. *Cyclops* as a separate, slim volume (*Two Satyr Plays*, 1957) and was often out of print.

scale and reliable critical edition of all the ancient testimonia and textual fragments of Aeschylus, Sophocles, and Euripides plus the other, "minor," tragic playwrights;[17] and meanwhile Richard Seaford published a first-rate new edition (with Introduction and Commentary in English) of *Cyclops*.[18] In due course, good new Loeb editions were published of all three of the great tragedians, including most of the readable fragments.[19] These in combination made the study of the remains of satyr drama much more feasible and welcoming. In 1998 an excellent full-scale, single-volume collection of all the significant satyric fragments, along with discussion of the archaeological and visual evidence (mainly vase paintings), by Krumeich, Pechstein, and Seidensticker was published, with introduction, Greek texts, and translations, with commentary (in German).[20] This provided for the first time a reliable and fairly complete "one-stop" repertory of material that could serve as a basis for methodical study of the genre. Shortly thereafter (2001–2002) a thoughtful monograph (in French) by Pierre Voelke, and two valuable survey articles (in English), one by Mairit Kaimio et al. and another by John Gibert, signalled at last the belated "arrival" of this genre to take its place among Anglophone scholars and students as a proper counterpart to the long-favored and densely-populated fields of tragedy and comedy.[21] Meanwhile, detailed studies of satyrs and silenes in Athenian visual culture in general were also proliferating, especially from the pens of François Lissarrague and Guy Hedreen;[22] and a brilliant new play, *The Trackers of Oxyrhynchus*, loosely based on Sophocles' *Ichneutai* while also fantasizing about the operations and imaginations of the pioneering British papyrologists Grenfell and Hunt, was written by Tony Harrison and produced at Delphi and then on the South Bank, London.[23] Satyr drama was suddenly in style.

Another crucial factor in this (re-)discovery of satyr drama has been the paradigm-shift within humanistic studies towards more anthropologically oriented analyses and the rise of "cultural poetics." Among Classicists, Athenian drama

[17] *TrGF* I = *Tragici Minores* (Snell 1971), II *Fragmenta Adespota* (Kannicht-Snell 1981), III Aeschylus (Radt 1985), IV Sophocles (Radt 1977), V Euripides (two vols, Kannicht 2004).

[18] Seaford 1984; he also since the late-1970s has contributed several important articles on Dionysian ritual and theater at Athens.

[19] Loeb volumes of the tragic (and satyric) fragments: Sophocles vol. III (ed. H. Lloyd-Jones 1996); Euripides vols. VII and VIII (ed. C. Collard and M. Cropp 2008); Aeschylus vol. II (ed. H. Weir Smyth [1922], rev. with Appendix by H. Lloyd-Jones 1957); now superseded by A. Sommerstein's new Loeb vol. III (2008).

[20] KPS 1999. In 2013 there appeared a useful edition of all the substantial remains of Greek satyr drama in the Aris & Phillips series, with Greek text, English translation, and commentary by P. O'Sullivan and C. Collard.

[21] Voelke 2001; Kaimio et al. 2001; Gibert 2002.

[22] Lissarrague 1990, 1993 (and see now also Lissarrague 2013); Hedreen 1992 (and see now also Hedreen 2007).

[23] Harrison [1988] 1991.

by the 1970s was beginning to be considered in more open-ended and multi-dimensional, less formalist and literary, ways, as critics sought to explore the social, economic, material, and political dynamics of these performances as well as their literary and philosophical/aesthetic meanings and value.[24] Elements of the festival occasion (the Great Dionysia in Athens),[25] the Athenian sex-gender system and its relation to the performances of young men in the Theater,[26] and the ritual and musical elements embedded within the plays themselves (prayers, laments, sacrifices, oaths, magical incantations, celebratory hymns, etc.), all of these increasingly came to be recognized as mirroring and reinforcing, or perhaps in some cases inverting or questioning, the performative realities in the "actual" world of Athenian social life.[27]

Both tragedy and Old Comedy (Aristophanes and his rivals) attracted a profusion of studies along these lines during the 1980s and 1990s. One current of criticism emphasized the "political" angles—especially the relationship between tragedy and democracy in Athens—while another focused more on the religious/social aspects of the whole festival event and of the plays' plots and outcomes within that larger context; in both cases, scholars often liked to propose models in which the key to understanding the intended or actual psycho-social effects of tragedy for the Athenian community at large was supposed to reside in the correct/normative vs. incorrect/disruptive/anti-democratic political and ritual behavior of the characters and actions represented in these theatrical performances.[28] At the same time, from a different angle, feminist and queer approaches to these dramatic texts

---

[24] Much of the pioneering work on these fronts took place in France during the 1960s and 1970s, among the followers of Louis Gernet and Jean-Pierre Vernant. Earlier, George Thomson had already been opening up some of these perspectives (see n. 13 above). A landmark moment (esp. for Anglophone scholars and readers) for this anthropological turn in the study of Athenian drama was the publication of Jack Winkler and Froma Zeitlin's co-edited *Nothing to Do with Dionysos?* (1990), a volume which, though it focused primarily on tragedy, contained stimulating essays on satyr drama by David Konstan and Winkler himself, as well as important discussions of theater spaces, bodies, and gender by Zeitlin and Ruth Padel. Meanwhile, outside Classics, the work of Clifford Geertz, Victor Turner, Richard Schechner, Pierre Bourdieu, Judith Butler, and others was transforming the ways in which "performance" was regarded and studied in many fields within the arts, humanities, and social sciences at large.

[25] Pickard-Cambridge 1968/1989, Goldhill 1986/1990; also Winkler and Zeitlin 1990 *passim*.

[26] Winkler 1990, Padel 1990, Zeitlin 1990, 1995, Hall 1997, etc.; also Travis 1996 (focusing esp. on the chorus, and building on the psychoanalytic and "object relations" work of Melanie Klein and D. W. Winnicott, as well as Janet Adelman; see Adelman 1992).

[27] Athenian drama thus could be interpreted, extending and literalizing the metaphor of Erving Goffman's classic, pioneering work of "performance studies," *The Presentation of Self in Everyday Life* (1959), as a rehearsal-room for Athenian social reality outside the Theater space.

[28] For a useful, though opinionated, survey of several of these approaches and the debates among their chief proponents—mostly British and/or Oxford-based (S. Goldhill, M. Heath, C. Sourvinou-Inwood, J. Griffin, P. Rhodes, W. Allan, T. Harrison, S. Scullion, et al.)—see now Allan and Kelly 2013; cf. too Carter 2011.

were opening up rich new dimensions of shifting subjectivities, non-hegemonic discourses, unconventional emotional affect, and psychological complexities that challenged, modified, or subverted entrenched masculinist habits of thought, both ancient and modern.[29] To these gender-oriented readings were soon added post-colonial and ethnically-focused analyses of the "Other" and of Athenian theater as a locus for the exploration of "difference" of various kinds.[30] These included a number of studies of "the body" in tragedy—male or female, Greek or foreign, damaged, suffering, abjected, and/or redeemed or purified.[31]

Few of these studies took much—or any—account of satyr drama: but two important exceptions were Jack Winkler's playful but insightful investigation of possible connections between ephebic ritual and choral performance in Athens, and Edith Hall's provocative suggestions about the male adolescent mentalities exhibited and licensed by the Athenians in publicly dressing-up and performing as ithyphallic satyrs in the Theater.[32]

My own interest in satyr drama grew out of the work I was doing in the 1990s on the sociology, politics, and psycho-social dynamics of Athenian tragedy, especially the plays of Aeschylus and Sophocles. I had been engaged in trying to trace the ways in which the theater audience's sympathies and imaginary "identification" with different individuals, groups, and situations within the plays seemed often to be "split" between upper- and lower-class characters (and sometimes between (an) actor(s) and the chorus), with each spectator alternating (imaginatively, pleasurably...) between adopting/identifying with the subject position of a larger-than-life elite figure, such as Agamemnon, Ajax, Xerxes, or Antigone, and that of a regular, anonymous person of lower status such as a Watchman, Nurse, Guard, or chorus-member.[33]

This way of "reading" and imagining Greek tragedy seemed to me to reveal a dimension that had been rather neglected in other kinds of socio-political inter-

---

[29] E.g. Zeitlin 1990, 1995; Foley 1985, 2001; Hall 1997, 1998; Padel 1990; Loraux 1987 [1991], 1995, 1998, [1990]; Wohl 1998; and see n. 26 above.

[30] Hall 1989, Zeitlin 1995; cf. too B. Seidensticker's *Palintonos Harmonia*, a valuable study of comic elements in Greek tragedy (1982).

[31] E.g. Loraux 1998 [1990], Rabinowitz 1993, Zeitlin 1995, Wohl 1998; cf. Foley 2001, Holmes 2013 with further references.

[32] Winkler 1985/1990; Hall 1998. Regrettably, I did not encounter Hall's stimulating article until after I had completed and published my own first article on satyr drama (Griffith 2002); see further my discussion in Griffith 2005 (= Chapter 2, pp. 94–96 and 103 below).

[33] Griffith 1995 (on the *Oresteia*); Griffith 1998 (focusing esp. on A. *Persians* and S. *Antigone*); Griffith 1999 (commentary on S. *Antigone*); cf. too Griffith 2006/2010, where I attempted a more thorough-going discussion of psychoanalytic readings of Greek tragedy in general, with a particular focus on *Antigone*. In these articles I have suggested that the experience of split identification, while being subjectively somewhat variable from one audience-member to another, and constantly shifting from one moment to the next in the theater, was—and is—characteristic of the theater-going experience in general.

pretation of these plays. Most of those studies tended to posit an imagined democratic Athenian citizen body that they saw as being constructed through the witnessing of fictional actions performed in the theater, actions involving ambitious aristocratic family-members crashing to ruin while collective judgment and critique was passed on them by the citizen body both (implicitly, or explicitly) within the play, and/or outside it, among the spectators. Such analyses were often framed within theories of a social reintegration that was supposedly brought about by the hero's demise/expulsion or salvation in relation to the restoration or purification of his/her larger community; and extensive debate was devoted to the question of a/the Chorus' status and authority, as a representative (or not) of the/a wider community and/or the theater audience itself.[34] Sometimes such interpretations were expressed in plainly didactic and normative terms, as if the moral-political "lessons" of tragedy were entirely straightforward and unequivocal; in other cases the readings were more open-ended, multi-voiced, and skeptical, with theater regarded as being not so much a simple endorsement of Athens' democratic institutions and mentalities as a kind of testing-ground, a school of critical inquiry for budding citizens.[35]

Largely lacking in almost all of these critical approaches was a serious consideration of class and status differences within the Athenian audience. The ideal spectator tended implicitly to be standardized and normalized as a member of a rather homogeneously democratic community ("Athenian" = "male, adolescent/adult, pro-democracy, citizen").[36] It was a sense of this lack that led me, during the 1990s, under the influence especially of reading Aristotle's *Politics* on the one hand, and such critics as Raymond Williams, Antonio Gramsci, Pierre Bourdieu, and Catherine Belsey on the other, to set about trying to investigate Athenian theater-going society in terms of a more complex and conflicted social mixture of traditional and new, aristocratic and democratic (and servile), "dominant" and "emergent," attitudes and behaviors. I proposed a model (derived partly from the political sociologist David Kertzer, and ultimately from Emile Durkheim) of "solidarity without consensus" within an Athenian theater audience—i.e., texts and performances that would draw the assembled spectators together in shared engagement and enjoyment even while different, even somewhat contradictory "messages" might be drawn by different constituencies within that one audience.[37]

Borrowing from both literary narratology and film criticism—the former for its strategies of tracking different kinds of "internal focalization" within the

---

[34] For discussion of the chorus' "authority" and relationship to the theater audience, see esp. Gould 1996 vs. Goldhill 1996, Mastronarde 1998, 1999, 2010, Foley 2003; and Chapters 1 and 2 below.

[35] See references in n. 28 above.

[36] For critique of this tendency, see esp. Roselli 2011, who offers a much "thicker" description of the imagined and actual audiences both within the Theater of Dionysos at Athens and outside it.

[37] Kertzer 1988; Durkheim 1912; cf. R. Williams 1977, Belsey 1985.

process of telling a story,[38] the latter for its techniques of measuring audience response and tracking a director's/editor's manipulation of their "subject position" throughout the course of a movie through choices of camera angles and cuts, etc.[39]—I attempted to analyse/track the various different levels of identification that a Greek tragedy seems to invite from its audience members, suggesting that one of the special delights and fascinations (lessons?) of theater-going was (and still is) the possibilities it presented for imaginatively occupying a number of previously unfamiliar—exciting, troublesome, unusual—subject positions, even while each spectator remained safely in his/her seat, physically immune from the dangers that were being experienced by the main characters onstage. Such shifting of subject-position and experimentation with different kinds of "identification," I have argued, might allow an audience member to experience simultaneously, or in alternation, both the immediacy and horror/pride of an elite hero's predicament/achievement, and the more distanced, yet still emotionally powerful and affective, feelings of admiration, disgust, or pity, approval or disapproval, anxiety or relief, expressed by the minor characters and chorus;[40] and we might also even be brought to share occasionally the perspective of the gods on the human action unfolding in front of (below) us. Audiences thus could enjoy the excitement and surprise of sometimes "identifying" with characters of a different gender or status from their own[41] and of experiencing previously unimaginable crises and dilemmas, even while sitting securely among a group of fellow-spectators, immune from harm.[42]

As I began to look more closely, out of curiosity, at the fragments of satyr drama (to which I had not previously paid much attention), it dawned on me that these plays seemed to involve similar dynamics of class/status difference, but in even starker and more blatant terms. The contrast, yet mutual dependence and constant interaction and cooperation, between elite characters (heroes, gods) and low-class, abjected satyr chorus is ever-present and undisguised, while the musical, visual, and linguistic elements seemed likewise to invite further anal-

---

[38] Particularly Mieke Bal (after Genette) and Irene De Jong (after Bal).
[39] See esp. Metz 1977, Mulvey 1975, Silverman 1983, and esp. L. Williams 1995, Clover 1992.
[40] Cf. Stallybrass and White 1986, Travis 1996, McCarthy 2000, etc.
[41] A process well described, e.g., by Zeitlin 1995, Clover 1992.
[42] Such an approach to interpreting the processes of theatrical "identification" with the characters and situations of Greek tragedy is rather different from the more familiar humanistic readings that focus more exclusively on "the hero" and his/her choices and struggles (e.g., Jauss 1974; also Bradley 1910, Whitman 1951, Knox 1964). It is different too from the "ritual substitute" (*pharmakos*) school of criticism (referenced above), in which a group (audience) is imagined as focusing its violent desires and feelings of collective guilt on a particular individual and thereby sublimating them, as a way of absolving the group itself from harm, purifying it, and restoring it to its full psychic strength. My readings of the typical tragic-theater experience have tended to emphasize instead the troubled but mutually attractive relationship between elites and non-elites, both within the plays and among the audience members.

ysis along these lines. And simultaneously, I found myself exploring in a separate, but not wholly unrelated project, the "class" and species dynamics of ancient Greek engagements, real and imaginary, with their equids—horses, donkeys, and mules[43]—, which of course involved several of the same issues as their fantasies about satyrs, humanoid creatures that are themselves half-horse; subhuman, yet wholly "daimonic"; and physically gifted beyond the capabilities of human beings. Satyrs as children, as slaves, as animals, as divinities—the Athenians seemed to find them strangely good to think with, and to "play" with: an unusual and intriguing kind of *mimêsis*. This was not a marginal activity for those Athenians, but one of the central components of their biggest annual festival. I found myself drawn to trying to explain why. What were these satyr dramas doing for them?

*****

The articles in this collection were conceived and written over the course of about a dozen years (beginning around 1998), and they are presented here with only very minor revisions. I have not tried to bring them systematically up to date with regard to bibliography, nor to revise them in light of subsequent scholarship or my own evolving ideas. Overall, I think that the articles and chapters should best stand (or fall) in their original form, and I have presented them in the order in which they were written and published. In just a few places, when I feel that it would be seriously misleading to leave the original version as my "last word" and considered opinion on a particular topic, I have added important new references or brief supplements, in square brackets.

The first chapter ("Slaves of Dionysos," from 2002) covers several of the themes mentioned above, attempting above all to modify prevailing notions about the purely ludicrous, gross, and frivolous nature of satyr drama and to suggest a more nuanced and multi-layered reading of the original audience's relationship to the satyr-chorus. The chapter draws from Peter Stallybrass and Allon White's insightful book, *The Poetics and Politics of Transgression*, which explores the remarkable appetite of nineteenth-century bourgeois British viewers for exotic and deviant or socially abjected behaviors and body-types, as displayed in museums, carnivals, freak-shows, theaters, and elsewhere.[44] The mixture of disgust and fascination, repulsion and attraction, traceable within those audiences suggests analogies with the Athenians' appetite for viewing the ithyphallic, riotous, irresponsible—yet highly musical, exuberant, and harmless—satyrs in the theater, i.e., an imaginary group of childish and slavish—yet curiously engaging and temptingly transgressive—dancers and singers played by actual Athenian male citizens. At the same time, I suggest, the language, comportment, and behavior of the elite (heroic and/

---

[43] M. Griffith, "Horsepower and Donkeywork: Equids in the Ancient Greek Imagination," *CP* 101.3 (2006) 185–246, 101.4 (2006) 307–58.

[44] Stallybrass and White 1986.

or divine) characters in these plays conforms fairly closely to the more proper norms of tragedy, thus confirming in even more exaggerated form the class distinctions and mixed responses which (I have argued) were characteristic of Athenian spectatorship of tragedy as well. At the same time, I point out a number of respects in which the conventions of satyr drama, and the responses elicited from an audience, appear to be quite different from those associated with Attic Old Comedy (Aristophanes et al.). The last part of this chapter focuses on one satyr play in particular, Aeschylus' *Proteus*, suggesting how this play (only small scraps of which actually survive) may have worked as a complement to the rest of the *Oresteia*, the tetralogy of which *Proteus* comprised the fourth and final part.

Chapter 2 focuses in more detail on the psychological dimensions of what it meant for citizen Athenians to impersonate satyrs in the Theater. Inspired by Eric Lott's now-classic book, *Love and Theft: Blackface Minstrelsy and the American Working Class*,[45] I suggest that the dynamics of American nineteenth-century Blackface performance may provide helpful insights into the ways in which the hyper-active, musically and choreographically adventurous, sexually transgressive, and verbally impertinent satyrs may have appealed to Athenian men who were constantly subjected to expectations of good behavior, proper speech, and modest deportment in their lives outside the Theater: for them, theater-satyrs seem to have represented some of the same alternatives (temptations/threats) that the "Black" body and its imagined performance idioms signified to working-class White Americans of the industrial North East. The chapter concludes with a more explicitly psychoanalytic reading of the fragmentary remains of Aeschylus' *Netfishers (Diktyoulkoi)*.

In Chapter 3, the focus shifts away from the dynamics of choral performance and the childish-slavish character of the satyrs, to issues of language and the thematics of plot. In particular, I show first that the vocabulary of satyr drama is in general very closely aligned with that of tragedy (and not with that of comedy), most notably in the usage of compound adjectives; and then I proceed to discuss the "romantic" elements of plot and scene-type in Sophocles' satyr dramas, suggesting that a high proportion of these plays (whose plots admittedly in many cases are largely a matter of speculation) contained scenes in which characters fall romantically in love and engage in the conventional manners and activities of courtship—a theme almost completely absent from our surviving tragedies, and from Aristophanes' comedies too.

Chapter 4 ("Greek Middlebrow Drama: Something to Do with Aphrodite?") develops this "romantic" angle further, while also expanding the critical horizon somewhat beyond the satyr plays of the fifth century (unlike the first three chapters). I explore some of the ways in which satyr drama seems to have anticipated

---

[45]Lott 1993, a book which itself builds skillfully on Stallybrass and White 1986; see also Lhamon 1998, Rogin 1996.

various developments in Greek (and Latin) literature that later came to be known as "pastoral poetry" and (in modern terminology) "prose romance," or "the novel"; and I suggest that the notion of a "middle" style of poetry and fiction-making that involved rustic settings, love stories, and exotic adventures may have found some of its earliest expressions in fifth-century Greek satyr drama. I note also that other forms of drama were being performed in different regions of Greece (i.e., outside Attica) that seem never really to have conformed to the Athenian or Aristotelian binary distinction between tragedy and comedy.

The essay that now comprises Chapter 5 was written for an Oxford conference in 2007 devoted to discussion of the Pronomos Vase, a famous late fifth-century Athenian painted pot excavated from Ruvo (South Italy), on which scenes of Dionysian activity are depicted: on one side, Dionysus and Ariadne in the wild, surrounded by satyrs, nymphs/maenads, and animals, and on the other, Dionysus and Ariadne reclining on a couch, in the presence of, or at least visually surrounded by, actors and choreuts costumed for performance in a theatrical tragedy-satyr play competition, including a group partially or fully attired as satyrs (and also a small winged figure labeled *Himeros* [Desire] hovering nearby). The pot was apparently first produced in honor of the virtuoso Theban aulos-player Pronomos, who is named on the vase and placed by the artist as the focal figure of the whole composition. My essay discusses the relationship between satyr drama and tragedy in the light of these scenes, focusing especially on the musical, erotic/romantic—and possibly eschatological—implications of this type of performance from both an Athenian and a South Italian perspective.

*****

In the years since the articles/chapters in this collection were written (i.e., since 2010), several important new studies of Greek satyr drama have appeared. In particular, mention should be made here of Rebecca Lämmle's monumental and comprehensive monograph,[46] which covers an impressive range of topics and themes in an even-handed way and with scrupulous attention to previous scholarship; a new edition, with English translations and extensive introduction and commentary, of *Cyclops* and all the major surviving fragments of satyr drama, by Patrick O'Sullivan and Christopher Collard;[47] Emmanuela Bakola's stimulating monograph on Cratinus that includes a chapter on his *Dionysalexandros* (an Attic comedy of the mid-fifth century featuring a chorus of satyrs), as well as further discussion of satyr drama;[48] and Carl Shaw's *Satyric Play*, exploring the interfaces between comic drama (both Athenian and Sicilian) and satyr drama skillfully and

---

[46] Lämmle 2012.
[47] O'Sullivan and Collard 2013.
[48] Bakola 2010.

from multiple perspectives.[49] One further article of my own has also appeared, in which I discuss the relationship between Athenian satyr drama and dithyramb in the fifth century, focusing especially on the self-referential remarks made by the satyrs to their own (often rather adventurous and innovative) performance style and bodily/social hexis, and their possible geo-political implications for Dionysian performance in general at Athens.[50]

By this point, it can be said that Greek satyr drama is firmly back in the place that it deserves—next to, subordinate to, but not completely eclipsed by, tragedy.[51] This is a genre with its own distinctive appeal, its own particular energies, and its own value.

---

[49] Shaw 2014; see too the Toronto PhD dissertation (2011) by Donald S. Sells, *Old Comedy and its Performative Rivals of the Fifth Century*.

[50] Griffith 2013b.

[51] The first international conference known to have been devoted entirely to Greek satyr drama was the one at Xavier University, Cincinnati, organized by G. W. M. Harrison and Jane E. Francis in 2003 (which gave rise to the publication of Harrison 2005). In April 2014 a conference on Aeschylus' satyr plays was held at U. C. Davis, organized by Anna Uhlig. In July 2016 a conference entitled "Greek Satyr Play: Reconstructing a Dramatic Genre from its Remnants," is to take place at the University of Patras, Greece, organized by Andreas Antonopoulos.

CHAPTER 1

Slaves of Dionysos

Satyrs, Audience, and the Ends of the Oresteia

INTRODUCTION

The social function and aesthetic-emotional appeal of the Athenian fifth-century satyr plays have been of only marginal interest to most scholars of tragedy. While attention has been given to the alleged "satyric" origins of tragedy, and to the changing role of satyr plays within the Great Dionysia during the eventful period between ca. 535 and 486 BCE, for the most part the two genres have been treated separately, and the importance of the satyric component of the annual tragedy-competition has been downplayed.[1] This is understandable, given the scanty (and mostly fragmentary) nature of the surviving satyric texts, and the cultural |[196] chasm that stands between twentieth-century scholars and a direct appreciation of the grotesque, half-animal choruses that pranced across the orchestra in the concluding phase of each tragic performance. But I think this neglect has had a distorting effect on the appreciation of both genres—especially tragedy—and has sometimes given rise to misleading assumptions as to the prevailing aims and character of the festival performances as a whole.

---

[1] A version of parts of this article was presented as a Carl Schlam Memorial Lecture at Ohio State University in April 2001. I am very grateful to my hosts and audience there, and in addition I should like to thank Leslie Kurke, Toph Marshall, Donald Mastronarde, Bridget Murnaghan, Andrew Stewart, Roger Travis, Nancy Worman, and two anonymous referees, for helpful comments and corrections.

Few books on the interpretation of Greek tragedy in general, or of the dramas of Aischylos, Sophokles, or Euripides in particular, pay serious attention to satyr plays. On the other hand, significant progress has been made over the last fifty years in the recovery and interpretation of individual satyr plays and in the understanding of the satyric genre as a whole: see especially Buschor 1943–1945, Guggisberg 1947, Collinge 1958, Brommer 1959, Conacher 1967: 317–39, Chourmouziades 1974, Lasserre 1973/1989, Rossi 1972/1989, Sutton 1980, Seaford 1976, 1978, 1984, Ussher 1977, Steffen 1979, Seidensticker 1979, 1989, Maltese 1982, Biehl 1986, Lissarrague 1990a, 1990b, 1993, Winkler 1985/1990, Hedreen 1992, and the excellent and comprehensive recent study edited by Krumeich, Pechstein, and Seidensticker (henceforth KPS 1999). Valuable too are S. Radt's editions of the satyric fragments of Aisch. and Soph. in *TrGF* vols. 3 and 4, together with Steffen 1935, Lloyd-Jones 1963, 1996, Kovacs 1994, and Pechstein 1998. For a full bibliography, see KPS 1999: 643–60.

Since antiquity, satyr plays have been viewed primarily as a contrast to, or relief from, the tragedies that preceded them. I shall not dispute this view, for it is obviously correct, at least in some respects. But it is an over-simplification, and does not get us very far in explaining the particular characteristics of the satyric form. Furthermore, by consigning the satyr play to a quite separate generic category from tragedy and analyzing it in radically different terms from its more revered companions, we risk misjudging its function and significance. In particular, there has been a curious asymmetry here, as scholars have consistently read the satyr play *against* tragedy, as a kind of commentary on the more august genre, while their readings of tragedy and the tragic occasion for the most part have taken no account at all of the satyric sequel. Yet in the fifth century (and presumably the late sixth century too),[2] satyr plays were regarded as an integral component of the whole competition in *tragôidia*. The same poets, *chorêgoi*, choruses, actors, and performance-space were involved; meters, staging conventions, and diction were broadly similar (and quite different from those of comedy); and even the plots themselves were cut from the same mythological-heroic cloth.[3] Although certain dramatists were admired above others as specialists in satyric drama (notably Pratinas and Aischylos; later also Pratinas' son, Aristias, and Achaios),[4] no |[197] tragic poet before Euripides is believed to have ventured to omit satyrs from his tetralogy.[5] "Playing satyrs" was thus not merely a deeply traditional Dionysiac rit-

[2] I shall not explore in this paper the difficult question of the relationship between the earliest (sixth-century) satyr-rituals and -dramas and those tragedies composed before ca. 490 BCE. Some of the key dates for these discussions: 535 (the date traditionally given for the first competition in *tragôidia* at the Great Dionysia), 510–508 (the reforms of Kleisthenes), 505–502? (the arrival of Pratinas and his satyr plays from Phleious, as an addition to the tragic dramas), 486 (the first competition in *kômôidia* at the festival). See esp. Pickard-Cambridge 1968/1989, Lesky 1983: 17–48, Rossi 1972/1989, Seaford 1976, 1978, 1981, 1984, Seidensticker 1979, Winnington-Ingram 1985: 258–63, Hedreen 1992, Csapo and Slater 1995, KPS 1999: 6–9, Wilson 2000; also W. R. Connor *C&M* 40 (1989) 7–32. For my purposes, it is sufficient to know that at least from the 490s on, satyr plays were incorporated into the tragic competition, and that they remained a requirement throughout the rest of the fifth century. My focus will be on the plays produced between ca. 475 and 400, i.e., the period of our surviving tragedies, with particular emphasis on the earlier period and Aischylos.

[3] The overlap in theme, diction, and style between the two genres has contributed, of course, to scholars' difficulties in determining whether particular fragments from plays, and play titles, attributed to the three great "tragedians" were in fact tragic or satyric. For example, as many as 35 of the 120 or so known Sophoklean play titles may be satyric; but only about 15 are securely identified as such (Lloyd-Jones 1996: 3–9, KPS 1999: 224–26, with further references). The suggestion by Seaford 1984: 4 that the satyrs may have been played by different chorus members from those of the preceding tragedies has found no supporters.

[4] On Pratinas, see *TrGF* I 4, Seaford 1978, KPS 1999: 74–87; for Aischylos' popularity as a satyr playwright, see *TrGF* III T 125a and b; for Aristias, *TrGF* I 9 (esp. T 4 = 4 T 7 = Paus. 2.13.6), KPS 1999: 213–23; for Achaios, *TrGF* I 20 (esp. T 6 = Diog. Laert. 2.133), KPS 1999: 491–545.

[5] In 438 Euripides produced *Alkestis* as fourth play of the tetralogy, apparently instead of a satyr play (2nd *hypothesis*). Some have suggested (in antiquity and more recently) that *Helen* and/or *Orestes*, or even others in addition, were likewise "prosatyric" (e.g., Sutton 1980: 180–90, Pechstein 1999: 12,

ual, but also generally accepted as the most appropriate and satisfying conclusion to the city's most complex and prestigious cultural event of the year.

In what follows, I will begin by reviewing current critical opinions about the aesthetics and social function of satyr plays in fifth-century Athens. Then I shall focus on some important features of these plays that seem to me not to be adequately addressed by these critical opinions—in particular, the issue of the audience's relationship to the satyr-chorus on the one hand and to the main "heroic" characters on the other—in an effort to trace more precisely how these performances contributed to the on-going Athenian cultural projects of individual masculine subject-formation and collective sense of group-membership and class struggle. This reading will involve some reassessment of the relationship between satyr play and tragedy, and will propose a closer bond of similarity and interdependence between the genres than is usually recognized. Finally, I will turn to take a fresh look at *Proteus*, the fourth and concluding play of Aischylos' *Oresteia*, in light of our findings and of some previously neglected pieces of evidence that may be relevant to the reconstruction and interpretation of that play and tetralogy.

CURRENT VIEWS OF THE SATYR PLAY

Scholarly explanations for the popularity and social function of the fifth-century satyr play have generally fallen into one or more of six broad categories. (1) "comic" or (2) "romantic" relief from tragic tensions, (3) a negative paradigm for civic behavior, (4) persistence of primitive fertility ritual, (5) reaffirmation of rustic values, (6) enactment or imitation of Dionysiac initiation ritual.

(1) Many critics have compared elements of the plays to Old Comedy, especially their incongruous twists of plot, shameless and grotesque stage figures, emphasis on grosser bodily functions (phallus and sexual pursuit, food and drink, energetic physical antics), and non-human choruses;[6] and both genres also exhibit

---

19–29, KPS 1999: 400–402); but there is ambiguity as to what this might mean; see below (pp. 57–70 on *Proteus*), and for strong arguments *contra*, D. F. Sutton *RCS* 21 (1973) 117–21, Sansone 1978, Marshall 2000. In general, Brommer's bald statement (1959: 5) remains true: "Das Satyrspiel ist in seiner Blütezeit also nicht ohne die Tragödie denkbar, die Tragödie aber auch nicht ohne das Satyrspiel." See too Easterling 1997b: 37–39, 48–53 ("Tragedy... through this early period... was inseparable from satyr drama," 37); likewise Rossi 1972/1989: 245 speaks of a "Grundaffinität" between early tragedy and satyr play, not shared by comedy.

[6]Demetrius (*Peri Herm.* 169) calls satyric drama "tragedy having fun" (*tragôidia paizousa*); Horace (*AP* 220–39) situates satyr plays midway between tragedy and comedy, but for the most part emphasizes the light relief that they provide from the rigors of the preceding tragedies (226: *vertere sêria lûdo*, cf. schol. 216: *satyrica drâmata, in quibus... iocôs exercêbant*). In general, see, e.g., Rossi 1972/1989, Seidensticker 1979, Sutton 1980, Zagagi 1999. Aristotle characterizes early drama as having "small, trivial plots (*mikroi mûthoi*) and ludicrous language (*lexis geloia*)" and claims that tragedy only "became serious late on (*opse apesemnunthê*) in its development out of the satyric" (*Poet.* 4.1449a19-21); but it is far from clear what evidence he had for these early stages of the two genres. Elsewhere in the *Poetics*

|[198] (though not in identical manner) an ironic and parodic relationship to tragedy, especially in their treatment of heroic myth and the juxtaposition of high and low characters and behavior.[7] On a separate, but related, trajectory, (2) satyr plays, with their predilection for rustic/exotic settings and conventional narrative structures, including unexpected discoveries and recognitions, miraculous rescues, and happy endings, seem clearly to belong to a "romance" tradition that can also claim the *Odyssey*, Euripides' "tragi-comedies," New Comedy, Theokritean pastoral, and Longos' *Daphnis and Chloe*.[8] Both the comic and romantic elements within the textual and visual remains of the satyr plays are too obvious to require further discussion here, and the appeal of both to their audience in terms of humor and wish-fulfillment is equally transparent. But it is important to bear in mind how different and separate these two modes (comedy and romance) were generally felt to be from one another.

"Romance," though it bore no generic name and occupied no particular performative niche of its own in archaic and classical Greece, can be clearly traced as a narrative form back to the "high" traditions of dactylic epic[9] and choral |[199] lyr-

he completely ignores satyr drama, but has plenty to say about *kômôidia*.

[7] See esp. Sutton 1980, but also the important distinctions outlined in KPS 1999: 36–37. Several critics have pointed out analogies between Greek satyr drama in its relation to tragedy and Japanese *kyôgen* in relation to *nôh*-plays: e.g., Smethurst 1989, Sutton 1980: 7, 179, and *QUCC* 32 (1979) 53–64. *Kyôgen* (literally "mad-words") are short farces performed as interludes between *nôh* dramas and sometimes containing parodies of *nôh* characters, themes, and scenes; see, e.g., Keene 1966, Tyler 1992: 7–11, N. Masnaku in Brandon 1997: 173–82. Sometimes a *kyôgen*-actor (*ai*) will play a minor character (Villager, Innkeeper, Boatman, Servant) in a scene of a *nôh* play; such characters are thus sharply distinguished from the (more socially elevated) others (*shite*, *waki*, *tsure*: see below, n. 47). In the medieval period, *kyôgen* appear to have evolved as lower-class spoofs of aristocratic *nôh*-performances. In the modern era, the schools and actor-troupes for the two forms, along with their costumes, language, music, choreography, and conventions of masking, continue to be kept completely separate (*kyôgen* actors do not use masks or dance, and there is no chorus), though certain groups of *kyôgen* actors will frequently be attached to a particular school of *nôh* performers and will regularly collaborate with them on productions. By contrast, the same actors and chorus were employed for both satyr plays and tragedies; and the costumes and language of the main characters in each were apparently almost indistinguishable. Thus, while the "low" and parodic relationship between the genres—including the use of comic "relief"—had something in common, the degree of overlap and continuity between the two was far greater in the Athenian context.

[8] Rossi 1972/1989, Seidensticker 1979; see further Burnett 1971, Knox 1979: 264–70. This "romantic" narrative tradition is usually taken to have little to do with the plots or settings of Aristophanes, Kratinos, or Epicharmos, though a few of their plays apparently did contain some "bucolic" and/or "romance" elements (e.g., Kratinos' *Dionysalexandros*, which even had a chorus of satyrs). For an approach that emphasizes the continuities and similarities between satyr play, Old Comedy, and New Comedy, see Zagagi 1999. [See now Shaw 2014.]

[9] The Argonautic epic tradition seems to have been at least as old as the Trojan Cycle (Hom. *Od.* 12.61–72, cf. K. Meuli, *Odyssee und Argonautika* (Berlin, 1921), G. Crane *CA* 6 (1987) 11–37. In addition to Jason and Odysseus, such figures as Perseus, Pelops, Herakles, Theseus, etc., also present many of the features of the romantic "quest" and/or rite of youthful passage: see, e.g., Propp 1929, Raglan 1936. On the pedigree of the prose romance ("novel"), see Hägg 1983; also Frye 1976 (and further, Chapter 4

ic.¹⁰ By contrast, Old Comedy, with its shameless characters, padded costumes and outsized phallus, gross language, and aggressively topical plots, belonged to the "low" traditions of iambic and epodic invective (Archilochos, Hipponax, etc.).¹¹ In their parodic relation to tragedy, too, romance and comedy differed: Old Comedy often incorporated whole scenes of "paratragedy" that absurdly replayed typical or specific material from epic or tragedy, while "romance" generally eschewed such direct confrontation with the serious-heroic world, preferring a more subtle process of allusion, revision, and mythic modification. It will be important to try to distinguish as precisely as possible where satyr plays stand on this parodic-allusive spectrum if we want to determine the nature of its relation to tragedy.¹²

(3) Given the strongly didactic purpose that many ancient and modern critics have attributed to Attic drama in general, and the powerful engagement with social and political issues that the extant tragedies and comedies exhibit, it might be expected that satyr plays also would perform some kind of educational or ethical function. At the simplest level, critics have found this in the social inversion represented by the undisciplined, uselessly self-indulgent satyrs, and have concluded that the Athenian citizen audience was thereby reminded (by contrast) of its own military and civic potential and responsibilities.¹³ Doubtless this analysis too is correct. Yet, if this is supposed to be the unequivocal message |[200] of the plays, it is curious that the satyrs themselves (unlike, e.g., centaurs in art and literature, or the animal and human targets of comic abuse in iambos, fable, and drama)

---

below]. And on the "origins" and character of Euripides' romance-tragedies, see esp. Knox 1979 [1970]: 264–70, Burnett 1971, Whitman 1974.

¹⁰For Stesichoros in particular, see Campbell 1991, and below pp. 57–74; cf. too the hexameter narratives of the "Hesiodic" *Catalogue* and "Homeric" *Hymns to Hermes, Demeter,* and *Aphrodite*.

¹¹Rosen 1988.

¹²See KPS 1999: 36–37. In general, attempts to read the surviving fifth-century satyr plays as detailed parodies of particular tragedies, or of the Homeric epics (notably E.'s *Cyclops* as parody of, or commentary on, the *Odyssey*) can be said to have yielded only limited fruit, as compared with the dazzling specifics of, e.g., Aristophanes' *Thesm.* and *Frogs*. "Anders als die gleichzeitige Komödie parodiert also das Satyrspiel weder die Tragödie noch den Mythos..." (KPS 1999: 37). In general, satyr plays seem no more, and no less, derivative of previous literary treatments of myth than tragedies do.

¹³See esp. Seidensticker 1979, Winkler 1985/1990, Lissarrague 1990a, 1993. Thus KPS 1999: 38–39 conclude: "Diese Anti-Ethik, die dem Publikum in Gestalt der Satyrn vor Augen rückt, wie es nicht sein und was es nicht tun sollte, und ihm zugleich in Erinnerung ruft, wie nahe und lebendig unter der zivilisatorischen Haut die animalische Natur des Menschen immer noch ist... dient aber zugleich auch der kritischen Diskussion und Affirmation der Polisordnung und ganz allgemein der menschlichen Zivilisation"). Collinge 1989 explores the "anti-authoritarian" tendencies of stage-satyrs and concludes that their behavioral excesses and attempts at social disruption would have struck the Athenian audience as being merely absurd and innocuous, never amounting to a radical or serious social critique of the status quo. As early as Hesiod (*Ehoiai* fr. 123.2 M-W), satyrs are described as *outidanoi kai amēchanoergoi* ("worthless nobodies, incompetents"). For analogies with Hesiod's Silver Generation of perpetual children (*WD* 127–37), see below n. 66 (though the Silver Race seem to be far more impious and threatening than the satyrs).

are never punished, never pay any price for their foolishness and cowardice, but rather find themselves invariably protected from harm and finally rewarded with the blessings they crave (mainly wine and idleness), even though they never seem to have learned anything useful. Furthermore, while the satyrs may often be found briefly resisting or misunderstanding the activities of the main heroic/divine figures, they seem for the most part (again, unlike the centaurs) to work in harmony with the hero and/or god towards the same happy outcome—an outcome desired also by the theater audience.[14] That is to say, the audience comes to feel itself on the same side as the satyrs, for all their grotesque and shameless characteristics: they are members of the same (imaginary) community, subject to some of the same fears and desires, and privileged with the same rewards and blessings. The satyrs are not villains or monsters, nor even stock comic buffoon-types; and rarely—or only temporarily—do they serve as "blocking" figures or opponents to the hero's efforts (though this role seems not infrequently to be filled by their sleazy father). So, if they are meant to be a negative example, it is striking that they are presented as being so successful.

(4) With their erect phalluses and close association with Dionysos, satyrs were obviously believed to contribute (like several of the dancing "fat-men" and animal choruses that were popular in many parts of Greece during the Archaic period) to the promotion of fertility in general, and of wine-production in particular.[15] Many such rituals from all over the world are known to anthropologists, and several include ceremonies in which grotesquely disguised individuals or groups perform mischievous pranks or enact bawdy stories, with a view (it seems) to ridding the community of harm and/or preparing the soil, animals, and humans too, for procreation and abundance in the coming year. It is a plausible assumption that |[201] satyr-choruses served originally as part of such a fertility-ritual, and that this

---

[14]Examples of satyrs as allies to the hero: E. *Cyclops passim* (assisting Odysseus vs. Polyphemos); A. *Dikty.* (helping to land the chest), *Prom. Pyrk.* (helping to distribute and celebrate fire), S. *Ichn.* (at first as trackers, aiding Apollo; then diverted by music and persuaded by Kyllene to help protect Hermes). Plays on the "Return of Hephaistos" would likewise normally have satyrs cooperating with Dionysos and the Olympians (see Figs. 1 and 7, and Hedreen 1992, Carpenter 1997). For characteristic language of cooperation, e.g., A. *Dikty.* F 46a 17–20, F 46c 6: βοηδρομεῖτε, 821–32, A. *Isthm.* F 78c 58: ξυνισθμιάζειν, A. *Prom. Pyrk.* F 204b *passim*, S. *Ichn.* F 314.48–49: προσφιλὴς εὐεργέτης θέλων γενέσθαι (and 84–85), E. *Cycl.* 471: πόνου γὰρ τοῦδε κοινωνεῖν θέλω, 483–84, 634: ὡς ἂν τῆς τύχης κοινώμεθα, 652–55, 708: συνναῦταί γε τοῦδ' Ὀδυσσέως. In some plays, the satyrs resemble those choruses of Comedy, who start out in an antagonistic posture, but during the course of the play are placated and/or reeducated, and thus come to be included within the circle of the hero's associates (e.g., *Acharnians, Wasps, Lysistrata*; and cf. the frog-chorus of *Frogs*); they thus end up also sharing in the joys of the final *kômos* (while the discomfited enemies are excluded and disgraced: Lamachos, Kreon, informers, war-mongers, etc.): so, e.g., A. *Amymone, Isthmiastai* (and the later stages of *Diktyoulkoi*, when the satyrs attempt to "marry" Danae); perhaps too S. *Helenês Gamos*? See further below, pp. 52–55.

[15]See esp. Pickard-Cambridge/Webster 1962: 115–16, 171–74 (contradicting Pickard-Cambridge's arguments in the 1st ed. [1927]), Hedreen 1992. [See now also Csapo and Miller 2007 *passim*.]

"original" function may have persisted even into the fifth century. But traditions do not normally persist very long if they are not still felt to be effective; and there are relatively few traces in the surviving satyr plays of such an agricultural and procreative emphasis (fewer, we may say, than in Old Comedy).[16] More to the point, the satyrs of fifth-century tragedy appear to have lost much of their original potency; unlike the irresistible bands of phallic, masked marauders in other (rural) contexts, the satyrs are constantly being rejected and disappointed, and whatever power of fertilization and/or male sexual dominance the satyrs may have exercised in the seventh- and sixth-century Peloponnesian countryside, in the Athenian urban theater it has been transmuted into something rather different.[17]

(5) L. Rossi has argued that among the reasons for the (re?)introduction of satyr plays into the Theater of Dionysos in the late sixth century and their continuation during the fifth century, we should recognize the specifically rustic, and thus more authentically "Dionysiac," appeal of the plays, as a contrast to the (by now) more sophisticated and urbane tragedies.[18] The satyr plays were thus intended to increase the sense of community and inclusion among all inhabitants of Attika, whatever their geographic or social origins. Certainly, satyr plays tend to affirm the cultural and religious value of the countryside, and the simple "bucolic" pleasures of non- (or pre-) political existence; and Rossi is surely right |[202] to

---

[16] Old Comedy has ritual abuse, cross-dressing, obscenity, etc.; often a final *kômos* and "marriage" (e.g., the endings of *Ach., Birds, Lys.*). In New Comedy, of course, such a conclusion is almost obligatory.

[17] For the relative impotency of the Athenian ithyphallic theater-satyrs, see further below, pp. 33–37. For an interesting comparison between rural and urban "fertility" rituals, see, e.g., Kinser 1990: 221–23 (on nineteenth- and twentieth-century New Orleans), who observes that ithyphallic and grotesque masqueraders in rural communities seem usually to maintain a strongly hetero-sexual focus (males harrassing females, and vice-versa), whereas in urban contexts the harrassment may be diverted into a process of male bonding and/or male rivalries. For Modern Greek traditions of *kallikantzaroi*, in comparison to the Athenian Anthesteria, see Lawson 1910: 221–32, Seaford 1984: 7–8 (and below, p. 34).

[18] Rossi 1972/1989 suggests further that the complaint, "Nothing to do with Dionysos!" (οὐδὲν πρὸς τὸν Διόνυσον), which is said to have prompted the "back-to-the-roots" movement at the end of the sixth century to bring in Pratinas of Phleious and his more overtly Dionysiac plays, may have come primarily from residents of the Attic countryside who felt themselves culturally and politically disadvantaged by the Athens-centered political culture of the new democracy (on which see e.g. Jones 1999, Wilson 2000). The ancient sources disagree, in fact, as to whether the complaint was directed against tragedy or dithyramb: Zenob. 5.40, *Suda* o 806 (referring to Chamaileon), Plutarch *Symp.* 1.1.5, 615a. In any case, it should be noted that, whatever Pratinas' satyr plays were like before he started producing them in Athens (he was a native of Phleious, a small town in the Argolid, near Corinth), they must have undergone some modification for the Attic audience: in particular, the stage-satyrs represented on vase-paintings are always *silênoi*—i.e., more horsey, less goatish, than the usual Peloponnesian images: see Buschor 1943–1945, Guggisberg 1947, Brommer 1959, Hedreen 1992, KPS 1999, and below pp. 37–44. After the 490s, however, satyr plays were generally composed and produced by Athenians (i.e., the tragic poets)—in contrast to the dithyrambs, which seem almost invariably to have been composed by outsiders (especially Thebans): see Wilson 2000: 66–67.

emphasize the importance of this basic distinction of setting and context.[19] But within this dichotomy (urban vs. rustic), even though the cheerful innocence and simplicity of the "romance" plots and their boisterous satyrs might indeed cater to low-brow country sensibilities, the dynamics of the plays seem if anything to reinforce, rather than mitigate, the stereotypical view of rustics as buffoons and incompetents. For it is not the country-folk themselves, but the other members of the traditional Olympian and heroic cast of (tragic) characters (Odysseus, Poseidon, Theseus, Diktys, Herakles, etc.) that take care of the serious business, while the satyrs prance and shuffle in and out of the way.[20] So here too some further refinement of the interpretive model seems to be required.

(6) As elementally Dionysiac companions of the god and embodiments of his spirit, satyrs/silens possess a vitality, a semi-divine status, and perhaps even a kind of wisdom, that are lacking in mere human beings. (Or perhaps we might say that satyrs embody permanently the qualities that human beings can only achieve briefly and intermittently through the rituals of Bacchic celebration.)[21] In addition, the plot of a satyr play characteristically involves a progression, from deprivation and toil to liberation and celebration, and from childish helplessness and victimization to empowerment and high or blessed status, a progression that is naturally shared to some degree by the audience watching the play, and may well be a reflex of the myths and rituals of Dionysiac initiation.[22] Thus the "demonic" powers and privileged status of satyrs are of key importance: they are not merely buffoons (even though they are usually buffoonish). Yet it must be admitted that the satyrs of drama seem rarely, if ever, to speak wisely or act in a morally significant way (they do not display, for example, the insight of a Shakespearean Fool or of Mozart's Papageno), and it was certainly not in order to see or hear divine truths emanating from their mouths that the Athenian audience stayed to watch

---

[19] The invention and development of scene-painting (*skēnographia*) reinforced this distinction through subsequent centuries: royal palace for tragedy; urban street with two houses for (New) comedy; pastoral grotto for satyr play; so (e.g.) the famous Boscoreale illustrations (Bieber 1961, E. Simon *The ancient theatre*, Eng. tr. [London, 1982] plate 11).

[20] By contrast, Aristophanes' choruses of farmers and charcoal-burners are solid, sensible, and reliable, the very backbone of Marathonian Athens; and at least by mid-play, they are staunch allies to the resourceful hero. In the urban setting of Old Comedy, it is usually the hyper-sophisticated city-types (Sokrates, sophists, sycophants, poets, demagogues) whose judgment is the more impaired. For town/country oppositions in Aristophanes, see, e.g., Ehrenberg 1961: 73–94.

[21] Recognition of the satyrs' beneficently demonic and potentially inspired nature is first explicitly attested by Plato (*Symposium*: Sokrates as Silenos), and later, e.g., by Virgil (*Eclogue* 6: the wisdom of Silenus). But it appears to be implicit in the stories of Midas and Marsyas from an earlier date. In the modern era, the motif was promoted especially by Friedrich Nietzsche in his *Birth of Tragedy* (1879), and has been explored further by Henrichs 1982, Seaford 1984; cf. too Lissarrague 1993: 217–18, Easterling 1997b: 42–44, 48–53, Wilson 1999.

[22] Henrichs 1982, Seaford 1984, Burkert 1985: 290–93.

the fourth play.[23] |[203]

Each of these six critical explanations for the persistence and popularity of the fifth-century satyr play seems to contain some truth; and there is no need for us to insist on a single "satyric pleasure" or "function" that trumps or cancels out the others.[24] But none of them seems to take us very far in accounting for the genre's curious and distinctive combination of "high " and "low" elements and in mapping the audience's engagement with, and response to, the interactions between satyric chorus and heroic characters.[25] These interactions clearly lie at the heart of this dramatic form and must have constituted a significant component of its appeal to the original Athenian audience. So it is to these that I now turn.

SATYRS AND HEROES, CHORUS AND AUDIENCE

The world of the satyr play (like that of romance, as we noted above) is much more self-consciously "fantastic" than that of tragedy. By "fantastic," I mean not only that the setting, events, and several of the characters—especially the satyrs themselves—are far-removed from the Athenian here-and-now and the normal laws of human cause and effect, but also that escapist fantasies and the gratification of desires play a much larger role in the motivations of the characters and twists of the plot than they do in the more political and serious medium of tragedy.[26] Satyr plays are usually set out in the wilds; amazing and delightful discoveries are made (a baby in a floating box, fire in a fennel-stalk, the first lyre made from a tortoise-shell, etc.); and the spirit and power of Dionysos are felt never to be far away, even though the satyrs may temporarily be suffering from the loss of his presence and pleasures. Thus satyr plays, as several critics have observed, often display the logic and flavor of *Märchen* ("fairy-stories, folk-tales"), with their simple motivations, resourceful and invulnerable heroes (often including children and damsels

---

[23] A certain sympotic "wisdom" of a traditional and ironic kind is offered at, e.g., *Cycl.* 495–502, following on 488–93, where the chorus claim to "educate" (παιδεύσωμεν) the recalcitrant Polyphemos (and see below n. 68); likewise the "instructions" (κελεύσματα) of S. *Ichn.* 231, E. *Cycl.* 656–62, etc., and see too S. *Oineus* F 1130.12–17, as well as the drunken Herakles in E. *Alk*. On the ironic, yet efficacious, operation of the chorus' "Orphic song" at E. *Cycl.* 646ff, see below, pp. 32–33.

[24] Similarly Rossi 1972/1989. For an outline of the multiple "pleasures" provided by tragedy, according to Aristotle, see Rorty 1992, and cf. Griffith 1999: 25–66.

[25] Most commentators restrict themselves to pointing out the humor deriving from the incongruity of having the satyrs continually interfering with "higher" activities of the other characters. Perhaps this humor is justification enough, and needs no further analysis. But I am curious as to why this particular form of incongruity was felt to be so rewarding, and so necessary in the context of tragic performance, that it continued to be reenacted with the same formula year after year.

[26] In what follows, when I generalize about "tragedy," I will for the most part exclude from my account those "romantic tragedies" that are seen by many as overlapping in several respects with satyr play: *Alkestis, IT, Ion, Helen*. I shall return to these later in this article (below, pp. 55–57). [Also Chapter 5 below.]

in distress), and benevolent divine supervision; and of course they always end happily, often with a marriage and/or some kind of restoration of social norms and promise of rewards for the larger community.

Within this satyric fantasy-world, the heroic story unfolds through the interactions of two groups of characters, sharply distinct, yet incongruously and |[204] inextricably linked. Or we could say, in Aristotle's terms, that a single "action" (*praxis*) or "story" (*muthos*) is "imitated" (enacted, represented) simultaneously by two different classes of performer, one "serious" (*spoudaios*), the other "low" (*phaulos*) or "ridiculous" (*geloios*).[27] At one level, divine and heroic figures from the traditional epic-tragic repertory employ conventional tragic diction and stage behavior in making their (for the most part) sober and respectable way through the conflicts and challenges of the plot towards a conclusion that reaffirms the value and authority of guest-friendship and hospitality, personal honor, marriage and the family, religious cult, and other traditional norms of Greek aristocratic life.[28] These characters are often found delivering speeches of quite serious ethical and rhetorical content (unlike those of Old Comedy, where even morally and politically serious speeches always have to be spiced up with jokes, allusions, and some comic hyperbole); and, even though they sometimes may eat, drink, and indulge in social interactions and trickery that would be indecorous for most tragic heroes, they seem generally to maintain their dignity and moral integrity even in the face of distractions.[29] Simultaneously, yet on a different existential level, we

---

[27] Aristotle in fact says nothing in the *Poetics* about the mature fifth-century satyr play (just as he says nothing about trilogies, or the context and procedures of the Dionysian festival). He appears to think satyr drama important only as a preliminary stage in the evolution of tragedy towards "its own proper nature" (*phusis*); and by the time that he was composing the *Poetics* (mid-fourth century) satyr plays had indeed become quite a separate entity from tragedy. Earlier in the fourth century, Plato likewise, in warning against the pernicious effects of "imitation" or "pretending" (*mimêsis*) for young men (*Rep.* 3.394e-398a, 10.605a-608b), talks consistently in binary terms of tragedy and comedy, and does not think to mention satyrs among the many kinds of disreputable objects of dramatic impersonation (tyrants, women, slaves, animals, etc.).

[28] The institutions of (esp. democratic) *political* life, on the other hand (armies, assemblies, laws and law-courts, public edicts, etc.), seem largely to be absent (though, e.g., Odysseus and his crew confirm at least their military valor and discipline in overcoming Polyphemos, *Cycl.* 650-51, 694-95): see Rossi 1972/1989, Seaford 1984: 18-19, 30-33 (with reference to Plato *Laws* 815c οὐ πολιτικόν). Upon seeing the satyrs shortly after his arrival onstage, Odysseus remarks τί χρῆμα; Βρομίου πόλιν ἔοιγμεν ἐσβαλεῖν ("What's this? We seem to have come to Dionysos' town!," a nice oxymoron: E. *Cycl.* 99-100).

[29] This is one reason why it is often impossible to determine whether a particular dramatic speech-fragment from a lost play was tragic or satyric; see above, p. 15. Examples of serious speeches in satyr plays: Odysseus at E. *Cycl.* 285-312, Dionysos at A. *Isthm.* F 78c, Dike at A. F 281a, Danae at A. *Dikty.* F 47a 773-85. (There are also "serious" speeches of more questionable moral caliber, sometimes in agonistic contexts—as in tragedy: e.g., Sisyphos at Kritias [or Euripides?] F 19 [see KPS 1999: 552-61], Polyphemos at E. *Cycl.* 316-46.) By contrast, the diction, speech-patterns, and metrical habits of Aristophanes' Lysistrata, Dikaiopolis, or Peisetairos, however earnest their message, never sound "tragic" even for a moment (apart from occasional phrases of blatant paratragedy). The metrical character of the iambics of satyr play is likewise only slightly "freer" than that of tragedy (much less so than

|[205] encounter the satyr-chorus: childish, animalistic, shameless, and irresponsible, running constant interference with these characters and frequently on the verge of derailing their heroic plot, but no less successful in reaching their own goal—i.e., release from toil and restoration to the blessed state of drunken union with Dionysos and renewed pursuit of the (always available, yet never quite attainable) Nymphs.

Satyr plays thus present a peculiarly skewed set of variations on the theme of dynasts and masses, leaders and led, masters and slaves, already familiar to us from the world of tragedy.[30] Like a tragedy, every satyr play is dominated by one or two leading characters[31] of noble or divine status (whom we may for convenience's sake call the "hero(es)"), whose responsibility it is to take decisive action, banish danger, and reestablish order and prosperity. The superior understanding, moral seriousness, and (in the case of male figures) valor of these elite characters command the audience's respect—and usually approval—in contrast to the ignorance, brutishness, and occasional outright lawlessness of the satyrs (and in some cases, of a villain or two as well); and these characters are seen to come from, and return to, positions of honor and authority within a legitimate kind of social structure, once this brief interlude in the wilds is concluded. The "progress" of the temporarily oppressed (or unrecognized, or lost, or new-born) mythical-divine hero indeed represents a familiar fantasy-narrative, one with which spectators of all social backgrounds can readily identify—and one that seems to be closely related to that of an initiate's ritual passage.[32]

In a much more blatant manner than tragedies, satyr plays reaffirm the childish and/or slavish dependency of the majority of the surrounding community (i.e., satyrs and audience) upon the resolute and responsible actions of their masterful

---

that of comedy): in Aischylos' surviving satyric trimeters, the rate is roughly one resolution per 10 lines; it is significant, too, that metrical resolutions are noticeably less frequent in the speeches of heroic characters than they are elsewhere in the iambics of satyr drama (Seaford 1984: 47–48 on E. *Cyclops*; and the same is true of, e.g., Kyllene and Apollo in S. *Ichn.*, or Danae, Dike, and Poseidon/Apollo [?] in Aischylos. [On these dictional and metrical details, see further Griffith 2006 = Chapter 3 below]). Nor do satyr plays seem to offer anything equivalent to the choral parabasis of Old Comedy, which was another vehicle for a kind of comic "seriousness," involving an address directly to the audience concerning matters external to the plot of the drama itself (cf. Sifakis 1977).

[30] See especially Griffith 1995, 1998, Wilson 2000: 194–97.

[31] To judge from the surviving plays and fragments, it was rare for a satyr play to contain more than two or three main characters altogether, though, e.g., S. *Inachos* may have had more (KPS 1999: 313–43).

[32] See above p. 22 on romance and *Märchen*; also Seaford 1984, Winkler 1990. We may ask, what about those victimized female characters who often in satyr drama begin by being threatened (by the satyrs, or a villain, or Herakles, or an unknown visitor...) but are soon "rescued" and/or found to be pregnant with a divine-heroic baby (e.g., Danae, Amymone, Io)? Perhaps, by conventional male Greek standards, the "discovery" in itself (as in several surviving tragedies) may be cause enough for happiness and pride (in the prestigious maternal future), though modern sensibilities might respond differently (cf. A. *Prom.* [Io], S. *Tr.* [Iole], etc., and Pindar *passim*: cf. Wohl 1998: 3–16, 46–56).

leaders.³³ And it may be significant that satyr plays appear to have made little use of such minor characters as messengers, guards, nurses, herdsmen, attendants, prophets, etc., who generally function in tragedy as representative and |[206] normative non-elite members of the larger community.³⁴ The sympathies of the theater audience are thus all the more sharply divided between, on the one hand, the heroes (superior moral agents, capable of decisive action—like ourselves—yet distinguished clearly from us by their royal-heroic or divine birth, resplendent costume, elevated diction, and prominent stage-presence),³⁵ and on the other hand, the dependent-inferior chorus (an anonymous and powerless group of excitable by-standers—like ourselves—intently watching, reacting, and responding to the actions of those heroes).³⁶ Yet we note that these two constituencies are not *opposed*; rather, they *collaborate* in their different ways to provide an outcome that is mutually beneficial, and we are thus required as spectators to experience the action simultaneously on two somewhat separate, yet overlapping and complementary, planes.

In the case of tragedy, the distinction between the (impressively, sometimes transgressively) active main characters and the (mildly, safely, dependently) passive minor characters and chorus involved the diverse members of the Athenian audience in mixed, even conflicted, responses to the fierce and emotionally wrenching action on the stage.³⁷ Such dissonances were perhaps less acute in satyr plays than in the preceding tragedies, given the reassuring presence within or around the periphery of the orchestra of the benevolent figure of Dionysos, patron of the whole dramatic occasion and ultimate reconciler of social tensions and class differences. But the split between higher and lower objects of identification is all the more blatant and peculiar, especially as so many of the main characters of

---

[33] As Lissarrague 1993: 213–14 points out, satyrs normally seem to constitute a dependent group in attendance on Dionysos, rather than a self-contained society of their own.

[34] Griffith 1995: 72–81, 1999: 55–58. In Euripides' "prosatyric" *Alkestis*, we do find two Servants, each with a significant role, as well as a rare example of a singing Child (though overall, no more than two actors are required for the play).

[35] The main characters go in and out of the central *skênê*-door, for example, which the chorus almost never do; and a heroic character is usually the center of visual and gestural attention, while the chorus spends much of its time on the periphery.

[36] On the exaggerated "responsiveness" of the satyr-chorus, see below, pp. 42–44. In E. *Cyclops*, members of Odysseus' crew are present on-stage for at least part of the action (650–53, 679–84); and two of them get eaten by the Cyclops off-stage; but they never speak, and thus for most of the play amount to no more than "dumb" parts (*kôpha prosôpa*), like the attendants of many royal characters in tragedy. (See further below, n. 39, on the alternating processes of separation and integration of the crew's role with that of the satyrs as "allies," "companions," and "fellow-sailors" to the hero, and the resultant "splitting" and reintegration of the audience's psychological identification.)

[37] For attempts to trace some of these mixed psychological responses and the resultant shifts in subject position within the Athenian audience, see Zeitlin 1995: 341–74, Griffith 1995: 72–81, 1998, Lada 1993. For discussion of similar instabilities of subject position in audience responses to movies, see Neale 1983, Silverman 1992, Mayne 1993, Williams 1995.

satyr drama are divine and the chorus is so alien.[38] |[207]

In Euripides' *Cyclops*, our only complete satyr play, it is possible to distinguish quite precisely a three-tiered structure of causation and engagement that brings about the happy ending: (1) the hero Odysseus, through his own superior intelligence and military resolve (including the supervision of his well-trained, but non-speaking, soldier-sailors, 650–53, 694–95) punishes an impious violator of guest-host norms and then departs to resume his role as ruler of Ithake (689–95, 701–703); (2) the satyrs, friendly allies and specialists in the use of wine and efficacious song (646–65), assist in the tricking and humiliation of a cruel master and are restored to their normal carefree existence (620–22, 709, cf. 38–40 etc.); (3) a divine spirit, whether imagined as "Marôn" (141–43, 412, 616), or "a divine something" (411: *theion ti*, cf. 285: *theou to prâgma*, 606–607: *ta daimonôn*) or Dionysos himself (519–30, 590, 678, 709), contrives to rescue those who deserve it and to guarantee them a life of future happiness.[39]

In normal tragic-causative terms, the dramatic plot depends on its "elite" characters (as well as the gods) to provide the desired outcome. If left to their own devices, the satyrs and their scurrilous father will never succeed. Not only are they too foolish, ineffectual, and cowardly, but they are not even sufficiently interested in the proper social goals or moral norms. Their minds run only on wine, food,

---

[38] To some of the more prosperous spectators at least, an Odysseus or Herakles (if not a Poseidon or Apollo) might appear quite accessible as a moral and behavioral paradigm, someone "of those in high reputation" yet still "like us" (Ar. *Poet*. 13.1452b34-53a10); the divine-heroic babies too, common in satyr plays (Dionysos, Hermes, Herakles, Perseus, etc.), are doubtless to some degree "like us" and engagingly cute, though their miraculous childhoods and brilliant future careers tend to elevate them already somewhat above the audience. Presumably, however, to those from the lower and less sophisticated end of the social spectrum (including the simple-minded rustics discussed by Rossi 1972/1989), the gaudily-dressed heroes and divinities will all have seemed quite remote from their own experience ("better than us," Ar. *Poet*. 2.1448a1-5), and in some cases—as in tragedy—potentially rather distasteful or threatening in the "tyrannical" assertiveness of their behavior. See Griffith 1995, and Mastronarde 1999 "factor (5)" (pp. 28–29 below).

[39] The conventionally fortuitous interweaving of these separate (divine vs. human, heroic vs. satyric) strands of causation is neatly exposed in the first encounter between Papposilenos and Odysseus:

[Od.] "Blasts of wind violently drove me here."
[Pap.] "Papai! You are struggling with the same fortune (τὸν αὐτὸν δαίμονα) as I."
(*Cycl*. 109–10)

Although in Homer it is Odysseus' own curiosity that leads him to land on Polyphemos' island, in a satyr play it is Dionysos that implicitly (or explicitly, 110: *daimona*) supervises every event: he is the "same spirit" for both, yet works in different ways for each (cf. Horace *AP* 225–29). Similarly, in the final lines of the play, Odysseus is credited with two distinct sets of "fellow-sailors": his regular Greek companions (705: συνναύταισι) and his temporary play-mates, the satyrs (708: συνναῦταί γε τοῦδ' Ὀδυσσέως). Insofar as the audience's fantasies of identification have previously been split between these two groups of "allies, companions" to Odysseus (642: σύμμαχοι = satyrs; 650: τοῖς οἰκείοις φίλοις, 653: φίλων = crew), this curious verbal and imagistic merging of the two groups may be said to constitute a reintegration of the audience's subject position into one of whole-hearted inclusion and participation in this final sympotic "voyage"; see above n. 36, and further below, pp. 47–49.

music, and sex. Yet it is also undeniable that every play *needs* its satyric chorus, to watch, react, collaborate, anticipate, and ultimately share in the guaranteed blessings of Dionysos. It is not just that "the chorus" is a conventional requirement in the Theater (though this is certainly true), but that in an important sense the satyrs' presence and involvement are essential to the dramatic fantasy—and in some sense, to the audience's engagement with the |[208] action. This is not to say that the chorus of a satyr play elicits dramatic tension or audience engagement equivalent to those of a tragedy, or that the audience situates itself whole-heartedly within the chorus' subject position and frame of reference: far from it—the satyrs' expectations and emotions tend to be wildly exaggerated and are often premature or groundless; and in general, the level of uncertainty or anxiety among the spectators of a satyr play remains quite low, so sure are they of the guarantee of divine protection and happy outcome (Polyphemos will not in fact eat Odysseus; Amymone and Danae will each be rescued from the satyrs' unwelcome advances; Apollo will not hurt Hermes; the Sphinx's riddle will be solved; etc.).[40] Nonetheless, as in tragedy, the chorus' responses to the action do contribute significantly to shaping those of the audience, in terms both of their own aspirations, and of their approval and support of the main (heroic) character(s).[41]

Some of my readers may perhaps be reluctant to concede that the audience's (our) sympathies were (are) in any way to be aligned with the satyrs, or that our imagination would stray at all in the direction of "identifying" with such abjected characters and adopting their subject position. Indeed, many critics write as if the only identification going on in the theater (whether tragic, comic, or satyric) is with the hero.[42] But we have already noted several respects in which the Athenian audience was necessarily drawn to share the choral perspective, and it is time now to return to that issue and to explore it in more detail.

The general question of the relationship between the theater audience and the dramatic (especially tragic) chorus has been extensively debated over the years.[43] While it still perhaps cannot be said that universal agreement has been achieved, recent contributions to the topic have clarified the issues considerably. In particular, Donald Mastronarde, in a study focusing primarily on the Euripidean tragic

---

[40] For some observations about possible retrospective wrinkles of uncertainty, even surprises, in the audience's understanding of the preceding tragic "trilogy," in cases where the action of all four plays was linked, see below pp. 57–74 (on A. *Proteus*).

[41] An obvious example is the chorus' gloating over Polyphemos' downfall (*Cycl.* 663–88). And on the similar function performed by tragic choruses, see below pp. 28–30 (with further refs.); cf. too Lissarrague 1993 on satyrs as spectators, and Travis 1996 *passim*, on the tragic chorus' peculiarly intimate relationship to the theater audience.

[42] E.g., Jauss 1974, Green 1979, Lada 1993; but for less monolithic approaches, see Travis 1996, Griffith 1995, 1998, Hall 1997 (and n. 37 above).

[43] In recent years, see esp. Vernant 1965/1983, Henrichs 1995, Gould 1996, Goldhill 1997, Travis 1996, Griffith 1999: 55–58, 65–66, Mastronarde 1998, 1999, Calame 1999; on Old Comedy, see Sifakis 1972.

chorus, has developed a useful checklist of "factors that contribute to the authority of the tragic chorus or tend to create a close identification of the external audience with the chorus"—along with a set of "countervailing factors" that tend to do the opposite, i.e., undermine the chorus' authority and/or distance the external audience from them. Of the eight "factors" on Mastronarde's list, the |[209] first three involve primarily the chorus' "authority."[44] The other five concern the degree and nature of the audience's identification with the tragic chorus, and are worth exploring here with regard to satyric choruses. Here (in paraphrase) are the five factors:[45]

(1) As an audience within the play, the tragic chorus serves as a spatial, temporal, and communicative intermediary for the external audience in the theater. (2) The chorus' status as a group, set over against the individual characters, links them to the audience (another corporate group) and tends to promote an analogical relationship with those characters. (3) The chorus, like the theater audience, conventionally survives the tragic catastrophe that usually engulfs the main character(s), and is able at the end of the play to return (like the audience) relatively unscathed to everyday life.[46] (4) The chorus usually have the final words of "summation" to deliver, often more or less directly to the audience. (5) In the Athenian (democratic) context, the interaction/opposition of such a (less socially elevated, and implicitly democratic) group with an elite (and implicitly "undemocratic") individual (king, hero, etc.) carries a particular ideological burden, which may be present also in the opposition between the (passive, observing) audience and

---

[44] These are: (1) the traditional nature of choral performance in general, with its analogue in the divine chorus of Muses (to which we might add the ethical and disciplinary power of the musical modes and choreography in eliciting automatic or culturally conditioned corporal and mental responses from an audience); (2) the conventional power of the choral voice to transmit a message both "vertically" from on high and "horizontally" amongst a community of peers; (3) the semiotic authority conventionally assigned to performative utterances, gnomic wisdom, and mythological narrative of the kinds commonly employed in choral lyrics. It should be acknowledged, certainly, that in these terms the "authority" of the satyric chorus is considerably smaller than that of tragedy; for those satyric lyrics that survive are relatively short, contain little gnomic or mythological material, and usually remain much more mimetic and less reflective or narrative than the stasima of tragedy (see Rode 1971, Seaford 1984 on E. *Cycl.* 356–84, KPS 1999: 19–23). But see n. 53 below.

[45] Mastronarde 1999; cf. 1998: 56–62. I have rearranged the order of these five, for the sake of convenience in my subsequent argument. Although Mastronarde does not specifically define what he means by "identification," I will take it broadly speaking to involve the readiness of a spectator (or reader) mentally to adopt the subject position of this or that character or group of characters on stage, and to imagine him/herself (re)acting (thinking and feeling) in the same way in this immediate context. See further Silverman 1992, Williams 1995, Lott 1993: 136–58, Griffith 1998: 39–43, with further references.

[46] Mastronarde does not discuss tragedies with happy endings from this perspective; but the same basic distinction can be observed between the big rewards of the heroes (recognition of family members, recovery of status and power, etc.) and the more modest gains of the chorus. A comparable process is found among the satyr-choruses, as we shall see.

those (active, speaking) characters.[47] |[210]

[47] Several of these functions of the non-elite "survivor" are also performed by some of the ordinary, minor characters, of course: see Griffith 1995: 72–81. In non-Greek tragedy (e.g., Shakespeare, or Japanese *nôh*-drama), this phenomenon tends to be more conspicuous. Thus in the closing scene of *Hamlet*, Horatio is prevented by the dying hero from joining the array of noble corpses and instructed instead to make sure that Hamlet's story reaches its proper public audience: "As thou art a man / Give me the cup: let go; by heaven, I'll have it! / O good Horatio, what a wounded name, / Things standing thus unknown, shall live behind me. / If thou didst ever hold me in thy heart, / Absent thee from felicity awhile, / And in this harsh world draw thy breath in pain / To tell my story…" And Horatio indeed begins this story-telling, with Fortinbras' support, before the play closes: "Let me speak to th' yet unknowing world / How these things came about… all this can I / Truly deliver…. But let this same be presently performed…." The noble hero's extraordinary sufferings are thus memorialized by lesser figures who explicitly are said to resemble and anticipate the members of the theater audience (and the playwright): "Bear Hamlet, like a soldier, to the stage…." In *nôh* drama, the life-and-death struggles and psychic agonies of the elite main character (*shite*, lit. "actor") conventionally form the focus of attention and commentary from a subsidiary interlocutor (*waki*, lit. "person at the side" or "witness") and from occasional other minor characters (e.g., a Villager or Innkeeper; see n. 7 above); meanwhile the chorus sit to one side, outside the acting/dancing space, and make no direct contact with the *shite*, while their voices generally speak and sing as an extension of his. Nothing usually *happens* to any of these by-standers/participants, as they witness the death, spiritual release, or transformation of the *shite*. The interest is overwhelmingly on the *shite*, and it is this character's consciousness that fills and dominates the theater; yet this consciousness is experienced from (or created and represented by) several different perspectives simultaneously. It is important to note that this main character (who traditionally is always played by a masked male actor), while invariably noble in status, is often female and/or dead (a ghost or demon), whereas the (non-masked) *waki*-character is invariably male and of middling social status (often a travelling monk)—i.e., much closer to the status and situation of the implied "ideal/normal/typical" audience member. (Occasionally, as in Zeami's *Matsukaze*, there is a second, subsidiary main [masked] character [*tsure*, "companion," male or female]; in which case the dynamic may become somewhat more complex, but not essentially different: cf. Tyler 1992: 181–92.) The "splitting" of the audience's perspectives on the *shite*'s experience is further enhanced by a peculiar linguistic convention, whereby the verb-forms frequently shift back and forth between 1st and 3rd person, so that everyone on stage may appear to be speaking (or singing) from the "same" viewpoint, or with reference to the same inner psychological awareness: see further Keene 1966: 19–21, Smethurst 1989, Tyler 1992: 7–12. It has been argued in an influential essay (Nogami 1930: 1–42) that because the *shite* is the sole focus of attention, *nôh* does not properly qualify as "drama": rather it is a "vehicle for display" of the main character's person and consciousness. On this reading, the *waki* as "onlooker" is more a "representative of the audience" or "interpreter" than a true character ("second performer") in the play. But Tyler 1997 argues persuasively that the dynamic between *shite* and *waki* (as between *shite* and *tsure*) is often one of inter-dependency, involving observed and observer, object and subject, "two yet not two" (a traditional Chinese and Buddhist concept), in which "*waki* and *shite* are co-dependent… The *shite*'s relationship with the *waki* is therefore crucial. Not only do the *shite*'s own qualities, as witnessed by the *waki* and the audience, arise from it, but the *waki* himself, as a person, is inevitably affected by his encounter with the *shite*. Their existences are interdependent. No doubt this interrelationship goes unnoticed, at least consciously, by most readers or spectators. Still, the words and images are there, and so is the human reality that informs them" (Tyler 1997: 66, 87). I cite these two (admittedly remote) forms of dramatic performance at such length here only because in each of them the distinction—and interplay—between higher and lower social levels on stage, and the resultant splitting of audience sympathies and subject position, seems to correspond so closely to, and hence

In assessing the "countervailing" factors (i.e., those that make it harder, or less likely, for the audience to identify with a tragic chorus), Mastronarde (following John Gould) rightly emphasizes the diversity of these choruses (which renders generalizations imperfect and sometimes misleading), and points in particular to the tendency for Euripides and Aischylos to prefer socially marginalized choruses made up of females and/or foreigners and/or slaves. Such choruses are much less straightforwardly representative of the community or the social norms of their respective plays than (e.g.) the old men of *Agamemnon* and *Antigone*, or the soldiers of *Ajax* and *Philoctetes*, and may accordingly be less likely to adopt |[211] the perspectives and command the sympathies of a predominantly male citizen audience. Yet overall, Mastronarde concludes that the degree of identification even in these cases is relatively strong.[48]

How about satyr-choruses, then, which would seem to stand even further off, at or beyond the margins, than the most abjected tragic chorus? Certainly their "authority" as a speaking or acting presence is small, as we have noted: they are indeed *outidanoi* ("nobodies"). Does this mean that the degree of identification with them experienced by the Athenian audience was equally small? Most critics have assumed so.[49] Yet not only did these satyrs share the conventional bond of fellowship with the audience enjoyed by every choral group in the theater, but they seem in fact to have held a peculiarly strong conscious or unconscious claim on the male Athenian imagination. Indeed, of Mastronarde's five positive "factors" contributing to the audience's "identification," at least three seem to apply no less to satyrs than to tragic choruses, while the other two present a more mixed—but far from unequivocally negative—dynamic of their own.

(1) As an "audience within the play," the satyr-chorus are constantly found watching, listening, commenting, and applauding as highly impressionable "spectators" of the wonderful inventions, achievements, and adventures of the main characters. To a greater degree than their tragic counterparts, they appear to have maintained an almost continuous corporeal commentary on the stage action, even when they were not speaking or singing. Thus, in spatial and communicative terms, they are intermediaries, "standing in" for the wider audience, which sits

---

illuminate, the multiple identifications for which I have been arguing in the case of Athenian tragedy and satyr play. I do not claim or believe that this is a universal effect of all forms of theater: rather, that certain "high" forms may derive their enduring appeal in part from their peculiar ability to appeal simultaneously to different social strata and to deliver mixed messages and emotional satisfactions to a varied body of spectators.

[48] See below, n. 126, for discussion. For a more thorough-going attempt to downplay the notion of a "collective" response to Athenian tragedy, however, and to emphasize instead each audience member's separate and individual reaction, see Griffin 1998.

[49] But see, e.g., Sutton 1980: 178–79, Seaford 1984: 7–10, 30–33, for reminders of the numinous value of satyrs. Toph Marshall suggests to me also that the satyr-chorus may well have enjoyed some measure of "carry-over" of authority from the preceding trilogy.

motionless at a greater distance from the action and never speaks.⁵⁰ And although their naive spectatorship is more childish and unreliable than that of the theater audience, so that an element of ironic distance frequently creeps in between the two perspectives, nonetheless for the most part the emotions of the satyrs are *exaggerations*, rather than negations or contradictions, of the audience's emotions.⁵¹ As for the temporal relationship, satyrs exist in a different dimension from the choruses of tragedy, in as much as the latter represent particular groups of men or women, tied to the moment of that tragic action, whereas the satyrs, |[212] though likewise caught for a moment in the place and time of this long-past mythical event, are nonetheless essentially "timeless" and ubiquitous—they are always the "same" satyrs, who always were and always will be getting into and out of trouble, then and now. (As Odysseus remarks, "I've known since long ago (*palai*) that you were like that...," *Cycl.* 649.) This timeless and unchanging quality may be said to bring the chorus even closer to the audience, as it bestows on both groups the capacity to stand apart from the immediate action and to contemplate their usual (continuous, extra-dramatic) status, separate and untroubled, a status to which they will be restored as soon as the play ends.⁵²

(2) Despite the tendency for choral utterances in satyr plays to be broken up into separate little phrases from different choreuts, and for the dances to be less strophically regular and orderly than their tragic counterparts, the satyrs do comprise a cohesive (corporate, and anonymous) group—like other choruses—in clear distinction from the individual (named) characters.⁵³ Satyrs burst easily into song, and their ready access to exclamatory language, music, dance, and ritual gesture gives them a more potent and emotive connection with the audience than

---

⁵⁰Lissarrague 1993: 212 comments on the "perpetual motion" characteristic of satyrs (as of children), both in drama and in vase-paintings; see too KPS 1999: 21–22 with n. 107, and further below, pp. 42–44 (on satyric song- and dance-rhythms).

⁵¹The satyrs' characteristic air is one of "unexpected... curiosity... astonishment, panic, bedazzlement... especially in satyric drama, where they are like naifs who discover what the spectator knows all too well.... In this sense, their status is close to that of children... The world of satyrs has its source, too, in *play*" (Lissarrague 1993: 218–19); cf. Seaford 1984: 36–37, KPS 1999: 28; also Burnett 1971 for tragic comparanda.

⁵²Several scenes in satyr plays include a nostalgic reference to a previous time when things were different and better; e.g., A. *Dikty.* F 47a 826–31, *Isthm.* F 78a 34–35: τρόπους καινούς, 48, 69; S. *Ichn.* F 314.223–24: τίς μετάστασις πόνων οὕς πρόσθεν εἶχες δεσπότηι χάριν φέρων, E. *Cycl.* 63–81: οὐ τάδε Βρόμιος, οὐ τάδε χοροί κτλ., 439–40: ὡς διὰ μακροῦ ... χηρεύομεν.

⁵³On the characteristics of satyric meter and choral expression in general, see Seidensticker 1979, Seaford 1984: 46–47 and ad locc.; also KPS 1999: 21–23 (who aptly compare the Furies' lyrics in the first half of A. *Eum.*, on which see also Griffith 1995: 101 n. 126). [For the general colometric and lexical similarities between the lyrics of Aischylos' satyr plays and tragedies, see Griffith 2006 = Chapter 3 below.] The closest tragic parallels to satyric style, with their high rate of trochaics, cretics, and dochmiacs, and frequent exclamations and interjections, are found in the more mimetic and/or anxious outbursts of (usually) female choruses (esp. in their entrance-songs); cf. Rode: 1971: 91–97.

the sober iambic utterances of the individual actors.[54] Choral anonymity and musical-choreographic collectivity were further reinforced by identical costumes; and indeed the satyrs seem even less capable than a tragic chorus of imagining |[213] themselves except as part of such a group; they have not even a potential existence as individuals.[55]

(3) Even more than the theater audience, the satyrs bring with them an aura not only of conventionally-guaranteed survival and invulnerability but also of markedly improved fortunes by play's end. The stage action is thus felt to be taking place in some sense *for their and our benefit and enjoyment*—even if the main agents are characters who have previously had, and in future will have, nothing to do with us (or the satyrs) at all.[56] The chorus of Euripides' *Cyclops* characteristically sum up their conflicted (yet unproblematic) relationship to the impending crisis on-stage with the proverb, ἐν τῶι Καρὶ κινδυνεύσομεν ("We'll let the Karians take the risks for us!" *Cycl.* 654): i.e., others more foolhardy and/or heroic will expose themselves to danger, while the satyrs wait to enjoy the fruits of a vicarious victory.[57] Odysseus recognizes—without apparent surprise (649: πάλαι μὲν ἤιδη

---

[54] Exceptions: the drunken Polyphemos sings a stanza of sympotic anacreontics (E. *Cycl.* 503–10), in epirrhematic response to the chorus; at A. *Prometheus Pyrkaeus* F 204b (= fr. 278 Lloyd-Jones), this could be (as Radt suggests) Prometheus singing about the celebration of fire; but most commentators assign both song and refrain to the chorus: "Good-willed favor (*charis*) makes me dance... Often, one of the Nymphs will hear and pursue me by the hearth's bright flame.—Indeed, I too am sure the Nymphs will establish choruses in honor of the gift of Prometheus.—Fine is the song that I expect them to sing about the giver, saying that Prometheus is the life-bringer and gift-bestower for mortals..." In general, although the use of melody and marked dictional and dialectal expressions can be said (Gould 1996) to distance choral utterance from the audience's normal and everyday speech, it is generally agreed (e.g., by Aristotle, Nietzsche, and many since) that the rhythmic, melodic, and visual effects of choral song and dance were felt to be more, not less, engaging to most audience members than the dialogue—especially given the notoriously exciting effect of the aulos, with its distinctive timbre; see, e.g., Anderson 1966: 44–47, 64–66, 136–38, West 1992: 31–36, Henrichs 1995, Wilson 1999. For helpful analogies (and differences) in the role of dance in *nôh*-drama, see Bethe and Brazell 1982, esp. 49–68, 163–78.

[55] In some vase-paintings, satyr-silens are given individual type-names (usually referring to their sexual behavior: e.g. Peôn, Posthôn, Styôn, Eratôn, Psôlas, Dophios, Terpekêlos, etc.; see also below, pp. 39–40, but these seem quite interchangable; cf. D. F. Sutton *AJP* 106 (1985): 107–10. On the Pronomos Vase (Fig. 5) citizen names are inscribed next to each satyr-choreut—but these refer to the human choreuts (and piper, lyrist, and poet), not to the satyr-characters. (Interestingly, the choreuts' names seem to be predominantly upper-class: Eunikos, Nikomachos, Kallias, etc.; see esp. Fig. 5b = Csapo and Slater 1995: plate 8; also Wilson 2000: 129–30, and further M. Osborne in Taplin and Wyles 2010.) Only Papposilenos has his dramatic name inscribed, like the main characters (Herakles, Dionysos, etc.). On the "in-between" status of Papposilenos—is he the chorus-leader? or a separate character, played by an actor? did his status vary from play to play, or did his conventional role perhaps evolve during the course of the fifth century, esp. after the introduction of the third actor?—see Seaford 1984: 4–5, G. Conrad *Der Silen* (Trier, 1997), KPS 1999: 24–25. [On the Pronomos Vase in general, and these questions in particular, see now Taplin and Wyles 2010.]

[56] For this process in the tragic context, see Griffith 1995; and see n. 47 above.

[57] The proverb is found also at Plato *Laches* 187b, *Euthyd.* 285c, where the scholiasts cite Archilochos

σ' ὄντα τοιοῦτον φύσει, "I knew long ago that this is what you are like")—that the satyrs are after all "useless men, nothing, <as> allies" (642: ἄνδρες πονηροὶ κοὐδὲν οἵδε σύμμαχοι), who have "no power in your arms" (651: χειρὶ ... μηδὲν σθένεις); yet at the very moment when they reveal their physical and military incapacity, they also promise the miraculous powers of their music:

> ἀλλ' οἶδ' ἐπῳδὴν Ὀρφέως ἀγαθὴν πάνυ,
> ὥστ' αὐτόματον τὸν δαλὸν ἐς τὸ κρανίον
> στείχονθ' ὑφάπτειν τὸν μονῶπα παῖδα γῆς.
>
> (Cycl. 646–48)
>
> But I know a really good incantation of Orpheus,
> So that the branch will move on its own accord into his head
> And set light to the one-eyed son of earth! |[214]

And in what follows, they sing their magical "exhortations" (646: ἐπῳδήν, 652: ἐπεγκέλευε, 653: κελευσμοῖς, 655: κελευσμάτων, cf. 664: παιάν, μέλπε...) as an accompaniment to the (offstage) handiwork of Odysseus and his crewmen. Indeed, they confidently boast:

> κελευσμάτων δ' ἕκατι τυφέσθω Κύκλωψ.
>
> (655)
>
> "As far as words go... let the Cyclops be consumed in flames!"[58]

Not only are their incantations fully in tune with Odysseus' wishes and needs, but they are fully effective: for immediately after their magical stanza (656–62), we hear Polyphemos' shriek, ὤμοι, κατηνθρακώμεθα.... ("Aagh! I've been incinerated!"). Whether Odysseus and his crew manipulated the burning branch, or it flew into the Cyclops' eye on its own (or a little of both), this chorus shares in the victory as surely as any of their tragic counterparts.[59]

(4) Like the tragic chorus, we can assume that the satyr-chorus normally delivered the last lines of the play, and made the final exit (as in *Cyclops*, the only play whose ending survives).[60]

---

fr. 216 West, and explain that Archaic Greeks used to employ Karians as cheap mercenary cannon-fodder in their battles. Similarly Porphyrios on Hom. *Il.* 9.378 (τίω δέ μιν ἐν καρὸς αἴσηι) interprets Achilleus' dismissive remark as referring to "a Karian." (The sense and context of Soph. F 540: Καρικοὶ τράγοι, from the satyric *Salmoneus*, are unknown.)

[58] On the force of ἕκατι, see Seaford 1984 ad loc.

[59] Likewise, the "Tracking" chorus of S. *Ichn.* succeeds in finding the cattle (and the baby Hermes), and consequently comes to enjoy the new benefits of lyre-music and (presumably) freedom; the "Net-fishing" chorus of A. *Dikty.* succeeds in landing the strange catch and strikes up a cosy rapport with little Perseus and his mother; and so on.

[60] For the analogous function in Shakespearean tragedy of closing words from one or more minor characters, confirming the theater audience's identification with them, see above, n. 47. See too n. 39 above on the multivalence of *sunnautai* in the closing lines of E. *Cyclops*: if the satyr-chorus is thus

By these first four criteria, at least, the satyr-chorus would seem not to have elicited a significantly different set of responses than their tragic counterparts. But at this point we need to confront the obvious question of the radically alien and abjected status, appearance, and behavior of this particular choral group. Can we really expect the audience to have identified to any significant degree with such a subhuman and disreputable bunch?[61] Most critics have assumed that the audience's attitude towards the satyrs must have been unequivocally superior and distant (whether amused or contemptuous or both), in recognition of the gulf between their rustic and childish—even slavish and animalistic—behavior and the citizens' own more civilized standards. But for all their absurd and grotesque aspects, the satyrs of drama seem in fact to have been presented in such a way as to engage the sympathies and fantasies of their male citizen audience to quite a significant degree. Indeed, I suggest that these choruses represented a playfully disguised ("misrecognized"), but imaginatively powerful and multivalent, mechanism for exploring and |[215] reconciling, on the one hand, the internal psychological pressures of male ego-formation and, on the other, the sharp divisions between the competing democratic and aristocratic ideologies that permeated Athens' larger political and cultural arena.

As Richard Seaford has emphasized, satyrs were *daimones*, with numinous powers of their own, and they represented in effect a *thiasos* of Bacchic celebrants, a role familiar to every member of the audience and directly experienced by many. Furthermore, the plots of the plays often involved the rescue of the satyrs from captivity and/or forced labor, encounters with a precious and transformational new invention or person, and their eventual restoration to the company of Dionysos himself; thus the theater audience became witnesses to, even participants in, a process of Bacchic salvation and empowerment.[62] And if, as Jack Winkler argued in a characteristically brilliant and provocative article, the members of the tragic and satyric chorus were always of ephebic age, then the level and nature of the process of identification and/or representation between audience and chorus would have been still further enhanced, as these young men by definition comprise the city's best and brightest, chosen representatives of the community at large.[63] |[216]

---

momentarily merged with Odysseus' human companions, the audience's sense of connection with him as "fellow-travellers" in his successful nostos is thereby doubled.

[61] At A. *Dikty.* 775 they are referred to as *knôdala* ("monsters, creatures"); cf. S. *Ichn.* 147, 153, 221, E. *Cycl.* 624: *thêres*, etc.

[62] Seaford 1984: 26–44. He suggests additional ritual (salvationist-initiatory) elements too, including celebration/participation in someone's emergence from the underworld (*anodos*), witnessing amazing sights and sounds, and finding and/or educating little children. Several of these motifs may be specifically linked to the Athenian festival of the Anthesteria (Seaford 1984: 7–8, referring also to Lawson 1910: 221–32; see above, n. 17). But Seaford's further suggestion that the animality of the satyrs may also reflect the totemistic character of an initiatory group or tribe seems to me less plausible.

[63] Winkler 1985, 1990. (The 1990 version omits the discussion of satyr plays.) Winkler's argument

Winkler himself argued for a heavily "educational" function for the plays (both tragic and satyric), in teaching the ephebes appropriate civic and military behavior through the presentation of paradigmatic performances of successful and unsuccessful youthful conflicts and challenges within the world of traditional myth.[64] On this "educational" score, the satyrs might seem at first glance to serve as a strongly negative paradigm, for they are not merely "non-political," but often downright subversive of civic and military values.[65] Yet, in a less overtly educational or didactic mode, the combination of "daimonic" inviolability and choral privilege may be said to protect—even to legitimize—this exuberant musical group in its chaotic enthusiasm and irresponsible hi-jinks. And not only are the satyr "children" disarmingly innocent and naive (markedly less treacherous, and slightly more soldierly, than their reprobate father—and even willing on occasion

---

is based primarily on the following considerations: (a) On the Pronomos Vase (Fig. 5), the two main actors are bearded adults, while the chorus-members are all younger and unbearded, i.e., apparently adolescents. The same is true of the three beardless satyr-choreuts shown rehearsing on a South Italian bell-krater of the 390s (Fig. 7 = Sydney #47.05 = Trendall and Webster 1971: 28, pl. II.2), not mentioned by Winkler. (On the other hand, as one anonymous referee points out to me, "the figure sitting at the bottom of the couch, who is most plausibly interpreted as the actor of a female part, is clean-shaven. It is worth noting that in the great majority of vase paintings showing actors, the actors are clean-shaven. Perhaps it was necessary to be clean-shaven to wear a whole-head mask? In that case, the Pronomos Vase becomes the exception with its bearded actors, who seem to have 'merged' with their parts in a type of merging between drama and reality that is found in other aspects of this vase"; see too Csapo and Slater 1995: 352.) (b) Greek choruses generally fell into three age-groups: adults (*andres* or *gynaikes*), youths (*neoi/kouroi* or *parthenoi/korai*), and children (*paides*). At the City Dionysia, choruses of "men" and of "boys" performed in the dithyrambic contests; but we hear nothing about choruses of "youths" (*neoi, kouroi, ephêboi*): the dramatic choruses of tragedy and comedy would be an obvious possibility for this. (No other choruses are known to have performed at that festival.) (c) The rectangular formations of the dramatic chorus, as contrasted with the circular choreography of dithyramb and most other choral dance, resembles the formations of military training and battle; and ephebic training was primarily intended as military training. (d) The ephebes were assigned a central role in the procession and Theater seating arrangements. (e) The goat (*tragos*) was associated with young men, both for its straggly beard and for its bleating voice. Of these arguments, (e) is the least convincing (esp. since it was the horsey, rather than goatish, aspects of the satyrs that seem to have been emphasized in Attic drama: see n. 71 below); but the first four are quite substantial.

[64]"These festivals were the occasion for elaborate symbolic play on themes of proper and improper civic behavior, in which the principal component of proper male citizenship was military... A central reference point for these representations—the notional learners of its lessons (*paideia*) about the trials of manhood (*andreia*)—were the young men of the city, and they were also the choral performers at least of tragedy [sc. and satyr play], and perhaps also of comedy," Winkler 1990: 20–21; likewise 1985: 51–53.

[65]So, e.g., KPS 1999: 38–39 (quoted above, n. 13). See too Seaford 1984: 8, 30–33 (with reference to Plato *Laws* 815c) on satyric rituals as being *ou politikon*. Satyrs do from time to time experiment briefly with athletic and even military training (e.g. A. *Isthm.*, Achaios *TrGF* I. 20 F 4; and cf. Collinge 1989, Lissarrague 1993, and, e.g., KPS 1999: Taf. 14a, 16b, 19b for images of satyrs engaged in more or less "civic" and/or military activities): but they always relapse into their previous life-style before play's end.

to receive "instruction" from others with enthusiasm and good will), but their harmless and ineffectual aggression, though it verges on *hybris*, is of a kind that (as we shall see) appealed strongly to the men of Athens.[66]

It is important to note that theater-satyrs never actually sustain or complete the assaults, rapes, or ambushes they begin; unlike the centaurs of myth, or the characters and choruses of Old Comedy, they are not by nature capable of serious violence or damage to others.[67] Instead, they posture incessantly, and live in a state of permanent excitement and playful anticipation—like children or the less |[217] sophisticated members of a drunken *kômos*—and by play's end they are rewarded with their longed-for release from toils, with all the dancing, singing, and drinking that the occasion demands. As in the finale of a Comedy, the audience are thus drawn in to share the expulsion of danger and enemies and to celebrate the resultant increase in social solidarity and *homonoia*, to which the satyrs have contributed their puny but magical share.[68] The satyrs are our friends. Indeed, if

---

[66] See, e.g., Aristotle's discussion of *hybris* and *neoi* in the *Rhetoric*. The more outrageous (and often anti-democratic) Athenian *hetaireiai* ("Men's Clubs") often chose nick-names for themselves that connoted a similar mind-set: *Ithyphalloi, Triballoi, Kakodaimonistai, Autolekythoi*, etc.; see Jones 1999: 223–27, Keuls 1985; and cf. C. W. Marshall *G&R* 46 (1999) 194, Wilson 1999 on the scandalously "satyric" figures of Alkibiades and Sokrates (and see further below, p. 133). In some respects, we might think of this group of eternally childish and irrepressible males, aggressive and selfish in their behavior, yet entirely dependent on a parent (and esp. fond of their mother), as resembling Hesiod's Silver Race (*WD* 127–37). But that Race, although curiously privileged, like the satyrs, in their relationship to the gods, has been removed from the face of the earth, whereas the satyrs are tolerated and even encouraged by the Olympians. The analogy should certainly not be pressed. [At the time of writing this article, I was unaware of Edith Hall's valuable 1998 article on "Ithyphallic Males Behaving Badly." In Griffith 2005 (below, Chapter 2) I do take this article into account.]

[67] Lissarrague 1990b: 61–66 observes that visual representations of satyrs (especially after ca. 500 BCE) rarely show them achieving successful intercourse with young women (maenads or nymphs) or men; instead they usually have recourse to somewhat degraded or solitary acts: exhibitionism, bestiality, group-sex, or masturbation; see too Simon 1982, Keuls 1985: 360–71, and below, n. 103; also pp. 54–55 (with Figs. 8a and 8b) on Amymone.

[68] It is significant that the crucial ethical and strategic error committed by Polyphemos is his acceptance of Odysseus' (deceitful) suggestion that he hog all the wine for himself and not share it hospitably with his fellow Cyclopes (E. *Cycl.* 445–46, 451–53, 507–10, 519–44); cf. Rossi 1971, Hamilton 1979. By contrast, the satyrs seem happy, there and elsewhere, to share with each other and anyone else: they are properly "social" in at least this one respect. At the end of the play, the chorus' celebration includes tormenting the blinded ogre and revelling in his humiliation (663–88), a process also (presumably) enjoyed by the Athenian audience. In Old Comedy, the final demonstration of male domination likewise frequently involves both chorus and main character(s) in a shared celebration (*kômos*) that includes violent or insulting rejection of outsiders. While we do not possess enough endings of satyr plays to generalize with confidence, it appears that the satyr-chorus and human heroes (unlike their comic counterparts) usually went off to separate final destinations to celebrate (see above, n. 39). In this respect, satyr plays are more similar to tragedies, which usually maintain the clear distinction between elites and commoners (chorus, messengers, polis at large) to the bitter end. Even the *Eumenides*, with its most inclusive and civic-minded of all tragic endings, sends its elite characters (Orestes, Apollo—and Zeus) off at the end to rosy futures in distant residences, while the local inhabitants (*chôritai*) are

we happen to be leisured young Athenian men, they may be said to be versions (inversions, caricatures) of ourselves.[69]

What did these stage-satyrs look like? Just how gross and subhuman were they? Obviously, if the audience found them too physically repulsive or contemptible, they would be unlikely to feel any sense of identification with them at all.[70] Satyrs and silens were represented on hundreds of sixth- and fifth-century Athenian vases, in many different shapes, ages, activities, and degrees of grotesqueness, ranging from the bestial and disgusting to the engagingly childlike |[218] or even near-respectable.[71] Indeed, the sheer profusion of such visual representations of satyrs, whether on their own, or in the company of nymphs, maenads, and Dionysos, or interacting with purely human characters, confirms the familiarity and powerful resonance of these images within the collective and individual Athenian imagination.

In the sixth century, Black-Figure representations tend to concentrate on particular mythological scenes, especially the Return of Hephaistos (as in Fig. 1) and Dionysos with Ariadne on Naxos.[72] But by the later sixth and throughout the fifth century, the Red-Figure repertoire expands steadily, and satyrs show up in a wide range of mythological and heroic scenes, and increasingly in connection with ev-

---

enlisted as "escorts" (*propompoi*) to lead the August Goddesses (*Semnai Theai*) to a new home beneath the Areopagus, where they will dwell for ever more as *metoikoi* (= permanent, non-citizen, resident aliens). It is unclear whether or not Athena accompanies her citizens in this procession.

[69]"From satyrs, we learn not about the Athenians' sexual behavior, but rather about their fantasies": Lissarrague 1990b: 66. It may be noted, too, that the dignified female figure seated next to Dionysos and Ariadne at the top-center of the Pronomos Vase (Fig. 5), dressed in tragic robes, holding a mask, and in conversation with the svelte, winged, nude figure of Desire (*Himeros*), appears to represent the "personification of Satyr play" herself: Csapo and Slater 1995: 69. [But I am now more inclined to regard this figure as being Aphrodite: see Griffith 2010 (= Chapter 4 below).]

[70]Ugliness and grotesqueness can sometimes, of course, be made the source of much pathos: e.g., Shakespeare's Caliban or Hugo's Quasimodo. But in those cases, the victimization of the character through social ridicule and exclusion, along with the audience's growing recognition of the character's potential for moral awareness and sympathetic behavior, are vital prerequisites, whereas the satyrs are neither victimized nor moralized to any significant degree. On the mixture of revulsion and desire, hatred and sympathy, in spectators' responses to cross-dressed, monstrous, black-faced, or otherwise "deformed" and abjected bodies on the stage, see further Stallybrass and White 1986, Clover 1992, Lott 1995: 136–68.

[71]In Athens, the preference for the silenos-type (with horse-tail, pointed ears, but otherwise human aspects) in itself tended to produce a more genteel image, even in the sixth century; and by the mid-fifth century this tendency was very pronounced, with Red-Figure satyrs sometimes becoming quite "bourgeois": see Brommer 1959, Simon 1982, Lissarrague 1990a, 1993, Carpenter 1997, KPS 1999, and nn. 73, 92 below.

[72]Buschor 1943–1945, Hedreen 1992 *passim*.

eryday human activities too.[73] The reasons for this evolution are debated,[74] as is the question of the relationship between the iconography of satyrs on vases and their physical appearance and movements in the theater.[75] Fortunately we do not have to resolve all these problems here. But it is generally agreed that the most reliable evidence for the appearance of fifth-century theater-satyrs consists of those paintings that clearly depict men wearing satyr costumes, i.e., those in which the actor's briefs (*perizôma* = trunks with phallus and horse's tail) are clearly visible, and in some cases his mask too. (If a costumed aulos-player and/or |[219] actor is present too, all the better.)[76] Such representations are not numerous;[77] but they do yield a fairly consistent picture, and it is from these that we should proceed.[78]

[73] By the mid- and later fifth century, satyrs sometimes come to be represented in quite mild and well-mannered guise; on occasion, indeed, the same painter has illustrated two versions of the same scene, one with a heroic or normal male figure engaged in athletic or sympotic-sexual activity, the other with a satyr in identical posture (e.g., KPS 1999: *Taf.* 12a and b = ARV^2 524,28 and 524,29 (Jason/satyr and Golden Fleece), KPS 1999: *Taf.* 16a and b = ARV^2 221,14 (athletes/satyrs training); cf. too KPS 1999: *Taf.* 17a = ARV^2 835,1 (satyr at an altar), etc. The effect seems not to be specifically parodic, merely good-humored and quaint: "look, satyrs can even do this too...!" [See now also Lissarrague 2013.]

[74] Hedreen 1992 thinks that it was Athenian dramatic performances (not only satyr plays, but other ritual impersonations too) that were primarily responsible for extending the range of contexts in which satyrs (or men dressed in satyr-costumes) could be imagined by vase-painters and their clients (so too Brommer 1959, Simon 1982). Others (e.g., Sutton 1980, Lissarrague 1990a, 1993) have argued that the visual field of vase-painting evolved quite separately from the theater, and that the changes in subject and style should be explained in terms of artistic and cultural factors, not imitation of stage-practice. Probably both sets of factors played a part; cf. Green 1991, KPS 1999: 41–73.

[75] The further question, to what degree individual vase-paintings of satyrs and other characters may represent particular scenes (or combinations of scenes) from recent theatrical productions, is even more troublesome, but less crucial to my present argument; see Green 1991, KPS 1999: 41–73 (R. Krumeich) for judicious surveys of the evidence. For discussion of the differences between satyrs, Comic choruses, and other "fat-men" and padded dancers from this same period, see Pickard-Cambridge/Webster 1962: 60–131, Seaford 1976, Hedreen 1992, and below pp. 39–40.

[76] It is not uncommon, however, to find a costumed aulos-player depicted in a satyr-scene that could not possibly have been thus staged, and that contains satyrs with no visible "trunks": e.g., KPS 1999: *Taf.* 10 = ARV^2 612,1 (satyrs excited by a female figure rising out of the earth). So this is not in itself a reliable guide (any more than it is for tragedy).

[77] About a dozen instances in all (in a couple of cases the presence or interpretation of a costume is uncertain): Brommer 1959: nos. 1–10, 20 (and cf. no. 15b); KPS 1999: *Taf.* 1b-c, 2a, 3–6, 8/9, 28a-b. Pride of place goes of course to the Pronomos Vase (Fig. 5); and valuable too is the Sydney krater (Fig. 7)—despite the relatively late date of both (ca. 400 BCE), and the latter's South Italian provenance—because they specifically depict actors and choreuts trying out their satyr costumes in rehearsal, rather than representing a particular scene from a mythologically based story.

[78] It is probable that satyr-choruses and silenoi performed also on occasions other than the City Dionysia, e.g., in the Attic demes. If so, we have no idea whether the same or different conventions governed satyr-costumes in these various performative contexts. (Notoriously hard to "place" and evaluate in particular is the Red-Figure bell-krater of Polion from ca. 430–20 BCE (KPS 1999: *Taf.* 15b = ARV^2 1172,8: New York Met. Mus. 25.78.66), a representation of old-men-satyrs in diaphanous, furry costumes performing with lyres at the Panathenaia, with an aulos-player in attendance.) Nor can we even be sure how much diachronic or synchronic variation there was among the dramatic satyrs of

In general, the chorus members' satyr-costume (Figs. 4–7) appears to have been simple and (as satyr-silens go) relatively "human"—much more so, for example, than that of the actors or choreuts of fifth-century Old Comedy (Fig. 2) and fourth-century Italian Comedy or Phlyax-plays (Fig. 3), with their padded and/or animal costumes and huge (usually non-erect) phalluses; and more so too than most of the representations of non-dramatic satyrs on vase-paintings from the sixth or early fifth century.[79] Although the mask was certainly grotesque, with its bald forehead, pointed horse-ears, snub nose, and bushy beard, it was not repulsive—ugly enough, we might say, to mark its wearers as members of a completely different, subhuman class from the heroes of the play (who wore normal tragic masks, as e.g. in Fig. 5),[80] and to remind us constantly that this chorus could never be equal drinking buddies or sexual partners with self-respecting humans, but not so hideous as to repel all human feelings of sympathy or affection. Before ca. 450, stage-satyrs usually appear to be of uniform age:[81] |[220] all are bearded, and also bushy-haired (because they are part-horse), but most look in other respects quite youthful, slim, and athletic (as in Figs. 5, 6, and 7).[82] Indeed, the slender legs, delicate arms, and athletic posture of the boyish, spear-toting, Giant-fighting satyr represented in Fig. 6 (ca. 500 BCE; ARV^2 121,23, by Apollodoros), marked as a dramatic chorus-member by his briefs, are more suggestive of Ganymede than of Silenos—earning the appreciative inscription Ο ΠΑΙΣ ΚΑΛΟΣ ("the boy is

---

the fifth century.

[79] See further Taplin 1993, Green and Handley 1995, Trendall and Webster 1971, A. D. Trendall *Phlyax Vases* = *BICS Suppl.* 19 (1967). In many cases it is uncertain whether the comic scenes represented on South Italian vases of the early fourth century (such as Fig. 3, a burlesque of the birth of Helen) come from indigenous Phlyax-plays or from imported Athenian (Old or Middle) Comedies: see Taplin 1993, Csapo and Slater 1995: 54–55, 66–69, KPS 1999: 43 and n. 9 with further refs.

[80] See too the Prometheus scene, by the Painter of the Athenian Dinos (KPS 1999: *Taf.* 6b = ARV^2 1180,2); and for an equivalent contrast, n.b. also Figs. 8a and 8b below.

[81] Variation of age increases markedly as the fifth century proceeds, and we begin to find gray-haired, balding satyrs, little child satyrs, and whole satyr families: see Lissarrague 1993: 215–16, KPS 1999: *Taf.* 22–24, and n. 73 above.

[82] An exception is the gray and balding "chorus" of the (possibly Aischylos-inspired?) Sphinx scene on a Red-Figure kalpis from the mid-fifth century (Würzburg ZA 20: see Simon 1982, KPS 1999: *Taf.* 22b). Sometimes satyrs on vases look a little paunchy (e.g., the Prometheus scene by the Nikias Painter, Gotha AVa 110 [75] = ARV^2 1334,19 = KPS 1999: *Taf.* 21b); but these are not necessarily stage-satyrs. The well-known Lucanian Polyphemos painting (London BM 1947.7–14.18 = KPS 1999: *Taf.* 26b, late fifth century; also in Seaford 1984: 23) represents slightly pot-bellied satyrs, in contrast to the slim and youthful humans who are physically helping Odysseus with the blinding (cf. E. *Cycl.* 624–55): but this painting cannot closely resemble any scene enacted in the Athenian theater, since the actors are "heroically" naked, rather than clothed in the conventional long-sleeved garment, the satyrs do not wear briefs, nobody wears a mask, and (despite the satyrs' vigorous movements) there is no sign of an aulos-player (even though, as a referee reminds me, satyr-actors are represented on the other side of the vase). Likewise e.g. the oinochoe of a satyr creeping up on a sleeping mainad named "*Tragôidia*" (Oxford 534 = ARV^2 1258; also Seaford 1984: fig. 4, p. 55; cf. Marshall 2000) is of little value as evidence for drama, as briefs are not indicated and the phallus looks more "realistic."

fine!"). The phallus attached to the choreuts' briefs was relatively small (Figs. 4, 5, 6, 7): though permanently and conspicuously erect, it was neater and less gross or obtrusive than that depicted on many of the non-dramatic satyr-scenes, and (as we noted above) much less offensive than those of Old Comedy or of earlier vase-paintings.[83] For the rest, the choreut's upper body and legs were either left naked, or covered with a thin body-stocking that imitated bare skin.[84] Thus each chorus-member, apart from his mask and tail, "looked" for the most part like a young man.

In contrast to this sprightly chorus, their Daddy, Papposilenos, was covered with a full-length furry, padded costume (*mallôtos chitôn*).[85] A clear distinction is thus maintained between the sleazy, selfish, old father and his innocent children: |[221] it is he who lies and betrays Odysseus to Polyphemos; he who collaborates with Skeiron in brutalizing travelers; he whose greed and untrustworthiness are ludicrously exposed in the early scenes of Sophokles' *Ichneutai*; and he whose implausible oath of comradely loyalty likewise turns false in Aischylos' *Diktyoulkoi*, whereas the chorus in each case seems to have been much less unscrupulous and malicious.[86] It is fitting, therefore, that Papposilenos' costume should be more an-

---

[83] See Figs 1, 2, and 3. In particular, we may contrast the early fifth-century "stage-satyr" of the Vienna calyx-crater (*ARV*² 591, 20A = KPS *Taf.* 28a: Altamura Painter, ca. 470/60 BCE) with the sixth-century satyrs of Fig. 1 (in each case, participating in a Return of Hephaistos). On the Greek aesthetic and homoerotic preference for small penises, see Dover 1978, Lissarrague 1990b, Stewart 1998. N.b. too the neatly tied-up penis (termed inaccurately by some scholars "infibulation") of the Kleophrades Painter's satyr-athlete (*ARV*² 183,7 = Lissarrague 1993: 209–12 with his fig. 14); and cf. A. *Isthm*. F 78a 27–28, *Dikty*. F 47a 786–820 (discussed below, in n. 103).

[84] See Simon 1982, KPS 1999: 53–54. In the later fifth century, the trunks apparently sometimes changed from being patterned cloth (e.g., Figs. 4 and 7—and also the choreut at the top on the far left of Fig. 5) to being furry and more animal-like (like the rest of the choreuts in Fig. 5). But the phallus remained "human" and of moderate size (i.e., not equine or asinine—contrast Figs. 1, 2, and 3). Simon 1982 suggests (following Kossatz-Deissmann 1982) that the trunks were adopted from female athletes and acrobats, while the body-suit was taken over from Comedy (see below, pp. 40–41).

[85] It is not certain whether Papposilenos always, sometimes, or never served as *koryphaios* (leader of the Chorus), or whether instead he was a separate character played by an actor; the conventions probably changed during the course of the fifth century. See Collinge 1958, Seaford 1984: 13–14, 24–25, G. Conrad *Der Silen* (diss. Bochum, 1996) [*non vidi*], KPS 1999: 24–25.

[86] E. *Cycl*. 228–315; E. *Skeiron P. Oxy*. 2455 fr. 6. 81–83 (= *hypoth*. fr. 18 Austin); S. *Ichn*. F 314.142–212; A. *Dikty*. F 47a 765–72, etc. On some vases, however (esp. later in the fifth century), Papposilenos is represented as an amiable and respectable tutor or friend (e.g., receiving the baby Dionysos, as in a White-Figure krater, Rome Vatican Mus. 16586, ca. 440–430 BCE = KPS 1999: *Taf.* 24b); and it is he who is apparently compared to Sokrates and interviewed by Midas in Plato and Vergil, and hence incorporated into Nietzsche's Dionysiac view of tragedy. So we should not rule out the possibility that the surviving evidence may present a distorted picture, and that in some plays he may have played a more creditable role. Likewise, as we noted earlier, it is possible that the chorus may occasionally have comprised "older" satyrs (gray-haired and/or costumed in the "fleecy-coat"). But the preponderance of evidence nonetheless indicates the clear distinction I am drawing here between "children" and "Daddy" (cf. n. 103).

imalistic and gross than theirs, closer to the world of Comedy or invective—just as it is he, not they, who is singled out for the painful humiliation of anal rape by a drunken and lascivious ogre.[87] It seems that he is to be regarded more as a small-minded and truly servile *paidagôgos*, or déclassé family-retainer, than as a true father—a social and symbolic role better reserved for Dionysos or Zeus.[88]

In assessing the physical appearance and behavior of the fifth-century satyr-chorus, it is particularly illuminating to compare them, on the one hand, with the sixth-century iconography of satyr-silens, and on the other, with the evidence of contemporary Old Comedy. On the François Vase (Fig. 1), the satyrs that escort Hephaistos in his Return sport huge erections (as does Hephaistos' mule) and horses' legs and hooves rather than human limbs; one carries a compliant Nymph in his arms. The class tensions within the scene are palpable, as the craftsman-god and his boisterous lower-class retinue are shown assertively claiming their new place in the political community of Olympos.[89] Hephaistos has used his new |[222] technology to compel Zeus, Hera, and the stylish aristocrats on Olympos to come to terms and provide him with a choice bride (Aphrodite, waiting disconsolately in the foreground); and it has taken Dionysos to reconcile their oppositions and bring about a mutually beneficial outcome. By contrast, in the fifth century, the satyrs (at least in drama, and perhaps in general too) appear to have shed most of this confrontational and assertive capability. For representations of aggressive (and often still ithyphallic) lower-class opposition to the authorities and/or the aristocracy, we have to turn to Aristophanes,[90] whose Comic Everyman (and

---

[87] E. *Cycl.* 581–89: ἐγὼ γὰρ ὁ Διός εἰμι Γανυμήδης, Κύκλωψ; ... ἀπόλωλα, παῖδες· σχέτλια πείσομαι κακά ... οἴμοι· πικρότατον οἶνον ὄψομαι τάχα. Such a fate might befall a comic slave (e.g., Chalinus in Plautus' *Casina*; and cf. the physical indignities mentioned and experienced by Xanthias in Ar. *Frogs*); but no member of a satyr-chorus ever suffers any comparable indignity. See further Hamilton 1979.

[88] What about their "mother"? The satyr-chorus does from time to time voice its delight at the prospect of a maternal figure (esp. S. *Isthm.* F 78a 13, A. *Dikty.* F 47a 810–11, 816–20), and they seem to blend their aggressive and domineering sexual urges with a more childish autoeroticism and desire to be played with and taken care of. This aura of infantile dependency is further enhanced by their affection for babies, as well as by their constant desire to suck on a wineskin. See further pp. 43–44 and n. 103 below. [And further Chapter 2 below.]

[89] Hephaistos had been banished from Olympos by his mother Hera because of his ugliness; in retaliation, he built a mechanical golden chair that enfolded Hera (and Zeus?) and refused to release her/them. After Ares tried unsuccessfully to force Hephaistos to capitulate, eventually Dionysos got him drunk, and he agreed to relent, if the gods would receive him back and give him Aphrodite as a bride. So Dionysos escorted him back to Olympos with attendant satyrs (the scene most frequently illustrated in Black-Figure vases). The story is narrated in Paus. 1.20.3; cf. Alkaios fr. 349 Voigt, Pindar fr. 283 S-M, Plato *Rep.* 2.378d3. For the "class-conflict" between "aristocratic" Olympians and "parvenu" craftsman-god, we may compare the (roughly contemporary) Homeric *Hymn to Hermes*; and for other Archaic representations of this mythological scene, with similarly potent satyrs, see Hedreen 1992.

[90] As G. de Ste Croix points out, however (*The Origins of the Peloponnesian War* [Ithaca, 1980] App. xi), the old aristocracy seems to be exempt from Aristophanic ridicule. For another avenue of class-conscious social criticism, we may look to the figure of Aisop and the traditions of the prose

sometimes his outrageous chorus too) gets in the face of authorities, outwits all opponents, and wins the prizes of food, drink, and sexual conquest:[91] and these Comic heroes and choruses are characterized by far more flamboyant physical and linguistic ugliness and shamelessness than the theatrical satyrs.[92]

As for the dances, postures, and gestures of the satyr-chorus, though these were of a distinctively vigorous and undignified kind, as compared with the more stately movements of tragedy, they were regarded as being much less gross and lascivious than those of comedy.[93] The most characteristic dance of satyrs, the *sikinnis*, was remarkable above all for its athletic, even acrobatic, |[223] leaps and contortions. To judge from the vase-representations (e.g., Figs. 4, 5, 8a and b), these movements, and the distinctively angular presentation of hands, legs, and torso, were exuberant and exaggerated, but not bestial, obscene, or ludicrous.[94] Some scholars (both ancient and modern) have suggested that the *sikinnis* was derived from military exercises.[95] But its chief associations seem to have been

---

fable: Kurke 2003 [and 2010].

[91] The comparison between satyric and comic drama, and their respective choruses, could be pursued further. Both types of drama frequently employ one or more opponents—"blocking" figures, villains, temporary obstacles to the happy ending—who must be overcome by the hero in the course of the play. In satyr plays, these opponents may include Papposilenos, and sometimes another mythological villain or ogre too (e.g., Polyphemos in *Cycl.*, Skeiron and Bousiris in their eponymous plays, Argos in S. *Inachos*); but more often, it seems, an opponent may be amenable to persuasion or may succeed in persuading the satyrs to cooperate amicably: e.g., Kyllene in S. *Ichneutai*, Herakles in several plays? Poseidon in A. *Isthm.*?); cf. Burnett 1971, KPS 1999: 26–27. Often an *agôn* takes place, whether between two parties, or between one party and the satyrs themselves; and the chorus, however intransigent and exuberant its initial opposition, seems invariably to end up siding with the victorious hero. (See above, pp. 25–27.) But the object and nature of the dispute between hero and chorus are usually very different in the two genres (as are their diction and metrical-rhythmical flavor: see Griffith 2006 [= Chapter 3]). [For fuller and more recent discussion of the relationship between Comedy and Satyr drama as genres, see Shaw 2014.]

[92] Another angle on this "domestication" and depoliticization of the satyrs: on the François Vase (and in many other vase-paintings), satyrs are strongly associated with donkeys and/or mules (Hedreen 1992: 14–17, Lissarrague 1990a: 54–56, 61–62), which belong for the most part to contexts of labor, sexual aggression, and lower-class rusticity; but on the stage, the equine aspects of Athenian silenoi tend to take over from the asinine, and contribute to the stage-satyrs' less resolute, more skittish and adolescent—perhaps also more pretentious?—mannerisms; cf. nn. 71, 100. [On actual and imaginary distinctions between horses, donkeys, and mules in Greek culture, see M. Griffith *CP* 101 (2006) 185–246, 307–58.]

[93] Most of the literary and lexicographical evidence comes from a much later period (Athenaios, Lucian, Hesychios, etc.) and is of dubious value; and some of it is self-contradictory. But if we rely primarily on the contemporary fifth-century evidence (both literary and iconographical), we find a fair degree of agreement on this. For fuller discussion, see Festa 1918, Lawler 1964, KPS 1999: 21–23.

[94] Presumably the *sikinnis* is being practiced by the satyr to the left (= behind) the seated aulos-player (Pronomos) in Fig. 5; see further Festa 1918 (with many illustrations), Lawler 1964, Seaford 1984 on E. *Cycl.* 37, KPS 1999: 21–23 (with *Taf.* 6b, 28b, etc.). N.b. too Pratinas *TrGF* I 4 F 3.15: ἅδε σοι δεξιᾶς καὶ ποδὸς διαρριφά (referring to some dance-movement?). [See now Seidensticker 2010.]

[95] Hesychios s.v. states that the *sikinnis* can be "soldierly" (*stratiôtikê*); cf. Lawler 1964: 111–12. It was

with young animals, especially horses. At *Cyclops* 37–40 the chorus as they dance the *sikinnis* are described by Papposilenos as *sauloumenoi*, a term elsewhere applied to the walk of horses or Bacchants and to the "swaggering" or "prancing" of high-class *hetairai* and fashionably luxurious men.[96] The sexual and (by some standards) "unmanly" associations of this dance were indeed quite strong; but it seems to have been clearly distinguished from the cruder hip-rotations and buttock-shaking of the Comic *kordax* (a dance also associated with lower-class *hetairai* or *pornai*).[97] In addition to the *sikinnis*, satyr plays did apparently employ other dances too, including some shared with tragedy;[98] and they undoubtedly made much use of hand-gestures (*cheironomia*) and mimetic choreography, e.g., for searching and tracking (S. *Ichn.*), net-pulling (A. *Dikty.*), athletic-training (A. *Isthm.*), etc.[99] The prevalent characteristics of the satyrs' dances seem thus to have been incessant movement, |[224] imitativeness, and exaggerated vigor: like children or young animals, they can never keep still.[100]

This childish, or coltish, body-language is basic to the satyric persona and constitutes one of its more attractive aspects. Like children, satyrs are frequently sur-

---

compared by others to the armed dance of the Cretan Kouretes. Possibly S. *Ichn.* F 314.173–74: ἐφίστω τριζύγης οἴμου βάσιν refers to a "three-rank formation": but other interpretations are possible (e.g., Lloyd-Jones 1996, "Take your stand where the three paths meet").

[96] Anakreon *PMG* 411: σαῦλαι Διονύσου Βασσαρίδες, *PMG* 458 (Clem. Alex. *Paid.* 3.11.69): σαῦλα βαίνειν (associated with γυναικεῖοι κινήσεις, τὸ ἀβροδίαιτον, and ἑταιρικά); Semonides 18: ...καὶ σαῦλα βαίνειν ἵππος ὥς...; Ar. *Wasps* 1173: σαυλοπρωκτιᾶν (of a man dressing in a Persian cloak and Spartan slippers, in an attempt to ape an upper-class life-style); grammarians also mention διασαυλούμενος (Aristophanes *PCG* 635 = fr. 624 Kock, in uncertain context, and glossed ἀβρυνόμενος, διαθρυπτόμενος = "behaving/dressing/walking luxuriously, being hopelessly extravagant"); cf. L. V. Kurke *CA* 11 (1992) 91–120.

[97] Lawler 1964: 69–86. See too Soph. F 772 Radt for a case of an ancient scholar (Demetrios Lakon) citing the *sikinnis* as "a type of comic dance " (*orchêseôs kômikês eidos*), but then quoting as confirmation a line of Sophokles that must come from a satyr play.

[98] Lawler 1964: 118–20. Little is known about the *strobilos* or *sobas*, or the *konisalos*, all of which are said to have been used in satyr plays—as was the *emmeleia*, a more stately dance, characteristic of tragedy. The *kordax* was also used in satyr plays, but apparently not nearly as extensively as in comedy. Of course we should remind ourselves once again that satyr plays went through several distinct evolutions during the period 500–200 BCE, and we cannot usually pin down any of these ancient scholarly descriptions to any particular period of theatrical performance.

[99] On S. *Ichn.*, see Zagagi 1999; and we may compare too KPS 1999: *Taf.* 4a and 4b (= ARV^2 571,75, kalpis by the Leningrad Painter, in Boston's Museum of Fine Arts, which depicts satyrs carrying pieces of furniture (?) and dancing exuberantly to a costumed aulos-player—perhaps a scene from Aischylos' *Thalamopoioi*.

[100] Lissarrague 1990a and b, KPS 1999: 21–23. The Greeks attributed such friskiness and irrepressible energy above all to colts or fillies, heifers, and fawns (*pôlos, moschos, nebros*), and regarded these young animals as especially highly-charged with erotic potential, frequently as objects of male desire (witness Anakreon, Ibykos, Alkman, and later Theokritos, Daphnis and Chloe, etc.); they are never considered as sexually crude as goats or donkeys. For the aristocratic associations of horses, see above, nn. 71, 92; and we may recall the conspicuous presence of Himeros (*Desire*) on the Pronomos Vase (above, n. 69).

prised, sometimes terrified—but eventually delighted—by new sights and sounds, and they are always at the mercy of their immediate feelings and appetites.[101] Their lack of restraint and inhibition and their constant state of expectation and desire, however absurd and incongruous these may be in the heroic contexts into which they have strayed, are more endearing than off-putting, and also make them all the more exemplary as spectators[102]—less jaded and sophisticated than the adult humans in the Theater, more naive, excitable, engaged, and impressionable, and ever ready to surrender themselves to the dramatic illusion. Nothing holds them back:

> ἀλλ' αἰὲν εἶ σὺ παῖς· νέος γὰρ ὢν ἀνὴρ
> πώγωνι θάλλων ὡς τράγος κνηκῶι χλιδᾶις·
> παύου τὸ λεῖον φαλακρὸν ἡδονῆι πιτνάς…
>
> (S. *Ichn.* 365–70)[103] |[225]

> You are always a child; young man (*neos anêr*) that you are,
> Like a goat, with that yellow beard sprouting, you are so full of yourself.
> Stop stretching out that smooth knob of yours in pleasure!

As virtual children, the satyrs are tolerated, even treated kindly and affectionately, by the heroes and divinities upon whom they rely; and they are accountable to nobody for their behavior—unless they attempt briefly to behave in more heroic mode and to perform actions that are beyond their powers (i.e., any significant action at all on stage, apart from drinking).[104]

---

[101] E.g., fire in A. *Prom. Pyrkaeus*, lyre music in S. *Ichn.*, mask-likenesses or busts (?) in A. *Isthmiastai*; babies or toys in A. *Dikty.*, S. *Dionyskos*, *Ichn.*, *Herakliskos*, etc.; cf. Sutton 1980, Seaford 1984, KPS 1999, etc.

[102] The Greek term θεατής ("spectator"), like the related θεωρός, implies engagement and mental/cultic participation as well as mere "watching"; see Ker 2000, with further references.

[103] This last remark seems to refer to the extending of the head of the penis beyond the foreskin: cf. S. *Dionyskos* F 171, Henderson 1978: 110. Other references to satyrs as "children" are common: A. *Dikty.* F 47a 807, S. *Ichn.* 161, E. *Cycl.* 587, 590, etc., Lissarrague 1993. Conversely, they fail to measure up as true "men": *Cycl.* 595, 642. [For discussion of A. *Dikty.* F 47a 786–832, where the chorus anticipate their imminent "marriage" to Danae and refer to her eager contemplation of this event, and then seem (though the text is badly mutilated) to imagine some kind of "primal" scene of "Oedipal" fantasy, see further Chapter 2.]

[104] The satyrs are allowed to be active in *assisting* an elite character (e.g., netting a casket, tracking cattle and finding a baby, distributing fire, etc.); but they never seem to succeed in formulating or executing an independent course of action that succeeds and makes any difference to anything. In many respects, we may be reminded of Longos' simple-minded and erotically inflamed adolescents, Daphnis and Chloe, whose bucolic natures likewise combine the animalistic with the childish, and render them quite clueless as social agents (and even as sexual partners), and yet divinely blessed and invulnerable to harm. In their case too, the happy ending requires eventually the intervention of an adult nobleman from the polis, Dionysophanes (!)—all under Pan's benevolent supervision: the rustics cannot manage it on their own. Cf. too Theokritos' love-sick Polyphemos (*Id.* 11), another inept yet daimonic, even charming, adolescent, despite his monstrous deficiencies.

aien su pais... Childish, certainly; but also slavish. Several of the immature and irresponsible attributes that mark children as incomplete or unripe adults were also conventionally regarded as distinguishing slaves more permanently from free men. In the Greek imagination, slaves were cowardly, bibulous, lacking in initiative, ugly, and to some degree less than fully human—all of which characteristics are conspicuously true of theatrical satyrs. Likewise, the movements and physical self-presentation of satyrs often incorporate typically slavish aspects: in many vase-paintings, they appear in full-face, with legs apart, staring straight out at the viewer; often they are placed in physical positions of great indignity and/or sexual accessibility, unthinkable for free men (or respectable children); and by the fifth |[226] century their sexual energies usually end up expending themselves (if at all), not on nymphs or mainads (as in the representations of the sixth century), but on animals, each other, or solitary masturbation.[105] The ambiguity as to which of these two human types the satyrs more closely resemble, children or slaves, seems to be an additional source of their socio-aesthetic value and psychological interest to the theater audience. For if their old and ugly facial features, subhuman pedigree, and incorrigibly foolish mentality belong to the (imagined) world of slaves, their exuberance, naiveté, invulnerability, and blessed aura of good humor and divine favor seem incompatible with such a status and more appropriate to children. This indeterminacy, or overlap, between the two statuses allows the audience's mixed feelings of affection and disgust, fellow-feeling and disassociation, plenty of room to be deployed. Do we despise these immortal "slaves (of Dionysos)" and perpetual "children (of Papposilenos)" for their inability to act independently and their subservience to the mastery of others, or envy them for their carefree reliance on their doting masters/parents? Perhaps both.

Above all, of course, in addition to being dependent, pleasure-seeking, musical, undignified, irrepressible, horny, and useless, the satyrs are always thirsty. Their unquenchable desire for wine, indeed the fact that their very existence revolves around its constant intake, provides the keynote to the predominantly positive vibe that emanates from this choral troupe. Slaves do not (in the Greek imagination) drink wine in all-male groups; nor do they dance, pursue young women, and sing songs to Dionysos: these are all activities for free men, especially young men. On the other hand, respectable young Greek men do not drink wine straight out of the skin, unmixed, while they are standing upright or running around. Sympotic dances and songs in Athens seem often to have employed some of the same (predominantly aeolic and iambic) rhythms, colometries, and structures (short stanzas, simple and repetitive cola) as those of the rustic satyrs, though as we have noted, the choreography of the latter is apparently distinctive and exaggerated in its postures and their language tends to make freer use of interjections, exclama-

---

[105] Collinge 1989, Lissarrague 1990b; contrast e.g. Fig. 1. (What are the associations of S. *Ichn.* 367 "goat"?—cf. Winkler 1990; and Lissarrague 1990a on donkeys, deer, etc.)

tions, and alternations of singer. (Of course, we know relatively little about the "rules" of drinking and song that were or were not observed during the final stages of a *kômos*, when the drunken young men left their prescribed sympotic space and roamed the streets looking for fun, sex, and/or trouble.) The conventions of the symposium normally restricted full participation to free male adults: no slaves, no respectable women, no children could recline or partake in the mixed wine. And these ever-immature satyrs (and their slavish father) can never belong at the same table as the heroic characters into whose stories they have intruded; yet they will be granted the blessings of Bacchic indulgence—in a mode appropriate to socially disadvantaged rustics or adolescents. Children and slaves are (always) in need of responsible adults (= |[227] heroic actors), who can take care of the serious decisions and actions for the community at large; similarly, the satyrs can keep their boyish little minds on drinking and playing.[106]

Boys (unlike slaves) are supposed to grow up into men and then to take on responsibilities of their own. So for them "play" includes an element of learning, and their irresponsibility is thus only temporary. By contrast, the satyrs are permanently childish; and while this status reduces their potential as objects of moral approval or emulation, it may add to their mystique and attraction as objects of conscious or unconscious psychological identification. For them (and for any audience members who can identify with them) wine, escape from toil, and fun are always available at someone else's trouble and expense—provided we are willing to abandon all self-respect and sense of social responsibility (ἐν τῶι Καρὶ κινδυνεύσομεν). This is the true freedom of "slavery" to Dionysos.

To sum up: the satyrs, even as they are ridiculed and despised by the Athenian audience, nonetheless engage them in an appealing fantasy, suggestive both of a return to childhood, and of a drunken *kômos*, i.e., the final stage of a symposium and/or erotic sortie. The audience thus buys into a double dynamic of identification. At one level, they aspire to and need the resolute, effective activity of the serious (heroic) characters, with their splendid clothing and correct tragic language, and recognize this as being the proper adult mode of behavior. From that perspective, the satyrs are a joke and a scandal: absurd, unreliable, immature. At another level, however, the impressionable, ineffectual, pleasure-seeking chorus draws the audience down with them, to share a more childish fantasy of dependence, pretence, desire, irresponsible spectatorship, and instant gratification—all at no risk

---

[106] On the François Vase (Fig. 1), Hephaistos and his crew carry a wineskin; and it was traditionally by this means that Dionysos confused Hephaistos' wits and persuaded him to end his anger. But Olympians would normally follow the more decorous procedures of the mixing-bowl; cf. E. *Cycl.* 149, Ar. *Knights* 105 (unmixed wine for slaves and/or Scythians and Thracians). [Indeed, true Olympians would not normally drink wine at all, but nectar.] Symposiasts have learned to recline, drink in moderation, take turns, etc. Are satyrs radically different and declassé? or just a couple of stages further into the *kômos*?

and in complete devotion to the salutary divinity (or Father) of the theater.[107]

On the basis of this analysis, I should like to proceed by tentatively proposing three (coexisting and mutually compatible) ways of reading the psychological "split" that appears to have been induced within the Athenian citizen audience by the satyr-chorus and heroic actors. The first involves the internal subject-formation of each audience-member; the second, the management of male sexual desire within the context of public performance and the theater; the third, the complex and shifting interactions between mass and elite within Athenian society at large. I suggest that all three derive much of their peculiar efficacy from their intimate relationship to the preceding tragedies. |[228]

(1) It has been said that satyrs existed in the Athenian imagination as "a countermodel to humanity."[108] In the theatrical context, we might revise this formulation (after Peter Stallybrass and Allon White), to say that satyrs and heroic/divine main characters co-existed in the Athenian theater to provide visual and audible expression to certain extremes of behavior that lay either above or below normal human limits, and thereby to define and reinforce implicit standards of civic performance and self-presentation.[109] Such a formulation obviously has much in common with the ethical-political reading of Winkler 1990 and others (above, p. 18, #3); but it places greater emphasis on the audience's unconscious desires for the exotic, forbidden, and abjected, and less on the conscious choice of behavioral models for emulation and avoidance.

In psychoanalytical terms, we may surmise that the mixture of attraction and revulsion elicited by the satyr chorus was especially appealing to repressed elements within the Athenian adult male psyche during the first half of the fifth century. The precious civic entitlements bestowed on all male citizens by the (still relatively new) democratic constitution brought with them corresponding responsibilities, demands, and fears: citizenship was thus simultaneously the source of intense individual and collective pride and of competitive male anxiety to perform, conform, and measure up to conventional standards of masculine comportment (an anxiety previously concentrated for the most part among the elite). Satyr plays presented a comforting medium within which to confront this

---

[107] For more detailed discussion of the role of the real and fantasized Father in such theatrical processes, see Griffith 1998: 57–80, with further references.

[108] Lissarrague 1990a: 66; cf. Keuls 1985: 357–71. Similarly, Stewart 1997: 191, "The... satyr is both a foil and a subhuman antitype to the tightly disciplined *kouros*. By constantly inverting and deforming the rules of culture, he helps to reaffirm its value."

[109] "Th[e] act of rediscovery itself, in which the middle classes excitedly discover their own pleasures and desires under the sign of the Other, is constitutive of the very formation of middle-class identity... The carnivalesque was marked out as an intensely powerful semiotic realm precisely because bourgeois culture constructed its self-identity by rejecting it. The 'poetics' of transgression reveals the disgust, fear, and desire which inform the dramatic self-presentation of that culture through the 'scene of its low Other,'" Stallybrass and White 1986: 201–202, with further reference to Bakhtin 1981, Kristeva 1980.

anxiety, through the splitting of the audience's focus between higher and lower objects of identification. The impressive and "heroic" actors, with their sumptuously decorated costumes, deliberate movements, and "high" iambic utterances occupied one (superhuman) end of a spectrum of appearance and behavior at whose other (subhuman) end pranced the unclothed, animalistic, musical, and acrobatic chorus. And unlike the "polyphonic" world of tragedy, which presented a fair number of more ordinary characters along the middle range of this spectrum,[110] with whom the theater audience can identify fairly directly in terms both of their appearance and of their patterns of speech and behavior, satyr plays seem to have offered no |[229] such middle ground: only a dialogically polarized world of "heroes" and satyrs.[111] In allowing themselves to adopt—even to a limited degree—a subject position that oscillated from one end to the other, the spectators were perhaps brought to occupy an intermediate (and thus appropriately "normal" and comfortable?) social and sartorial position—that of the Athenian male citizen-soldier; or perhaps they may have found it unnecessary, or impossible, fully to reconcile these competing desires, enjoying instead a more open-ended and indeterminate relationship to the performers.[112] We cannot be gods or heroes; and we should be ashamed to be satyrs: yet at some level we yearn to be both.[113]

---

[110] Towards the higher end, there are friends and minor relatives of the chief characters and several of the male choruses (e.g., A. *Ag.* and *Pers.*, S. *Ant.* and *Phil.*, E. *Alk.* and *Hks.*); towards the lower end, messengers, nurses, tutors, watchmen, female and foreign choruses, etc. See further Seidensticker 1982, Hall 1997, Griffith 1995, 1999 (on the Guard of S. *Antigone*).

[111] I am here borrowing, and adapting, the notions of "polyphonic" and "dialogic" from Bakhtin 1981 and Kristeva 1980: both employ the terms especially to describe the competing voices and perspectives represented in the discourses of carnival and satire.

[112] As compared with the various forms and locations of the fascinating-grotesque studied by Stallybrass and White 1986 (the pig, the sewer, the maid, etc.), by Clover 1992 (slashers, aliens, and their movie-victims/opponents), and by Lott 1993 (black-face minstrels), the satyrs of drama are relatively innocuous and benign in their manners and contexts: they do not seem to arouse the same degree of horror or hatred as is intermittently invoked in each of those other media, and their stories are placed far from the "here-and-now" of the Athenian polis. This would appear to mean that the audience's fantasy could afford to dwell more comfortably and extensively in the subject position of the satyr-chorus (since it was relatively less threatening) than, e.g., in that of the "black" minstrel or Victorian slum prostitute. Nonetheless, the dynamics of mixed disapproval and affection, repulsion and attraction, seem to be similar and comparable. See too Stewart 1997: 187–92. [See further Chapter 2.]

[113] By "we" (and "us, our own," etc.), here and intermittently in what follows, I mean "the implied/actual spectators," i.e., primarily the mainstream male fifth-century Athenian audience, but also that mental-emotional component of a modern reader that is able to put itself (with more or less conscious effort) into a similar psychological state to those Athenians. I realize that the use of such a universalizing expression threatens both to homogenize unjustifiably the original audience's (doubtless diverse) response and—worse still—to essentialize that historically specific (Athenian, male, mainstream) response into a timeless consciousness (or subconsciousness) implicitly shared by all theater-goers and readers, male and female, then and now. But I trust my readers to resist these threats, and I think that such expressions of implied common experience can help to indicate some of the familiar subject positions and deeply ingrained linguistic and cultural habits on which these theatrical texts depend for

So do we settle for what lies in between, the life of ordinary human citizens—the one constituency not represented on the satyric stage? Or do we each consciously or unconsciously find our |[230] own individual subject position, higher or lower, on the continuum of audience responses, thus participating in, and contributing to, the process of "solidarity without consensus" that I have explored elsewhere?[114]

There is another dimension to be considered as well, within this process of citizen identity-construction: slavery. We have noted the many conventionally "slavish" features of the chorus' (and still more Papposilenos') appearance, demeanor, and conduct, and it would be hard not to conclude that at some level the radical distinction between noble hero and subhuman satyr was experienced by the Athenian audience in terms of the deep and omnipresent psycho-social divisions between free and slave that permeated their society. In these terms, the satyr plays would have provided an opportunity to experiment with the slave's subject position and to imagine an unproblematic servile existence in which a benevolent master will take loving care of his "boys," actual work is rarely required, and the slave's life consists mainly of music, drinking, and sexual fantasies.[115] At the same

---

their effect(s): see further Griffith 1998. The yearning for a return to infantile ("pre-Oedipal") irresponsibility and dependency (on an ever-present mother's body) is postulated as a powerfully persistent fantasy by much Freudian psychoanalytic theory. In particular, the work of Melanie Klein has provided a suggestive model for the ways in which the child's painful process of learning to differentiate him/herself from the mother, and to find substitutes for the nourishment and comfort of the maternal breast, gives rise in adults to persisting subconscious fantasies of a "return" to sensory-alimentary-ludic plenitude, which may come out in dreams, in play, in art—or in neurosis. For applications of Klein's theories to drama and public spectacle, see esp. Adelman 1992, Lott 1993: 145–48, Travis 1996. Particularly pertinent to our analysis of the "childish-slavish" satyrs is Eric Lott's account (1993: 146) of the responses of white, northern working-class audiences to "the totalizing, and thus terrorizing, connectedness of pre-Oedipal bliss" that they encounter in the spectacle of an abjected black subject whom they find both enviable for his "infantile" capacity to *enjoy* (and to find reliable sources of pleasure—e.g. in outrageous physical movement and sexual innuendo, in misuses of language, in musical and gastronomic exuberance, in switching of gender roles) and also thoroughly contemptible in his uninhibited refusal to sublimate his desires.

[114] See Griffith 1995, and n. 125 below. For the notion of an "ordinary," middle-of-the-road collective identity that is constructed by means of representations of abjected others, see esp. Stallybrass and White 1986, who argue that during the eighteenth and nineteenth century the constitution of conformist, monochromatic, middle-class British consciousness and self-image was facilitated by the public presentation—and moralistic rejection—of "colorful" but degraded and/or exotic and grotesquely imagined alternatives. In fifth-century Athens, the democratic versions of civic identity likewise entailed a rejection both of (debased) slavish, feminized, and non-Greek behaviors and images on the one hand (Hall 1989), and of the "colorful" excesses of Eastern and/or old-style aristocratic life-styles on the other—though the luxurious and elitist appeal of the latter never entirely vanished (cf. Griffith 1998: 20–57).

[115] As Lissarrague observes (1993: 212–14), satyrs enjoy "membership in a collective," yet (sc. unlike, e.g., centaurs, who form "a real society") they "do not form an isolated society... They have a subordinate status, like that of slaves"; thus they are "artisans at the forge of Hephaistos, sculptors; cooks; servants of Herakles; thieves and gluttons; incorrigible and unrepentant drunkards," etc. See above, esp. pp. 44–46 and nn. 106–107; also Lott 1993: 136ff.

time, the natural superiority of the master-culture is reaffirmed at every turn, and the (iambic/tragic) world of the heroes and gods is presented as the only legitimate, or even imaginable, métier for responsible social living. Yet the differences between the frisky, animalistic, rustic satyrs and the conventional slaves of Old and New Comedy are quite striking. Comic slaves are for the most part pragmatic and worldly-wise, accustomed to hard labor and physical punishment, and never found operating in groups.[116] In Old Comedy, too, unlike satyr drama, slaves never gain their freedom, and always continue their existence at play's end within the same orbits (household, city) as their hero-masters. Perhaps we should say, then, that the animalization, collectivization, and, above all, infantilization, of the satyrs' servile bodies contrives both to render them less immediately recognizable to the Athenian audience as human |[231] "slaves" at all (and thus easier to have fun with, without any sense of anxiety or guilt) and by the same token less easily distinguishable from other "childish" and under-developed components of the Athenian citizen body.

(2) The satyrs provided an opportunity for male sexuality, which tragedy kept securely buttoned- and bottled-up, to be both flaunted and defused. In the whole surviving corpus of Greek tragedy—at least, before the later years of Euripides' career—it is hard to find a single scene in which a good, respectable man expresses feelings of sexual love or desire, or is seen choosing to risk danger and death to win a bride or defend a beloved.[117] That is not to say that eros has no place in tragedy—far from it: women commit atrocities out of sexual desire and jealousy (Klytaimestra, Deianeira, Phaidra, Medeia, Hermione, etc.) and choruses and

---

[116] Perhaps the Scythian Policeman of Ar. *Thesm.* comes closest to satyric behavior and demeanor, though he still utterly lacks the exuberance and joyful naiveté of the satyrs. Although the evidence is disputed and inconclusive, it appears that in Classical Athens (unlike Rome), slaves were not extensively employed in herding or agricultural activities, which were mostly handled by free farmers themselves.

[117] Out of 31 extant plays, I find the following instances: Haimon loves Antigone (S. *Ant.*); Achilleus loves Iphigeneia (E. *IA*); Agamemnon presumably feels desire for his captive slave Kassandra (A. *Ag.*); likewise Herakles for Iole (S. *Tr.*), Neoptolemos for Andromache (E. *Andr.*); and in each of these cases the man's desire is thematically significant for the plot of the play, but none of these men explicitly mentions it himself. Aigisthos may love Klytaimestra (A. *Ag.*, *Cho.*; S. *El.*, E. *El.*), but he too never says so (though Klytaimestra declares their love); the sons of Aigyptos desire their cousins, but never appear on stage to speak in A. *Supp.*; nor does Zeus, lover of Io, in *Prom.*; Jason may desire his new bride (E. *Med.*), or may be marrying her merely out of expediency; as for Oidipous, what does he feel for Iokaste (S. *OT*)? E.'s *Andromeda*, with its focus on Perseus' "falling in love" with the damsel in distress, and eventually marrying her, thus appears to have represented a startling innovation for tragedy: see now Gibert 2000. Other apparent exceptions are significant too: Admetos (E. *Alk.*) and Menelaos (E. *Helen*) both express love for their wives—in quasi-satyric plays (see below, pp. 55–57); Theoklymenos clearly lusts after Helen (E. *Hel.*)—but he is a gross and tasteless barbarian; Pylades in the end gets to marry Elektra (E. *El.*, *Or.*), and Orestes marries Hermione (*Or.*), but neither has hitherto shown any sign of interest or desire for this at all. Regrettably, we do not know how the love between Achilleus and Patroklos was handled in A.'s *Myrmidons* trilogy.

messengers sometimes relate the catastrophic (or occasionally blessed) results of heroes' love affairs. But male tragic heroes (unlike their counterparts in epic or New Comedy) rarely present themselves in a state of physical desire or emotional yearning or jealousy. By contrast, the ithyphallic satyrs are permanently in a state of sexual arousal and ever quick to mention the urgency of their desires even if they never succeed in finding and winning a truly desirable partner. Here again, the bifurcation of imagery and activity between actors and chorus seems absolute (and distinctly different from Old Comedy):[118] the satyrs may brandish their tumescent phalluses, boast of their charms and even threaten rape or "marriage," but they achieve no worthwhile satisfaction or significant sexual relationship (let alone marriage or progeny),[119] whereas the heroes (whose physical appetites, like those of their tragic counterparts, remain discreetly hidden and unspoken) end up ||[232] marrying choice brides, siring babies, and founding important dynasties.[120] The satyrs' very identities and costume signify naked and indiscriminate lust,[121] and they can barely (or sometimes cannot at all) contain their desires; yet (like slaves, like children) they have to give way to the mature and capable—but more polite and restrained—adult figure of the symbolic Father (the Law, or true Phallus) and watch as he wins the bride instead. This they do with good humor and no rancor, in full awareness of their proper station.

What about the theater audience? In which directions and through what forms were (are) their desires channelled? Their conscious judgment doubtless ridiculed the shameless exhibitionism of the satyrs and noted with approval their failure to achieve instant sexual gratification. This same conscious judgment will have endorsed the more decorous (and successful) conduct of a Poseidon or Odysseus

---

[118] In Aristophanic comedy, both hero and chorus wear the over-sized phallus, and although the hero is generally rewarded with the choicest sexual prize, there seems to be little difference between them in their attitude or approach to the objects of their desires. Likewise, all are usually included in the final *kômos*, feasting, peace, etc.

[119] On vases, a few later fifth-century examples of satyr-families are found (Lissarrague 1993, KPS 1999: *Taf.* 23b, etc.); otherwise satyrs remain unattached, unmarried, and usually erotically rejected (but ever hopeful): Collinge 1989, Lissarrague 1990b: 61–66. For sexual boasting in satyr drama, cf. A. *Dikty.*, E. *Cycl.*; for attempted or threatened rape, A. *Dikty.*, A. *Amymone* (cf. Fig. 8a), E. *Cycl.* 179–87.

[120] I count 14 satyr plays by Aischylos or Sophokles in which a marriage or productive sexual relationship for the hero probably resulted at play's end: A. *Amymone, Diktyoulkoi, Kirkê, Ostologoi, Prôteus* (see below), *Sphinx*; S. *Achilleôs Erastai, Admêtos, Krisis, Helenês Gamos, Inachos, Kêdalion, Pandôra/Sphyrokopoi, Oineus* (cf. F 1130 R). This number represents roughly half of the total number of satyr plays by these two playwrights whose plots are known or can be surmised with any degree of probability. It should perhaps be added that several satyr plays were written around the exploits of Herakles, whose mythological record of productive couplings was notoriously prodigious; but we know the details of almost none of these plays. In iconographic terms, Dionysos has Ariadne, Hephaistos is given Aphrodite: but (as we noted above) the satyrs rarely in the fifth century seem to gain the access to nymphs or mainads that they seek.

[121] See above, n. 55 (names of satyrs). [See further Chapter 3 below, on romantic and erotic themes in Sophokles' satyr dramas.]

(or even Herakles).¹²² But as watchers and fantasists, the members of the audience (like their sympotic counterparts, gazing at the satyric figures painted on their drinking-cups and mixing-bowls) also could not help recognizing a distorted reflection of themselves in the insatiable and ineffectual chorus. The Dionysiac licence of the theater allowed (even required) them vicariously to expose their sexuality for all to see and to jettison all restrictions and inhibitions in an (imaginary) pursuit of gratification—secure in the knowledge that a satyr never really suffers pain or humiliation or serious loss, merely momentary frustration, and that the pleasures of (theatrical, imaginative, satyric) anticipation and male self-assertion are their own reward. In combination, this "split" experience of satyric exhibitionism and heroic consumption may be said to have satisfied, in a roundabout and complementary way, a comprehensive male sexual fantasy, without breaching the code of decorum that governed the behavior of tragic characters in the Theater.¹²³ For if the tragedies were designed to present the |[233] political and moral rewards that accrue to a community through the magnificent self-assertion, self-denial, and even self-destruction of its elite members,¹²⁴ the ensuing satyr plays provided a reassuring picture of erotic and/or marital bliss and familial restoration, that is achieved not (as in Comedy) at the expense of tragic values and decorum, but side by side, as a romantic complement and reward for tragic labor and suffering. Whether every audience member felt himself equally entitled to occupy the subject position of the victorious hero or god, or whether some found themselves settling for something closer to the satyrs' role of cheerful spectator—this will be the topic of our next section.

(3) In socio-political terms, the split-level action and mixed audience-response of the satyr play provided an exaggerated and distorted version of the prevailing dynamic of tragedy, in which the brilliant achievements and hideous con-

---

¹²²Herakles to some degree perhaps bridges the gap between satyr and "tragic" hero, as his voracious appetites and lack of restraint bring him closer than most heroes to the satyrs' way of doing business (cf. E. *Alk.*). But at least his penis is kept under wraps, and he does not dance the *sikinnis*.

¹²³As we implied above (pp. 20–21), this process seems to have imparted a peculiar twist to what may formerly have been a simpler ritual of rustic fertility, in which the satyrs were more potent and less involved with, and constrained by, the decorum of another (tragic) discourse. See Stewart 1997: 200 (on the "splitting" of the Athenian symposiast's erotic response to visual representations involving desirable female figures combined with both satyrs and gods or heroes); also Lott 1993. An analogous phenomenon has been observed by Steve Neale, in his analysis of the competing images of masculinity in certain mainstream American movies (esp. Westerns). Frequently (as, e.g., in *The Man who Shot Liberty Valance*, or *Shane*, or most of Sam Peckinpah's films) the audience is presented with two prominent male characters, of whom one (rather tame) will survive the crisis and live on to prosper in a conventional married relationship, the other (more flamboyant, and problematically wild and super-masculine) possesses talents that ensure victory over the bad guys, yet will prevent him from ever settling down into a conventional bourgeois family life-style (Neale 1983). The audience (both male and female) thus find themselves responding to two different objects of desire and/or identification, each attractive in its own way, yet ultimately incompatible with one another.

¹²⁴Griffith 1995, Wilson 1999: 194–97; see too Seaford 1994.

vulsions of great dynastic families were played out before the shocked and awed gaze of attendants, messengers, nurses, prophets, and choruses, while the shifting viewpoints and sympathies of the spectators likewise played into a mutually reinforcing relationship of rivalry and interdependence between high and low, leaders and led, reflective of the larger contours of Athenian life.[125] For inside the theater, as outside it, the elite was both criticized and treasured for its dangerous but indispensible dominance; and during the course of the plays the more democratic viewpoints of the lower-class observers were simultaneously marginalized (since choruses and minor characters, like the theater audience |[234] itself, are never granted the power to determine the outcome or take control of their own lives, but always placed in a position of dependency on the actions of the nobility) and yet also comfortably validated (since it is generally the messengers' or attendants' narrations, and the chorus' lyric speculation and commentary, that shed the brightest light on the true state of the heroes' affairs, and thus illuminate the strengths and weaknesses of those doomed dynasts). Thus it is often the lowest and least personally impressive or admirable individuals and groups that come closest to representing the viewpoint of the majority of the theater audience.[126]

This pattern of "tragic" action, and of divided and shifting audience identifica-

[125] I have argued elsewhere (Griffith 1995) that this process helped to generate a kind of "solidarity without consensus" among the Athenians. The term is borrowed from Kertzer 1988, and derived ultimately, one might say, from Emile Durkheim and Clifford Geertz; it refers to a social phenomenon in which a sense of community and fellow-feeling is fostered within a diverse, even sharply divided, society (e.g., by a publicly performed ritual, or by the effective use of appropriate verbal and visual symbols in speeches, advertising, or other cultural productions), without the various members of that society all necessarily attaching the same precise meanings or values to that ritual or those symbols. In the Theater of Dionysos, the mixed messages and shifting class-dynamics of the tragic texts and stage action, by providing alternative subject positions and emotional/intellectual appeals to different segments of Athenian society, might thus simultaneously reinforce both democratic and aristocratic ideologies in a manner that would alleviate, rather than exacerbate, social tensions, without actually resolving any of the deeply entrenched contradictions that underlay and caused them; cf. too Easterling 1997b, Wilson 2000.

[126] On messengers as representatives of a sympathetic "lower-class" point of view, distinctively oriented towards the audience's perspectives, see De Jong 1991; for the sharp "relief" cast by "comic" characters in tragedy, see Seidensticker 1982; on the Watchman, Herald, jurymen, and other subordinate viewpoints in A.'s *Oresteia*, see Griffith 1995: 72–81; on the Guard and Chorus as reflective/determinative of the audience's response to the heroine of S. *Ant.*, see Griffith 1999: 54–58; and for examples of foreign/female/servile choruses who nonetheless forge strong sympathetic links with the audience, we may cite A. *Supp., Cho.* (and perhaps *Eum.*); E. *Hek., Tro., Ion, El., IT, Hel., Pho., Or.* and (above all) *Ba.*; and to a less abjected degree (i.e., citizen women choruses) A. *Th.*; S. *Tr., El.*; E. *Med., Hipp., Andr., Hik.*; cf. too A. *Pers.* (Persian old men). For the "splitting" of responses within an individual audience member, see nn. 37 and 38 above. During a single tragic performance, one and the same spectator might well encounter different elements that would pull him/her in opposite directions: on the one hand, towards experiencing unfamiliar or extreme subject positions (e.g., ruler/slave, victim/killer, woman/man), and on the other, towards recognizing and reaffirming long-standing and familiar ("normal") social and psychological tendencies and attitudes: see e.g. Clover 1992.

tion and sympathy, is typical of fifth-century tragedies, and plays directly into the ideological context of the Athenian polis, in which citizens tended to look to their aristocratic leaders with mixed expectations while those leaders themselves (who apparently included, or were closely associated with, several of the playwrights and *chorêgoi* themselves) trod a thin line between the "timocratic" lure of their personal and dynastic ambitions and the more egalitarian rhetoric and practice of the dominant democratic ideology. And, as we have seen, the same pattern of dependent/useless spectator-choruses and dominant hero-actors is present also—in exaggerated form—in most of the satyr plays whose plots we know or can surmise. With few if any minor characters to share the lower-class perspectives as "internal audience,"[127] the childish-slavish satyrs occupy an even more determinative position, as the main focalizing device for the theater audience in its relation to the heroes and the heroic action. The "split" in their responses, i.e., the double-consciousness of simultaneously imagining themselves empowered like these mythological heroes or divinities (Herakles, or even Dionysos himself), while also surrendering themselves deliciously to the fantasy of satyric (infantile, drunken) irresponsibility and self-indulgence, becomes all the more irreconcilable and comforting. For the overriding message of the satyr play is that someone else (a hero, a god, a playwright) will adjust and redefine our (tragic) world for us—temporarily at least—into terms that guarantee absence of pain |[235] and toil. We are expected to collaborate in this process, of course, but only by watching and by following our appetites. The reward for our acquiescence will follow, in the shape of a miraculously happy ending. Thus, even as the theater has provided a space and opportunity (in the tragedies) to unpack and explore some of our deepest anxieties and fears, the obligatory satyr play ensures that we will conclude that exploration with a reassuring (imaginary) rearrangement of our human and civic predicament. This, as I have attempted to argue, is both a "relief from" the tragic experience and in a sense an intensification of it.

Figs. 8a and b (two Red-Figure bell-kraters from the second half of the fifth century) both depict Amymone and satyrs. Whether or not these paintings reflect a scene or combination of images from any particular drama,[128] they serve to illustrate well the status and relationship between satyrs, actors, and spectators as we have analyzed them so far. On both vases, the satyrs are dancing around Amymone; yet even in the first (Fig. 8a) there seems little danger of sexual conquest: she looks unfazed; their phalloi are limp, and their attempts to embrace her seem

---

[127] See above, pp. 24–26 and n. 110.

[128] Amymone was one of the Danaids; she went to fetch water from a spring, but was assaulted by one or more eager satyrs; Poseidon rescued her, and in turn persuaded (?) her to become his bride instead; she became the Nymph of the spring and bore Nauplios. A satyr play on this topic formed the fourth play of Aischylos' Danaid tetralogy: on this, see further Garvie 1969, Winnington-Ingram 1981, Friis Johansen and Whittle 1980, KPS 1999: 91–97.

more energetic than threatening;[129] and in the second (Fig. 8b), the difference in scale and dignity between Poseidon and the surrounding satyrs emphasizes the gulf between their respective social statuses. It is towards Poseidon alone, her savior and new lord/husband, that Amymone's gaze and gesture are directed, and the marriage of the heroic pair is the focus of the whole scene. The other bystanders (the satyrs, and we, the external observers) are welcome, in our subordinate and supporting roles, to dance, sing, and drink around the periphery—while the whole occasion is orchestrated by Dionysos, the master of ceremonies, whose thyrsos lies in the foreground of Fig. 8a, and whose liquid fills the interior of the vessels themselves.

It has been suggested by many critics that Euripides, at a certain point during the fifth century, took it into his head to steer *tragôidia* in a new direction—or perhaps, to be more precise, to channel it into the course previously filled by satyr plays.[130] First *Alkestis* (438 BCE) and subsequently *IT*, *Ion*, and *Helen* (all apparently composed between 420 and 410) follow the trajectory of a "romance" plot and contain various similarities to the traditional satyr play; and a didaskalic record even informs us that *Alkestis* was performed fourth "in place of a |[236] satyr play."[131] At around the same date, Euripides' *Andromeda* made a sensation with its heroic love-interest and rescue scene.[132] *IT* and *Helen* in particular involve the retelling, and untelling, of a familiar story, along with miraculous and/or divinely manipulated deception, phantoms, mistaken identities, and recognition scenes, and virtual or actual returns from the dead. In a real sense, therefore, we may say that the plots and characters of these "romances" constitute an allusive revisiting and revision of already established tragic plots. When (or to the extent that) such "revision" is accompanied by reliable guarantees of divine/elite capacity to resolve human crisis and conflict, and to provide salvation and renewed faith even after betrayal, loss, separation, and death itself, it may be said to be truly "romantic" and reintegrative. But to the extent that questions and doubts may be raised as to the credibility of key events and as to the human and divine motivations within the new version, this revision may be felt rather to be "ironic," adding layers of uncertainty and ambiguity rather than providing a definitive and clear-cut new picture of reality. Most critics have ascribed to Euripides' romance-plays fairly

---

[129] It is unclear what the satyr's hand is doing near Amymone's breast in Fig. 8a; but no actual contact appears to be taking place, and the assault is certainly less violent or effective than equivalent rape-scenes from mythology (esp. those involving centaurs); see above, pp. 42–43, on the energetic, but generally non-aggressive character of satyric choreography. See too Simon 1982, for an interesting re-reading of another satyric assault scene (ARV^2 370.13).

[130] So Burnett 1971, Whitman 1974, Sansone 1978, Knox 1979: 250–74, etc. On the dating of Euripides's plays, see Cropp and Fick 1985; also now Gibert 2000, Mastronarde 2000.

[131] Now see Marshall 2000. Ancient scholiasts make a similar suggestion about *Orestes* too; but see n. 5 above. (In what follows, I have little to say about *Orestes* or *Ion*, whose romance features follow a slightly different pattern from the others.)

[132] See Gibert 2000 for full discussion.

massive doses of such irony, and have seen this as a distinctively fin-de-siècle turn, a symptom (or result) of the decadence of the tragic genre, of the demoralizing effects of the Peloponnesian War, of sophistic scepticism, or a combination of all three.[133]

In combination with ancient scholars' comments about a "prosatyric" function to some of these happy-ending tragedies, such interpretations have led many twentieth-century critics to conclude that Euripides introduced a radical new wave of theatrical sophistication and self-awareness with these happy-ending plays.[134] But there are good reasons for thinking that this "ironic" mode of narration and presentation may predate Euripides by several generations and may indeed have been especially and intrinsically characteristic of the satyr play throughout its history.[135] By the latter part of the fifth century, playwrights |[237] (including Sophokles and Euripides) seem very seldom, if ever, to have presented connected tragic trilogies in the manner of Aischylos' *Oresteia*, Danaid-trilogy, etc.[136] Perhaps Euripides' "revisionist" mode of combining satyric and tragic conventions represented an attempt to recover some of the dramatic possibilities exploited in the earlier part

---

[133] E.g., Whitman 1974, Foley 1985; cf. Mastronarde 1999.

[134] Cf. Knox 1979: 264–70, Michelini 1987, Mastronarde 2000, for review of scholarly opinions about the generic status of "tragedy," "tragicomedy," "romance," etc., and about Euripides' individual contribution to the evolution of these "happy-ending" forms. It should be noted, however, that it was for his *unhappy* endings that Eur. was esp. distinguished in Aristotle's eyes (*Poet.* 13.1453a27-30), and that of all the features of new-fangled Euripidean technique that we find criticized in Aristophanes and elsewhere, none has anything to do with inappropriately happy endings or surprise twists of plot (apart from gods *ex machinâ*).

[135] I should perhaps make clear that on the available evidence it is not possible to draw definite conclusions about the content or tone of most of these pre-Euripidean satyr plays or their relationship to the tragedies to which they were affiliated. In what follows, I will try to make a case for treating Aischylos' satyr plays as possessing some of the ironic sophistication that we normally reserve for Euripides; but I accept of course that such a case must for now remain somewhat speculative. The scholars of antiquity knew and understood little about fifth-century satyr plays—and even less about connected tetralogies; and this makes it especially hard to reconstruct the work of Pratinas, Aischylos, Aristias, Sophokles, and the others against whom Euripides is supposed to have been reacting with his new kinds of *tragôidiai*. After the fifth century, the individual plays even of a connected tetralogy were routinely treated as separate dramas (e.g., catalogued alphabetically, as four separate entries, and copied separately, as in our medieval manuscripts). Old satyr plays were rarely performed (in contrast to old tragedies), and their texts—if they were read at all—were apparently studied and quoted along with the tragedies, i.e., without much awareness of their peculiar conventions. So it was hardly to be expected that a sensitive critical assessment of Aischylos' or Sophokles' achievement as a satyr playwright would survive into the Alexandrian era or later.

[136] The three plays of the Trojan "trilogy" (*Alexander, Palamedes, Trojan Women*—the sole attested example of Euripidean plays on a related theme being performed together in the same year) do not appear to have been at all closely connected (and the satyr play that accompanied them, *Sisyphos*, may well have had no connection at all with Troy: KPS 1999: 442–48). For Sophokles, neither Radt (*TrGF* vol. 4) nor Lloyd-Jones 1996 finds any evidence at all for trilogic organization among the 120 known plays.

of the century by Aischylos (and others too, doubtless) through the sequence of three tragedies and a satyr play all on one continuous theme.[137]

With this idea in mind—i.e., the notion that Aischylean tetralogies were complex and integrated wholes, whose final (satyric) component belongs in any assessment of their overall meaning and may shed crucial revelatory and/or ironic light on the preceding tragic action—let us turn to the *Oresteia*, and see what more we can make of it.

FINALE: AISCHYLOS' *PROTEUS* AND THE ENDS OF THE *ORESTEIA*

According to the anonymous *hypothesis* to Aischylos' *Agamemnon* (*TrGF* III T 65a), "The play was produced in the archonship of Philokles in the second year of the 80th Olympiad. Aischylos came first with *Agamemnon*, *Choephoroi*, *Eumenides*, and satyric *Proteus*. Xenokles of Aphidne was producer (*chorêgos*)."[138] The surviving fragments of *Proteus*, the fourth play of the *Oresteia*, amount to |[238] a total of two complete but partly unintelligible lines, quoted by Athenaios for their gastronomic interest (F 210 = Athen. 9. 394a), plus one half-line and four isolated words, quoted by late lexicographers for their grammatical or lexical oddity (F 211–215). This is not a promising basis on which to build a reconstruction of the play or its relation to the preceding three tragedies; but fortunately we possess a number of clues, of varying degrees of reliability, that allow us to draw several fairly firm conclusions, as well as to indulge in a number of tantalizing speculations.

In Book 4 of the *Odyssey*, Menelaos recounts how, in the course of his eight-year journey home from Troy, the gods and bad winds combined to delay him (and presumably Helen too, though she is not mentioned at all in this episode)[139]

---

[137] In many respects, Euripides' dramatic technique likes to emphasize its traditional and conventional character (in contrast to the more seamless plays of Sophokles); cf. Michelini 1987. Several of his plots and individual scenes present themselves as self-conscious responses to the work of Aischylos in particular.

[138] It is not known whether this Philokles was Aischylos' nephew of the same name, himself a playwright of note (*TrGF* I p.88, *TrGF* III p.39); nor whether this Xenokles was related to the tragedian who later defeated Sophokles when he produced *OT*. The title *Proteus* is included in the alphabetical list of A.'s plays included in the anonymous *Life of A.* (T 78), which is transmitted with several of the medieval manuscripts of his seven surviving plays. The list omits *Prometheus Pyrkaeus* (the satyr play performed with A. *Persians* in 472 BCE, F 204a-207) and *Thalamopoioi* (possibly satyric: see Radt's nn. on F 78). Altogether 73 plays are listed, and at least 9 omitted, perhaps as many as 17 or 18: see Radt on T 78.

[139] In light of the rest of the *Odyssey*, we might infer that she was with Menelaos, but not involved in the capture of Proteus. It is possible that alternative versions already existed, however. In the *Iliad* it is remarked that Paris and Helen stopped in Sidon on their way from Sparta to Troy (*Il.* 6.289–92); in the *Odyssey* she is said to have acquired her blissful opiate from an Egyptian medicine-queen (*Od.*

on the island of Pharos, at the mouth of the Nile. This was the home of the "Unerring Old Man of the Sea, Proteus the Egyptian" (γέρων ἅλιος νημερτής, 4.384–85).[140] Menelaos and his men began to starve; but eventually Proteus' daughter Eidothea took pity on him, and told him how to capture Proteus and force him to divulge how he might return home. Following her instructions, he and three companions hid on the beach under seal-skins (provided by Eidothea), at the spot where Proteus brought his herd of seals every day to sleep (νομεὺς ὣς πώεσι μήλων, "like a shepherd with his flock," 4.413). After Proteus arrived, counted his seals, and went to sleep, Menelaos and his comrades jumped on him and then held on tightly while he changed shape into a lion, leopard, snake, boar, water, tree, and finally himself again. Then he finally informed Menelaos that the adverse winds were caused by Zeus and the other gods, who were angry at his failure to sacrifice a hekatomb. He also told him of the fates of other Achaian heroes returning from Troy (notably Aias Oiliades and Agamemnon), and advised him to hurry to Argos to exact vengeance on Aigisthos, or, if he should find that Orestes had already done this, at least to join in the funeral rites (4.543–45).

At *Agamemnon* 636–80 the Herald describes the storm that destroyed much of the Greek fleet as it was sailing home from Troy, and mentions specifically (671–79) that he does not know whether or not Menelaos's ship survived. This passage must be preparing us for the appearance of Menelaos in Egypt in the fourth play, in accordance with the *Odyssey* narrative. Furthermore, we are informed that the name "Eidô" was employed in Aischylos' *Proteus*, as equivalent to the Homeric Eidothea; so Proteus' daughter may well have played a role of some kind |[239] (whether or not this role was as significant as that of Eidô-Theonoê in Euripides' *Helen*).[141] There is nothing more that we are entitled to regard as definite about this satyr-finale.[142] Yet it is by no means all that we can plausibly infer.

Virtually all scholars have assumed that this Egyptian excursion followed the story of *Odyssey* Book 4 quite closely, providing little more than a cheerful ap-

---

4.219–34). See Gantz 1993: 571–72, and below, pp. 59–60.

[140] The narrative begins with the word Αἰγύπτωι (4.351), but quickly specifies, "There is an island just off Egypt, that they call Pharos...," and at the end of the narrative Menelaos is instructed to sail "to Egypt" and perform sacrifices there (4.570–87). Thus Pharos and Egypt are virtually, but not quite, elided into one (as they are by subsequent authors, such as Herodotos and Euripides).

[141] F 212 = *Etym. Gud.* s.v. εἰδώ. In E. *Helen* 4–16 we are informed, "Proteus, king of Egypt ... had two children, one male, Theoklymenos, and a noble maiden Eidô, pride of her mother when she was a baby; after she came to the ripe age for marriage, they called her Theonoê, for she knew all the present and future things of the gods (τὰ θεῖα), having obtained this privilege from her ancestor Nereus." See too Nonnos *Dion.* 43.269, and Kannicht 1969: 2.20–21.

[142] The other surviving fragments include references to "a wretched pigeon eating..." or "being eaten..." (F 210: σιτουμένην δύστηνον ἀθλίαν φάβα / μέσακτα πλευρὰ πρὸς πτύοις πεπληγμένην[?]), and a "fish-paste" (F 211: καὶ τὸν ἰχθύων γάρον), which may recall Aulis and starving sailors in A. *Ag*. But we possess no clue as to the role of the satyr-chorus: perhaps they assisted in the minding of Proteus' smelly flock.

pendage to, or parody of, the grim trilogy that preceded: so, in contrast to his brother, the fortunate Menelaos resolved the problem of the adverse winds, starving sailors, and angry gods, and returned home unharmed.[143] Only rarely has the possibility been entertained that Aischylos might have presented the "alternative" story, most famously presented by Stesichoros and Herodotos (in two quite distinct and independent versions), according to which Helen spent the duration of the Trojan War in Egypt with Proteus.[144] Such a counter-version (or "recantation," *palinôidia*) was certainly available to Aischylos and offered intriguing possibilities for a "satyr-romance" set at the end of, and in response to, one or more of the preceding tragedies (possibilities that Euripides fully exploited in his *Helen, IT,* and *Orestes*);[145] and the text of the three surviving plays of the *Oresteia* in fact presents several curious linguistic and structural hints that seem to point precisely to such an Aischylean detour.

The Egyptian sojourn of Helen, as we find it attested by the mid-fifth century, took several different forms. In Book 2 of Herodotos' *Histories* (composed presumably between 450 and 425), we are told that King Proteus (now a conventional monarch, not a shape-shifting sea god) was so disgusted to learn of Paris' behavior in seducing his host's wife and stealing both her and much treasure, that he kept Helen and the treasure in Egypt until Menelaos should come to reclaim them, and meanwhile sent Paris on his way to Troy empty-handed. The siege of Troy still took place, however, because Paris and the Trojans could not persuade the Greeks that they did not in fact have Helen and the treasure; only after the city was |[240] captured did Menelaos realize what had happened and sail to Egypt to retrieve Helen.[146]

A century earlier, the choral lyric poet Stesichoros had produced, it seems, no fewer than three accounts of Helen's career. One was fairly orthodox (i.e., along the lines of the *Kypria* and *Iliad*). In two others, Stesichoros made a point of contradicting the standard versions of Homer (the *Iliad*) and Hesiod (presumably the *Ehoiai*), though we do not know how precisely similar or different these two vari-

---

[143] "A lighthearted parody" (Sutton 1980: 26–27), "Menelaos' cheerful and inconsequential adventure in Egypt, and the prophecy of his happy homecoming represent, as untragic parallels, a striking contrast to the tragic homecoming of his brother Agamemnon" (R. Germar and R. Krumeich, in KPS 1999: 181), etc.

[144] Stesichoros *PMG/PMGF* 192–193; Hdt. 2.112–20. See Gantz 1993: 571–76.

[145] Cf. Whitman 1974, Seidensticker 1979. We may note that all three of these plays make use of an image/replica/phantom (as does *Alkestis*), and deal with Iphigeneia, or Helen, and Orestes; cf. too E. *El.* 1278–83, and below pp. 60–70.

[146] Hekataios too mentions Helen's presence in Egypt (*FGHist* 1 F 308–309); but we cannot tell for what reason. Herodotos discusses in some detail the relative likelihood of his own version (which he says he was given by Egyptian priests) vs. Homer's Iliadic version (and that of the *Kypria*). He does not mention Stesichoros (or drama) at all, a neglect that is characteristic of his approach throughout the *Histories* (only Homer and Hesiod merit rebuttal). For discussion of Hdt.'s possible sources, see Kannicht 1969, Lloyd 1988: 46–47, Fehling 1989: 59–65.

ant versions were.¹⁴⁷ In the most famous one, if we interpret the opening words literally, Helen is said never to have traveled with Paris at all: "That story is not true. You did not even set foot (οὐδ' ἔβης) in the benched ships, nor did you come to the towers of Troy..." (*PMG* 192). This would imply her aerial transportation to Egypt in a manner similar to that described at Euripides' *Helen* 44–46, "Hermes took me in folds of air (αἰθέρος), covered me in cloud (νεφέληι καλύψας)..., and settled me in this house of Proteus...." But this is incompatible with what we are told about other aspects of Stesichoros' treatment (unless this represents a garbling of his "two different palinodes"): for several sources confirm that Stesichoros (like Herodotos) had the disapproving Proteus himself take Helen away from Paris, and supply him instead with an "image of her (εἴδωλον αὐτῆς) painted on a board, so that by looking at it he should assuage (παραμυθοῖτο) his own desire."¹⁴⁸ (We are not told whether Helen in the first place left Sparta with Paris voluntarily or not; but in Herodotos it is implied that she had responded positively to his advances: 1.115.4.) Thus the "phantom/image" of Helen that accompanied Paris to Troy seems to have been significantly different in the two versions: one was a deceptive replica, the other a consolatory picture. (How Stesichoros handled the revelation of the identity of the phantom and the guilt or innocence of Helen, we do not know.) |[241]

According to one ancient source, Stesichoros was not the inventor of this Helen-phantom: "Hesiod was the first to introduce the phantom of Helen."¹⁴⁹ This report has been condemned by many as a simple mistake (Tzetzes should have said "Stesichoros"). But this is not a likely error, and there is no good reason to mistrust the statement.¹⁵⁰ Precisely the same kind of *eidôlon* substitution takes

---

¹⁴⁷Hesiod fr. 358 M-W (see further below, n. 149). In *P. Oxy.* 2506 fr. 26 col. 1, the commentator on Stesichoros states (*PMG/PMGF* 193): "<In one poem> he finds fault with Homer for having Helen and not the phantom of her be in Troy, while in the other he finds fault with Hesiod. For there are two different palinodes, one beginning ... the other ....." It seems that only one of these poems came to be regularly known and canonized in later times as *The Palinode* (*PMG* 192 = the version cited by Plato etc.). Some scholars have rejected the testimony of this commentator (who appears to be based on the fourth-third-century Peripatetic critic, Chamaileon) and have limited Stesichoros to just one *Palinode*: e.g. Kannicht 1969 (who even sees the *Palinode* as being part of the same poem that contained the original Helen-narrative; see below, n. 160).

¹⁴⁸Schol. Aristid. *Or.* 1.212; cf. Tzetzes on Lykophron 113 (2.59 Scheer). Dio Chrysostom asserts, "Stesichoros in his later poem says that Helen never sailed anywhere at all, while others say Helen was snatched by Alexandros, but arrived here among us in Egypt" (*Or.* 11. 40f [1. 125f von Arnim, 1.159 de Budé]).

¹⁴⁹Tzetzes on Lykophron 822 (1.71 Scheer) = Hes. fr. 358 M-W (among the "*fragmenta dubia*"); cf. West 1985: 134–35. The date of the composition of the (pseudo?)-Hesiodic *Ehoiai* (also known as *The Catalog of Women*) is much debated, of course. It may not be much, or at all, earlier than the time of Stesichoros. Herodotos asserts that he believes Homer (i.e., the author of the *Iliad*) was aware of the story of Helen's sojourn in Egypt, but suppressed it: δοκέει δέ μοι καὶ Ὅμηρος τὸν λόγον τοῦτον πυθέσθαι ... ἠπίστατο τὴν ἐς Αἴγυπτον Ἀλεξάνδρου πλάνην (2.116.2, 6).

¹⁵⁰Another similar case of agreement between Hesiod and Stesichoros is mentioned by Philodemos

place in a Hesiodic account of Iphimedê/Iphigeneia; and it is worth noting carefully the technique by which that "variant" is introduced:[151]

> γῆμ[ε δ' ... ἄναξ ἀνδρ]ῶν Ἀγαμέμνων
> κού[ρην Τυνδαρέοιο Κλυταιμήσ]τρην κυανῶπ[ιν·
> ἣ τ[έκεν Ἰφιμέδην καλλίσφυ]ρον ἐν μεγάροισιν
> Ἠλέκτρην θ' ἣ εἶδος ἐρήριστ' ἀ[θανά]τηισιν.
> Ἰφιμέδην μὲν σφάξαν ἐυκνή[μ]ιδες Ἀχαιοὶ
> βωμῶ[ι ἔπ' Ἀρτεμίδος χρυσηλακ]άτ[ου] κελαδεινῆς,
> ἥματ[ι τῶι ὅτε νηυσὶν ἀνέπλ]εον Ἴλιον ε[ἴσω
> ποινὴ[ν τεισόμενοι καλλισ]φύρου Ἀργειώ[νη]ς,
> εἴδω[λον· αὐτὴν δ' ἐλαφηβό]λος ἰοχέαιρα
> ῥεῖα μάλ' ἐξεσά[ωσε, καὶ ἀμβροσ]ίην [ἐρ]ατε[ινὴν
> στάξε κατὰ κρῆ[θεν, ἵνα οἱ χ]ρὼς [ἔ]μπε[δ]ο[ς] ε[ἴη,
> θῆκεν δ' ἀθάνατο[ν καὶ ἀγήρ]αον ἥμα[τα πάντα.
> τὴν δὴ νῦν καλέο[υσιν ἐπὶ χ]θονὶ φῦλ' ἀν[θρώπων
> Ἄρτεμιν εἰνοδί[ην, πρόπολον κλυ]τοῦ ἰ[ο]χ[ε]αίρ[ης.
>
> (Hes. F 23a 13–26 M-W)

Agamemnon, king of men, married
Dark-faced Klytaimêstra, daughter of Tyndareus;
And she bore beautiful-ankled Iphimedê in the halls,
And Elektra, who rivaled the immortal goddesses in her appearance.
Iphimedê was slaughtered by the well-greaved Achaians
At the altar of Artemis of the loud cry and golden distaff,
On that day when they were sailing off to Troy in their ships
To exact retribution for the Argive woman of beautiful ankles—|[242]
Her phantom (*eidôlon*), that is; she herself (*autên*) was quite easily rescued
By the arrow-loving deer-shooter, who poured lovely ambrosia
Down over her head, so that her flesh should be undamaged,
And made her immortal and ageless for evermore.
Now the races of men on earth call her "Artemis in the road,"
Servant of the famed archer goddess.
[There follows next the birth of Orestes, and his killing of Klytaimestra.]

The "adding-on" narrative style, common in hexameter epic (particularly in enjambement, as here), makes such a deviation from tradition especially effective

---

(*De Piet.* p.24 Gomperz = *PMG* 215): "Stesichoros in his *Oresteia* followed Hesiod <in saying> that Iphigeneia, daughter of Agamemnon, is now named Hekate"; see below, pp. 63–65. It should be borne in mind that "Hesiodic" poetry embraced a huge range of material, some of it of local origin and focus, some more Panhellenic and systematic. Thus multiple "Hesiodic" versions are not rare. See (e.g.) Nagy 1990, West 1985.

[151] The supplements in the (seriously lacunose) papyrus text are mainly supplied by E. Lobel, and are obviously highly speculative. But the general sense of the lines, and the trajectory of the narrative, are not in doubt. [This is now fr. 19 in G. W. Most's Loeb edition of Hesiod, vol. 2.]

and inclusive: we hear the usual version (Ἰφιμέδην μὲν σφάξαν...), and then, four verses later, hear the contradiction of it (εἴδωλον· αὐτὴν δὲ ... ἐξεσάωσε...). Thus both stories get told, and held in tension with one another; neither is guaranteed the author's or audience's unequivocal assent, both are left open for future exploitation.[152]

The normal (orthodox) version of the sacrifice of Iphigeneia thus appears to be the one with the substituted phantom (*eidôlon*) or hind. That is how Hesiod, Stesichoros, and Euripides tell the story; and no certain example survives from earlier than Aischylos in which Iphigeneia is unequivocally killed. In *Agamemnon*, the Chorus paint a lurid picture of Agamemnon and the other "war-loving judges," as they ordered her to be gagged and lifted "on high above the altar, like a goat" (*Ag.* 232); and later in the play neither Klytaimestra nor the Chorus express any doubt that she was indeed cruelly killed by her father, in a crime that cries out for vengeance (1412-20, 1525-29, 1555-62).[153] But the moment of the sacrifice is narrated quite evasively: "What happened then, I did not see, and I do not say" (*Ag.* 248). Given the Chorus' intense focus on the moral contradictions involved in this scene at Aulis—a discomfort shared by Agamemnon and all modern scholars[154]—we may be sure that this evasion did not pass unnoticed by the Athenian audience. Did Artemis indeed allow this innocent to be slaughtered, |[243] as the necessary means to enforce retribution for Zeus' and Agamemnon's brutal destruction of Troy? Or did she intervene to rescue her (as we might expect from a divinity devoted especially to young animals and women)? The subsequent scenes of this play—and of the trilogy—say nothing directly to contradict the prevailing impression that Iphigeneia is dead.[155] But of course that is the whole point of an

---

[152] The same technique is found e.g. at Hom. *Od.* 11.601-602 too, presenting the figure of Herakles in the underworld: at first it appears to be Herakles himself (601), but quickly he is "replaced" by his phantom (602: *eidôlon*)—with the "real" hero now up on Olympos (602-604), as several traditions preferred. But the subsequent description of Herakles' appearance, entourage, and behavior is extremely vivid and by no means wraithlike or insubstantial, as he recognizes Odysseus, weeps, and tells him how "I suffered misery... etc." (605-27). See further Griffith 1990: 196-200, Gantz 1993: 582-87.

[153] Klytaimestra's language at 1415ff is curious, however: "He sacrificed his own child, even though sheep were abundant in woolly flocks... as a charm (ἐπῳδόν) for Thracian winds." The option of an animal substitute, and the term *epôidon* (suggesting magical spells), are enhanced by the reference to "Thrace," which, in addition to being in the north and hence the origin of these unfavorable winds, is also the source of many of the most powerful Greek incantational techniques—including telekinesis and necromancy; cf. Burkert 1962.

[154] Scholarly articles continue to debate Agamemnon's choice: "Which of these actions (is/was) without evils?" "Why is Artemis angry?" etc. For a good recent discussion, laying out previous critical views and steering a sensible path among them, see Käppel 1998, with whose assessments I largely concur—though he does not consider the possibility that the sacrifice might not in fact have been completed; nor does his book make any mention of the satyric sequel.

[155] Certainly Klytaimestra seems to be convinced that Iphigeneia's spirit underground will welcome her act of vengeance; and a ghastly network of images and phrases in *Ag.* links the Chorus' intimations and Kalchas' prophecies with the imagined activities of an *alastôr* or *teknopoinos mênis*, etc.

eidôlon. Everyone must believe that the intended victim has died (as they continue to do in Euripides' *IT* until Iphigeneia reveals herself); otherwise the *eidôlon* will serve no purpose. Thus Agamemnon was indeed guilty of meaning to kill his daughter, and of actually killing a helpless victim whom all believed to be her: so he still deserved to be punished. But Artemis' intervention will turn out to have been less heartless, and the "theodicy" of the *Oresteia* a little more palatable, if it is finally revealed in the fourth play (perhaps from the mouth of the prophetic Proteus, or his daughter Eidô(!)) that Iphigeneia is after all—and as half-expected—safe and sound, whether now reunited with her brother or still presiding over a cult somewhere as a virtual divinity in her own right.[156]

Fig. 9 shows a Pompeian wall-painting from the House of the Tragic Poet (presumably based on one or more Greek originals), depicting the sacrifice of Iphigeneia.[157] At the center, Iphigeneia is being lifted up for sacrifice by two warriors (Diomedes and Odysseus, presumably), under the supervision of Kalchas: her eyes, and Kalchas' too, are fixed on the huddled and shrouded figure of Agamemnon off to our left, who at this point cannot bear to watch or participate. Above—in a different spatial and/or temporal (or generic?) dimension, as it were—Iphigeneia is being whisked towards the heavens on the back of a deer. As for Artemis/Diana, she appears twice: once in sternly regal posture above Agamemnon's shoulder (standing as a statue on a broken pillar that has no apparent connection with the rest of the surroundings), and again on high, receiving Iphigeneia into the clouds. Both versions of the story, and of Artemis' treatment of this family, are thus simultaneously presented to our view. Similarly, in Fig. 10 (a mid-fourth-century Italian Red-Figure volute krater from Tarentum),[158] Iphigeneia is represented as half-woman, half-deer—or rather, as *both* woman *and* deer—in the very process of being sacrificed/transformed/substituted/replicated.

Such a technique of alternative or contradictory story-telling, refuting and unsaying—yet simultaneously alluding to and thus reaffirming—the "standard" story, was well-established in the epic repertoire at least by the seventh century, and was perhaps as old as the epic itself.[159] The continuing notoriety of Stesichoros'

---

[156] This suggestion has been previously advanced by Griffith 1990: 199 and n. 53, Cunningham 1994, but in each case with only brief discussion. See E. Fraenkel on A. *Ag.* 247 for references to earlier discussions.

[157] See *LIMC* s.v. "Agamemnon" 41 (= "Kalchas" 9 = "Iphigeneia" 38). For detailed discussion of the composition and style, see, e.g., Curtius 1929: 290-92, who claims to recognize at least three distinctly different styles and compositional components in the painting's human figures ("ein Pasticcio"), which he attributes to a clumsy adaptation of older "originals." (Curtius is especially scornful of the depiction of Artemis' statue and the scenes in the clouds, "...wie aus einem franzözischen Ballett"). But perhaps we should think instead of an artfully *doubled* pictorial narrative, i.e., a purposeful disjunction of styles and manners in the simultaneous presentation of a story and its variant within the same frame; see Fig. 10, and below, pp. 63–65.

[158] See further Green and Handley 1995: fig. 22 = *LIMC* 5.712 no. 11, pl. 467.

[159] Griffith 1990. The related Homeric technique of having gods rescue heroes from the battlefield

Palinode was thus due perhaps more to the flamboyance and autobiographical color of its self-advertisement (i.e., the claim that, since Helen had blinded the poet for speaking ill of her, now she must give his sight back, since he is changing his tune and salvaging her good name) than to the intrinsic novelty of the story itself or its narrative tactics.[160] Indeed, the same ancient commentator who informs us of the existence and opening lines of two separate *Palinodes*[161] also remarks that Stesichoros' poems in general were remarkable for their "innovations" (*PMG* 193. 17 = *P. Oxy*. 2506 fr. 26 col. Ii, 17: οὗτος δὲ ἐκαινοποίησε τὰς ἱστορίας...), and that they were a prime source of material for the fifth-century tragedians (*PMG* 217 = *P. Oxy*. 2506 fr. 26 col. Ii, 5–27: με[τὰ γὰρ] Ὅμηρον κα[ὶ] Ἡσίοδον [οὐδενὶ] μᾶλλον Στησιχόρου [συμ]φων[οῦσι]· Αἰσχύλο[ς μὲν γὰρ] Ὀρέστ[εια]ν ποιήσα[ς τριλο]γίαν [Ἀ]γαμέμνον[α Χ]οηφ[όρ]ους Εὐμεν[ίδας... τὸν ἀναγ[νωρισμὸ]ν διὰ τοῦ βοστρύχο[υ· Στ]ησιχόρωι γάρ ἐστιν [...], Ε[ὐ]ριπίδης δὲ τὸ τ[όξον] τὸ Ὀρέστου ὅτι ἐστὶν δε[δομέ]νον αὐτῶι δῶρον πα[ρὰ τ]οῦ Ἀπόλλωνος ... [Εὐριπίδ]ης δὲ καὶ τὴν Ἰφ[ιγένειαν ἐ]ποίησε γαμουμέ[νην Ἀχιλλεῖ] ... σατ[ ]ρ..[. "After Homer and Hesiod <they agree> most with Stesichoros; for Aischylos, in composing his *Oresteia* <trilogy? story?>,[162] |[245] *Agamemnon, Choephoroi, Eumenides*, <took over>[163] the recognition (*anagnôrismon*) by means of the lock of hair; for this is in Stesichoros. And Euripides <took over> the bow of Orestes that has been given him as a gift from Apollo... [The commentator quotes E. *Or*. 268]...; and Euripides

---

in clouds of mist, or send doubles down to fight in their place, is discussed by Kannicht 1969: 1; but he insists that such techniques were never applied to the figure of Helen before Stesichoros in the sixth century—impelled by pro-Spartan loyalties to clear her name for cult purposes. On the "doubling" tendencies of Homer's Helen in Homer and elsewhere, see Zeitlin 1995: 403–16; and on the indeterminate quality of her agency and perspective, Worman 1997.

[160] The traditions of the fake Helen and guiltless Helen continued to flourish, of course: even before E. *Helen*, we find E. *Elektra* 1278–83 (from the late 420s), Gorgias (later fifth century), Isokrates (early fourth century), etc.; and cf. Griffith 1990 for discussion of sophistic and older poetical habits. Kannicht 1969: 1.21–44 argues at length, however, in favor of the traditional view that Stesichoros was the first to introduce this novelty; see too Gantz 1993: 582–87. Furthermore, he suggests that, so far from composing three separate poems on Helen, Stesichoros presented his blinding and recovery of sight within one and the same poem: thus the "palinode" represented the "immediate" recantation (εὐθύς, Plato *Phaedr*. 243a) of a mistaken account that he had only begun to sing about, but never completed. Whether or not this ingenious hypothesis is correct (which seems to me unlikely), it would be consistent with the techniques of telling/untelling I have outlined. It is notable too that several ancient commentators on Homer's *Iliad* (including Herodotos) surmised that its author was aware of the counter-tradition about Helen: see above, nn. 147 and 149.

[161] *PMG* 193.17 = *P. Oxy*. 2506 fr. 26 (Page 1963). This commentator appears to be following the Peripatetic scholar Chamaileon, of the late fourth century BCE.

[162] The ink traces do not support the reading of gamma (for τριλογίαν) here. Rho looks possible, so perhaps ἱστορίαν (cf. col. ii, 18)? See next n.

[163] The space in the first half of line 11, before ΤΟΝ ΑΝΑΓ[ΝΩΡΙΣ / ΜΟ[Ν, has room for ΠΡΩΤΕΑ; but we need a finite verb (e.g., παρέλαβε, "took over, borrowed"); so probably the commentator is ignoring (or ignorant of) the satyric fourth play of "the *Oresteia*."

also made Iphigeneia <come to Aulis> to marry <Achilleus?>...").[164]

Altogether, in the two surviving columns of the papyrus (= *PMG* 193 and 217) there are seven specific innovations and/or quotations of Stesichoros listed by this commentator. The five we have so far mentioned all refer to his *Palinode(s)* and *Oresteia*, i.e., to his treatment of Helen and the families of Agamemnon and Menelaos.[165] There are therefore strong grounds for supposing that the other two references that can be partially deciphered from the papyrus may likewise refer to this cluster of stories. I will quote the whole passage as it continues:

> αὐτὸ[ς δ]έ φησ[ιν ὁ] Στησίχορο[ς] τὸ μὲν ε[ἴδωλο]ν ἐλθεῖ[ν ἐς] Τροίαν, τὴν δ' Ἑλένην π[αρὰ] τῶι Πρωτεῖ καταμεῖν[αι· οὕ]τως δὴ ἐκ[α]ινοποίησε τ[ὰς ἱστορ[ί]ας [ὥ]στε Δημοφῶ[ντα μ]ὲν τ[ὸ]ν Θησέως ἐν τ[ῶ]ι νόστωι με[τὰ] τῶν Θεσ[τια]δῶν [ ] ἀνενεχ[θῆναι λέγ]ειν [ἐ]ς [Αἴ]γυπτον, [γενέσθα]ι δὲ Θη[σεῖ] Δημοφῶ[ντα μ]ὲν ἐξ Ἰό[πης] τῆς Ἰφικ[λέους, Ἀ]κάμαν[τα δὲ ἐκ] Φαί[δρας] κτλ.
>
> ...Stesichoros himself says that the phantom went to Troy, but Helen remained with Proteus. Indeed, so innovative was Stesichoros in his narratives that he even said that Demophôn, son of Theseus, during his return home <from Troy> with the Thes<tia>dai was brought to land in Egypt; and also that Demophon was Theseus' son from Iopê, daughter of Iphikles, while Akamas was from Phaidra....

After this, the papyrus becomes even more lacunose; but before it gives out completely (nine lines later), it is possible to read, in successive lines, the names "... Helen....," "Agamem[non]" and "A]mphilochos...."[166] In a separate Appendix below I explore some of the possible implications of these papyrus scraps, and suggest some likely (and other less likely, but not inconceivable) connections that we may draw between these names (especially that of Demophon and by |[246] implication also his mother, Aithra) and the fourth play of the *Oresteia*. But even if we decide that the reference must be instead to one or more quite separate Aischylean dramas, the evidence we have already considered concerning Iphigeneia and Helen seems solid and substantial enough to invite some reassessment of the conventional view of *Proteus* as merely an insignificant afterthought to the trilogic *Oresteia*.

Few scholars apparently have been willing to entertain the notion that an

---

[164]The last line of the column, before the papyrus breaks off, contains the traces of just four letters, which Page reads tentatively as ΣΑΤ.Ρ' (i.e., *saturoi? saturikôi?*) The mind boggles... (e.g., ΕΝ ΔΕ ΤΩΙ ΣΑΤΥΡΙΚΩΙ ΠΡΩΤΕΙ...).

[165]As we noted above (n. 150, on *PMG* 215), Stesichoros also appears to have narrated in his *Oresteia* a version of the sacrifice of Iphigeneia in which she was not killed but became (an associate of?) Artemis-Hekate. We also know from yet another source (schol. Pind. *P.* 11.26 = *PMG* 218) that Stesichoros (like Aischylos in *Cho.*) gave a significant role to Orestes' nurse.

[166]*P. Oxy.* 2506 fr. 26. col. i (and see further Page 1963). For further speculations about the possible contents of this papyrus, and its implications for the reconstruction of A. *Proteus*, see below, Appendix.

Aischylean satyr play might have pursued such radical dramatic convolutions as these.[167] Almost all have been content with a cheerful satyric romp among the seals, culminating in a bland narrative from *Proteus* that would make no difference at all to our understanding or appreciation of the preceding trilogy. This is in part, no doubt, because of a (commendable) reluctance to speculate about a play of which so little survives. But it is also undoubtedly the result of a deeply rooted prejudice as to the nature of Aischylean drama (and of satyr plays in general, too), together with an ingrained habit of reading Greek culture as a steady evolution from primitive to sophisticated and from simple to complex (or from "Archaic" through "Classical" to "Hellenistic"). Critics shrink from ascribing too much subtlety, self-consciousness, or allusiveness to Greek authors and audiences before the arrival of Euripides and the sophists in the later fifth century. Thus if Euripides presents us (from the late 420s onwards) with a barrage of Helen- and Iphigeneia-phantoms, contradictory speeches, and other tantalizing human and divine apparitions and doubles, it must be because he (and/or the Spirit of his Age, or the sophists in particular) has suddenly discovered the delights of paradox, the power of theatrical illusion, and the limits to human certainty and control.

Yet, for at least a century before the production of the *Oresteia*, and probably long before that, Greek audiences had been familiar with the idea that the Trojan War might have been fought over a phantom, that Artemis might have preserved Iphigeneia, and that Egypt was the perfect place for false, modified, or fantastic stories. And it is obvious enough (to the unprejudiced eye and ear) that the first play of Aischylos' trilogy frequently exploits these uncertainties and fantasies.[168] |[247] In addition to the broken-off and open-ended narrative of Iphigeneia's sac-

---

[167] Of course, up until 1963 (when the Stesichoros commentary was published in *P. Oxy.* vol. 29), there was relatively little evidence available to demonstrate the detailed use of his poetry by both Aischylos and Euripides—which has since been further extended into the area of the Theban cycle by the publication of the Lille papyrus (*PMGF* 222A = Campbell 1992: 136–43). In a short but engaging article, C. W. Marshall has pointed out some of the similarities between E.'s *Helen* and the possible plot and characters of *Proteus*, but comes to a different conclusion, suggesting that we have here "a continual effort to rewrite the literary past: Stesichorus emended the Homeric version, which in turn is denied in Aeschylus' *Oresteia* (or so it would seem, lacking any conflicting evidence for Helen's role in *Proteus*).... Euripides follows the Stesichorean route and counters Aeschylus, writing his alternate literary history onto the physical setting of his own drama" (Marshall 1995: 77). In what follows, I try to show that "conflicting evidence" of a kind does in fact exist, shadowy and insubstantial though much of it is, and that Aischylos' affinities were probably closer to Stesichoros (and Euripides, and the *Odyssey*) than to Homer's *Iliad*.

[168] It should also be borne in mind that other dramatists had certainly staged versions of this myth over the previous 50 years and more. One tragic performance in particular may well have anticipated several of Aischylos' most memorable trilogic effects, including the net and bath for Agamemnon's murder, and the symmetry of the two killings (first Agamemnon, then Aigisthos), to judge from the "diptych" character of the two scenes depicted on the Boston krater by the Dokimasia Painter (*ARV*² 652: from the 470s BCE): see Davies 1965, Prag 1985.

rifice (*Ag.* 248-49, discussed above),[169] the language of the first play of the trilogy surrounds Helen repeatedly with a mysterious aura of evanescence and elusiveness:[170]

> πόθωι δ' ὑπερποντίας
> φάσμα δόξει δόμων ἀνάσσειν.
> εὐμόρφων δὲ κολοσσῶν
> ἔχθεται χάρις ἀνδρί.
> ὀμμάτων δ' ἐν ἀχηνίαις
> ἔρρει πᾶσ' Ἀφροδίτα.
> ὀνειρόφαντοι δὲ πενθήμονες
> πάρεισι δόξαι φέρου-
> σαι χάριν ματαίαν·
> μάταν γάρ, εὖτ' ἂν ἐσθλά τις δοκῶν ὁρᾶι,
> παραλλάξασα διὰ χερῶν
> βέβακεν ὄψις οὐ μεθύστερον
> πτεροῖς ὀπαδοῦσ' ὕπνου κελεύθοις.
>
> (*Ag.* 414-26)

> In yearning for the one across the sea,
> A phantom will seem to rule over the halls.
> From lovely-shaped statues (*kolossôn*)[171]
> The favor for the man/husband is hated:
> In the emptinesses of the eyes
> All desire (Aphrodite) has gone.
> Dream-fantasies, painful appearances
> Are there, bringing useless favor.
> In vain, when someone seems to see something good, |[248]
> Changing shape, the vision (*opsis*) is gone through his hands,
> No longer following along the winged paths of sleep....

---

[169] Perhaps it is mere coincidence that this same description also compares Iphigeneia to a young woman's painted image: πρέπουσά θ' ὡς ἐν γραφαῖς, προσεννέπειν θέλουσα ... ("looking like someone in a picture, wanting to address them...," *Ag.* 242-43); cf. Fig. 9 and n. 157 above. The break-off in the sacrifice-narrative is immediately followed by a further reference to a prophecy, "The arts of Kalchas are not fruitless. Justice assigns learning to those who have suffered. The future, when it happens, you will hear...." (*Ag.* 249-52). It is generally accepted that this hugely long choral ode serves as a kind of introduction to the themes and plan of the whole *Oresteia*; and this should probably include *Proteus*.

[170] On this phenomenon around the figure of Helen in this and other contexts, see further Loraux 1995: 195-210.

[171] *kolossos* is not found in Greek literature before this. In Herodotos, the word is used specifically of Egyptian statues (2.131, etc.). At this date there is no particular connotation of exceptional size; and probably the term would suggest to an Athenian audience a *korê*-statue, more or less life-sized: see Fraenkel ad loc. (who also refers to Wilamowitz' discussion of Protesilaos and Laomedeia in Euripides). Such statues or dolls were used extensively in magical spells and oaths; cf. S. I. Johnston, *Restless Dead* (Berkeley, 1999). (Some scholars, however, have preferred to take the *kolossos* here as referring to Menelaos.)

> πάραυτα δ' ἐλθεῖν ἐς Ἰλίου πόλιν
> λέγοιμ' ἂν φρόνημα μὲν
> νηνέμου γαλάνας,
> ἀκασκαῖον δ' ἄγαλμα πλούτου,
> μαλθακὸν ὀμμάτων βέλος,
> δηξίθυμον ἔρωτος ἄνθος.
> παρακλίνασ' ἐπέκρανεν
> δὲ γάμου πικρὰς τελευτάς ...
> ... πομπᾶι Διὸς ξενίου,
> νυμφόκλαυτος Ἐρινύς.
>
> (Ag. 736–48)

> At once I would say that there came to Troy
> A thought of windless calm,
> A gentle ornament (*agalma*) of wealth,
> Soft shaft of the eyes,
> Heart-biting bloom of desire.
> But changing course, she/it ordained
> Bitter final rites of marriage...
> ... by the sending of Zeus of hospitality,
> The bride-wept Erinys.

In both these choral passages, a feminine subject, who appears at first to be Helen, undergoes a "change" (426: *parallaxâsa*, 744: *paraklinâsa*) and is explicitly revealed as, in one case, a "vision" (*opsis*), in the other "an Erinys." The first passage seems to be describing the mental agonies (both waking and sleeping) of Menelaos and his household; yet it could also describe the experience of Paris awakening to find that his night of sexual bliss with his stolen bride is over ("not to return again") and has in any case been a fraud—he will have henceforth nothing more to hold "in his arms" than Helen's "face/vision" (*opsis*).[172] We are told, too, that the arrival of the "Helen-apparition" in Troy is "by Zeus' sending" (748: *pompâi Dios*)—like the saving of Menelaos' ship from the storm "through Zeus' plan" (677: *mêchanais Dios*, cf. 663–65: *tuchê de sôtêr*)—further reminders that |[249]

---

[172]This was, we recall, the twist of one of Stesichoros' *Palinodes*, as Proteus gave Paris a painting "to assuage his desire": above, pp. 59–60. We are reminded too of other misguided and illusory sex-acts, usually involving clouds, mist, or dreams (Ixion, Endymion, Iasion); above n. 159; cf. Kannicht 1969: 1.35–38. Hovering round the fringes of this same cloud of associations we may note also *Ag.* 1500 *phantazomenos gunaiki...* (referring to Helen's sister, Klytaimestra, who claims to have been "impersonated" by the avenging spirit of Atreus' house). (In Book 3 of the *Iliad*, when Paris succumbs [again] to the irresistible beauty of Helen, he recalls their first act of love-making, "on the island of Kranae" [3.443–45]—which ancient scholars assumed must be near the Peloponnese [why would Paris wait longer?]. So Proteus' substitution of the phantom-Helen on Pharos presumably occurred a few nights later.)

the Trojan War (in the notorious "counter-version" of the *Kypria*) was all part of Zeus' "plan" to lighten the earth of the weight of too many mortals.[173]

The *Oresteia* began with a Watchman, whose direct and confidential address to the theater audience drew us immediately into an almost conspiratorial closeness with him. He bemoaned the passing of "the old days... when the house was still being properly managed..." (*Ag.* 19), and looked forward to "grasping [his] master's loving hand" upon his return home (*Ag.* 34–35). Since that scene, our perspectives have quickly bifurcated and multiplied, as we came to share the subject positions of the Argive Elders, the Asian slave-women, even the Furies, as well as a number of higher- and lower-class characters, as they agonized, speculated, suffered, acted, and watched their way through the tribulations of this house. In the final scenes of *Eumenides*, we (along with the rest of the Athenian observers) find ourselves represented onstage by a dominant Athena and a silent human jury working in tandem (another "split" perspective for us), and eventually also by a singing chorus of Escorts (*Propompoi*) whose simulation of a Panathenaic procession brings us again into the strongest possible identification with the events and participants in the orchestra. The "king" (*Ag.* 35) has indeed "come home" for us, though not now in the person of Agamemnon (the Watchman's human "master"), but rather that of Athena and her father, Zeus, who "sees all" (*Eum.* 1045: *pantoptâs*, cf. 1025: "the eye of the whole land of Theseus...") and "watches over and protects" her citizens (997–1002).[174] Thus our split perspectives are merged again and focused into a shared, reflexive vision of a united Athenian community contemplating itself and talking/singing to itself: the Escorts (*Propompoi*) thus finally respond to the Watchman's opening concerns.[175]

And so the trilogy ends, amidst the political fervor and pageantry of Athens and its people. But the tetralogy continues, and carries us off at once to a place where our fantasies may experience a different kind of conclusion to the complexities of this age-old saga of betrayal, loss, and domestic mayhem. In Egypt, the twelve young choreuts will reappear as satyrs (perhaps revisiting some of the cretic rhythms so insistently hammered home by their trilogic predecessors); maybe we get to see Helen at last—or she (and her double) may be merely described (again), as she is reunited with the husband she never deserted? A satyr play restoring Helen to her husband and reaffirming the joys of conjugal fidelity and bliss would be welcome after the horrors involving Paris, Klytaimestra, |[250] Aigisthos,

---

[173] Ancient scholars argued about the meaning and reference in *Il.* 1.5 of *Dios boulê*. Some connected it to Zeus' plan in the *Kypria* (fr. 1); cf. Hesiod fr. 204 M-W, E. *Tro.*, and Gantz 1993: 567–68.

[174] On the paternal role of Zeus (and of Athena, as virtual *basileus archôn*) in this final scene, see Sommerstein 1989 on *Eum.* 1001–1002, Griffith 1995: 104–107; and on the royal/paternal "eye" elsewhere in tragedy, see also Griffith 1998: 57–74.

[175] The citizen chorus sings cheerful instructions for all (*Eum.* 1043, 1047: εὐφημεῖτε ... ὀλολύξατε νῦν ἐπὶ μολπαῖς), in contrast to the "silence" and avoidance of unpropitious utterance of the Watchman (*Ag.* 16: ὅταν δ' ἀείδειν ... δοκῶ ..., 36; τὰ δ' ἄλλα σιγῶ· βοῦς ἐπὶ γλώσσῃ μέγας, 38–39).

Agamemnon, and Kassandra; and it might do something to mitigate the level of misogynistic fervor that dominated parts of the first three plays. Whether such restoration would allay all worries, we may doubt, however: the tragic trilogy is not erased, merely revised. But perhaps this might be the play in which that celebrated, but hitherto unplaced, Aischylean verse was originally delivered:

> ἀπάτης δικαίας οὐκ ἀποστατεῖ θεός.
>
> (Aisch. *TrGF* 3 F 301)[176]
>
> God does not object to just deception.

The "deception" of Paris by a god-sent phantom was for the good of Helen (and Menelaos too), and for the good of the institution of marriage—as well as for the reputation of the Olympian gods, who otherwise must bear the responsibility for the Judgment of Paris and resultant sack of Troy. A "just deception" is also what Gorgias recommended as the most desired and pleasurable accomplishment of a tragic playwright, vis-à-vis his audience.[177] Barring further discoveries from the sands of Egypt, we are unlikely ever to know just how the *Oresteia* ended. But I think we can be confident that it left its audience both more confused, and more comfortable, as a result of its romantic and depoliticized revisions. We have been faced with two contradictory alternatives, in effect: the tragic world of the trilogy and the romantic sequel of the satyr play—and in the altered state of Dionysiac consciousness, such double vision is quite acceptable, even required. |[251]

---

[176] The verse was quoted by the sophistic author of *Dissoi Logoi* (3.10 DK), as well as by Stobaios and various Homeric scholiasts. Radt, like his predecessors, includes it among the "*incertae fabulae*," and cites attributions by various scholars to *Danaids, Aiguptioi, Prometheus Pyrkaeus, Thalamopoioi,* or *Philoktetes*. On metrical grounds, it is more likely to be from a satyr play than a tragedy: the initial resolution—especially of a trisyllabic word, *apatês*, not followed by an enclitic or postpositive particle—would be extremely unusual in Aischylean tragedy, less so in satyr play (e.g., F 281a 9); see Griffith 1977: 77–78.

[177] Gorgias F 23 DK (Plutarch *de glor. Ath.* 5.348c): ἤνθησε δ' ἡ τραγῳδία καὶ διεβοήθη, θαυμαστὸν ἀκόαμα καὶ θέαμα τῶν τότ' ἀνθρώπων γενομένη καὶ παρασχοῦσα τοῖς μύθοις καὶ τοῖς πάθεσιν ἀπάτην, ὡς Γοργίας φησίν, ἥν ὅ τ' ἀπατήσας δικαιότερος τοῦ μὴ ἀπατήσαντος καὶ ὁ ἀπατηθεὶς σοφώτερος τοῦ μὴ ἀπατηθέντος. ... In his *Defence of Helen* (!), Gorgias claims "deceptions of opinion (δόξης ἀπατήματα), inducing pleasure and dispelling pain," as the function of "inspired incantations through words" (ἔνθεοι διὰ λόγων ἐπῳδαί) and "magic" (γοήτεια): F 11a 10 DK.

APPENDIX

STESICHOROS *P. OXY.* 2506 F 26 AND AISCHYLOS' *PROTEUS*

The mention of Demophon's arrival in Egypt, in the same passage of Stesichoros commentary that discusses that poet's *Oresteia*, raises some intriguing questions.[178] As Denys Page (the first editor of the papyrus) has noted, no other author, before or after Stesichoros, is known to have brought Demophon to Egypt, for any reason.[179] There is no trace of such a story anywhere else; and it is impossible to be certain what the Stesichorean context or motive was for this Egyptian detour. The reference to his "return" (ἐν τῶι νόστωι) must mean that Demophon (like Menelaos) was travelling back to Athens from Troy when he was carried to Egypt. A poem entitled *Nostoi* (*The Returns* = PMG 208–209) was attributed to Stesichoros, along with another entitled *Iliou Persis* (*The Capture of Troy* = PMG 196–205): both presumably involved reworkings of material from the Cyclic Epics. But the use of the singular here (νόστωι) seems to refer to Demophon's individual "journey home," not the title of a work (which would be plural). Such a journey could have been mentioned in either of those poems. Yet in light of the surrounding references in the papyrus to Helen, Proteus, and Agamemnon, we must consider the possibility that the arrival of Demophon in Egypt (and the question of the two different mothers for Theseus' two sons) was connected in Stesichoros' narrative to the story of the phantom Helen, and that it may belong to his *Oresteia*, or one or other of the *Palinodes*.

What would Demophon have been doing "in his return from Troy"?[180] The sons of Theseus, Demophon and Akamas (who are usually found operating as a unified pair, though a few authors, in addition to Stesichoros, do distinguish

---

[178] See above, p. 65.

[179] "Demophonta ad Aegyptum esse devectum unus auctor Stesichorus," Page 1968: 35. (Page 1963 acknowledges in his preface a large debt to the preliminary editorial work of E. Lobel; so we may assume that Lobel was equally baffled.)

[180] And how should we fill in the missing letters in line 20: ΜΕ[...]ΤΩΝΘΕ.[....]ΔΩ.[("...Demophon on his return home ? with the ...")? Page tentatively suggested μετὰ τῶν Θεστιάδων (and indeed, it is hard to think of any other plausible restoration). The "children of Thestios" would normally refer to the uncles of Meleagros, who were best known for being killed in the Kalydonian boar-hunt—an event that seems to have absolutely nothing to do with Demophon or Egypt. Perhaps the fact that these were also brothers of Leda might have given them reason to help go and find Helen? (Leda and Althaia were both daughters of Thestios, king of Aitolia.) Or else Θεστοριδῶν? Thestor was father of Kalchas, chief seer of the Greek army at Troy. After Kalchas died, Mopsos and Amphilochos became the seers during the return from Troy; and Amphilochos is mentioned in *P. Oxy.* 2506 col. i, line 30.... But Amphilochos does not appear to be descended from Thestor and Kalchas. And a TLG search produces no example of a plural Thestoridai—only the singular Thestorides (= Kalchas—or else Homer's reputed Ionian teacher).

between them in birth and attributes),[181] are not mentioned in the *Iliad*.[182] But the |[252] Cyclic Epics and subsequent mythographical and iconographical traditions gave them important roles in the late stages of the Trojan War: they were present inside the Wooden Horse and participated in the sack of the city; they were involved in bringing the Palladion from Troy to Greece;[183] and (a matter of particular interest to Athenians) they found and recovered their grandmother Aithra (mother of Theseus), who had become a slave of Helen's before the War and had gone with her to Troy.[184] The recovery of Aithra was a popular topic in sixth- and early fifth-century Athenian art; and the episode often involved Helen, whose permission was required before Aithra could be freed from slavery and reunited with her Athenian family.[185]

Is it conceivable that in one Stesichorean version—and then in Aischylos' *Proteus*—not only Helen but also Aithra was missing when Troy was captured, so that Demophon was required to visit Egypt in order to recover her? This idea may seem far-fetched: yet there is a curious reference in *Eumenides* that may possibly be preparing for just such a scene. Here are Athena's first words of the play:

> From afar I heard the summon of invocation,
> As I was taking possession of the land near Skamandros,
> Which the leaders and champions of the Achaians
> Distributed entirely to me,
> A great portion of spear-captured possessions,
> Chosen gift to the children of Theseus.
>
> (*Eum.* 397–402)

Part of the point of these lines is clearly to establish Athena's credentials as rep-

---

[181] See in general *RE* art. "Demophon," and *LIMC* articles "Akamas," "Aithra."

[182] The Athenian leader in the *Iliad* is Menestheus (*Il.* 2.546–56), who has often been suspected (since antiquity) of being a late interpolation into the tradition.

[183] See Gantz 1993: 642–47. The Palladion was a statue of Pallas that was supposed to have fallen from heaven and was housed in Athena's temple at Troy. Possession of it guaranteed control over the city of Troy. After Diomedes and Odysseus stole the Palladion from the citadel one night, various disputes over it took place among the Greeks, before eventually it was brought to Greece. (In some versions, a replica was also manufactured (!), and both Palladia were in circulation for a while.) Several different Greek (and Italian) cities claimed to possess the original Palladion. In Athens, the sanctuary of the Palladion became the site of trials (ἐπὶ τῶι Παλλαδίωι) for involuntary homicide (φόνος ἀκούσιος). In Athenian iconography, the statue(s) carried by Demophon and Akamas, or by Demophon alone, or by Diomedes and Odysseus, often consists of a bearded male figure; but presumably the more usual idea was that the statue was female, i.e., Pallas Athena herself (like the image of Artemis in E. *IT*).

[184] Hom. *Il.* 3.53. cf. *LIMC* s.v. "Aithra," M. Anderson, *The Fall of Troy in Early Greek Poetry and Art* (Oxford, 1997) 242–45. This last purpose was sometimes cited as the only reason that the two youths came to Troy at all. In Apollodorus (*Epit.* 5.22), the recovery of Aithra by the sons of Theseus is mentioned in the next sentence after the recovery of Helen by Menelaos.

[185] See Paus. 10.25.8 (and 5.19.3, on the chest of Kypselos); Quint. Smyrn. 13.496–543, Diktys of Crete 13, schol. E. *Hek.* 123, schol. E. *Tro.* 31.

resentative of Athens' interests (she seems to be standing in for, or collaborating with, the "children of Theseus"), as well as to remind the Theater audience of recent events around Sigeion.[186] But the words αἰχμαλώτων ("spear-captives," 400) |[253] and ἐξαίρετον δώρημα ("chosen gift," 402), in conjunction with the "children of Theseus," would necessarily remind an Athenian audience of Aithra (since she was famously the only prize that interested Theseus' sons) and would add yet another strand to the rapidly multiplying links forged in the course of this trilogy between contemporary Athens and mythical Argos and Troy.[187]

On the face of it, it must be confessed, we should hardly expect to find Demophon or Aithra (or indeed any other elements from Athenian mythology) showing up in the midst of Menelaos' adventures in Egypt (whether or not these included Helen and a phantom); and such a development might seem especially unlikely in Stesichoros, a poet who had no particular interest in Athens. Yet, given the remarkable (and quite unexpected) Athenian twists in *Eumenides*, we can hardly rule out such a turn to the Aischylean sequel. Connections between Demophon and Orestes or Helen are in fact not hard to find. For example, in several versions of the Orestes story (including E. *IT*), Demophon is ruler of Athens when Orestes arrives, pursued by the Erinyes, and the awkward, but effective, guest-host interactions between Orestes and Demophon provide an aitiology for the Choes ceremony of the Anthesteria.[188] A fourth play (*Proteus*) might have introduced further Athenian resonances for this Argive story, with one or both of the sons of Theseus predicting or explaining future civic—or perhaps festal Dionysiac—practice. If so, was the recovery of Aithra also represented (perhaps with a recognition-scene)? And was the arrival of the Palladion perhaps included as the basis of a new cult for Athens' patron goddess, comparable to the founding of the Areopagos Court and Panathenaic procession in the preceding play? We can only guess—while taking due note of the reference to "those who guard my statue justly" (αἵτε φρουροῦσιν βρέτας τοὐμὸν δικαίως, *Eum.* 1024-25) in the closing ceremonies of the trilogy.

By this point in our speculations, we have admittedly amassed rather a large cast of characters for a short satyr play, if Menelaos, Proteus, Helen, Demophon, Aithra, and Eido were all to be given speaking parts. And we have the further embarrassment of no fewer than three possible *eidôla*: Iphigeneia's (presumably only in narrative), the fake Palladion (more likely, perhaps, in Diomedes' possession,

---

[186] See Sommerstein 1989 ad loc, with further references; also Griffith 1995: 98–100.
[187] The additional allusion to Kassandra (cf. A. *Ag.* 954-55: πολλῶν χρημάτων ἐξαίρετον ἄνθος, στρατοῦ δώρημα...) would add further resonance between Agamemnon's choice and Demophon's at the moment of Troy's capture, and their different familial and civic consequences.
[188] Cf. Burkert 1985. In A. *Eum.*, however, no human rulers of Athens are present, only Athena as virtual "Queen Archon," presiding over the Court of the Areopagos and the founding of the Panathenaic procession; cf. Sommerstein 1989: 132, Griffith 1995: 96–98.

not Demophon's), and Helen's (whether of cloud, or a painting, or whatever...).[189] So, until such time as the sands of Egypt may yield us further new evidence, we should perhaps rein in our speculations and resign |[254] ourselves to knowing less than we should like—though perhaps more than we realize.

---

[189]For the sake of completeness, I should also mention that E.'s *IT* likewise employs a cult statue (βρέτας, ἄγαλμα: 87, 1176), which "fell from heaven" to the land of the Taurians (87–88) and must now be carried back to Greece by Orestes and Iphigeneia (with the help of a deceptive ritual), so that it can form the basis of a new cult in Attika (see above, p. 60–62).

FIGURES

FIG. 1: Return of Hephaestus with satyrs. "François Vase"; Museo Arch. Florence.
From A. Furtwängler and K. Reichhold, *Griechische Vasenmalerei: Auswahl hervorragender Vasenbilder*, vol. 1 (Munich 1904).

FIGURE 2

FIG. 2: Scene from an Athenian comedy: costumed aulos-player with two choreuts or actors dressed as fighting cocks.

Athenian Red-Figure calyx-krater (late fifth century BCE). Formerly in The J. Paul Getty Museum; now the property of the Superintendency of Naples.
Drawing by Elizabeth Wahle.

FIG. 3: Comic scene of Birth of Helen. South Italian Red-Figure vase from Bari (fourth century BCE).
From M. Bieber, *Die Denkmäler zum Theaterwesen im Altertum* (Berlin 1920).

FIGURE 3

FIGURE 4

FIG. 4: Theater-satyr standing by a mixing-bowl. Athenian Red-Figure cup (early fifth century BCE). Courtesy of the Staatliche Antikensammlungen und Glyptothek, Munich. Photograph by Krueger-Moessner.

FIGURE 5a

FIG. 5a: "Pronomos Vase": Aulos-player, poet, actors, and satyr-chorus.

Athenian Red-Figure volute-krater (late fifth century BCE).

Facsimile of obverse of vase, by Furtwängler-Reichhold vol. 3. 143/144. Photograph by Jerry Kapler.

FIGURE 5b

FIG. 5b: Pronomos Vase; drawing of same scene as 5a, by E. R. Malyon.

Reproduced courtesy of E. Csapo.

FIGURE 5c

FIG. 5c: Pronomos Vase: obverse and reverse scenes combined.

Composite facsimile from Furtwängler-Reichhold, number-key supplied by Thomas Mannack.

Courtesy of T. Mannack (Beazley Archive) and the Oxford University Press.

FIGURE 6

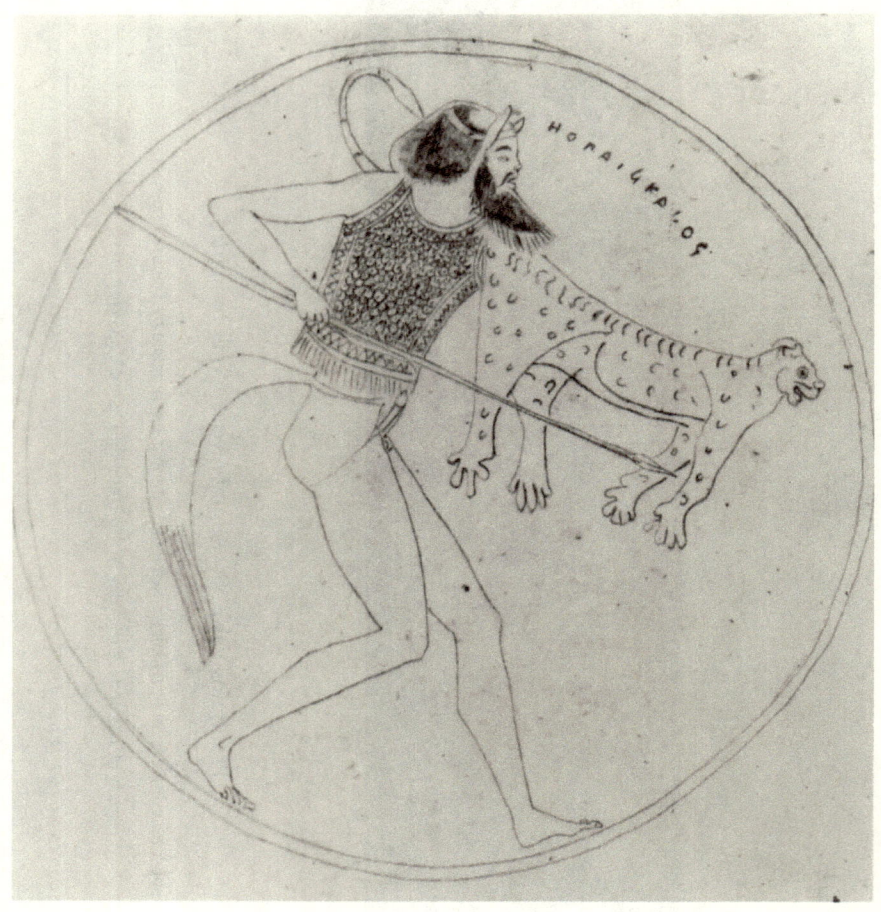

FIG. 6: Theater-satyr helping Dionysus in war against the Giants.

Attic Red-Figure cup by Apollodorus (*ARV*² 121, 23; early fifth century BCE).
Lost; formerly in Rome. From Brommer 1959.

FIGURE 7

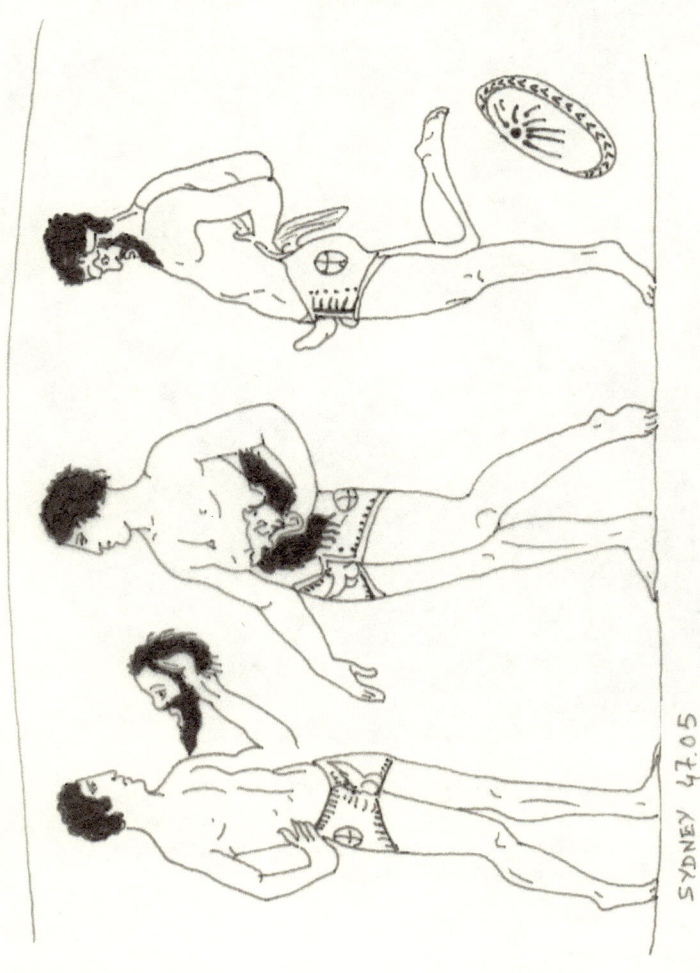

FIG. 7: Three youthful satyr-choreuts, rehearsing.

Apulian Red-Figure bell-krater (early fourth century BCE). Sydney, Nicholson Museum. Drawing by François Lissarrague.

FIGURE 8a

FIG. 8a: Amymone surrounded by satyrs.

Athenian Red-Figure bell-krater (ARV^2 1155,6; mid-fifth century BCE).
Courtesy of the Kunsthistorisches Museum, Vienna.

FIG. 8b: Amymone and Poseidon, surrounded by satyrs.
Athenian Red-Figure bell-krater (ARV^2 1440,1); mid-fifth century BCE.
Courtesy of the Martin von Wagner Museum, Universität Würzburg. Photograph by K. Oehrlein.

FIGURE 9

FIG. 9: Sacrifice of Iphigenia.

Pompeiian wall-painting, from the House of the Tragic Poet (first century CE).
National Museum, Naples.
Image from WikiCommons.

FIGURE 10

FIG. 10: Sacrifice and transformation of Iphigenia. Tarentine Red-Figure volute-krater (fourth century BCE). Courtesy of the Trustees of the British Museum.

FIGURE 11

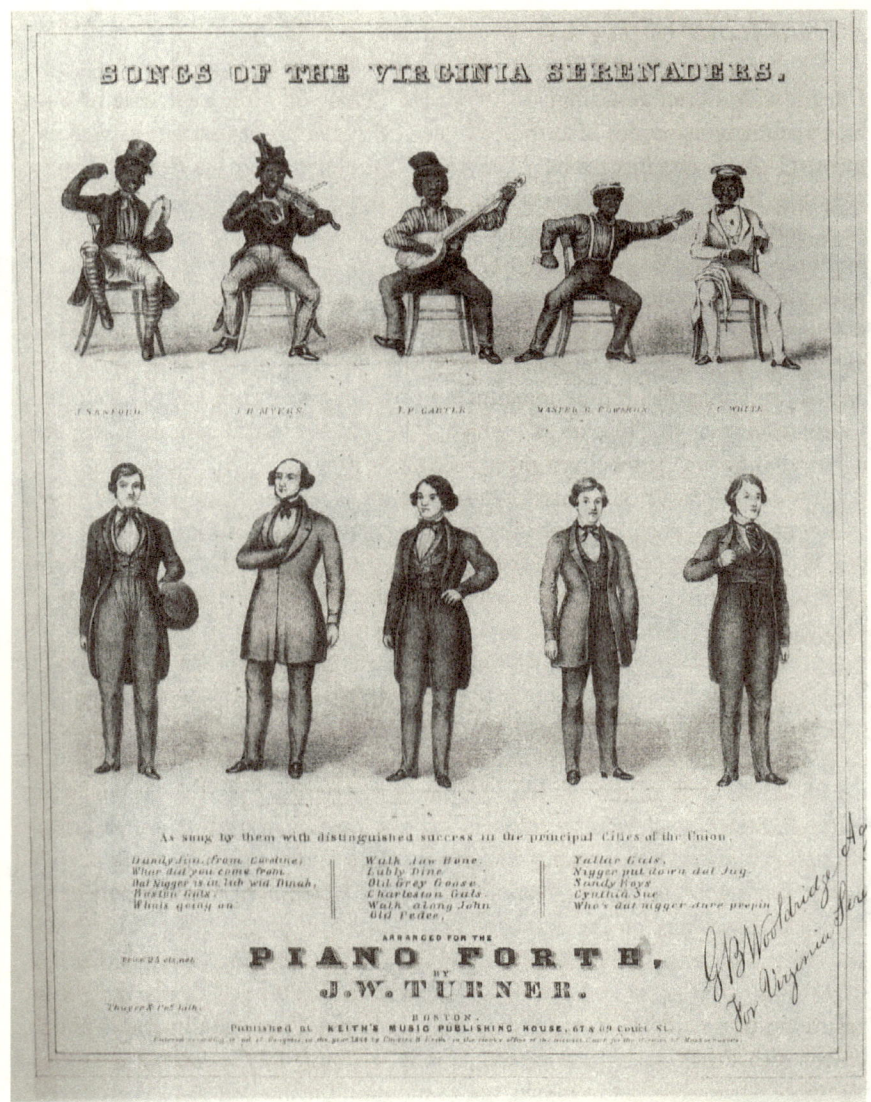

FIG. 11: The Virginia Serenaders, 1844

Courtesy of the Houghton Library, Harvard University.

FIGURE 12

FIG. 12: William Henry Lane ("Juba") dancing at Vauxhall Gardens, London. (Woodcut from the *Illustrated London News*, August 5, 1848.)

Photograph courtesy of the Houghton Library, Harvard University.

CHAPTER 2

Satyrs, Citizens, and Self-Presentation

INTRODUCTION
Athenian Theater and Citizen Performance

Since the 1970s there has been a steady stream of books and articles dealing with the City Dionysia in Athens as a civic ritual, and with the role played by tragic and comic drama in constructing collective and individual male Athenian identity.[1] Some critics see fifth-century Greek theater as a carnival of inverted roles and temporarily subverted values, in which citizens could use disguises, masks, and fictional stories to experiment with extremely alternative types of behavior and explore otherwise risky and forbidden challenges to social and moral norms.[2] Others see Attic drama instead as a delightfully mystified "Ideological State Apparatus" that reinforces (in more or less subtle ways) conventional gender, ethnic, and class distinctions.[3] In either case modern scholarly discussion has focused intensively on the festival context, on audience responses, and on the social function of these plays within Athenian culture at large. Earlier generations of more literary—especially New Critical—analysis had concentrated on the relationship between the dramatic hero and the gods, or on the interplay of images, themes, and moral values within the text. But the advent and incorporation into departments of literature and Classics of cultural studies (including gender studies, performance studies, and film studies), along with the use of increasingly refined psychoanalytic approaches to literature and culture, have resulted in a vigorous critical discourse about Athenian theater that recalls Plato's concerns about the social (psychagogic, pedagogical) impact of musical and dramatic performances. Thus the activities in the Theater of Dionysos are seen as contributing centrally to the formation and self-presentation of good (or less-than-good) Athenian citizens.[4]

[1] On the conditions and conventions of fifth-century production in the Theater of Dionysos, see Pickard-Cambridge 1968/1989; Goldhill 1990; Csapo and Slater 1995; Wilson 2000, Foley 2003: 2–12.
[2] So, e.g., Goldhill 1990; Zeitlin 1995; Hall 1997; cf. Bakhtin 1981; Turner 1982.
[3] So, e.g., Zeitlin 1977 and 1995; Hall 1989; Winkler 1985/1990; Case 1990; Wohl 1998; Roselli 2002. For a good discussion of Althusser's "Ideological State Apparatus" (ISA) in relation to Greek tragedy, see Wohl 1998: xxx-xxxiii, and also Wohl 2002: 23–25, 220–23.
[4] See esp. Winkler and Zeitlin 1990; also Hall 1989; Rose 1992; Seaford 1994; Griffith 1995, 1998; Goldhill and Osborne 1999; Bassi 1998; and for broader (non-Greek) perspectives, see e.g. Montrose

Until very recently, satyr plays received little or no mention in these discussions, as experts on tragedy and comedy rarely paused for more than a few moments to discuss this third genre, unless of course they |[162] were concerned with the *origins* of tragedy. Whole books and long articles continued to be published on Aischylos or Sophokles that never mentioned the fact that a quarter of their plays were satyr dramas; and even Euripidean scholars have tended in their discussion of *Cyclops* to concentrate on analysis of the play's parody and inversion of tragic or epic norms, and to engage repeatedly with the question of the quasi/pseudo-satyric nature of *Alkestis*, or *Orestes*, or other Euripidean tragedies.[5] As a result, satyr plays were left largely to satyr-specialists. More recently, however, significant progress has been made towards the integration of the study of satyr drama (and also of dithyramb) into what might be called the mainstream of Athenian cultural studies; and the playing of the satyric "Other" is coming to be more widely recognized as a central—not merely marginal or vestigial—feature of Athenian theatrical performance.[6]

The competition in *tragôidia* at the City Dionysia gave the opportunity to selected poets and wealthy *chorêgoi* to pick from a wide variety of topics and themes, and to costume their tragic chorus and actors in many different masks and clothes in their exploration of the classic stories of their distant past. This past was imagined and represented as an age of kings, queens, heroes, and divine apparitions, far removed from the here-and-now of Athenian civic life, and yet recognizable in many respects as a commentary or distorting mirror of contemporary real-life problems and issues.[7] The choruses of these tragedies, as many critics have noted, rarely comprise young citizen men: instead, they are women (young or old, free or slave), old men, foreign visitors, or slaves within the community where the play is set.[8] The effect of having such marginalized groups (Bacchantes, Furies, Suppliant Women, Trojan captives) speaking and singing with the special authority exercised by a chorus in such performative contexts has been much discussed; and critics have linked this apparent paradox to the prevalence of prominent and assertive, often conspicuously victimized, female lead characters in tragedy. Indeed,

---

1980; MacAloon 1984; Appel and Schechner 1990. For a disapproving reaction to such critical tendencies in the field of Greek drama, see, e.g., Griffin 1998.

[5] See, e.g., the studies of Ambrose 2005 and Slater 2005.

[6] For reviews of recent scholarship on satyr plays, see esp. Gibert 2002 and Griffith 2002 [= Chapter 1]. Much credit for the revival of interest is due to Seidensticker 1979 and 1989; Sutton 1980; Seaford 1984; Konstan 1990; Lissarrague 1990a and 1990b; as well as the superb editions of the fragments of Aischylos and Sophokles by Stefan Radt. Most recently, see Hall 1998; Voelke 2001; Kaimio 2001; Sommerstein 2002 and 2003; Griffith 2002 [= Chapter 1]; and the invaluable volume of Krumeich, Pechstein, and Seidensticker 1999 (KPS).

[7] See, e.g., Vernant 1981: 23–48; Goldhill 1990; Griffith 1995, Easterling 1997b.

[8] Gould 1996; Mastronarde 1998 and 1999; Hall 1998; and Foley 2003 for a thorough survey of the evidence. If the chorus *are* young men, they are generally soldiers abroad on campaign (Sophokles *Ajax*, *Philoktetes*). On the age of the male chorus of Euripides *Alkestis*, see Ambrose 2005.

this insistent "Playing of the Other" seems to have been a highly attractive aspect of the Dionysian occasion, and one that the citizen performers had come to expect and even relish.[9]

The Comedy competition was conducted on a different day, and by a different set of *chorêgoi*, poets, actors and choreuts from the tragedies and satyr plays.[10] The costumes, language, rhythms, plots, and behaviors of Comedy belonged to a separate repertoire—one that often parodied and played off and against tragedy, but never for a moment could be mistaken for it, and was not supposed to share performers with it.[11] Thus Aristotle, for example, even if he may be a little obsessive in his binary oppositions and dichotomous categories, is surely speaking for |[163] all Athenians when he defines Tragedy as depicting human activity that is *spoudaios* ("noble, worth taking seriously"), whereas Comedy is *phaulos* ("lowly, good-for-nothing"), and when he proceeds to derive each of them from completely different origins and assign them opposite social and ethical functions (*Poetics*, chapters 4 and 6).

Many critics write as if satyr plays occupied a middle ground between tragedy and comedy,[12] and most have tended in fact—like most modern performers of satyr plays—to lean heavily in the direction of comedy, often succumbing to the temptation to treat satyr plays simply as burlesque and parody, and as providing an essentially comic inversion and contrast to the serious and often disturbing tragic prequels.[13] But in fact both Athenian institutional practice and the compositional technique of the playwrights placed satyr plays squarely alongside the tragedies. The plots were taken from the same repertoire; the main actors wore exactly the same kinds of costumes and masks as they did in the tragedies (see the Pronomos Vase [Fig. 5a, b, c]); the language, meters, and performance style of the actors' dialogue scenes were for the most part closely similar to those of tragedy.[14] The one major difference was the chorus—which was the core of the civic

---

[9] Zeitlin 1995; Hall 1989; Segal 1997; Griffith 2001; Roselli 2002. For some broader (non-Greek) dimensions of such cross-dressing performances, see Garber 1993; Orgel 1999.

[10] Sokrates seizes on this point in Plato's *Symposium*, and at the end of the dialogue is found questioning Agathon and Aristophanes as to why the same poets should not be experts in both genres (*Symp.* 223b-d).

[11] See, e.g., Taplin 1986, for the self-conscious oppositions presented by comedy and tragedy; further Willi 2002; Sommerstein 2003.

[12] For good formulations of the "in-between" status of satyr drama, see, e.g., KPS 32–4; Lissarrague 1990a; Voelke 2001.

[13] This was notably true of the performance of *Cyclops* which the participants in our conference attended at Xavier University in April 2003 (directed by Peter Karapetkov, and designed by Boryana Kostadinova). It is also somewhat true of *The Trackers*, Tony Harrison's brilliant adaptation (1990) of Sophokles' *Ichneutai*. I much regret that I have never seen a performance of this play; illustrations and discussion of its first production from Delphi in 1988 are available in McDonald 1992: 97–113.

[14] KPS, 14–17, 32; Seaford 1984: 44–8, López-Eire 2003, Redondo 2003; further Griffith 2006 [= Chapter 3]. The character Papposilenos is something of an exception to this rule, as his language tends

occasion, it might be said, but at the same time the single element that was always the most open to performative extremes. The function of the satyr-chorus thus presents a curious challenge, as critics seek to explain this obligatory and peculiar sequel to the tragic trilogy. This chapter will propose a fresh way of explaining the significance and appeal of this particular mode of "Playing the Other," by paying close attention to the considerable overlap between tragedy and satyr play, and noting their sharp formal and stylistic separation from Comedy.[15] At the same time, it examines the peculiar dynamics of the relationship between satyr-chorus and main characters in the light of the prevailing social structures of fifth-century Athens.

The first part (largely positivistic) of the chapter surveys the diction and metrics of the surviving satyric texts, by way of confirming the stylistic affinities between tragedy and satyr drama. Objective, quantitative, and fairly reliable criteria exist (as ancient critics recognized) that can be used to measure the level of "elevation" of Greek poetical expression, and thereby to place any piece of verse, at least from the fifth century, quite precisely on a fixed stylistic scale. This scale ranges from the highest flights of Aischylean or Pindaric lyric at one end, to the crudest or most extravagant vulgarities of Hipponaktean iambos or Aristophanic burlesque and paratragedy at the other.[16] Classical Greek ears, and Athenian ears in particular, were expertly attuned to the fine calibrations of word-choice, dialogue rhythms, and colometric patterning (and presumably of musical mode too, though we are less capable of tracking this), just as their eyes were well-educated in the |[164] different registers of costuming, choreography, and gestural semiotics.[17] The existence of these relatively stable aesthetic criteria allows fairly confident conclusions to be drawn about the associations and flavor of satyric diction and metrics, as these are preserved in the surviving texts, as well as about the costume and chore-

to strike a lower note than that of the other characters, but even so his language is still closer to tragedy than to comedy.

[15] This is not to ignore the presence of satyrs in some Old Comedies (so Storey 2005). Satyrs can indeed show up almost anywhere in Athenian representational arts: see Lissarrague 1990a [and 2013]; Stewart 1997; and Carpenter 2005. But satyr *plays* as a dramatic genre adhere closely to tragic, not comic, norms in almost all respects. [But see further Shaw 2014.]

[16] Aristotle in the *Rhetoric* and *Poetics*, ps.-Longinus, and Horace in the *Ars Poetica*, for example, all write confidently about the various techniques for calibrating degrees of "ornamentation" (*kosmos*), "elevation" (*hupsos*), and "grandeur" (*megaloprepeia*), in relation to the style "proper and appropriate" to each genre (*prepon, decorum*).

[17] Thus Aristophanes' chorus (*Frogs* 1114) compliments the audience for their peculiar expertise and discrimination (*manthanei ta dexia*); and Thucydides' Perikles (2.40) likewise remarks that the Athenians were distinguished for their exquisite taste (*philokaloumen*); see Wohl 2002, and below, pp. 88–90. Greek notions of correctness of linguistic usage (*orthotês*), "high" vs. "low" style, proper delivery (*hupokrisis*), and deportment (*hexis, schêmata, eukosmia*), were already well developed by the time of Protagoras and Aristophanes, and were discussed in ever more minute detail by rhetoricians, educationalists, and moralists throughout antiquity: in addition to the standard rhetorical handbooks, see e.g. Wehrli 1946; Bremmer 1991; Gleason 1995; Zanker 1995; Bassi 1998; Worman 2002.

ography, as these are recorded in the visual arts, in relation both to comedy and to tragedy, and also in relation to the larger conventions of public and semi-public citizen self-presentation.

The second part of the chapter changes gears from such positivistic stylometrics, to a more speculative inquiry into the psychic life of the Athenian audience of these plays. The annual self-presentation of satyrically cross-dressed choruses of citizens, interacting with the more sober and "serious" (*spoudaios*) lead-characters in these satyr dramas, played into Athenians' fantasies of infantile, adolescent, and adult male desire, and also, I suggest, into anxieties and prejudices about slaves. The aim here is to trace in particular how these performances contributed to the on-going cultural projects of individual masculine subject-formation[18] and collective sense of group-membership and class relations—i.e., to the construction and maintenance of what we might call citizen identity.

The third and final part of the chapter looks in detail at one particular scene from Aischylos' *Diktyoulkoi* (*The Net-Fishers*: F 46-7), which I take to be exemplary of the lexical, metrical, and performative characteristics that I have outlined. This scene may serve as a test-case of my larger claims about the presentation of a fantasized Athenian male self through the mechanisms of satyric performance. Parts 1 and 3 focus rather narrowly on fifth-century Athens and on the particular characteristics of the surviving satyric texts. Part 2 steps back a little from the dramatic texts themselves to consider some of the broader aspects of Athenian self-presentation through theatrical performance, and proposes some modern analogies that may help to illuminate the peculiar institution of the Athenian satyr play.

The classic study of "self-presentation" by Ervin Goffman, *The Presentation of Self in Everyday Life* (1959), was a pioneering document of the discipline that subsequently emerged and became institutionalized as "Performance Studies."[19] Goffman employs the term "self-presentation" with reference to the speech-patterns and types of behavior ("routines") employed for particular occasions and interactions in everyday life. These he compared to the performance of a dramatic role, designed to be played within a pre-constructed and mutually recognized system of conventions—that is, everyday life regarded as if it were a dramatic script, along with requisite props, sets, and costumes. A person's whole character and personality may thus be seen as a composite of these social roles and performanc-

---

[18] For explanation and justification of this notion of an adult male "subject," who has to be formed (or "constructed") through a process of physical maturation, psychological indoctrination, and habituation, so as to conform to a set of pre-existing social and linguistic norms, see especially Goffman 1959; Althusser 1972; Silverman 1983; Bourdieu 1990.

[19] For a useful survey of the field of performance studies, see, e.g., Appel and Schechner 1990; Carlson 1996; and further Bourdieu 1990 (including his important account of *habitus*); De Lauretis 1987; Butler 1990 and 1993; Parker and Sedgwick 1995. For discussion focused on ancient Greek and Roman performance, see esp. Gleason 1995; Stehle 1997; Bassi 1998; Griffith 2001; Wohl 2002; Worman 2002.

es, and the theater is made a metaphor for real life (as |[165] Goffman explicitly states). More recent work within Performance Studies has reversed this polarity, so that theatrical self-presentation itself, taken in its broadest sense of "playing," including all kinds of ceremonies, rituals, and performances, is analysed for the contribution that it makes to the formation both of the actors' and of the audience's "identity" as a group or as a collection of individuals.[20] This chapter thus combines both modes of analysis in attempting to assess the dynamics and social function of fifth-century Athenian satyr drama.

It must be conceded from the start that any attempt to describe, even in general terms, the characteristics and effects of satyr drama might seem over-optimistic, given the desperately deficient nature of the surviving evidence. In the case of Aischylos, we have only a tenth of his tragedies, while the recent collection in KPS cites fragments from fifteen fairly securely attested Aischylean satyr plays, plus a few more scraps from a further six that are more dubious. In most cases these fragments amount to no more than a single word or phrase, or a couple of trimeters quoted from the play. But five satyr plays do survive in somewhat more substantial bits: *Diktyoulkoi* (*The Netfishers*), the doubly-titled *Theoroi* or *Isthmiastai* (*The Spectators*, or *Visitors to the Isthmus*), *Prometheus Pyrkaeus* (*Prometheus the Firekindler*), *Sisyphos* (whether *Sisyphos the Runaway*, or *Sisyphos Rolling the Rock*), and the so-called *Dikê*-play. The papyri that preserve bits of *Diktyoulkoi*, *Isthmiastai*, and *Prometheus Pyrkaeus* contain both lyrics and dialogue trimeters and are thus especially valuable for what they tell us about the structure, metrics, and style of Aischylean satyr plays.[21] The grand total of Aischylean satyric production amounts, in fact, to roughly 320 verses, or parts of verses (340 if we count the fragments of "uncertain" provenance). Over half of these verses are incomplete. For Sophokles the situation is both better and worse. It is better, because we do possess a large continuous chunk of one satyr play, *Ichneutai* (*The Trackers*), amounting to about 350 lines complete enough to talk about with some confidence. It is worse, because even though we must assume that some 30 or so of the 120 or so known Sophoklean play titles must have been satyr plays, we can in fact identify only about a dozen of them for sure, and we possess very few fragments from most of these.[22] And the very fact that it is so difficult to distinguish between satyr play and tragedy on the basis of a few lines of dialogue or iambic rhêsis randomly quoted out of context is itself a proof that the two genres are indeed closely related in language and style. As for Euripides, although we possess the entire *Cyclops*, we are far from sure that this is a representative example of the genre as

---

[20] See e.g. Orgel 1975; Schechner 1977, 1985; Turner 1982; Geertz 1990; Greenblatt 1980; Montrose 1980; Garber 1993; also Goldhill's introduction to Goldhill and Osborne 1999.

[21] It is interesting to note that Aischylean satyr plays were still being read and copied in Greek Egypt during the 1st and 2nd century CE.

[22] See Lloyd-Jones 1996: 3–9; KPS 224–6; Sommerstein 2003; Griffith 2006 [= Chapter 3].

it had flourished during the first half of the century.²³ |[166]

PART 1

Vocabulary, Stylometrics, Colometry

The main characters of satyr play, who are usually gods or goddesses, kings or queens, heroes or their relatives, express themselves for the most part in iambic trimeter dialogue that is very similar in style to that of tragedy. Although satyric expression rarely, perhaps never, aspires to the highest flights of Aischylean "sublimity,"²⁴ the more dignified satyric characters (e.g. Danaë or Kyllene, Poseidon or Apollo, or Odysseus)²⁵ generally pitch their discourse on a relatively high plane of tragic elevation. A quick glance through the longer passages of continuous dialogue or rhesis among the surviving fragments, as well as Euripides' *Cyclops*, will confirm this, e.g., Aischylos F 47a 770–85 (*Diktyoulkoi*), F 78c (*Isthmiastai*), F 281a (*Dikê*-play), Sophokles F 314 218–89 (*Ichneutai*), Kritias (?) F 19: there is very little in the diction of any of these to mark their non-tragic provenance. Even the chorus in dialogue with other characters for much of the time maintain a fairly standard, non-colloquial (and non-parodic) level of poetic discourse, and employ rhythms, vocabulary, and rhetorical figures comparable to those of tragedy.

One should not exaggerate the closeness and continuities between the diction of satyr play and that of tragedy. Obviously satyr plays contain a fair sprinkling of ridiculous and indecent (or at least undignified) language and activity—mostly from the satyrs themselves and especially their gross Daddy-figure, Papposilenos, whose language, behavior, and costume seem generally to be coarser and lower than anyone else's, including those of the Chorus.²⁶ There is thus frequent reference to animals, foods, furniture (including chamber-pots), buttocks, and penises; colloquialisms and diminutives are common; and exclamations as well (such as the peculiar noises of Sophokles *Ichneutai* 176 and *Cyclops* 49–52).²⁷ Nonetheless,

---

²³See Pechstein 1998; and Gibert 2002 (with further references). There are various more or less reliable testimonia informing us that Euripides experimented with substitutions for traditional satyr plays on different occasions during his career, *Alkestis* being the most often remarked.

²⁴Part of what follows here was originally presented at an APA panel (Philadelphia, January 2002), on "Magniloquent Aiskhylos: Sublimity or Bombast...?," organized by Stephen Daitz and Elizabeth Scharffenberg. My thanks to the organizers for their invitation, and to the co-panelists and members of the audience for their comments on that occasion. For more extended discussion of satyric diction (esp. in Sophokles), see López-Eire 2003, Redondo 2003, Griffith 2006 [= Chapter 3].

²⁵It will be clear that in this, as in other respects, I do not agree with Hanna Roisman's heavily ironic interpretation of Euripides *Cyclops* in Harrison 2005.

²⁶See Seaford 1984: 46; and Griffith 2002: 220–1 [= Chapter 1]; and note the costume of Papposilenos on the Pronomos Vase ([Fig. 5a, 5b, 5c]).

²⁷See too *Ichneutai* 100, 131, 443. For detailed discussion of the overlaps and differences between tragic, satyric, and comic diction and syntax, see Sommerstein 2002; Willi 2002; López-Eire 2003;

the sprinkling of such "lower" stylistic elements is far from pervasive; in most places the register of satyric diction is almost indistinguishable from that of tragedy. Indeed, with regard to one particularly distinctive feature of "elevated" style, the high rate of compound adjectives and abstract nouns, the satyr plays show virtually no deviation from the practice of tragedy: in this respect the divergence from Aristophanic comedy is very sharply marked.[28]

The surviving texts, then, seem to occupy a lexical range that overlaps on one end with conventional "tragic" style but extends at the other into a somewhat more intimate and colloquial, but still "middle-brow," poetic style, especially suitable, it seems, for romantic, pastoral, childish, and domestic scenes.[29] Although erotic and sexually explicit language and situations are quite common, sometimes of an outrightly aggressive nature, nothing is violently disruptive, nothing as exaggeratedly low, ugly, |[167] or outspoken as is found routinely in Old Comedy, or in iambos and mime.[30] Nor are bombast or absurd coinages present of the paratragic kind so beloved by Aristophanes; and for all their tendency (sometimes exaggerated by modern critics) to invert the plots or specific episodes from tragedies,[31] satyr plays seem rarely to lower themselves to outright parody of the tragic genre. Indeed, those features that do set satyr plays apart from tragedy may recall, not so much Old Comedy or its antecedent invective genres, but such semi-serious narratives as the Homeric *Hymn to Hermes*, with its farts, odd animals, sneaky tricks, deceptions, and frequent references to food and laughter, or, from later periods, Theokritos' bucolic *Idylls*, with Polyphemos, and other love-sick and/or uncouth, but basically good-hearted and even intermittently inspired and inspiring, herdsmen, or Longos' *Daphnis and Chloe*, with its playful but elegant romance of hyper-rustic innocents.[32]

These lexical distinctions are confirmed by the metrical evidence of the dialogue. The iambic trimeter is the prevailing meter. The surviving Aischylean satyric fragments contain one passage of trochaic tetrameters (*Isthmiastai* F 78a 18–22), a meter associated with early "unserious" dramatic performance by Aris-

---

Redondo 2003; Slenders 2005; also Bers 1982: 202. López-Eire 2003 begins by asserting (386): "The language of satyr drama occupies an intermediate position between the language of tragedy and that of comedy," but soon goes on to state (387), more accurately, "The language of satyr drama is much closer to the language of tragedy than to that of comedy." Sommerstein 2002 points out that tragedy itself contains more comic diction than is usually recognized, especially in the mouths of lower or more villainous characters.

[28] See the detailed discussion in Griffith 2006 [= Chapter 3].

[29] Ibid., with particular focus on romantic themes in Sophokles' satyr plays; [and see too Chapter 5 below].

[30] On the question of the tone of the sexual language and situations found in satyr plays, see Hall 1998; Voelke 2001: 211–59; López-Eire 2003: 397–406.

[31] See, e.g., Sutton 1980 *passim*; Marshall 2005.

[32] For discussion of the pastoral settings and romance features of satyr play, see KPS, Griffith 2002 [= Chapter 1]: 198–9, 246–50, and 2006 [= Chapter 3].

totle, but also found in the tragedies of Aischylos and Euripides, while Sophokles' *Ichneutai* 298–329 contains iambic tetrameters, a meter not attested in tragedy or comedy. Otherwise, iambic trimeters are as standard for satyric as for tragic dialogue.[33] Within the trimeter, Porson's Bridge (that is, the requirement that a "heavy," or metrically "long," third anceps not be followed by word-break) is almost unfailingly observed in satyr plays, as it is in tragedy.[34] In the 150 or so satyric trimeters of Aischylos that can be measured for this phenomenon, there are only two major breaches of the Bridge (*Isthmiastai* F 78a 7 φωνῆς δεῖ, 78a 23 ὑμᾶς, ὠγαθοί); Sophokles *Ichneutai* yields only four cases (114, 120, 341, 353); and in Euripides *Cyclops*, there are likewise just four instances (210, 304, 681, 682).[35] By contrast, the trimeters and tetrameters of Aristophanes constantly disregard Porson's and Hermann's Bridges.[36] Likewise, Old Comedy allows metrical resolutions of all kinds freely within the iambic trimeter, whereas Aischylean and Sophoklean satyr plays are almost as sparing and strict with resolution as their tragedies. The one significant exception to satyr play's conformity to tragic practice is the occasional occurrence of an "irrational" first anceps (the so-called "1st foot anapaest"); but even this is admitted only sparingly, except in Euripides: just once each in Aischylos (*Dikê*-drama F 281a 9) and Sophokles (*Ichneutai* F 314 230); but 30 times in Euripides *Cyclops*.[37] The recitative anapaests of satyr play are likewise metrically indistinguishable from those of tragedy, with anapaestic dimeters occurring in steady synapheia, marked off by the |[168] usual clausular paroemiacs. Comic-style catalectic anapaestic tetrameters do not occur.[38]

Both the lexical expressions and the rhythms of satyric dialogue thus operate for the most part within, or close to, the same registers as tragedy, and are sharply differentiated from Comedy. Aristophanic dialogue and recitative verse are distinctive and instantly recognizable from their *sound* as non-tragic, even counter-tragic, even apart from their *sense* (obscenity and scatology, neologisms, topical references, paratragic spoofs). Satyr drama, by contrast, belongs squarely in the aural realm of tragedy.

---

[33] See further KPS 16–17, Seaford 1984: 45–6.

[34] On the function of these bridges, see W. S. Allen *Ictus and Accent* (Cambridge 1980).

[35] West 1982: 88 n. 40, cites only one of the Aischylean occurrences (F 78a 7), and from Sophoklean satyr plays he cites only *Ichneutai* 353 and possibly *Ichneutai* 114. On Euripides' practice, see Seaford 1984: 45.

[36] According to Seaford 1984: 45 n. 139, Aristophanes infringes Porson's Bridge roughly once per 5 trimeters.

[37] In addition, we find 17 times in Euripides' *Cyclops* (discounting proper names) a resolved breve or anceps outside the first two syllables ("first foot") of the trimeter: Seaford 1984: 45 n. 137. Such a rate of so-called "comic anapaests," while it is at variance with the tragic practice of Aischylos, Sophokles, and Euripides, is lower than what we find in Aristophanes; and in general the rate of resolutions in *Cyclops* is comparable to Euripides' later tragic style, in which resolutions of almost all kinds become increasingly frequent.

[38] See Dale 1968; West 1982; cf. Voelke 2001: 159–67.

With regard to song in satyr plays, comparison between Comedy and Tragedy is less revealing, for the lyric meters of Old Comedy overlap in colometry and technique with those of tragedy to a much greater degree than the dialogue. For the *range* of lyric moods and styles that find their way into the plays of Aristophanes, Kratinos, Eupolis, and the rest is broad enough to include a number of relatively "straight" songs of intermediate poetic elevation, whose metrical characteristics are broadly shared with some of the simpler songs of tragedy (especially Aischylos), as well as those of such lyric monodists as Anakreon, Alkman, and the Attic singers of skolia.[39] These songs often maintain a smooth and consistent poetical level that contrasts with the bawdy irregularities of the spoken and chanted passages for which Old Comedy is most renowned. They contrast too with several other sung passages (anapaestic tetrameters, epirrhematic syzygies, among others) that likewise tend to be much more disruptive and "low" than the strophic norms of tragedy. Even though Comedy never ventures as tragedy does into the more ambitious complexities of dactylo-epitrite, ionics, or enoplian-based aeolics, and comic stanzas generally remain relatively short and simple in their overall structure, there are several odes in Aristophanes that share a common colometric and structural technique with the "middling" levels of tragic lyric.[40]

The most distinctive characteristics of the extant lyrics of satyr drama are (i) the relative scarcity of strophic pairing, (ii) their tendency to be highly mimetic and action-oriented, and (iii) their metrical uniformity and consistency.[41] J. Rode identifies twelve passages of astrophic choral lyric in the surviving satyr-texts, versus only three of strophic choral lyric.[42] The astrophic passages are almost all highly mimetic, with the satyrs running, hunting, herding, questioning, and experimenting in various ways, rather than singing contemplative or speculative songs as is usual in tragedy.[43] Such constant intrusion of the chorus's musical and choreographic energies into the stage action is entirely characteristic of this incorrigibly childish and hyperactive group. It is notable, too, that in tragedies it is precisely at moments of extreme excitement (fear, searching, grief) that choruses

---

[39] On Aristophanic lyrics, see esp. Zimmermann 1984; Mathews 1997; L. P. E. Parker 1997; Bierl 2001.

[40] Thus it made good sense for A. M. Dale to write a single book, *The Lyric Metres of Greek Drama* (1968); and West 1982 likewise has a single chapter (pp. 77–137) on all of "Drama," both tragic and comic. On Aristophanes' rare forays into dactylo-epitrite, see Parker 1997: 89–90; on enoplians, Parker 1997: 77–8. As for ionics, Parker 1997: 61–4, remarks that they are "not a standard comic metre."

[41] See Rode 1971: 85–95; KPS 17; Voelke 2001: 159–79.

[42] The astrophic passages assembled by Rode 1971 are Pratinas F 3; Aischylos F 78a (*Isthmiastai*) 5–17, Sophokles F 314 (*Ichneutai*) 58–72, 94–117, 170–95, 207–210; F 269a 51–6, F 269c 25–39 (*Inachos*); Euripides *Cyclops* 49–54, 356–74, 608–623, 656–62. The strophic passages are Aischylos F 204b (*Prometheus Pyrkaeus*), Euripides *Cyclops* 41–81, 495–518. See further Rode 1971: 85–7, Seaford 1984: 46–7.

[43] For tragedy, Rode (1971) lists only 20 passages of astrophic choral lyric from the 31 surviving plays, in comparison to the 3–5 strophic songs contained within each play.

are |[169] liable to break down into astrophic and mimetic reactions.[44] Indeed, the lyrics of Aischylos *Eumenides* or Sophokles *Philoktetes*, where the chorus is recurrently engaged in physical encounters, confrontations, and collaborations with one or more of the actors, and cannot disengage itself enough to sing an entirely self-contained, multi-stanza aria on its own, contain many features in common with satyr drama. Such engagement of the chorus with the stage action, in short, vigorous, and metrically simple lyrics, may also perhaps be a reflection of contemporary forms of work-song and other rustic or lower-class refrains.[45]

In Euripides *Cyclops*, perhaps the most distinctive ode is the one in which the chorus undertake to "educate" the uncouth Polyphemos in proper sympotic behavior (anapaests 489–93) and proceed to launch into elegant anacreontics (495–502). The diction, topoi, and metrical technique of this passage are consonant with those of other extant sympotic songs from non-dramatic contexts, such as Anakreon *PMG* 356, 395, and 396; there is nothing intrinsically parodic about this stanza, however, which is a relatively straight komastic song.[46] The incongruity comes, not from the diction or rhythm of this passage in itself, but from Polyphemos' misguided rejection of the congenial ethos that is being espoused, and from his own subsequent perversion of sympotic conventions. The satyrs themselves are singing quite properly and engagingly—this is something (for once) that they know something about, even if they are a few years out of practice.[47]

As for the choice of lyric meters, the practice of the three major tragedians in their satyr plays may not have been uniform. In Aischylos, to judge from the meagre remains, the colometry of satyr play is found to occupy precisely that middle ground that is shared by tragedy and comedy. The lyric meters encountered there are primarily the cretic or iambo-cretic (as at *Isthmiastai* F 78a 14–17, F 78c 43–8; and also the ephymnic refrain at *Prometheus Pyrkaeus* F 204b 6–8 = 15–17); glyconic-aeolic (the strophic pair at *Diktyoulkoi* 802–11 = 812–20); and dochmiacs (the strophic pair at *Prometheus Pyrkaeus* F 204b 1–5 = 9–14). All three of these metrical types are common both to tragedy and to comedy, and they are all also found in the satyr plays of Sophokles and Euripides. One late source mentions that the combination of glyconic and pherecretean, as found at Aischylos *Diktyoulkoi* F 47a 805 ff., was especially favored by early satyr-dramatists.[48] The surviving re-

---

[44] For example, Aischylos *Seven against Thebes* 78–149, *Suppliant Women* 825–35, *Eumenides* 254–75, Sophokles *Ajax* 866–78; see too the monodies of Euripides *Ion* and *Hypsipyle*.

[45] Voelke 2001: 167–82; Rossi 1974; Griffith 2002: 222–4 [= Chapter 1]; see too Wilamowitz 1921: 330–3. The low-class and over-excitable language and actions of the Furies in Aischylos *Eumenides* are discussed in Griffith 1995: 101 n. 126 and Sommerstein 2002, who describes these as comic elements.

[46] Rossi 1971 sees parody; but see Seaford 1984 on vv. 483–518, 495–502; also Voelke 2001: 91–7, 177, 182.

[47] See further Rossi 1971; Hamilton 1979; Seaford 1984 ad loc.; Slenders 2005.

[48] West 1982: 96–7, quoting Aphthonius *GL* 6.151.24ff.: "*apud Graecos comoediarum veterum scriptores plurimum est* [sc. the combination *glyconic + pherecretean*], *et magis apud eos qui satyrica scripserunt; unde a nonnullis 'satyricum' prius vocabatur, verum postea abiit in consuetudinem ut priapeum*

mains of Aischylean satyr drama do not present any examples of the "lower" metrical types commonly found in Old Comedy, such as the anapaestic tetrameter, or the regular Eupolidean or Kratinan dimeters. Strings of resolved cretics (paeonics), another "low" type, are likewise not found in Aischylos, but they are found in Sophokles *Ichneutai* 176–202 and |[170] in Euripides *Cyclops*, along with highly resolved dochmiacs.[49] Whether their absence from Aischylos' surviving fragments is a sign that his lyrics were closer to tragedy than those of his successors, or is merely due to chance, it is impossible to tell. Another late source mentions that satyr-choruses used often to enter the orchestra with resolved anapaests (proceleusmatics): these too are not found in Aischylos, but occur in Sophokles' *Ichneutai* and *Inachos* (F 269c 16–20), as well as in Pratinas' famous Fragment 3.[50]

Not infrequently, the satyrs and Papposilenos (again, like Aischylos' Furies, or Sophokles' Philoktetes) resort to mere inarticulate noises: grunts, yelps, cooings, and squeaks, more appropriate to children or young animals than to adult humans. But overall, from the available metrical evidence, it may be observed that satyric lyrics for the most part fall within the rhythmical, as well as lexical, contours of tragedy, despite their often disruptive and even ludicrous content as the satyrs express their anticipation, dismay, consternation, lust, or terror at the amazing and/or heroic events unfolding around them. So, in general, while the dancers, and especially perhaps the aulos- and lyre-players, often got to show off in ways that they rarely could in tragedy,[51] the choreuts are not required to debase themselves in the gross physical or linguistic excesses expected of their comic counterparts.

As for the costumes, gestures, and choreography of satyr plays, in relation to those of tragedy and comedy, the main points may be summarized quite briefly here.[52] First, the main actors wore costumes identical to those they wore in the accompanying tragedies; and as far as we can tell, their deportment, like their language, was generally the same too. From time to time, a Polyphemos, or Herakles, or baby Hermes, may have indulged his bodily appetites in ways that clearly violated tragic norms, but this is occasionally even true of tragedy itself.[53] As for

---

appellaretur." West notes the similarities between this metrical form and the poetry of Anakreon, and even Archilochos in his less savage moments; see too Parker 1997: 22–5, 70–2.

[49] See West 1982: 123.

[50] M. Plot. Sacerdos *GL* 6.499.11–13 Keil, Aphthonius *GL* 6.99.19–20 Keil; also Aristid. Quint. 2.15, p. 82. 15–16 Winnington-Ingram; cf. West 1982: 123, Voelke 2001: 167–72.

[51] Consider, for example, the focus on the aulete Pronomos on his eponymous vase ([Fig. 5a, b, c]), and the fragment of Pratinas' choral song (F 3), if this is indeed from a satyr play. Pipe music, on- and off-stage, plays a prominent part in Sophokles *Ichneutai* and *Inachos*; and also in Eur. *Cyclops*. It appears that aulos-players in the theater were usually non-Athenians: Wilson 2003.

[52] For fuller discussion, see KPS 41–73; Voelke 2001; Griffith 2002: 217–25 [= Chapter 1]; Seidensticker 2003, with further references.

[53] E.g., the Pythian Priestess scrambling on all fours in Aischylos *Eumenides*; Polymestor likewise in Euripides *Hekabe*; the Phrygian Slave in Euripides *Orestes*; Herakles feasting and singing drunkenly in

the chorus, although the basic satyr costume, with balding, snub-nosed mask and briefs sporting horse-tail and phallus, obviously gave them a very different general appearance from that of any tragic chorus known to us, they nonetheless present a far less gross and "low" demeanor than the padded and deformed figures of Comedy, or even than most of the non-dramatic satyrs represented on vases. Indeed, the semi-nude bodies of satyric choreuts represented on Attic and South Italian Red Figure vases are generally slim and youthful (e.g., the well-known Attic hydria of an aulete and satyr-chorus carrying pieces of furniture [Boston MFA 03.788 = ARV^2 571,75 = KPS Tafel 4, Harrison 2005: Fig. 4], and an Apulian bell krater attributed to the Tarporley Painter, with its three youthful satyr-choreuts rehearsing [Fig. 7]); their masks, though grotesque, are not hideous or repulsive; and their phalluses, though erect, are small and relatively inoffensive.[54]

Some of the dance-steps of satyr drama were common to tragedy too. The most distinctive exception was the *sikinnis*, with its acrobatic, leaping movements. So far as it is possible to reconstruct this well-known dance |[171] from the available evidence,[55] it appears to have emphasized the youthful and exuberantly animalistic character of the satyr-chorus, in ways that apparently resembled the ephebic *pyrrhichê*, a naked shield-dance that formed an integral component of adolescent military training in Athens and elsewhere.[56] In *Laws* 2.653d-e, Plato mentions that "Bacchic choruses" were especially suitable for the young, because they cannot keep their bodies still. He may well have had satyric choreography in mind. Certainly, his discussion has little to do with the vulgar excesses of Old Comedy and its often brutish or violent choruses.

Tragedy itself quite frequently presents choruses composed of figures quite far removed from the normal role-models of Athenian youthful masculinity, such as decrepit old men, grief-stricken women, Asian household slaves, Phrygian Bacchantes, Egyptian refugees, even snake-haired Furies. That is to say, for all the intrinsically "normative" character of the tragic chorus *qua* chorus, it was not unusual for the choreuts to appear as a distinctly abjected contrast to the "high" heroic characters and in a form quite "Other" to the male Athenian citizen body.[57] Tragic choruses in the surviving plays are indeed predominantly female, or old, or both; many are additionally foreign or servile. Thus in respect to gender and age at least, the conspicuously male and youthful satyr-chorus consistently represented the Athenian citizen body to itself more faithfully than many of the tragic

---

Euripides *Alkestis*; cf. too Io's gadfly-induced leapings in [Aischylos?] *Prometheus Bound*.

[54] Foley 2003; Hall 1998; Griffith 2002: 218–24 [= Chapter 1].

[55] See especially Seidensticker 2003 [and 2010], with further references. For a good discussion of the problems facing modern scholars of ancient dance in general, see Naerebout 1997.

[56] See esp. Voelke 2001: 131–57, following Athenaios 14.630d and Ceccarelli 1998, with further references; also Griffith 2002: 221–4 [= Chapter 1], where the associations between satyr-choruses and young horses, heifers, and deer are discussed.

[57] See Gould 1996; Foley 2003.

choruses did.[58]

Finally, like the choruses of tragedy but unlike those of comedy, the satyrs rarely seem to come into any serious collision with the main characters of the play. This non-oppositional relationship presumably was reflected in the choreography, as it is in the innumerable visual representations of groups of satyrs cavorting around heroic characters in various contexts and activities, especially on Athenian vases. In this respect they are quite different from centaurs, for example, and other monstrous opponents of heroic characters in classical Greek verbal and visual narratives. Visual representations in vase painting or sculpture of satyrs being physically wounded or attacked by a hero, a standard role for centaurs and Amazons, seem never to occur.[59] Likewise the stage-satyrs' interactions with the other characters are predominantly collaborative. When they are not, the satyrs are either unsuccessfully amorous, or temporarily distracted by external constraints, or mildly chaotic, but never really challenging or threatening. It is as if the satyrs exist on a parallel plane of their own, intersecting with, but never seriously disrupting, the activities of the more serious and responsible human characters whose story is unfolding all around them.

Like perpetual children, or rustic simpletons, or skittish colts, the satyrs caper restlessly but harmlessly around in cheerful and blessed devotion to Dionysos (and Aphrodite), returning at the end to a separate world |[172] of their own, a world that is both timeless and apolitical, a world of perpetual childhood and release from toil and worry. Satyr-choruses are never in danger of inflicting or suffering real damage to themselves or others, and never act as nastily or aggressively as the shameless characters of Old Comedy.[60] The satyrs are indeed charmed and charming spirits (*daimones*), and lead a blessed life, of a kind unmatched by any other figures in Athenian drama. They are not presented or perceived as the audience's enemies, nor as the objects of strong disapproval or antipathy: rather, they are the audience's friends, and in certain respects the projections and embodiments of some of its most childish and simple desires.

---

[58] See Hall 1998; Foley 2003; and below, pp. 92–96, 101–103.

[59] See esp. Stewart 1997, for representations of Amazons and Centaurs as violent threats to social order, and the assimilation of Amazons to Persians in Athenian art post-490 BCE.

[60] In Aristotle's terms (*Poetics* 4.1449a19-21; cf. 4.1448b26-7, 5.1449a31-7), the satyrs are "little" (*mikroi*) and "laughable" (*geloioi*) in status, appearance, behavior, and language, but not really gross (*phauloi*), distorted (*diestrammenoi*) or ugly (*aischroi*) as the characters and choruses of Old Comedy are, with their exaggerated costumes, offensive language, and hostile attitude towards others: see further Griffith 2002: 217–24 [= Chapter 1].

PART 2
Fantasy, Identity, Self-Presentation

In the after-glow of the unexpected defeats of the invading Persians, and during the subsequent period of imperial expansion, the Athenians' pride in their achievements and growing sense of cultural uniqueness and entitlement were reflected in, and fuelled by, an increasing number of more or less nationalistic (and increasingly masculinist) cultural productions. These were visual as well as verbal, and among the most exciting, inclusive, and influential of them were the dramas that were produced annually in the Theater of Dionysos.[61] As the democracy, partly by means of the manipulation of its "coalition" (*summachia*) of more or less dependent and subordinated city-states, assembled ever richer and more elegant fruits for the gratification of its citizens, new forms of cultural expression kept evolving to justify and enhance the ideology of Athenian unity, superiority, and entitlement, in contrast to the imagined inferiority of their "barbarian"—and Greek—rivals and opponents. Indeed, it was precisely during this period that the polarities of barbarian vs. Hellene, and also of Spartan vs. Athenian, seem first to have been systematically articulated in the Attic imagination.[62] The annual Funeral Oration, innumerable public and private monuments and songs honoring the tyrannicides, visual and poetical representations of the adventures and (alleged) political career of Theseus, of Erechtheus, of the eponymous heroes, of Solon, and of the Marathonomachoi, together with the spectacular building program on the Acropolis, all contributed significantly to this escalating project of defining and reinforcing a cohesive and self-confident Athenian citizen identity.

At the same time, continuing struggles within the citizen body between rich and poor, urban and rural, oligarch and democrat, together with even more fun-

---

[61] See esp. Hall 1989; also, e.g., Stewart 1997; Bassi 1998. I employ the anachronistic term "nationalistic" for want of a better word to refer to the specifically Athenian claims to political and cultural hegemony among Greeks and non-Greeks in the fifth century BCE.

[62] See esp. Hall 1989: 1–76 (drawing on Said 1977); T. Harrison 2002, Rawson 1969. Distinctions between "barbarian" and "Greek" were most often articulated in terms of softness, luxury, effeminacy, and despotism/slavishness vs. toughness, simplicity, manliness, and equality/autonomy; conversely, Athenian cultural sophistication, outspokenness, and independent-mindedness were contrasted with Spartan crudeness, authoritarianism, and inarticulate boorishness (along with their excessively liberal attitudes, by Athenian standards, towards the power and visibility of women). Athenian taste, values, and "education" (*paideusis*) were thus conceived as occupying a position somewhere between these two extremes: so, e.g., "Perikles" at Thuc. 2.40; further Loraux 1986; Wohl 2002; and n. 75 below. In this context, we should bear in mind that the evidence for the date of the construction of the first Theater on the south side of the Acropolis, next to the sanctuary of Dionysos Eleuthereus, is quite inconclusive. Some scholars believe it did not take place until the 440s or even later. (Previously, productions of tragedy and satyr-plan may have taken place in the Agora or the Pnyx.) Thus the period of the building (or at least, the expansion and elaboration) of a bigger and better Theater for dramatic performances coincided precisely with the period of greatest Athenian pride and self-promotion.

damental and delicate issues of inclusion and exclusion vis-à-vis the citizen body, made the creation of a coherent collective identity for "the men of Athens" (*andres Athênaioi*) all the more elusive, yet all the |[173] more desirable and necessary. For there were many residents of Attica who might be included on occasion under the umbrella-term "Athenians," yet whose status was more or less sharply distinguished from that of citizen. "Bastards" (*nothoi*) had only one citizen parent (a status that in many other Greek cities would qualify for citizenship). Resident aliens (*metoikoi*) were eligible to pay taxes and fight in the army, but not to vote, hold office or plead their own legal cases. Adolescents below the age of 18 were still too young to vote and still to some degree under the control of their father or guardian, yet already conscious of their future entitlements. Above all, there were slaves and women, with whom Athenian men shared their daily living space but relatively few of their civic privileges. The Athenian imagination was thus intensely preoccupied with developing forms of cultural expression that would, if possible, simultaneously legitimize Athenian supremacy in the eyes of the rest of Greece, build a sense of solidarity among all the residents of Attica concerning their own stake and membership in this Athenian democratic project, and yet also maintain and justify existing distinctions of privilege and value within that Attic population.[63]

No form of cultural expression was as capacious, flexible, or influential to these ends as the Theater, with its mass audiences, emotive musical forms (Aristotle's *melos*, *harmonia*, and *rhythmos*), splendid costuming, spectacle, and choreography (*opseôs kosmos*), ornamental linguistic styles (*hêdusmenos logos*, *lexis*), deeply traditional and emotive stories (*mythos*), pointed intellectual and moral debates (*dianoia*), and vivid representations of high and low, admirable and disgraceful, human, superhuman, and subhuman character (*êthos*).[64] In engaging the Athenians each year with fictionalized and mystified representations of their conscious and unconscious anxieties concerning gender, ethnicity, class, and age distinctions, and at the same time presenting them with the competing attractions of traditional vs. innovative, indigenous/amateur vs. imported/professional musical idioms and techniques, these annual performances amounted to a virtual "workshop" on democratic citizen identity.[65] I would suggest that the enduring popularity of the satyr play during the period 505–ca. 420 BCE was due in large part to its distinctive and multifaceted contribution to this on-going process of creating and reinforcing Athenian identity, in all its multiple layers and guises, through the

---

[63] For analyses of these cultural processes in fifth-century Athens, see esp. Loraux 1986; Bassi 1998; Bäbler 1998; Wohl 2002; Roselli 2002 [and 2011].

[64] These terms are all employed and explained in Aristotle *Poetics* 6.1449b24-50a10.

[65] Critical discussion of gender and ethnicity in Greek tragedy has been extensive: less attention has been paid to issues of class conflict, the generation-gap, and slavery: see below, n. 78. On the social significance of the rivalries between old and new music and acting styles, see Wilson 1999; Csapo 2002, 2004.

performance of collective self-presentation and audience identification that the theater was uniquely capable of providing.[66]

Athenian tragedy, I have argued elsewhere,[67] provided its audience with split and shifting subject positions for them to occupy, as their |[174] sympathies and perspectives on the action oscillated between the high, elite heroes and the lower-status choruses and minor characters. The ensuing satyr plays presented an exaggeration of that tragic dynamic, by emphasizing the distance between the high and low characters onstage, and thus increasing the split between two processes of audience identification. At one level, there is identification with the august individuals who carry out the serious and effective action and, in the case of tragedy, frequently suffer its ghastly consequences. At the other, there is identification with a group of ineffectual, yet physically and musically hyper-active, dependents and by-standers who witness, comment on, and survive these actions, and then return to their usual hum-drum existence, immune from serious calamity, much like the theater audience itself. In the case of satyr plays, the guarantee of a happy ending, that is, its flavor of Romance, adds a distinctively different twist from most tragedies. Often indeed, a successful erotic encounter takes place among the elite characters, and more than half the satyr plays whose plots are known seem to have ended with the marriage of the hero and heroine.[68] Even those that have no marriage, like *Cyclops*, do generally affirm the return of the heroic character(s) to positions of social and political prominence and respectability, while the chorus of useless but harmless satyrs are restored to Dionysos, their beloved master and protector, and to the resumption of a life of irresponsible drinking and chasing after nymphs.

The sympathies of the theater audience are thus divided between, on the one hand, the heroes (superior moral agents, capable of decisive action, like ourselves, yet distinguished by their royal-heroic or divine birth, resplendent costumes, elevated diction, and prominent stage-presence), and on the other hand, the dependent-inferior chorus of semi-human creatures who behave like so many irresponsible children or useless slaves. Yet these two constituencies are not *op-*

---

[66] On the difficulties, but also the possibility, of talking about the unconscious of "the Athenians" in general, Wohl 2002: 27–8 has helpful observations: "If with [Judith] Butler we understand the unconscious as the remainder of ideology, then perhaps it will not seem strained to speak of the unconscious of an entire polis or people.... To speak of a civic unconscious thus does not necessarily mean reifying an abstraction or imposing a mechanical analogy between individual and collective; instead, it means taking seriously the discursive nature of the unconscious ("individual" or "collective") and trying to delineate the repressed of Athenian discourse in both its ideological specificity and its psychological complexity."

[67] Griffith 1995, 1998, and 2002 [= Chapter 1]. See too Easterling 1997b; Budelmann 2000; Roselli 2002.

[68] In general, see KPS 17–34; on Sophoklean "romance" in particular, Griffith 2006 [= Chapter 3]. In Griffith 2002: 235–7 [= Chapter 1], it is argued that Euripides' romantic tragedies may have borrowed from the miraculous and erotic themes of satyr drama. [See too Chapter 5.]

posed; rather, they *collaborate* in their different ways to provide an outcome that is mutually beneficial, and we are required as spectators to experience the action simultaneously on both levels. By means of this split dynamic, the audience is presented simultaneously with two kinds of male fantasy: one high, the other low, but both whole-heartedly endorsed by the dramatic logic of satyr drama. The parallel universes of heroic and satyric experience enable the spectators' fantasy, in psychoanalytic terms, to experience simultaneously *both* the adult attainment of the symbolic order (Logos, paternal authority, and marriage, as represented by the elevated diction and concealed phallus of the lead actor(s)), *and* the uninterrupted continuation of infantile, pre-Oedipal desires, emblematized by the small but erect phalloi of the satyrs and their restless physical movements, and confirmed by their inability ever to grow |[175] up, learn anything useful, take care of themselves, or even fully master normal (adult) patterns of speech. This ineffectuality of theirs, so far from being a source of serious criticism or disapproval, is perfectly acceptable, even expected. As virtual children, the satyrs within the plays are tolerated, even treated kindly and affectionately, by the heroes and divinities upon whom they rely. They are accountable to nobody for their behavior, unless they attempt briefly to behave in more heroic mode and to perform actions that are beyond their powers (that is, any significant action at all on stage, apart from drinking). It is this dichotomy of fantasies, and its implications for the self-presentation of young Athenian citizens, that will be our focus in the rest of this section.

Such "splitting" of audience identification has been analysed by critics of film, a medium in which camera-angles and editing techniques can be monitored quite precisely and the resulting manipulation, or construction, of the spectator's subject position can be traced in exact detail.[69] Shifts of identification and alternations between conflicting impulses within the same audience, perhaps even within the same individual spectator, may contribute powerfully to viewing pleasure, as well as multiplying the interpretive possibilities of any single film "text."[70] This process surely applies, with due modifications and reservations, to theater audiences as well.

The basic premise of such a critical model is that, for individual audience members, both movies and stage-plays, like other art-forms (and perhaps dreams, too),

---

[69] See especially Mayne 1993; Silverman 1992; Clover 1992; Williams 1995. Several of these critics employ an explicitly psychoanalytic framework, following Metz 1979; Mulvey 1975, in turn based on the work of Jacques Lacan; D. W. Winnicott (particularly Winnicott 1971); and Melanie Klein 1948, on which see also Jameson 1981; Silverman 1983 and 1992; Adelman 1992; Wright 1998.

[70] Mayne 1993; Hansen 1995; Clover 1992; Williams 1995; Mostkoff (forthcoming). Thus, e.g., Clover has shown how it is possible for the spectator both to take a sadistic pleasure in identifying with Peeping Tom or the (implicitly or explicitly male) predator as a female victim is pursued, and (simultaneously, or alternately) to share masochistically that victim's anxiety, her growing determination to fight back, and her eventual victory and self-vindication over the masculine/inhuman monster-predator. Such a dynamic of shifting subjectivities appears to allow, even require the spectator to switch imaginary genders, degrees of empowerment, and sexual orientation with remarkable speed and flexibility.

provide an outlet for their fantasies, anxieties, and wish-fulfillments, while often cloaking those fantasies in disguises and displacements that may render them almost unrecognizable, or perhaps "misrecognizable." The presentation of the narrative through the images on the screen, or the actors' bodies on-stage, draws the spectator's own fantasy into identifying with one or more of the characters, into adopting (one or more) character's subject position in relation to the action and to the other character(s), and into sharing (some of) his or her desires, anxieties, aspirations, and final disappointment or satisfaction. At the same time, for a theater audience as a group—to a greater degree, perhaps, than for the more individualized and passive film-viewers in a darkened movie-house—a stage drama, like other mass spectacles and public performances, whether religious, athletic, or political, can also operate as a powerful mechanism of collective self-presentation and self-definition of the group, by itself, to itself.[71]

The performers of satyr plays, the same citizen actors and chorus-members who performed the preceding three tragedies, were responsible for playing both the gods and heroes who dominated the main spoken dialogue and key actions of the plot, and also the satyr-chorus that sang, danced, yelled, grunted, and cavorted its way in and out of those dialogues |[176] and actions. Furthermore, despite their disreputable and abjected characteristics, the satyrs possessed a certain intrinsic authority and an inherent capacity to serve in some sense as the spectators' collective representatives, just like any other choral group performing at a major civic festival,[72] even as they engaged that audience in an appealing fantasy suggestive both of a return to childhood and of a drunken *kômos*, that is, the final stage of a symposium and/or erotic male sortie. The audience's dynamic of identification would thus draw them simultaneously in two separate directions. At the higher level, the resolute, effective activity of the serious (heroic) characters, with their splendid clothing and correct speech-patterns, is clearly recognizable as being the proper adult mode of behavior (from which perspective the satyrs are absurd, unreliable, immature—a joke and a scandal). But at another level, the spectators would be drawn "down" into the subject position of the impressionable, hyper-active, musical, and pleasure-seeking chorus, to share a more childish fantasy of repercussionless dependence, pretence, desire, and instant gratification, sharing the satyrs' cheerful devotion to the salutary divinity of the theatrical experience.

In real life, boys are supposed to grow up into men, and then take on respon-

---

[71]Key critical texts of performance/identity criticism along these lines include: Goffman 1959; Turner 1982; Schechner 1977 and 1985; Butler 1990 and 1993; Parker and Sedgwick 1995; and (for ancient Greece) Worman 2002; see too Kertzer 1988. For theater audiences in particular, see, e.g., Orgel 1975; Montrose 1980; Bennett 1998; Mostkoff (forthcoming); and for choral performances in classical Greece, see Stehle 1997; Kowalzig 2004.

[72]See Mastronarde 1999; also Calame 1999; Stehle 1997; Griffith 2002: 207–27 [= Chapter 1]; Foley 2003.

sibilities of their own.[73] For them, "play" includes an element of learning, and their irresponsibility is thus only temporary. By contrast, the satyrs are permanently childlike; and while this status reduces their potential as objects of moral approval or emulation, it may add to their mystique and attraction as objects of conscious or unconscious psychological identification. For them, and for any audience members who can identify with them, wine, sexual pursuit of any and all objects of their desire, escape from toil, and fun are always available at someone else's trouble and expense, provided one is willing to abandon all self-respect and sense of social responsibility. This is one vital component of the freedom bought by "slavery" to Dionysos.

Edith Hall has argued that, so far from presenting a negative paradigm of masculine behavior from which young Athenians were intended to learn better conduct,[74] the satyr-chorus instead reinforced and implicitly condoned adolescent male sexual aggression, drunkenness, and self-assertion through the plays' uninhibited presentation of satyric exuberance and irresponsibility.[75] Hall is surely right to emphasize the positive appeal (to male Athenian sensibilities) of these satyric representations, given the relative lack of inhibition manifested in fifth-century Athenian culture around male fantasies and displays of sexual aggression. She is right also to point out the considerable degree to which non-theatrical male adolescent behavior, especially in the symposium and *kômos* (two areas also closely identified with Dionysos) sometimes resembled that |[177] of satyrs in drama. Even so, the satyrs' ineffectual, cowardly, infantile, and self-defeating behavior is made so prominent in these plays, and is presented in such sharp contrast to the disciplined and successful action and speech of the major characters, that we should hesitate to conclude that the Athenian theater audience, however row-

---

[73] References to satyrs as "children" are common: e.g., Aischylos *Diktyoulkoi* F 47a 807; Sophokles *Ichneutai* 161, 365; Euripides *Cyclops* 587, 590. Frequently, the satyrs are instructed to "be men" (e.g., *Cyclops* 595, cf. 642). Sometimes they are called "beasts" (*thêres, knôdala*); see further Lissarrague 1990a, Griffith 2002:, 224–7 [= Chapter 1]. By contrast, "slaves" (*paides*, in another of this word's basic senses) are never expected to "grow up, mature" into free men (*eleutheroi andres*) or citizens (*politai*). This ambivalence in the signification of *pais* seems to be crucial to the appeal of stage-satyrs in the Athenian imagination; further Griffith 2002: 224–7 [= Chapter 1], and pp. 102–3 below.

[74] Such negative readings of satyrs as paradigms of anti-civic behavior ("counter-model to humanity," Lissarrague) have tended to prevail in recent scholarship; cf. KPS 34–9. These formulations often have much in common with Plato's observations about the (negative) social effects on the young of dramatic performances, and are often influenced, too, by the more recent ethical-political reading of tragic and satyric performance advanced by Jack Winkler (1990). For a survey of further opinions, see Griffith 2002 [= Chapter 1]; Gibert 2002.

[75] I regret that I was unaware of Hall's important 1998 article when I wrote my previous analysis of satyr plays, Griffith 2002 [= Chapter 1]. But whereas Hall sees a critical, "either/or" choice (*either* the audience disapproved of satyric misbehavior, *or* they were sympathetic to it), I believe we should accept "both/and," that is, a *mixture* of attraction and revulsion within the fifth-century Athenian adult male psyche at the prospect of such unbridled sexual aggression and display; cf. Stallybrass and White 1986; Lott 1993.

dily homosocial and adolescent its prevailing mentality, would have identified whole-heartedly with this choral group in all of its wilder aspirations and attempts at self-assertion. Rather, the audience's relationship to these satyrs may have been less straightforward, neither wholly negative, nor wholly positive. The satyr-chorus and heroic/divine main characters thus co-existed and interacted with one another, and with the spectators in the Theater of Dionysos, in such a way as to mimic, both visually and verbally, certain extremes of human behavior that lay both above and below normal adult limits, extremes that simultaneously provided quite different kinds of attraction for the fantasy of the spectators. Such representation of coexistent opposites may have served to define and reinforce an intermediate (if largely implicit) standard of proper civic performance and self-presentation lying between these extremes. Or perhaps the alternating occupation of opposed, but equally attractive, subject positions during the course of one and the same dramatic performance may have provided a peculiarly "theatrical" pleasure and value of its own. The precise psychological and ethical consequences of such a mixed response are difficult to determine.[76] In any case, the "splitting" of audience identification into higher and lower constituents seems incontrovertible.

In almost every arena of public expression, Athenian democratic ideology aimed at "aristocratizing" the Athenian demos. It did so by drawing as many (male) Athenians as possible, rich and poor alike, into an imagined, shared community of heroes, virtual noblemen, "lovers of beauty" and blessed beneficiaries of divine favor, and by contrasting this ideal community with a less fortunate, less masculine, less desirable alternative. This process necessarily involved some exclusions and mental erasure of differences, as all Athenians citizens, rich and poor alike, were encouraged to think of themselves as a single unified group, in distinction from foreigners (Persians, Spartans), women, and slaves—"a beautiful, harmonious whole."[77] Inevitably the fault lines and social distinctions within the

---

[76] We should bear in mind that the audience comprised a large and somewhat heterogeneous group of citizens and other public-minded celebrants of the festival, a group doubtless containing multiple social layers, multiple viewpoints, and multiple individual fantasies. It is unlikely that they all reacted in the same way: see Griffith 1995 [and also Roselli 2011].

[77] Loraux continues (1986: 198), "[the Epitaphios of Perikles] makes an aristocratic democracy the very symbol of unity"; cf. Bassi 1998; Wohl 2002: 30–72. Analysing this same speech of Perikles (as reported by Thucydides), Wohl points out (451–2) the ways in which the Athenian citizens are invited to imagine themselves as all included as members of the same elite, sophisticated, leisured group: "This citizen enjoys an easy, pleasurable, and aristocratic manliness. 'We love beauty with frugality and we love wisdom without softness' (*philokaloumen te gar met' euteleias kai philosophoumen aneu malakias*, Thuc. 2.40.1). The Athenians' loves are those elite staples, beauty and wisdom." And again (Wohl 2002: 37–8): "The democratic subject is... constructed within an elite framework. ... Thus the 'aristocratic principle' (as Loraux calls it) is not only the guiding principle of the democracy in this speech, but also the defining principle of the democratic subject. ...The dynamic of the oration may be cohesive in that it creates a unified community out of disparate interests. It is also coercive, though, for to refuse to identify with the speech's elitism is to fail to be Athenian. The speech forges a cathexis to an elite vision

Athenian populace revealed themselves nonetheless—by design or accident—in the structures and dynamics of the very discourses and performances that attempted to erase them. In the case of tragedy, recent studies have done much to illuminate the ways in which issues of gender and ethnicity fuelled and shaped their subject matter and dramatic treatment. There has been less attention paid to issues of class and slavery.[78] |[178]

The annual staging in the Theater of Dionysos of the puerile-servile satyrs, in their dissolute, yet amiable and harmless, encounters and collaborations with the more respectable figures of heroic myth, provided in exaggerated form precisely such a dynamic of social interaction and inclusion. For even as, according to one dramatic logic, the spectators were encouraged to approve and identify with the capable, adult figures of heroic respectability, and to reject the irresponsible and subhuman antics of the satyrs, according to another (at least equally strong) logic, they were also invited to share the chorus's irrepressible expressions of its desires, and to revel in their collective immunity to harm or shame. Disapproval and desire, self-improvement and self-indulgence, were thus deliciously mixed, in a musical and visual combination that both reinforced existing class distinctions (between heroes and satyrs, masters and slaves, adults and children), and yet embraced the collective sense of co-operation, inclusion, and sexual/sympotic well-being for all.

This is clearly exemplified by the confused and confusing dynamics of the satyrs' drinking and musical habits, perhaps their two most persistent and definitive features, apart from their sexual appetite. For while their devotion to wine, and to song and dance, is entirely characteristic of young elite male behavior, their readiness to drink their wine unmixed, even directly from the skin, along with their peculiarly boisterous choreography and simple song-rhythms,[79] seem to be more characteristic of "Thracians" or "Scythians," that is, of groups servile by nature and entirely unlike Athenian gentlemen, according to prevailing prejudices.[80] Ismaros, reputedly the first place at which Dionysos cultivated grapes and

---

of Athens.... If the citizens identify themselves as an elite, do they not also identify with the very idea of an elite, an idea that would seem to be antithetical to *dēmokratia*? This identification is the basis of the speech's hegemonic force."

[78] On issues of class and status in Greek tragedy, see esp. Rose 1992; Griffith 1995; Wilson 2000; Roselli 2002. [See further now Roselli 2011.]

[79] The rhythms, colometries (predominantly aeolic and iambic), and structures (short stanzas, simple and repetitive cola) of satyr drama often resemble those of Athenian sympotic dances and songs, though the satyrs' language tends to make freer use of interjections, exclamations, and alternations of singer, and their choreography is sometimes quite exaggerated in its postures: see pp. 84–87. Unfortunately we know relatively little about the rules of drinking and song that were or were not observed during the final stages of a *kômos*, when the drunken young men left their prescribed sympotic space and roamed the streets looking for fun, sex, or trouble.

[80] To drink wine unmixed was regarded as a "Scythian" habit. To lose self-control and start fighting when drunk was supposed to be typical of "Thracians." The Spartans were said deliberately to get their

made wine, was in Thrace; his son or grandson Maron hailed from there, and he is identified with the extraordinarily potent and sweet wine offered by Odysseus to Silenos (*Cyclops* 141). There are further Thracian and Scythian associations for the satyrs too, in the peculiar appeal of the Dionysiac, Orphic, and other exotic forms of music and dance associated in the Athenian imagination with the far north and east, where the sources of the most evocative modes of singing, piping, and spell-casting (*epôidai, goêteia*) were supposed to reside. Young male and female slaves were often employed in Athenian homes as auletes, exotic dancers, and singers at symposia, and the same place that produced the majority of Athens' slaves was thus also the home of wine, of demonic possession, and of the most emotive musical performances.

Rarely are groups of male slaves represented on the Athenian stage, or in visual art either. There were probably relatively few such groups to be seen operating together in the city center, rather than in the mines or fields, or indoors in factories. One group that may perhaps have influenced |[179] the conception of stage-satyrs is the 300 "Scythian Archers" (*toxotai*), who served as a rudimentary police force in the service of the Athenian magistrates between 490 and 390 BCE. These public slaves (*dêmosioi hypêretai*) had no autonomous jurisdiction, and no commanding officers of their own. Their job was merely to carry out the instructions of the civic authorities, stand guard over prisoners, act as ushers at crowded public events, and perform other such duties. With their distinctive "ethnic" clothing and somewhat despised responsibilities, these Scythians were a conspicuous reminder of division in a city where, for the most part, it was hard to tell citizen from slave in everyday life.[81]

An illuminating analogue to the function of these childish-slavish stage-satyrs in contributing to the formation of democratic Athenian identity is provided by American blackface minstrelsy.[82] In his already-classic study, Eric Lott analyses the mixture of desire and derision on the part of nineteenth-century White, Northern U.S. working-class performers and audiences at the spectacle of an abjected (imaginary) Black subject whom they find both enviable for his "infantile" capacity to *enjoy* (that is, to take pleasure in outrageous physical movement and sexual

---

Helots drunk as an exemplary spectacle to their elite youth (Plutarch *Lykourgos* 28.8). (I am grateful to Anton Powell for reminding me of this reference.) Hall 1998 rightly points out, however, that male Athenian audiences may well have enjoyed and sympathized with representations of adolescent male misbehavior, aggression, and sexual exploitation of others that would strike many modern audiences as demeaning and disgusting. The same is true, of course, for quite a number of modern cultural productions (*Porky, Animal House*; the Playboy channel, and the like) and of much homosocial male behavior in general.

[81] The "Old Oligarch" makes this complaint (ps.-Xenophon *Athenaiôn Politeia* 1.10). On the composition and responsibilities of the Scythian archers, see further Jacob 1928; Hunter 1994: 3–4, 145–7. Aristophanes presents a ludicrously inarticulate and horny Scythian archer at the end of *Thesmophoriazousai*, who is quickly outwitted and made drunk by the resourceful Athenians.

[82] See esp. Lott 1993; Rogin 1995; Lhamon 1998.

expression or innuendo, in misuses of language, in musical and gastronomic exuberance, in switching of gender roles), and also thoroughly contemptible in his uninhibited refusal to sublimate his desires and behave "properly" (Lott 1993: 6):

> Minstrelsy brought to public form racialized elements of thought and feeling, tone and impulse, residing at the very edge of semantic availability, which Americans only dimly realized they felt, let alone understood.... This articulation [of racial difference] took the form of a simultaneous drawing up and crossing of racial boundaries.... I depart from most other writers on minstrelsy, who have based their analyses on racial aversion, in seeing the vagaries of racial desire as fundamental to minstrel-show mimicry. It was cross-racial desire that coupled a nearly insupportable fascination and self-protective derision with respect to black people and their cultural practices, and that made blackface minstrelsy less a sign of absolute white power and control than of panic, anxiety, terror, and pleasure.

Two images (Figs. 11 and 12) reproduced here from Lott's book depicting the antics of blackface minstrels present several striking similarities to Athenian dramatic satyrs. In both cases the exaggerated childish traits and imaginary physical deformities, or inversions of "polite" posture and body-type, enhanced by musical and choreographical exuberance and lack of inhibition, mark the impersonated figures as simultaneously hyper-masculine and subhuman (Lott 1993: 116–17, 119–20, 140): |[180]

> The "black" body's dangerous power was remarked by nearly all observers of the minstrel phenomenon: it was probably mainly responsible for minstrelsy's already growing reputation for "vulgarity".... Dancers would exploit the accents of sexuality and of sexual ambiguity: the "jaybird wing"... was considered highly indecent for someone in skirts—perhaps even more so if this someone were male.... Insurrection and intermixture effectively mapped minstrelsy's transgressive range. Early minstrel songs simultaneously produced and muted the physical power of black men coded by such events. Exaggerations or distortions of dialect, for example, or gestures meant to underscore the complete nonsense of some songs might effectively dampen any too boisterous talk.... And all of the unspoken connotations of this bodily power were clearly wedded to an "inferior" people, played moreover by white men who could easily demarcate the ironic distance between themselves and their personae [see Fig. 11!]. Still, the power was made quite available, and could be provocative... More often the reminders came in sexual form. White men were routinely encouraged to indulge in fantasies about black women—which, however highlighted, and implicitly identified them with, the salacious black male characters who "authored" the fantasies, confusing the object of sexual interest... If the primary purpose of early blackface performance had been to display the "black" male body as a place where racial boundaries might be both constructed and transgressed, the shows that developed in the mid-1840s were ingenious in coming up with ways to fetishize the body in a spectacle that worked against the forward motion of the show, interrupting the flow of action with uproarious spectacles for erotic consumption.

Blackface minstrelsy contributed powerfully for over a century (from the 1820s to at least the mid-twentieth century) to the process of constructing and strengthening an American sense of national identity, based on a shared self-image of "whiteness," masculinity, and racial difference. Although blackface performance began among a specific sub-group |[181] of the working-class, mainly Irish, white population in the industrialized North East, it steadily spread to pervade all areas and levels of U.S. culture. Stage plays, vaudeville skits, musical comedies, movies, phonograph records, and radio shows continued to draw heavily on blackface routines and stereotypes right through to the 1950s, and it has persuasively been argued that no other form of cultural production contributed so heavily to the formation of "American" identity. As Michael Rogin says (1996: 29):

> Neither Africa nor southern slavery actually gave birth to American blackface...: it emerged in the early 19th century from the new cities of the market revolution. Democratized from the [European royal] court and the [Southern] |[182] plantation, minstrelsy enacted the urban white desire to acquire African American expressive power and supposed emotional freedom without actually freeing the slaves.... White predation was inverted and assigned to colored nature, most famously in the attribution to Indians of violence and lack of respect for the property of others, and in the assignment to black men of laziness and sexual desire for white women.... Hysteria over miscegenation and the mixing of bodily fluids operated alongside racial cross-dressing.... Racial aversion alone cannot account for the American history of race-based inequality. American identity was formed as well out of destructive racial desire.... Yankee, backwoodsman, and blackface minstrel, emerging simultaneously in assertions of American nationalism, were the first voices of the American vernacular to challenge aristocratic Europe. Just as each proclaimed a regional identity—Northeast, West, and South—each also came to signify the new nation as a whole. The Yankee became Uncle Sam, while the backwoodsman metamorphosed into the western hero of the frontier myth. Both these figures, however, were surpassed in national appeal by the minstrel. [After 1842] for the next half century, "our only original American institution," as one minstrel called it, remained the most popular mass spectacle in the United States.[83]

The obsessive re-performance by White males of fantasized "Black" bodies (both male and female), with their distinctively exaggerated and improper—yet exuberant and exciting—posture, choreography, vocabulary, elocution, musical rhythms, and disruptive but harmless misbehavior, served simultaneously to create a shared object of abjection and ridicule, and a mystified and harmless site of nostalgia and infantile desire ("the plantation," "Mammy," "all God's chillun"), in response to which White Americans could feel themselves united both by na-

---

[83] Rogin (1996: 29) goes on to observe that this popularity only gradually waned over the next sixty years; and he observes that "the four transformative moments in motion picture history [by which he means *Uncle Tom's Cabin* (1903), *Birth of a Nation* (1915), *The Jazz Singer* (1927) and *Gone with the Wind* (1939)] were founded on blackface."

ture (blood, skin-color, "race") and by historical and mythological tradition. Lott (1993: 53) puts it succinctly:

> The special achievement of minstrel performers was to have intuited and formalized the white male fascination with the turn to black, which Leslie Fiedler describes this way: "Born theoretically white, we are permitted to pass our childhood as imaginary Indians, our adolescence as imaginary Negroes, and only then are expected to settle down to being what we really are: white once more." These common white associations of black maleness with the onset of pubescent sexuality indicate that the assumption of dominant codes of masculinity in the United States was (and still is) partly negotiated through an imaginary black interlocutor. If this suggests that minstrelsy's popularity depended in part on the momentary return of its participants to a state of arrested adolescence—largely the condition to which dominant codes of masculinity aspire—one must also conclude that white male fantasies of black men undergird the subject positions white men grow up to occupy.[84]

For the performers themselves (Fig. 11), and for their audiences, blackface |[183] performance presented a unique mechanism for exploring fantasies—negative and positive, transgressive and normative—of gendered, sexual, and racial identity. This mechanism both confirmed pre-existing models of white (disciplined, restrained, "cultured") behavior, justified the existing (and still growing) social and economic practices of slavery, Jim Crow, and anti-miscegenation legislation, and yet at the same time provided opportunities for repressed and socially disadvantaged whites to tap into verbal, musical, and choreographical possibilities that would otherwise be "improper" and hence forbidden.[85] As Lott (148, quoting S. Zizek) succinctly observes:

> Because one is ambivalent about and represses one's own pleasure, one imagines the Other to have stolen it or taken it away, and "fantasies about the Other's special, excessive enjoyment" allow that pleasure to return. Whites get satisfaction in supposing the "racial" Other enjoys in ways unavailable to them—through exotic food, strange and noisy music, outlandish bodily exhibitions, or unremitting sexual appetite. And yet at the same time, because the Other personifies their inner divisions, hatred of their own excess of enjoyment necessitates hatred of the Other. Ascribing this excess to the "degraded" blackface Other, and indulging it—by imagining, in-

[84]On the role of nostalgia in minstrelsy (for the good old days, for the Old South, for the imagined harmony and bliss of the plantation and family, for the countryside, for white supremacy, *et alia*), see esp. Lott 1993: 190–3.

[85]In an intriguing and complicated further development, black performances of blackface in turn developed their own spins on this parodic tradition, as did subsequent Jewish immigrants in the early twentieth century (Rogin 1996). The dancer in Fig. 12 is in fact an African American, William Henry Lane, wearing blackface, who performed under the name "Juba." He was recognized as the most accomplished dancer of his time, and defeated the leading white blackface performers in competition, before they adopted the policy of refusing to compete against him (Lott 1993: 113–6). Thus blackface could operate as a floating signifier in many different ways and contexts, as it continued to do into the twentieth century.

corporating, or impersonating the Other—workingmen confronting the demand to be "respectable" might at once take their enjoyment and disavow it.

The coincidences and correspondences between nineteenth-twentieth century American Blackface and the operations of fifth-century BCE Athenian stage-satyrs are indeed striking. In particular, there is a similar emphasis in both on a hyper-active male body, on the use of extravagant and sexually suggestive choreography ("Jumping Jim Crow"), and on childish and solipsistic misuse of proper speech-conventions, all designed in both positive and negative ways to present contrasts to "normal" adult masculine behavior, as well as to stage an ongoing and irrepressible, yet absurd, incongruous, and comfortably ineffectual series of attempts by the abjected under-class at sophisticated behavior and sexual conquest and self-gratification. Fundamental differences between the dynamics of blackface performance and those of satyr drama cannot be ignored, above all, the fact that blackface, however distorted and imaginary its figures and conventions, was based on a representation of an actual exploited and severely victimized class of people, whereas horse-tailed silenes were self-evidently a fiction, a non-human and non-existent species, however much they might have in common with actual or imagined slaves, children, or sympotic adolescents in Athens. Nonetheless, it seems hard to avoid the conclusion that stage-satyrs did in significant ways serve to "represent" to the Athenians their own slaves, their own children, as well as their own less inhibited (adolescent, sympotic, Dionysian) male selves. |[184]

No subaltern's voice has survived from fifth-century Athens, no slave discourse, however muted or indirectly recorded. Slaves and women are frequently represented in Athenian art and drama, but their authors are always free men. Even the rural poor rarely are heard or seen in the surviving documents and monuments, their voices largely eclipsed by the abundance of material from the *astu*; when they are represented, it is usually with mockery or distaste.[86] Whatever "arts of resistance" may have been available to Athenian slaves (as to Athenian women), in the form of cultural productions, games, writings, or ceremonies that may have commented on and reacted to the terms of their own subjection, did not include access to any literary or performative mode that was able to transmit their own voices and opinions directly to future generations.[87] Instead, there remain a number of different media and mechanisms through which free Athenian men could represent to themselves figures who corresponded more or less exactly and

[86] See Jones 2004, esp. 157–8 (on the Rural Dionysia), 194–207 (on rustic life as represented in Old Comedy), and 161–73 (on "Realities"): esp. p. 172: "...for an Athenian citizen under the classical democracy, to be rural was to be uncivilized, to be rural was to be as good as a slave—at least in the estimation of urban writers and their urban readerships... Any country person... will have been instantly recognizable and marked as an inferior 'other.'"

[87] On these questions, see esp. Scott 1990; McCarthy 2000: 3–29, with further references. For illuminating discussion of the Aesopic tradition, as a low-class counter to elite perspectives on religion and cultural production in the sixth and fifth centuries, see Kurke 2003 [and 2010].

"realistically" to the slaves with whom they spent almost every waking hour of their lives, but whom they barely felt any need to mention in most of their literary, historical, or philosophical discourse.

In drama, where slaves naturally made constant appearances as attendants, messengers, nurses, and tutors, the opportunity presented itself for the exploration of the problems and anxieties of free-slave relations. Such exploration rarely occurs in tragedy, however, and even in Old Comedy the norms and normality of master/slave relations seem rarely to undergo continuous critique.[88] It may be that the satyrs of the theater constitute the most revealing reflection of Athenian fantasies and prejudices about the natural differences and capabilities of slaves and masters, as well as one of their most effective mechanisms for reassuring themselves of the benevolent and harmless character of slavery itself as an institution. The annual re-presentation and re-inscription of the heavily racialized and naturalized difference between humans and slave/satyrs took the form of a recurrent narrative and performative structure that cheerfully reasserted at every turn the mutual benefit and compatibility of their combined endeavors in a fantastic world of romance and happy endings. The subalterns' voices were thus heard, even their bodies were seen collaborating in vigorous group efforts, without a moment's concern that this chorus could ever get out of control or assert itself at its master's expense. Satyr-choruses often begin a play in a state of forced labor or imprisonment; but they easily escape from this state of oppression, usually through someone else's efforts. This regained freedom in no way involves any equalizing of the respective statuses of the two different types (humans, satyrs). The satyrs' true master, in the end, is Dionysos himself, whose symbolic "liberation" of his servants from toil may be felt to render unnecessary any and all actual |[185] (social, political, psychological) resistance to human authority in the world outside the theater.

It would be wrong to insist on a simple one-to-one correspondence between stage-satyrs and any particular type, gender, class, or species in the world outside the theater. They are (like) children, (like) slaves, (like) drunken adolescents, but there is no need to try to decide which of these they resemble most. Their identity can shift from play to play, or even from one scene to another of the same performance. It may even be possible to imagine them as actual spirits of the countryside, miraculous and enchanted agents of some god. Theatrical cross-dressing in general offers an especially fluid and multivalent opportunity for actors and audience to collaborate and experiment in "self"-presentation and identification with the Other. The Theater of Dionysos, as Froma Zeitlin and others have argued, was an ideal space in which the Athenians could experiment with all sorts of travesties,

---

[88] See Dover 1963; Willi 2002. [See now two excellent new studies of slaves in Old Comedy: Walin 2012, Akrigg and Tordoff 2013.]

not only of gender, but also of age, status, and class as well.[89]

The endings of satyr plays, it appears, were usually two-tiered, restoring both heroes and chorus to their respective desired and deserved social status. More often than not, this takes the form of marriage for the heroes, and renewed drinking and celebration of Dionysos for the satyrs. The "split" experience of satyric exhibitionism and heroic consummation thus reasserted, in a roundabout and complementary way, a satisfying and comprehensive Athenian male sexual fantasy without breaching the code of decorum that governed the behavior of tragic characters in the Theater. Like that other loosely related semi-public, semi-private phenomenon of male self-presentation, the *kômos*, satyr plays revelled in the affirmation of masculine sexuality, cameraderie, and more or less harmless aggression,[90] an affirmation that frequently teetered on the brink of hybris and self-indulgence, yet at the same time was felt to consolidate male bonds of comradeship and of shared and distinctive citizen entitlement.

Whatever the gender or age or social status of the choruses singing and dancing in the three tragedies that had preceded, the Athenians always knew who and what the fourth chorus of each tetralogy would consist of: young males—permanent "boys," like a group of Peter Pans or Mowglis. That is to say, despite their other animalistic and radically alien characteristics, with respect to gender they are invariably and unequivocally the *same* as the male Athenians who play them and watch them.[91] The plots of the plays too seem generally to have reimposed a more familiar male dominance after the disrupted gender relations that frequently marked the preceding tragedies. The ostentatiously male presence of the satyrs for the finale of every tetralogy provided a particularly strident reassertion of masculine entitlement and success, and of the legitimacy and efficacy |[186] (perhaps even attainability) of male desires, at several different levels of fantasy at once. At the same time, the sharp distinction between "higher" and "lower" forms of male desire that this satyric performance inscribes within the fantasy of the spectators appears to be both the source and the result of much of its social and aesthetic appeal.

---

[89] See Garber 1993; Zeitlin 1995; Roselli 2002.

[90] Hall 1998 draws attention to the repeated scenes of attempted or fantasized rape, especially group rape by the satyrs, in these plays. But both in the visual arts and in the theater, satyrs are generally represented as failing conspicuously in such endeavors, and as rarely eliciting much serious anxiety in their prospective victims; cf. Lissarrague 1990: 61–6, Griffith 2002: 216–7 [= Chapter 1], and above, p. 88.

[91] In their enjoyment of permanent leisure, too, the satyrs resemble specifically upper-class Athenian youths; and their favored pastimes include drinking and athletic endeavor. Any expectation that they might be compelled to perform serious work for others always turns out to be short-lived.

PART 3
Forms of Desire in Aischylos' Netfishers

One particular sequence of scenes from Aischylos' *Netfishers* (*Diktyoulkoi*) reveals in an illuminating way the split identification of the audience, the fluctuations between higher and lower registers of expression, and the alternative perspectives that are thereby provided on male sexuality. A reading of this sequence will thus combine the findings of the first two parts of this chapter, both underlining some of the positive stylistic points made in the first part, and also providing a good example of the simultaneous appeal of both infantile/servile ("pre-Oedipal") and ethically responsible ("post-Oedipal") desires. This simultaneous experience, as I have argued, seems to be especially characteristic of the theatrical processes of satyric self-presentation and audience identification.

The surviving fragments from *Diktyoulkoi* (*The Netfishers*), mostly recovered from three separate (and badly mutilated) papyrus finds, yield a fairly clear picture of the main outlines of the plot.[92] In an early scene, the satyrs assist in spotting an unexpected object floating in the sea, and call for assistance in netting and bringing it to shore; it is, presumably, the chest containing Danaë and Perseus. The satyrs' back-and-forth questions and answers indicate their eagerness and readiness to learn and be helpful (F 46a 1–21 = PSI 1209): ξυνῆκ[ας...; / ξυνῆκα... ("Did you notice...?"/ "Yes, I noticed...!"), δέρκου νυν ... / καὶ δὴ δέδορκα... κτλ ("Look over there...?" / "Yes, indeed, I'm looking...!"), βοὴν ἵστημι τοῖσδ' ἰύγμασιν... ("I'm summoning help with these cries..."). At some point, the local king Diktys (or his brother Polydektes, or perhaps both together) arrives to assist in the rescue.

In the second papyrus fragment (F 47a = *P.Oxy.* 2161), Danaë is confronted by Silenos and the satyr chorus, who have ideas about setting up house with her. She makes a formal, horrified appeal for help, in very much the tragic style:

> ...καὶ γενέθλιοι θεοί...
> ...τοῖσδε κνωδάλοις με δώσετε...
> ...λυμανθήσομαι...
> αἰχμάλωτος... |[187]
> ...ἀγχόνην ἄρ' ἄψομαι

> "Ancestral gods,
> <please don't> give me to these creatures...
> I shall be violated...
> ...a captive...
> So I will fasten a noose around my neck...!"

[92] I will not here be able to go into many details of the text and interpretation, which are problematic in many places. For expert discussion and further references, see especially Siegmann 1948; Werrede Haas 1961; Lloyd-Jones 1963: 531–41; Radt 1985: 161–74; Hall 1998: 27–9; KPS 17–24 (A. Wessels, R. Krumeich).

(F 47a 773–78)

But Papposilenos is not discouraged or deterred. He and the satyrs make friends with baby Perseus, and proceed to express their lewd hopes and expectations about the family life into which he and his mother are to be introduced (F 47a 786–820a). There ensues an intriguing "primal scene," as the baby boy (son of Zeus and Danaë, destined future slayer of the sea-monster and rescuer-husband of Andromeda) appears to respond enthusiastically to the physical and verbal overtures of Papposilenos and the chorus, and to the bright prospect of their prominent *phalloi*, dangled before his eyes:

> ...] γελᾶι μου προσορῶν
> ...] ὁ μικκὸς λιπαρὸν
> ...τὸ] μιλτόπρεπτον φαλακρὸν...
> ...ὡς] ποσθοφιλὴς ὁ νεοσσός...
> ὄλοιτο Δίκτυς...
> ...κτλ.

> The little guy is smiling so sweetly
> as he looks at my shining bright-red knob...
> ...What a willie-lover that little kid is...!
> ...Ruin take Diktys...!

(786–88, 795, 800)

The language is informal, friendly and encouraging, not gross or accusatory: "πόσθη is a small member or a young boy's member, and seems to have had an affectionate and somewhat respectable tone, in contrast to the vulgar and almost violent tone of πέος."[93] Inspired by this simple physical connection, the rapport between the baby boy and the rambunctious satyrs seems immediate and unalloyed.[94] As the scene proceeds (802–32), baby Perseus' intent focus on the phallus (φαλακρόν, 788; ποσθοφιλής, 795) is imagined by Papposilenos, in the course of a short and elegant strophic song (in glyconic-pherecretean cola), sprinkled with ornamental adjectives and images, as leading to a blissful future of fulfilled Oedipal desire, apparently involving collaboration and competition with, and eventual replacement of, his new "father" (F 47a 802–20):[95]

> ὦ φίντων, ἴθι δε[ῦρο   {ποππυσμός}
> θάρσει δή· τί κινύρηι; |[188]

[93]Henderson 1978: 109, with further references; see too Redondo 2003: 425–8; López-Eire 2003: 397–406; and Slenders 2005.

[94]Similarly, the baby Dionysos in Sophokles' satyr play *Dionysiskos* (F 171) shows his delight in the satyrs' prominent penis: "When I offer him something to drink [sc. wine], he immediately strokes my 'nose' (τὴν ῥῖνα) and raises (his? my?) hand to (his? my?) knob (φαλακρόν) and laughs...."

[95]On the meter, see Voelke 2001: 177–80; and above, p. 85.

δεῦρ' ἐς παῖδας ἴωμεν...
ἵξηι παιδοτρόφους ἐμάς,
ὦ φίλος, χέρας εὐμενής.
τέρψηι δ' ἴκτισι καὶ νεβροῖς
ὑστρίχων τ' ὀβρίχοισι...
κοιμήσηι δὲ τρίτος ξὺν
μητρὶ καὶ πατρὶ τῶιδε.

ὁ πάππας δὲ παρέξει
τῶι μικκῶι τὰ γελοῖα
καὶ τροφὰς ἀνόσους, ὅπως...
ἀλδὼν αὐτὸς...
χαλᾶι νεβρόφον-...ποδ...
μάρπτων θῆρας ἄνευ δ[ορὸς(?)
θῶσθαι μητρὶ παρέξεις
κηδεστῶν τρόπον οἷσιν
ἔντροφος πελατεύσεις.

Hey, little man, come over here! {*Burbling sound*}[96]
Cheer up! Why are you crying?
Let's go over here to my sons...
You'll be happy to come into my child-rearing hands, my friend!
You will sleep as the third in bed with
your mother and me, your <step>father.
And Daddy will give the little guy (*mikkos*) his fun and trouble-free
sustenance, until...
<And then>, when you grow up (?),
since your <step>father is losing (?)
the vigor of his fawn-killing foot,[97]
you'll catch beasts without (spear?)
and give them to your mother to eat for dinner,
in the manner of her husband's family,
among whom you'll be brought up as an adopted nurseling(?).

Then the rest of the satyrs chime in, with smooth, tragic-style recitative anapests (821–32):

ἀλλ' εἶα, φίλοι, στείχωμεν ὅπως
γάμον ὁρμαίνωμεν, ἐπεὶ τέλεος

---

[96] In the margin of line 802 the papyrus contains the word ποππυσμός. It is not clear whether this noise (which seems to be an extra metrum stage-direction, like e.g. the μυγμός, ὠγμός at Aischylos *Eumenides* 117–29) is made by Papposilenos, as an encouragement to the baby (as most editors have assumed), or is a raspberry-sound emitted by Perseus himself (as Philip Ambrose suggests [2005]).

[97] ποδός (816) seems to be a double-entendre: Henderson 1978: 129–30.

καιρὸς ἄναυδος τάδ' ἐπαινεῖ.
καὶ τήνδ' ἐσορῶ νύμφην ἤδη
πάνυ βουλομένην τῆς ἡμετέρας
φιλότητος ἄδην κορέσασθαι.
...νῦν δ' οὖν
ἐσορῶσ' ἥβην τὴν ἡμετέραν...
   ...γάνυται. νυμφ[...
   ...λαμπραῖς τῆς Ἀφροδίτης... |[189]

Come on, friends, let's go
and get started on the wedding,
since the perfect, proper moment approves this
without need for words!
...Now I see that the bride here is already really eager
to sate herself on our loving...
Now bright with joy, she looks at our youthful charms
...<and anticipates>
the brilliant bridal <...> of Aphrodite!

(F 47a 821–32)

The gleeful and self-satisfied anticipation of mass-marriage, or gang-rape, is at one level an expression of Athenian youthful male self-assertion at its most blatant and crude,[98] but at another it is a reminder of the inappropriateness and ineffectuality of such childish, adolescent, and servile aspirations, since the audience knows that in just a moment Danaë will be rescued and happily married to a hero, while the satyrs and their shameless father will (yet again) be disappointed, as Papposilenos' impatient curse at 800 already hints ("To hell with Diktys!" ὄλοιτο Δίκτυς).[99] The extent to which the Athenian (male) audience shared the satyrs' enthusiasm, and allowed itself to occupy their subject position at this excited lyric moment, is therefore quite difficult, if not impossible, to determine. But it seems a safe inference that, as in the case of the audience of American blackface performance, the feelings of desire, derision, and disgust were inextricably mixed.

---

[98] Hall 1998: 27–9, who points out that similar expressions are found at Euripides *Cyclops* 179–87, where the satyrs imagine the gang-rape of Helen. See too Griffith 2002: 235 [= Chapter 1] for discussion of the similar scenes (poetical and visual) involving the pursuit of Amymone by the satyrs, and her eventual submission to Poseidon.

[99] By the standards of ancient Greek or other Near Eastern societies, marriage with, or even rape and impregnation by, god or hero was generally described as a blessing for any young woman (thus a "happy" marriage). For most modern, Western (esp. female and feminist) readers and theater-goers, the notion that any new "heroic" husband will do just fine for Danaë, as for Amymone, or any number of other objects of divine and heroic desire, may be less appealing. (Ovid's *Metamorphoses* offers an especially vigorous battle-ground for such critical discussion.) My point here is simply that the notion ("How fortunate to be chosen as the 'bride' of this or that god/hero...!") is pervasive throughout ancient Greek culture, and is not confined to satyr plays.

Papposilenos' song is mere fantasizing, and the audience is fully aware that dramatic reality will turn out quite differently. Conventional reality (i.e., the world of politics, military achievement, and marriage) rarely intrudes into a satyr's fantasy. Instead, he indulges in a more primitive idea of bliss, consisting of eating, playing, hunting, and sexual pleasure. In its most infantile (Oedipal) form, such bliss may even involve fantasies of a return to the mother's body, as seems to be suggested in this scene. (This state of desire may well have been shared by baby Perseus too, of course, and it would be interesting to know how this tiny character was played on-stage.) As soon as Danaë's rescuer and future husband shows up, however, she will leave the satyrs behind and return to her proper place in the human social hierarchy, while her little son too will proceed to a more conventional (non-incestuous) heroic upbringing, as he deserves.[100] By contrast, the satyr-"boys" themselves will remain forever childish and incompetent, their Daddy too old and inebriated to achieve anything, their own careers and marital aspirations never advancing beyond the infantile and the imaginary.

The baby Perseus' delighted fixation on the visible "wee-wee" (*posthê, phalakron*) is thus merely temporary. He will soon enough grow up to |[190] bigger and better things. Likewise his "whimpering" (803 κινύρηι) and "burbling" (802 ποππυσμός) will evolve into articulate speech and rational argument. As a hero (or male elite citizen), he will make the transition beyond childish playfulness and yearning for instant gratification to a proper adult concealment of the physical penis, and will direct his desires instead towards symbolic forms of male power, military-political success, and marriage. But for the satyrs this transition will never take place: their development is permanently arrested, their *phalakron* always visible, shiny, and irresponsibly erect. Meanwhile, in the immediate present of the satyric fantasy-world, the Athenian audience, and the citizen actors and chorus who represent them, can enjoy the simultaneous experience of both subject positions and both trajectories at once. The splitting of self, and presentation of these multiple "selves" for the spectators' contemplation and delight, is the special function of the theater, and the peculiar pleasure of Dionysiac play.

---

[100] George W. M. Harrison reminds me, however, that several Greek heroes received quite unconventional upbringings far from home, e.g. with Cheiron (Achilles, Jason), or as a temple slave (Ion). Perhaps the predilection for babies that is exhibited by the surviving remains of satyr drama reflects another aspect of mixed feelings about slaves: after all, Athenian babies and small children (like the White children of the American South) spent much of their time being raised, educated, protected, entertained, and fed by male and female domestic slaves..

CHAPTER 3

Sophocles' Satyr Plays and the Language of Romance

1. INTRODUCTION

Satyr plays are usually regarded as occupying a middle ground between tragedy and comedy, and as constituting a mixture of the two that provided light relief after the emotional rigors of the preceding tragedies. But of course the term "comic" encompasses a wide variety of formal and generic categories, from the ritualistic invective, obscenity, and grotesque costumes of *iambos* and Old Comedy to the romance themes and "happy endings" of the *Odyssey,* Euripides' *Orestes,* and *Daphnis and Chloe,* and it seems to me that modern scholarly preoccupation with the broader and cruder elements of satyr drama (and with possible parodies of particular tragedies) has tended to result in a neglect of what we might term the "romantic" aspects of this dramatic genre, in terms both of its level of lexical decorum and of its representation of erotic attraction and relationships.[1]

Roughly one quarter of Sophocles' plays (some 30 or so, out of the 120 or so known titles) were presumably not tragedies but satyr dramas. Apart from the lengthy but damaged papyrus of *Ichneutae,* we have only tantalizingly small bits and pieces from any of them, and only |[52] about a dozen titles have been identified with any degree of certainty.[2] At least as many more of the plays that are

---

[1] In this paper I shall purposely use the terms "romance, romantic" to refer to two different but overlapping spheres of meaning: (i) works of fiction that include themes of travel, adventure, exotic location, and often erotic encounters too, culminating in a happy ending (see e.g. Frye 1957, esp. 51–52, 306, 319; 1976); (ii) erotic engagement, courtship, sexual passion, and falling in love (as in the contemporary English usage, "a romantic evening," "how romantic!"), as distinct from "low" and crudely anatomical or violent depictions of sexual conquest and activity on the one hand, and non-erotic representations of marriage and other intimate relations on the other. As will become clear in what follows, the overlap between (i) and (ii) seems to have been characteristic of Sophoclean satyr plays. By "happy ending," I mean primarily the (re)uniting of male and female lead characters (usually in marriage), and the prospect of familial and social harmony and prosperity to follow. Thus *hypothesis* 2 to Euripides' *Orestes* uses the term "comic" to describe the outcome of that play (κωμικωτέραν ἔχει τὴν καταστροφήν).

[2] Lloyd-Jones (1996) identifies thirteen titles; Krumeich, Pechstein, and Seidensticker (1999) (KPS)

normally listed as tragedies must therefore in fact have been satyric; and suggestions have varied wildly as to which these might be, concerning both plays whose titles alone are known and others for which some fragments survive in ancient quotation or papyrus remains.[3] This variation is in itself quite telling, for it brings home to us how little difference there often is between the dialogue of tragedy and that of satyr drama.

If an ancient commentator does not happen to specify that the Sophoclean passage he is quoting comes from a satyr play, we tend to assume it comes from a tragedy. But sometimes there is no way of telling, one way or the other. Even from the exiguous remains of the known satyr plays of Aeschylus and Sophocles, one could quote several continuous passages of iambic trimeters whose language and metrical character conform perfectly to the norms of tragedy (e.g. A. *Fr.* 46a.4–20 (*Dicty.*), *Fr.* 281a (*Dikê*-play), S. *Fr.* 314.221–232 (*Ichn.*)—to say nothing of the dialogue scenes of Euripides' *Cyclops* or the famous atheism-fragment from Euripides' or Critias' *Sisyphus* (*Fr.* 19 KPS). For while the language, meter, and stage-deportment of the satyrs themselves (and of their disreputable father, Papposilenus) are discernibly, and sometimes conspicuously, sub-tragic, the serious characters appear to conduct themselves linguistically and behaviorally for the most part very much as they do in tragedies—a distinction that is confirmed by the costuming and visual self-presentation of the actors, to judge from the Pronomos Vase (Fig. 5a, b, c) and the other surviving representations of stage performances and rehearsals.[4]

Ancient and modern critics alike, in assigning satyr drama to some kind of "middle" level between high tragedy and low comedy,[5] and |[53] thus regarding satyr drama as essentially half-comic, have tended to interpret all signs of "high" language or serious themes in satyr drama as necessarily burlesque or parody of tragedy.[6] Yet in most formal respects satyr plays belong quite squarely with trag-

---

eighteen; *alii alia*. See below, notes 22, 44.

[3] In what follows, quotations and references to Sophoclean fragments will be based primarily on Radt (1977); but reference will also be made to the editions of Lloyd-Jones (1996) and KPS.

[4] For discussion of the visual evidence, see esp. Brommer (1959); KPS 41–73 (R. Krumeich); Griffith (2002) [= Chapter 1], with further references.

[5] The account of Horace in *AP* 220–239, and other references to "tragedy at play" (e.g. Demetrius *On Style* 169), certainly encourage us to think in terms of an intermediate status for satyr drama between the two more familiar dramatic forms; and thus e.g. KPS; Voelke (2001); López-Eire (2003). But more often it is the comic connections that are emphasized in modern criticism, as e.g. Voelke (2003); see W. Allan (2003: 309): "The satyr play... has more in common with the comic tradition than with the tragic" (referring also to Zagagi 1999); contrast Seaford (1984), Griffith (2002 [= Chapter 1], 2005 [= Chapter 2]), and Demetrius *On Style* 163. A further kind of "middling" status for satyrs in the Athenian imagination has come more into vogue over the last twenty years or so, as they are viewed in structuralist terms as cultural "mediators" between god and animal (e.g. Lissarrague 1990, Voelke 2001).

[6] So esp. Sutton (1980), who emphasizes the function of the satyric genre as an on-going inversion

edy, and share very few of the characteristics of comedy. Furthermore, the notion of a "middle" style (which the ancients sometimes applied to this form, as to e.g. pastoral) is in itself quite ambiguous: for by the standards of Classical criticism, the "middle type" or "character" of style is usually thought of, not as a mixture of high and the truly low (i.e. the vulgar and colloquial), but as a sub-genre, or gradation, within the "high."[7]

The present article has two main goals: first, to establish more precisely what place on the high/low spectrum is occupied by the language of Sophocles' satyr plays, and second, to explore the language that is used in these plays to describe erotic and romantic relations (desire, passionate love, courtship, and sexual activity). In combination, these two avenues of investigation will reveal that Sophoclean satyr drama seems to have presented a high incidence of relatively "serious" and romantically-tinged erotic language and behavior; and my article will conclude with some brief suggestions as to the significance of this fact for the general character and dramatic impact of these plays.

2. ELEVATION OF LANGUAGE

A number of recent studies have focused on the non-tragic elements of satyric diction, sifting through the fragments to assess the use of diminutives, colloquialisms, vulgarisms, obscenities, and paratragic expressions in comparison with the practice of tragedy and comedy.[8] The results have been rather inconclusive (and sometimes circular): on |[54] the one hand there is no disputing the general point that satyr drama admits a higher rate of colloquial and mildly vulgar language than tragedy while eschewing the grossness and exaggerations of comedy; but on the whole no clear and consistent distinctions appear to have been established between the word-choice, syntax, and style of satyric dialogue and those of tragedy. That is to say, while it is easy enough to pick out particular passages (mainly those spoken or sung by the satyrs themselves, or by their scurrilous father/leader Papposilenus) that refer to animals, food, drinking, babies, body parts and functions (urinating, farting, masturbating), music, and dancing in ways that would not be encountered in tragedy, or that employ exclamations and stage antics of a sub-tragic type, these expressions and gestures are for the most part distinctly less "low" and disruptive than their equivalents in Aristophanes;[9] and the language of

---

of tragic norms.

[7] Thus "grand" (*megaloprepês*), "middle" (*mesos*) or "flowery" (*anthêros*) or "smooth" (*glaphuros*), and "thin" (*ischnos*) are all "types" (*charactêres*) of serious, formal prose style, quite separate from "low" mime or conversation. On the characteristics of the "smooth" and "charming" style, see esp. Demetrius *On Style* 128–178; further Wehrli (1946); Lausberg (1990); etc. [See further Chapter 5.]

[8] See esp. KPS 15–16; López-Eire (2003), Redondo 2003.

[9] On the mildness of satyr drama's language for sexual activity in particular, as compared with that of Comedy, see Henderson (1975); Griffith (2005) [= Chapter 2 above]. The costuming of the satyr-

the non-satyric characters, which comprises quite a high proportion of the dialogue of every play, appears to have adhered quite closely—like the metrical features of their iambic trimeters—in almost all respects to the level of tragedy, and to have contained very few indicators of colloquial, let alone comic, style.[10]

One simple and objective index of the level of elevation (*hupsos, semnotês, megaloprepeia*: "grandeur, magniloquence") of a given passage of Greek poetry is the frequency of compound adjectives.[11] The Greek critics from Aristophanes and Aristotle onwards recognized that this element of word choice was one of the most conspicuous kinds of "adornment" (*kosmos*) through which ordinary, simple language might be transformed into more elaborate and poetic expression;[12] and it is not surprising to find that the rate of compound adjectives per line consistently reflects in numerical terms the well-known |[55] distinction between the loftier style of Aeschylus and the more mundane diction of Euripides.[13] And although common-sense would perhaps suggest that all kinds of long words might contribute equally to "high" style, closer inspection soon reveals that polysyllabic verb-forms (both simple and compound) are in fact quite common in all levels of Greek expression, including comedy and prose,[14] whereas compound nouns and adverbs, and above all adjectives, turn out to be a far more reliable index of elevated style.[15]

I have assembled complete data on the compound nouns, adverbs, and adjectives found in the surviving satyric plays and fragments. But my analysis here, which employs comparative figures for the surviving tragedies and satyric fragments of Aeschylus, Sophocles, and Euripides, and also two sample plays of Aristophanes (*Acharnians, Clouds*), will focus only on the compound adjectives, since it is these that are the most consistently informative.[16] The results of this analysis are contained in Table 1.

---

chorus likewise was much less exaggerated and gross than that of Comedy, cf. Griffith (2002: 217–224) [= Chapter 1 above]. On exclamations and interjections, see Stevens (1945; 1976); Labiano Ilundain (2000).

[10] Seaford (1984: 47–48). On the metrical characteristics of satyric trimeters (especially their scrupulous observance of Porson's Bridge), see Griffith (2005) [= Chapter 2 above].

[11] See Griffith (1977: 148–150) (based in part on Clay 1958; 1960).

[12] The contest of Aeschylus and Euripides in Aristophanes' *Frogs* makes much of this feature; and see Aristotle *Poetics* 21.1457a31-1459a16, esp. 1459a10 τῶν δ' ὀνομάτων τὰ μὲν διπλᾶ μάλιστα ἁρμόττει τοῖς διθυράμβοις ("In the case of nouns [and adjectives], compounds are especially suitable for dithyrambs"); also Demetrius *On Style* 164.

[13] See Griffith (1977: 149–150).

[14] In the first 125 lines of Aristophanes' *Acharnians*, we may note seven polysyllabic, but quite prosaic, perfect passive participles: μεμιλτωμένον, παρεσκευασμένος, ἐσκηνημένοι, κατακείμενοι, κατακείμενος, ἐξυρημένε, ἐσκευασμένος.

[15] See Griffith (1977: 149–153).

[16] The complete lists of compound adjectives are reproduced in the Appendix. Lists of the rest of the (non-adjectival) compound words are not included because they are not distinctive.

TABLE 1: Comparative rates of compound adjectives per 1000 lines

Aeschylus' tragedies:	(highest)	316 (*Supp.*)
	(lowest)	248 (*Eu.*)
		247 (*Pr.*)
Aeschylus' satyr-fragments:		216
Sophocles' tragedies:	(highest)	200 (*Ant.*)
	(lowest)	126 (*Phil.*)
Sophocles' satyr-fragments		175
Euripides' tragedies:	(highest)	173 (*Pho.*)
	(lowest)	104 (*Heracl.*)
Euripides' *Cyclops*:		130
Aristophanes		ca. 66

It is immediately apparent from Table 1 that for each of the tragedians the rate of compound adjectives in his satyr plays is similar to |[56] that in his tragedies,[17] and that the rate of compound adjectives for all three tragedians remains consistently higher than that for Aristophanes. In the remains of Aeschylus' satyr plays (amounting to approximately 320 verses complete enough to be somewhat intelligible), there are 70 compound adjectives,[18] giving a rate of ca. 216 per 1000 lines. This falls slightly below the rate for Aeschylus' tragedies, but is still significantly higher than any of the plays of Sophocles or Euripides. In Euripides' *Cyclops*, we find 90 compound adjectives in 704 lines, a rate of ca. 130 per 1000 lines, squarely within the range of Euripides' tragedies.[19] By contrast, the first 400 lines of Aristophanes' *Acharnians* yield just 29 compound adjectives (a rate of ca. 74 per 1000 lines), while *Clouds* 1–200 yield only 11 (55 per 1000). Furthermore, a significant proportion of the Aristophanic compound adjectives are quite prosaic and/or "low" (e.g., (*Ach.*) μεσημβρινοί, ἀθάνατος, καταπύγονας, χαυνόπρωκτα, φιλαθήναιος, κακοδαίμων, Μαραθωνομάχαι, πεντέτεις, τριακοντούτιδες, (*Clouds*) ἄδικον, ἀμαθής, τρισμακάριος), while others are absurdly inflated and/or paratragic (e.g. *Ach.* 3 ψαμμακοσιογάργαρα, 119 θερμόβουλον, 181 ἀτεράμονες).

Turning to Sophocles' satyr plays: in *Ichneutae* (Fr. 314), we have approximate-

---

[17] It could be argued that the rate of compound adjectives in satyr plays may have been artificially elevated by the accidents of transmission, since many of the fragments are quoted by grammarians such as Hesychius, Pollux, etc. precisely for the rare words that they contain. But the papyrus fragments of Aeschylus and Sophocles, which survive only by chance, maintain a similar rate of polysyllabic words in general, and of compound adjectives in particular; so it does not appear that this argument is cogent.

[18] Occasionally, a word is incomplete or corrupt, but seems nonetheless almost certainly to be a compound adjective or noun: e.g. (*Dicty.*) ποικιλονωτ-, νεβροφον-; (*Isthm.*) ἐπιτροπ-, τριδουλ-, etc.

[19] Some of these 90 in *Cyclops* are quite humdrum (e.g. ἄδικος, εὐσεβές); but most are quite "tragic" and non-parodic, as a glance at the Appendix will confirm.

ly 350 lines that survive intact enough to yield usable material.[20] In these 350 lines, we find between 54 and 60 compound adjectives, i.e. a rate approaching 175 compound adjectives per 1000 lines of verse.[21] In the other indubitably or probably satyric Sophoclean |[57] fragments (perhaps 17 plays in all),[22] where the accidents and uncertainties of transmission are often even more problematic—though the quotations from Stobaeus, Plutarch, etc. do at least usually reach us as more or less whole lines—the rate is similar. In total, they amount to ca. 185 "lines,"[23] in which approximately 40 compound adjectives occur (many of them occurring in short lyric lines), yielding a rate of ca. 215 per 1000 lines. The grand total of compound adjectives per lines in Sophocles' satyric fragments is thus at least 94 (54 + 40) in ca. 535 lines, ca. 175 per 1000. This rate falls squarely within the rate for Sophocles' extant tragedies, which range from 200 (highest) to 126 (lowest) per 1000 lines.

As we have already noted, this criterion (frequency of compound adjectives) does seem to distinguish effectively and consistently between the different levels of elevation among the tragedians and comedians. Within each tragedian's work, the figures are consistent; and Aristophanes' plays yield figures of a completely different order from those of any of the tragedians. By this criterion, at least, the language of satyr play (and specifically of Sophoclean satyr plays) is not really "in the middle," between that of tragedy and comedy, but almost identical to that of tragedy.

Other markers of tragic elevation and/or distinctively Sophoclean diction yield less conclusive results when applied to his satyr plays; but none points to any sharp deviation. Thus, in accordance with the high frequency of polysyllabic adjectives, Sophocles' satyr plays also contain several examples of three-word trimeters—at least four in 535 lines (a higher rate than any of Sophocles's tragedies, in fact): *Ichn. Fr.* 314.122, 173; *Fr.* 329; *Fr.* 537.2—and perhaps two more, if *Fr.* 473 and *Fr.* 666 are satyric (as several scholars believe).[24] And it may be noted that Sopho-

---

[20] In cases of damaged or defective texts, I have defined a "usable" line as one containing at least six secure syllables and two or three clearly identifiable words. In deciding which of several possible readings to follow, I have generally compromised between KPS and Radt (1977).

[21] Of course, there might be a few more compound adjectives lurking in the missing parts of those 350 mutilated lines; so if anything these figures are on the low side overall. I am also making no distinction between lyric and dialogue, or between longer and shorter verse units, treating all of them simply as "lines" which makes the measurements all the more crude. But given the state of the evidence, we really have no choice.

[22] These seventeen are: *Achilleôs Erastai, Amphiaraus, Amycus, Dionysiscus, Helenês Gamos, Heracleiscus, Heracles, Inachus, Cedalion, Cerberus, Crisis, Momus, Oeneus, Pandora, Salmoneus, Syndeipni,* and *Hybris.* See above, note 1; and the discussions of Lloyd-Jones (1996); KPS.

[23] Here too the decision as to what should or should not count as a "line" is often somewhat arbitrary (esp. in the case of the mutilated *Inachus*); see above, note 21.

[24] Sophocles' highest rate is four per play (*Aj.*), his lowest is one (*Tr.*); Aeschylus ranges from three (*Pers.*) to thirteen (*Th.*); see further Stanford (1940), Griffith (1977: 91–92). On the basis of such small (statistically insignificant) figures, one would not want to claim that Sophocles regularly employed

cles' predilection for nouns suffixed with -σις and -μα appears to be equally strong in his satyr plays.[25] |[58]

3. SENTENCE LENGTH

A separate index of style is the number of words per sentence. I have surveyed all the surviving passages of Sophocles' satyr plays that are at least three lines long, do not contain a change of speaker, and are well enough preserved for us to tell whether or not they contain major punctuation, simply counting the total number of words (of any kind) that occur between one major punctuation mark (full stop, colon, or question mark) and the next; and I have compared the results with the figures that have previously been compiled for the three tragedians.[26] I have done the same for Aristophanes' *Acharnians*.

The one slight but consistent difference that was previously observed among the three major tragedians was Sophocles' smaller number of short sentences (1–10 words long) and generally higher proportion of long sentences (esp. those of 36 words or longer), as compared with both Aeschylus and Euripides. Thus in the case of Aeschylus' undisputed tragedies, 46% of the sentences (476 out of 1019) are between 1 and 10 words long; similarly for the six selected plays of Euripides the figure is 45% (772 out of 1645);[27] but for the four tragedies of Sophocles that were examined (*Ajax, OT, Antigone,* and *Trachiniae*) the figure is only 38% (348 out of 923).

For the satyric fragments of Sophocles, a slight but probably significant difference is the higher rate of short sentences (i.e. 1–10 words long): these comprise 44 out of the total of 79 eligible sentences, i.e. almost 56%, a higher rate even than Aeschylus and Euripides' tragedies and significantly higher than Sophocles' tragedies, approaching the rate of Aristophanes (61%). And strikingly, a high proportion of these sentences consist of only 1–5 words (25 in all = 32%; for |[59] Sophocles' tragedies the rate is only 12%)—presumably a positive index of greater

---

more three-word trimeters in his satyr plays than in his tragedies; but, for what it is worth, we may take this as a small piece of evidence that he did not use significantly fewer.

[25]These nouns are studied by Long (1968: 34ff); Griffith (1977: 152). In Sophocles' satyr plays, there are eleven occurrences of -σις nouns altogether (*Fr.* 171.1 βρῶσις; *Fr.* 181.2 βρῶσιν; *Fr.* 314.81 σύλησιν; *Fr.* 314.164 ἐλευθέρωσιν; *Fr.* 314.174 βάσιν; *Fr.* 314.223 μετάστασις; (*Fr.* 314.265 πύστις); *Fr.* 314.372 ξενόστασις; and *Fr.* 1130.15 μέτρησις, ὄρχησις, λάλησις. As for -μα nouns (plentiful in all three tragedians), I count no fewer than 31 in Sophocles' *Ichneutae* alone; and there are two in *Fr.* 149, and another in *Fr.* 941.

[26]The figures for the non-satyric plays of the three tragedians are taken from Griffith (1977: 214–217). It should be noted that in that earlier study I included only passages of eight or more lines (rather than three) from the same speaker—an unrealistic criterion when studying the fragmentary satyr plays. This may perhaps create a significant source of difference; but I see no alternative.

[27]The figures for *Rhesus* are 77 out of 170 (45%).

directness of expression, simplicity of style, and avoidance of complex syntactical subordination. This is confirmed at the other end of the spectrum, where we note the scarcity in Sophocles' satyr plays of very long sentences (those containing 36 words or more): I find only two such passages, *Ichn. Fr.* 314.151–160 (55 words, preceded by a 33-word sentence in 145–150) and *Fab. Incert* (maybe *Oeneus*) *Fr.* 1130.9–16 (36 words). And an interesting feature of these long sentences in the satyr plays is their relatively simple syntactic structure with extended anaphora and parataxis (esp. *Fr.* 1130), in contrast to the syntactically more elaborate strings of subordinate clauses preferred in Sophoclean tragic rhesis.[28]

In sum: by most of the available stylistic indices, the language of Sophocles' satyr plays stands very close to—indeed is often indistinguishable from—that of his tragedies, while deviating sharply from the practice of Comedy. This is especially the case for the diction and meter of the dialogue scenes. And while his satyr plays do deviate significantly from his tragedies in their preference for short sentences, the discrepancy is relatively small, and suggests a preference for simplicity and avoidance of syntactical complexity that is as characteristic of a smooth "middle" style of expression as it is of comic style. We may conclude that in terms of stylistic register and elevation, satyr play appears for the most part to inhabit the same world as tragedy. |[60]

4. SOPHOCLES' LANGUAGE OF SEX AND LOVE

As we have noted, scholars have looked long and hard—perhaps too hard—at the "comic" features of satyric diction,[29] focusing on expressions concerning food and drink (though satyr plays emphasize especially wine-consumption and sympotic behavior, whereas Comedy tends to focus more intently on eating);[30] interactions

---

[28] There are two further sentences in the satyr-fragments that extend beyond 25 words, both in *Ichn.* (*Fr.* 314.145–151, 223–228). These likewise are syntactically simple, the first especially so, a string of participles, nouns, and adjectives in apposition to subject of the main clause ("Why are you so scared, you dummies, frightened of everything, always working away at spineless stuff..., just bodies and tongues and phalluses...?"), though the second is a little more complex and closer to elevated tragic style. In Aristophanes' *Acharnians*, the overall rate of long sentences (over 30 words) is similar (6%) to that of Sophocles; but it is notable that most of the long sentences come in the Parabasis (626–718), where the style takes on a distinctive rhetorical flavor of its own, in some respects more elevated and political than normal comic dialogue: so 646–649, 34 words; 668–675, 33; 676–682, 35; 713–716, 33; 706–712, 48. (The other long sentences in the play are: 17–22, 38 words; 211–238, 31; 247–252, 31; 544–551, 40; 599–606, 46; 979–984 and 995–999, 38.)

[29] See above, notes 8 and 9. In what follows, I shall not try to maintain a consistent distinction between the language of the heroic characters and that of the satyrs and Papposilenus, since the fragmentary state of the surviving Sophoclean evidence simply does not make this possible. So I will refer in general to "satyric style," even though it was clearly not entirely homogeneous.

[30] Sympotic language in Sophocles' satyr plays is actually not as extensive as it is in Aeschylus or in E. *Cyclops*—perhaps merely a matter of chance. But see below, p. 119 (on *Fr.* 537).

with, and descriptions of, animals and rustic activities (herding, fishing, hunting, etc.); physical labor; diminutives and other colloquial expressions;[31] exclamations and interjections of excitement, chasing, wondering, and discovery,[32] along with many repetitions and insistent anaphoras.[33] Less often noted by scholars are the frequent references to other contexts of luxury, leisure, and high-living in addition to the symposium, especially weddings and betrothal ceremonies;[34] and in general the search for the comic seems to have blinded critics to some of the more sophisticated and romantic elements in satyric—and especially Sophoclean—descriptions of human interactions.

References to (lower) bodily processes seem in fact to be much less common in satyr play than in Old Comedy,[35] and the actual language employed is much less coarse.[36] Indeed, even when reference is made in satyr drama to undignified noises, postures, and loss |[61] of bodily self-control, the expressions seem to maintain a tone similar to that, e.g., of the Homeric *Hymn to Hermes*, where the baby farts, sneezes, and whistles loudly (280, 295–297), or of Aeschylus' *Libation Bearers*, where the Nurse describes the baby Orestes's peeing and puking (748–762) in affectionate and matter-of-fact terms. Sophocles' satyr plays rarely use low or obscene terms in their references to human anatomy and sexual activity.[37] Typical

---

[31] Stevens (1931; 1976); Seaford (1984: 47).

[32] Some of these exclamations are peculiar to satyr drama, e.g. *Ichn.* Fr. 314.131 ὗ ὗ ὗ ὗ, 176 ὗ ὗ ὗ, ψ ψ ἆ ἆ.

[33] E.g. S. *Ichn.* Fr. 314.100 θεὸς θεὸς θεὸς θεός, 107 ἰδοὺ ἰδού; cf. 177–178 ὑπέκλαγες ὑπέκριγες ὑπό μ' ἴδες. On the stylistics and tone of such anaphora, see below, pp. 119, 123–124. On Aristophanic interjections, see Labiano Ilundain (2000).

[34] See below, pp. 118–119.

[35] See also López-Eire (2003); O'Kell (2003), with further references.

[36] At S. *Ichn.* Fr. 314.147 the satyrs are reproached as being ὄνθια "manure" ("you lumps of dung!")—certainly not a compliment, and not an elevated word; but ὄνθος is found twice in Hom. *Iliad* 23 (775, 777), and the word occurs also in Aeschylus' tragedies (*Fr.* 275, regarding the death of Odysseus; likewise κόπρος is not uncommon in high poetry). The satyr plays appear in fact to refrain from using the lower registers of terms of shitting, farting, pissing, etc. (χεζ-, ἀποπερδ-, πιεζ-, κτλ.), in contrast to the practice of Aristophanes and Old Comedy (and before that, Hipponax and iambos): so e.g. the opening scene of Ar. *Frogs*, and Henderson (1975: 187–203 and *passim*). The lowest word we find of this kind in Sophocles is the hapax ἐνουρήθρα ("chamberpot"); and even in this case we note that ἐνουρέω is itself not an uncommon prose expression (Herodotus, Aristotle, etc.). At *Ichn.* Fr. 314.168 Lloyd-Jones interprets ψοφήσετε as "you'll fart" or "shit" (??) (sc. in terror); but the text here is too uncertain for any reliable conclusions to be drawn. At *Fr.* 1130.11 (probably from S. *Oeneus*, in a scene in which the satyrs are presenting themselves as suitors for the hand of Deianira), we find among a list of their alleged athletic skills (mostly quite conventionally admirable), the phrase ὄρχεων ἀποστροφαί "twisting of testicles" (sc. in the *pankration*). Here again ὄρχεις is the standard prose (scientific-medical) term for "testicles," e.g. in Herodotus and the Hippocratic Corpus—it is not slang, and is not disruptive of the rest of the formal speech.

[37] In Lloyd-Jones' edition (1996) of *Fr.* 483 (from S. *Pandora*) we read τρίψει (γέμοντα) μαλθακῆς ὑπ' ὠλένης. This restoration and interpretation as masturbation are far from secure.

is S. *Dionysiscus Fr.* 171.1-3 with its much-discussed reference to φαλακρόν.[38] We never encounter in Sophocles (or Aeschylus or Euripides either) any of the lower terms such as πέος, ψωλή, πρῶκτος, πυγή, κύσθος, χοῖρος, etc. Instead we find e.g. *Ichn. Fr.* 314.150-151 σώματα ... μόνον, / καὶ γλῶσσα καὶ φαλῆτες ("just bodies, tongues, phalluses!").[39]

Of course, the fact that we do find such frequent mention of the penis in a state of erection is significant and distinctive. In Sophocles not only are φαλακρόν and φαλῆτες prominently mentioned, but we are given also detailed descriptions of "stretching it out" and manipulating it (*Ichn. Fr.* 314.368-370 παύου τὸ λεῖον φαλακρὸν ἡδονῆι πιτνάς, |[62] "Stop stretching out that smooth knob in pleasure!"); and from the satyric *Momus* (*Fr.* 423) we encounter the word ἀποσκόλυπτε ("draw back the foreskin"). The linguistic and behavioral register in such contexts seems to be playful and affectionate, but not obscene, and it seems to be a certain childishness in the satyrs' character that is thus emphasized. In this respect, the excitable but perennially immature and ineffectual chorus occupies a special place on the Athenian erotic spectrum.[40] As quasi-adolescents or boys, exploring and fantasizing about their sexuality, always watching, hoping, and making advances, but still for the most part merely "playing" with themselves, these satyrs are contrasted with the more mature and well-directed human (and Olympian) participants in the romances and marriages that take place before their eyes, on the same stage and before the same audience.

As we noted above, Sophocles' satyrs—and other leading characters in his satyr plays—are often found in contexts of luxury, leisure, and high-living, especially at the symposium or participating in betrothal or wedding ceremonies. The plots of at least three—probably—satyric plays of Sophocles (*Helenês Gamos, Crisis* [i.e., the *Judgment of Paris*], and *Oeneus*, which dealt with the suitors for the hand of Deianira; cf. *Fr.* 1130), all involve language and situations of stylish living and social pretension reminiscent of Herodotus' account of the marriage of Megacles' daughter.

---

[38] Is this baby (Dionysus) accepting food, or drink (*brôsin*)? and is he reaching up to stroke someone's nose and bald head, or his penis and its glans? Editors take different views, as they do on the similar *Ichn. Fr.* 314.366-372. When is the "shiny, bald head" (φαλακρόν) just a bald head, when is it supposed also to connote, or denote, the shining tip of an erect phallus? (See now O'Kell 2003: 291-295.) But even if in *Fr.* 171 the latter is meant, we should note that (as in the similar scene in A. *Dictyulci*, where the baby Perseus is described as being "fond of the *posthê*" (ὡς ποσθοφίλης ὁ νεοσσός) and as reaching out to touch the phalluses of the nearby satyrs) the terminology is friendly and mild (πόσθη, φαλακρόν cf. φαλῆς, φάλλος) not coarse or vulgar; cf. Henderson (1975); Griffith (2005) [= Chapter 2 above]. Greek has plenty of coarse and vulgar terms to choose from, to refer to the penis, anus, vagina, etc., and to various kinds of sexual activity, as the text of Aristophanes exemplifies (and Henderson (1975/1991) discusses in detail); but satyr drama does not employ the cruder terms at all.

[39] See further Seaford (1984: on E. *Cycl.* 180).

[40] So S. *Ichn. Fr.* 314.366 ἀλλ' αἰὲν εἶ σὺ παῖς. See further Griffith (2005) [= Chapter 2 above], with particular reference to Aeschylus' *Dictyulci*.

Thus in *Fr.* 1130 (which is certainly satyric, and probably from *Oeneus*) the satyrs present themselves as suitors. The syntactically simple list of attributes, all nominatives and genitives, with six-fold anaphora (ἔστι μέν..., ἔνεισι δέ..., ἔνεστι δέ..., ἔστιν..., ἔστι..., ἔστι...) is especially striking, with its suggestion of limitless abundance of talent and epideictic exuberance, culminating in the three -σις abstracts (15–16 ἔστιν οὐρανοῦ / μέτρησις, ἔστ' ὄρχησις, ἔστι τῶν κάτω / λάλησις..., "There's measuring of the heavens, there's dancing, there's talking about the things below"), specifying the satyr-suitors' sophisticated intellectual accomplishments. Elsewhere (*Fr.* 361, from the *Crisis*), Aphrodite's gorgeous adornments, and her overwhelming effect on those who saw her, are described (πάντα συνεταράχθη) in language that contains no visible hint of parody or |[63] incongruity. Possibly (probably?) satyric too is *Fr.* 398 (*Manteis*), a description of a dinner-setting, again with anaphora used to emphasize the abundance of luxurious foods and furniture (ἦν οἰὸς μαλλός..., ἦν δ' ἀπ' ἀμπέλου / σπονδή τε καὶ ῥὰξ εὖ τεθησαυρισμένη, / ἐνῆν δὲ παγκάρπεια συμμιγής..., "There was a sheep's fleece, there was libation from the vine and grapes well-treasured, there was an all-abundant mixture of fruits..."). Likewise the (probably Sophoclean) Adesp. *Fr.* 656 (*P.Oxy.* 2804), although it is a papyrological mess,[41] certainly includes references to expensive perfume (βακκάρις), "Lydia," "Sardis" and other details of luxurious life-style, as well as perhaps to "intercourse" (ξυνεῖναι), and someone's "prime-youthfulness" (ἄκρηβον).

Fr. 537 (*Salmoneus*) contains an extended description of sympotic behavior: τάδ' ἐστὶ κνισμὸς καὶ φιλημάτων ψόφος· / τῶι καλλικοσσαβοῦντι νικητήρια / τίθημι καὶ βαλόντι χάλκειον κάρα, "Here are the itch and sounds of kisses: I offer prizes to the best *kottabos*-player and to the one who hits the bronze target!" The mention of *kottabos*-playing lends an upper-class tone to the proceedings, while the "itch, sting" of desire and "sounds of love-making" may indicate musical as well as amorous conduct.[42] Perhaps we should consider too in this context Sophocles' *Tyro* (*Fr.* 659), in which the young woman laments the cropping of her lovely hair and the consequent loss of her sexual attractiveness, as well as *Fr.* 769 (Incert.) with its reference to effeminate clothing.

These references to luxury, to sympotic behavior, and to weddings, all create contexts from which the language of sexuality and of the physical and emotional manifestations of desire (*erôtika*, *aphrodisia*) is never far away. Sophocles' fragmentary plays do indeed contain several descriptions of the bitter-sweet and positively exciting symptoms of "falling/being in love"; and a remarkably high proportion—possibly all—of these appear to come from satyr dramas.

In the dialogue scenes of the seven surviving tragedies there are no such "ro-

---

[41] Apart from Snell-Kannicht's edition (*TrGF* II F 656), see Carden (1974: 244–250); KPS 393: both agree with Lobel (*ed. princeps*) that the fragment is probably satyric, and probably Sophoclean.

[42] For the multiple associations of κνισμός, see KPS 384.

mantic" passages. As for the lost tragedies, these are of course difficult to evaluate in these terms, since in so many cases we know almost nothing of their contents, even of their cast of characters. But in surveying those surviving fragments that are either definitely tragic or of uncertain genre, I notice only a handful of plays in which a love affair and/or marriage, or even sexual desire, seems to have |[64] played a significant part in the plot.[43] The most probable candidates seem to be: *Colchides, Nausicaa, Oenomaus, Procris, Troilus, Tyro*, and *Phaedra*—i.e. seven plays. Of these, *Procris* and *Phaedra* clearly involved erotic conflicts that were not of the straightforwardly "romantic" and positive kind that I have outlined. Of the remaining five plays, I think it likely—as have several scholars before me—that at least three or four were satyr dramas (i.e. *Nausicaa, Oenomaus, Tyro*; perhaps *Colchides* too).[44]

Sophocles' satyr dramas appear to have been full of erotic language and love-scenes. The prime example is the *Lovers of Achilleus* (*Achilleôs Erastai*). In one fragment (*Fr.* 157) we encounter the phrase ὀμμάτων ἄπο / λόγχας ἵησιν ("s/he darts spears from his/her eyes"), in which probably it is "he"—i.e. the young Achilleus—who thus wounds with his glances. This play, along with two or three others of Sophocles', clearly introduced both homosexual and heterosexual desire as the focus of serious attention from the main characters. Several grammarians, in discussing the term παιδικά, cite *Fr.* 153 and give us the immediate context: …ἐπιδόντων γάρ τι τῶν Σατύρων εἰς τὴν γυναικείαν ἐπιθυμίαν, φησὶν ὁ Φοῖνιξ "παπαῖ, τὰ παιδίχ', ὡς ὁρᾷς, ἀπώλεσας" ("After the satyrs have given in a bit to their desire for women, Phoenix says, 'Hey, you can see you've lost your boyfriend!'"). The satyrs apparently have just transferred their affections from a male to a female object; i.e. presumably they have dropped out of the competition for the affections of the lovely young Achilleus, and are now (as usual) pursuing women and/or nymphs—though who exactly is being addressed by Phoenix, as having "lost" his *paidika* is far from clear. In any case, the play seems to have concerned itself with the different trajectories and dynamics of young male homosexual and heterosexual desire, a characteristically elite and leisured preoccupation at Athens.[45] |[65]

---

[43] In an unpublished paper on Aristotle's *Poetics* and the origins of the Greek novel, delivered during the early 1980s, John J. Winkler argued that a good number of fifth-century tragedies (now lost) may have followed a trajectory of "happy-ending" closer to the model of E. *IT* than to the disastrous closure of S. *OT* (whence Aristotle's discussion in chapters 13 and 14 of the *Poetics*). But Winkler does not explore the likely erotic component of such "romantic" tragedies. I am grateful to Francis Dunn for making a typescript of this lecture available to me.

[44] Other possibilities for romantic plots or scenes in lost tragedies might be *Aichmalotides, Alcmeon, Amphitryon, Andromeda, Dolopes, Hermione, Euryalus, Thyestes* <cf. *Fr.* 256?>, *Iphigenia, Lemniai*, and *Tympanistai* (i.e. another eleven possibles); but almost none of these is definitely known to have contained any such scene or description, and several in any case may have been satyric.

[45] An incidental reference to *paidika* occurs also in *Fr.* 345 (*Colchides*, a play dealing with Jason and Medea), as we are told of Zeus' passion for Ganymede's thighs (μηροῖς ὑπαίθων τὴν Διὸς

Apart from these brief but suggestive references to homoerotic romantic relations, we find three longer passages that describe the effects and feelings of love in more detail.[46] The first comes once again from *The Lovers of Achilleus*:

> τὸ γὰρ νόσημα τοῦτ' ἐφίμερον κακόν·
> ἔχοιμ' ἂν αὐτὸ μὴ κακῶς ἀπεικάσαι.
> ὅταν πάγου φανέντος αἰθρίου χεροῖν
> κρύσταλλον ἁρπάσωσι παῖδες εὐπαγῆ,
> τὰ πρῶτ' ἔχουσιν ἡδονὰς ποταινίους·
> τέλος δ' ὁ θυμὸς οὔθ' ὅπως ἀφῆι θέλει,
> οὔτ' ἐν χεροῖν τὸ κτῆμα σύμφορον μένειν.
> οὕτω δὲ τοὺς ἐρῶντας αὐτὸς ἵμερος
> δρᾶν καὶ τὸ μὴ δρᾶν πολλάκις προσίεται.

> "This disease is a desirable evil.
> Here's a comparison—not bad, I think:
> when ice gleams in the open air,
> children grab.
> Ice-crystal in the hands is
> at first a pleasure quite novel.
> But there comes a point –
> you can't put the melting ice down,
> you can't keep holding it.
> Desire is like that.
> Pulling the lover to act and not to act,
> again and again, pulling."

(Soph. *Fr.* 149, tr. A. Carson, slightly adapted)

This description of the bitter-sweet properties of Love deserves more detailed discussion than is possible here. Fortunately the reader can consult the extended analysis by Anne Carson,[47] who devotes more space to this passage than to any

---

τυραννίδα), in a line cited by Athenaeus together with the famous passage from Aeschylus' tragedy *Myrmidons* (*Fr.* 135 σέβας δὲ μηρῶν ἁγνὸν οὐκ ἐπηιδέσω, / ὦ δυσχάριστε τῶν πυκνῶν φιλημάτων). There is another reference to *paidika* from an unknown play (*Fr.* 841 (Incert.) ὅτωι δ' ἔρωτος δῆγμα παιδικὸν προσῆι). We do not know if the play is satyric or tragic. Still from the clearly homoerotic angle, *Fr.* 448 of Sophocles' *Niobe* also mentions a homoerotic relationship, as motivating one of the sons (τῶν Νιοβιδῶν βαλλομένων καὶ θνηισκόντων, ἀνακαλεῖταί τις τὸν ἐραστήν): this too is a play that, as several scholars have proposed, could well be satyric, with the gods so active on-stage, and a straightforwardly moralistic plot of divine punishment of the misguided.

[46] Further short passages of this type include: *Fr.* 537 (*Salmoneus*), discussed earlier, which occurs in the context of a symposium (...κνισμός καὶ φιλημάτων ψόφος...etc.); but beyond the conventional "sting" of love, we can say little more about the context or direction of this scene; also *Nausicaa*, though unfortunately nothing survives of the scenes between Nausicaa and Odysseus (a topic also treated in Old and Middle Comedy).

[47] Carson (1986: 111–116). In the first line, she reads ἐφήμερον with the MSS, not ἐφίμερον as most editors do.

other poetic text from ancient Greece, so exemplary and suggestive does she find it of Classical Greek sensibilities concerning desire and its effects, delights, dangers, pains, and |[66] attractions. Her discussion of the ice-simile is characteristically vivid and precise:

> "We hang upon the physical fate of the melting ice; it is, in a way, the protagonist of the simile and we are watching it perish. At the same time, we care for the hands of the children. Ice is cold, and the longer you hold it the colder your hands get. But this care reminds us of another. The longer you hold it, the more it melts.[...] As a conventional lover, you relish the sensation of melting, in your bittersweet way. <But> as an observer of ice, your feelings about melting are different, more complex[...]."[48]

We do not know who spoke the lines, nor to whom they refer (Phoenix or Heracles in love with Achilleus? Achilleus with Patroclus? or vice-versa? Achilleus with a woman? The satyrs with Achilleus, or now a woman? The possibilities are almost endless...). But the crucial point for the present purpose is simply that this passage, singled out as it is for being one of the most complex and engaging of all Classical Greek descriptions of "love the bittersweet," occurs in a satyr play.

A second extended passage of erotic language comes from S. *Oenomaus*: and in this case the romance is definitely heterosexual. The passage is very corrupt; and some of the restorations are less than certain. But the gist is clear, as Hippodamia describes the inflammatory effects of the meeting of Pelops' gaze with her own, in boldly figurative language:

> τοίαν Πέλοψ ἴυγγα θηρατηρίαν
> ἔρωτος, ἀστραπήν τιν' ὀμμάτων, ἔχει·
> ἧι θάλπεται μὲν αὐτός, ἐξοπτᾶι δ' ἐμέ,
> ἴσον μετρῶν ὀφθαλμόν, ὥστε τέκτονος
> παρὰ στάθμην ἰόντος ὀρθοῦται κανών.

> "Such a magic hunting-charm of Love,
> a kind of lightning-bolt of the eyes, Pelops has received.
> By this he himself is heated-up, and it (he?) is roasting me too,
> Measuring his eye (gaze) equally, just like a builder's ruler
> that is lined up straight along its level."
>
> (Soph. *Fr.* 474, Radt's text)

Many scholars have concluded that this play was probably satyric, with its ogrish villain, gruesome skulls, athletic competition, and winning of the bride.[49] In any case, there is no doubt that Sophocles' play |[67] provided a serious and engaging treatment of a romantic encounter, in language that belongs to the same register

---

[48] Carson (1986: 114).

[49] As we have seen, satyrs are often found in contexts of athletic competition and courtship contexts. We may note that this story was later the subject of New Comedies by Antiphanes and Eubulus.

as that of the mainstream erotic poets and novelists of Greek tradition.

Our third surviving continuous passage of romantic language is found in *Fr. 941* (Incert.—possibly, but not certainly, satyric), describing the power (and names) of Cypris.

> ὦ παῖδες, ἥ τοι Κύπρις οὐ Κύπρις μόνον,
> ἀλλ' ἔστι πολλῶν ὀνομάτων ἐπώνυμος.
> ἔστιν μὲν Ἅιδης, ἔστι δ' ἄφθιτος βίος,
> ἔστιν δὲ λύσσα μανιάς, ἔστι δ' ἵμερος
> ἄκρατος, ἔστ' οἰμωγμός, ἐν κείνηι τὸ πᾶν
> σπουδαῖον, ἡσυχαῖον, ἐς βίαν ἄγον
> ...
> εἴ μοι θέμις—θέμις δέ—τἀληθῆ λέγειν,
> Διὸς τυραννεῖ πλευμόνων ἄνευ δορός,
> ἄνευ σιδήρου· πάντα τοι συντέμνεται
> Κύπρις τὰ θνητῶν καὶ θεῶν βουλεύματα.

> "Children, the Cyprian goddess is not only 'Cyprian,'
> But she is called by many names:
> She is Hades; she is Eternal Life;
> She is Raging Madness; she is Unmixed Desire;
> She is Wailing. In her resides everything serious,
> Everything peaceful, everything that leads to violence....
> ... If it is allowed for me—and it *is* allowed—to state the truth,
> She rules without spear, without steel, over the heart of Zeus. Indeed,
> Cypris short-circuits all the plans of mortals and of gods."
>
> (Incert. *Fr.* 941.1–6, 14–17)

Although this passage is less striking than the previous two, the anaphora of ἔστι in 1–6 recalls *Oeneus Fr.* 1130 (quoted above), in which we observed the simplicity of satyric sentence structure and noted that this may have been a mannerism of the "middle style" of epideictic and descriptive writing in general.

In all these examples, we are engaged with the language and sexual dynamics of "romance": "boy meets girl" (or "boy meets boy"), "they fall in love," etc. (or "satyrs meet boy/girl, but s/he is saving her/himself for someone better"). Although, as we have noted, it is impossible to determine whether some of these passages are tragic or satyric (i.e., *Oenomaus Fr.* 474, *Fr.* 841 Incert., *Colchides, Niobe*), all the others—i.e. the clear majority of the surviving Sophoclean passages dealing with love and romance—indisputably are. And the language of all these "romantic" passages is quite straight and serious; there is nothing comic, parodic, or burlesque in any of them (although of course there may have been an element of incongruity present if the satyrs spoke the lines or were the subject of the description, or being |[68] referred to as potential lovers or suitors). The language itself seems quite appropriate to the expression of the bitter-sweet excitement of young love, and to the serious treatment of such romantic encounters—in a vein comparable to that of e.g. Anacreon, or later the bucolic lovers of Theocritus and the Greek novel (esp. Longus' *Daphnis and Chloe*).

Indeed, these two authors probably offer some of our best evidence for the Hellenistic *Nachleben* of satyric mentality and style, and it is striking that Theocritus in particular, in his poems of rustic romance and adolescent infatuation, makes use of similar techniques of anaphora and repetition to the ones we have noted in Sophocles' satyr plays, with a comparable blending of high and low-er (but not "low") elements:

> ἔντι δάφναι τηνεί, ἔντι ῥαδιναὶ κυπάρισσοι,
> ἔστι μέλας κισσός, ἔστ' ἄμπελος ἁ γλυκύκαρπος,
> ἔστι ψυχρὸν ὕδωρ...
>
> "There are laurels there, there are delicate cypresses,
> There is dark ivy, there is sweet-fruited vine,
> There is cold water...."
>
> (Theocr. *Id.* 11.47–49)

K. J. Dover comments that such forms of repetition and anaphora were characteristic of popular and traditional songs, lullabies, wedding-songs, forms which were (he says) "eschewed by Classical literature...."[50] I suggest that the Classical Sophocles did not entirely "eschew" such figures of speech, but used them in his satyr plays; and that in this respect, as in others that we have observed, his language of romance belonged to the smooth "Middle Style" that ancient theorists thought suitable for such topics.

5. CONCLUSION

It may be significant that the biographical tradition gives us a highly erotic Sophocles[51] (as distinct from the drunken, soldiering Aeschylus, |[69] and the reclusive, bookish, impious Euripides). As a boy, Sophocles is said to have performed a gorgeous naked dance in a choral celebration after the Battle of Salamis (T 28), and as a young playwright he scored a hit playing the role of the nubile Nausicaa as she danced and played ball with her friends, in his (possibly satyric) play of that name. In his mature years, Sophocles was well-known as an *erastês* who flirted frequently, though not always successfully, with young male waiters and other

---

[50]Dover (1971: xlvi-viii). For further examples, see e.g. Theocritus 1.71–72, 74–75; 11.22–23, and 24.40 ἔστι... ἔστι...; ps-Theocr. 8.11–12. Demetrius (*On Style* 140–141) remarks that the *charis*-providing figures of *anadiplôsis* and *anaphora* are especially frequent in Sappho; and he also remarks (132) on the intrinsic *charis* of such subject-matter (*pragmata*) as νυμφαῖοι κῆποι, ὑμέναιοι, ἔρωτες, ὅλη ἡ Σαπφοῦς ποίησις—exactly the same subjects as form the content for satyr drama. [See further Chapter 5.]

[51]The evidence (four pages' worth) for Sophoclean "*amatoria*" is collected in Radt (1977).

cute *paidika*; and late in life (as Plato and others record) he acknowledged that his sex life in general had been stressful and unrelenting.[52] Of course, little or nothing of this biographical tradition need actually be true (for we know how unreliable these *Lives of the Poets* tend to be); but we may surmise that the idea of Sophocles as a man intensely engaged in both homosexual and heterosexual pursuits (like his alleged Oedipal strife with his sons) found support in—and/or was originally suggested by—his writings, as with most of these poetic *Lives*. That is to say, Sophocles was thought of as a famous lover, because so many of his plays presented famous lovers and love-affairs.[53]

It appears that about half of the satyr plays of Aeschylus and Sophocles whose plots can be reconstructed even in outline with any degree of confidence were love-stories ("romances") that ended up with a male hero, human or divine, marrying a new bride (often after rescuing her from attempted capture and violation by another, or by the satyrs, or both). Love stories, of course, comprise the chief plot element of the majority of the dramas that the world has ever known. In Athens, the New Comedy of the fourth century BCE and later (as in Rome) certainly offered an unending spectacle of youthful romance. But in the fifth century, Old Comic sex and marriage were represented very differently. "Love" or "romance" would not be the word to describe the sexual appetite of an Aristophanic hero (even a husband, like Cinesias in *Lysistrata*): "desire," "horniness," or "lust" (even "sadism") might be closer to the mark, and the language of desire, courtship, sexual pursuit, and intercourse in Aristophanes is generally rough and crude in the extreme.[54] |[70]

Our surviving tragedies allow little room for sexual desire of a positive and successful kind: only occasionally for conjugal love (Alcestis-Admetus; Helen-Menelaus) and various last-minute betrothals (such as Electra to Pylades). After Euripides' break-through love-drama *Andromeda* of 415 (?) BCE things may have changed.[55] But for most of the fifth century, it appears to have been primarily the satyr plays that provided the most engaging and fertile field of romance for Athenian theater-goers—not necessarily as burlesque, nor as parody, but as an imaginary world in which a couple could meet, fall in love, and end up happily married. And Sophocles' satyric language was equal to the needs of such romantic occasions.

---

[52] Plato *R*. 328b, Soph. T 80a.

[53] Interestingly, Plato's language about Sophocles' erotic tribulations (T 80a) describes Love as λυττῶντά τινα δεσπότην ("a kind of raging slave-owner"), a phrase that recalls S. *Fr.* 941 (1–4 Κύπρις … λύσσα μανιάς, 15 τυραννεῖ, above p. 123).

[54] There is nothing like e.g. Ar. *Ach.* 271–279 in the surviving remains of satyr drama.

[55] See Gibert (2000), Griffith (2002) [= Chapter 1 above].

APPENDIX

COMPOUND ADJECTIVES IN SATYR PLAYS, TRAGEDIES, AND OLD COMEDY

AESCHYLUS

Dicty. Fr. 46a-c: ἐνάλιε, ἀμπελοσκάφοι, ἐγχώριος, μαρειλύτων; *Fr.* 47a-c: πρόξενον, προπράκτορα, αἰχμάλωτος, μιλτόπρεπτον, ποικιλονω-, ποσθοφίλης, ὑστρίχων, παιδοτρόφους, εὐμενής, νεβροφον-, ἀνόσους, ἄναυδος, -ντροπος, ὕφαλος; *Isthm. Fr.* 78a: εὐσεβῆ, πρόφρων, καλλίγραπτον, σεισίχθονος, ἄναυδον, ἐπιτροπ-, ἄναλκις; *Fr.* 78c: ἔνορκον, τρίδουλ-, πολυπ-, διστοίχων, νεόκτιτα, ἐμμελέστατον; *Prom. Pyrk. Fr.* 204b: εὐμενής, ἀκάματον, ἑστίουχον, φερέσβιος, σπευσίδωρος, νυκτιπλαγκτ-, βαθυξυλ-; *Fr.* 204c?: τηλέγνωτον; *Fr.* 205 ὠμολίνου; *Fr.* 288?: πυραύστου; *Fr.* 307: ἄναυδος; *Dikê-play Fr.* 281a: ἔνδικον, εὐδερκές, δύσαρκτον, ὁδοιπόρων; *Glaucus Pontius Fr.* 25e: ἄγραυλος, ἔπιχωρι-, ἄφυλλον ὑψηλο-; *Fr.* 26: ἀνθρωποειδές; *Fr.* 29: ἀειζώον; *Kerykes Fr.* 108: σεμνόστομον; *Fr.* 110: πυρσοκόρσου; *Circê Fr.* 113a: μανόσπορος; *Fr.* 114: αὐτόφορβος; *Leon Fr.* 123: ὁδοιπόρων; *Proteus Fr.* 210: δύστηνον, μέσακτα; *Fr.* 213: ἄεπτοι; *Fr. Incert.* 330: λεοτόχορτον, νεαίρετον; *Sisyphus Fr.* 225: θεοφόρων... λεοντοβάμων... χαλκήλατος; *Fr.* 226: σταθμοῦχος; *Fr.* 227: ὑπερφυής; *Fr.* 228: πολυξένωι; *Fr.* 230: αἱμόρρυτοι [φλέβες]; *Trophoi Fr.* 246d: πεδοίκου.

Total: 70 in ca. 320 lines, i.e. rate of ca. 215 per 1000 lines |[71]

SOPHOCLES

Ichn. Fr. 314.10 [δύσ]λοφον, 14 [βου]στάθμου, 16 ἐφημέρων (?), 19 παντελές, 21 ἐμμανής, 36 συμμαχ-, 41 νυμφογεννή[του], 48 προσφιλής, 51 χρυσοστεφές, 69 ὑπόνομα (?), 70 διανύτων, 78 ἀρίζηλα, 83 κατήκοος, 84 προσφιλής, 85 παωτεκής, 96 διπλοῦς, 97 ὕποσμος, 108 ἐπίσημον, 116 ἐναργῆ, 118 παλινστραφῆ, 123 [βοη-]λάτην (?), 146 ἄνευρα, 149 ἄνευρα, ἀκόμιστα, ἀνελεύθερα, 157 ὀρειτρόφων, 162 χρυσόφαντον, 173 κυνορτικόν, 174 τριζυγής, 203 ἀληθ[ές], 218 πέδορτον, 221 ὑλώδη, 222 ἔνθηρον, 225 ὕποινος, 226 εὐπαλῆ, 228 ἐγγόνοις, 233 ἀναιτί- (?), 243 βαθύζωνε, 245 ἄξενος, 255 ὀρθοψάλακτον, 270 βαθυζώνου, (285 ἄφραστα?), 290 ἔμμεστον, 300 ἄναυδος, 301 προμήκης, ἐπίκυρτος, 304 βραχυσκελές, 305 προσφερές, 308 προσφερές, 310 σύγγονος, 316 ἀρτίγομφα, 327 ξύμφωνον, 329 [χερ]οψάλακτος, 342 ἀληθῆ, 343 ἀληθῆ, 363 [ἄκ]αρπον (?), 372 ἀπόψηκτον, 375 ῥινοκόλλητον, 381 παμπόνη-, 383 ἀληθές.

Total: 54 (60?) in ca. 350 entire-enough lines, i.e. ca. 155 (175?) per 1000 lines

Other satyr plays (certain or probable): Amphiaraus Fr. 114 ἄγραυλος; *Fr.* 117

ἀλεξαίθριον; *Achilleôs Erastai Fr.* 149 ἐφίμερον, εὐπαγῆ, ποταινίους, σύμφορον; *Fr.* 152 διχόστομον, δίπτυχοι; *Fr.* 156 ἀρρῶξιν; *Dionysiscus Fr.* 172 ἄλυπον; *Helenês Gamos Fr.* 181 ἀχρεῖος; *Inachus Fr.* 269a 2 θεοστυγῆ, 43 λινεργ-, 46 ἄφθογγος, 50 ἄπιστα, 52 ἀξυνετ-, 53 πολυφαρμ-, 56 αἰολωπόν; *Fr.* 269c 16 πολυιδρίδας, 19 αἰδοκυνέας, ἄβροτον, 31 πορπαφόρος; *Fr.* 274 πάνδοκος; *Fr.* 278 εὐδαίμονες, ἀφθίτου; *Fr.* 284 ἀντίπλαστον; *Fr.* 288 κυαμόβολον; *Fr.* 289 παλινσκίωι; *Fr.* 292 ἀελλόθριξ; *Fr.* 294 ἄναντα; *Fr.* 295 ἀστολοκρατές, ἀναυδον; *Cedalion Fr.* 329 ἀλλοτριοφάγοι; *Fr.* 332 αὐτοκτίστους; *Cophi Fr.* 363 ἰσόπριος; *Oeneus Fr.* 1130 2 αἰχμαλ-, 8 ὄμαυλοι, 13 παντάγνωστα, 16 ἄκαρπος; *Syndeipni Fr.* 565 κάκοσμον; *Hybris Fr.* 670.2

Total: 40 in ca. 185 entire-enough lines, i.e. ca. 215 per 1000 "lines"

Total for Sophoclean satyr plays: 54 + 40 = 94 in ca. 535 lines i.e. ca. 175 per 1000 lines

EURIPIDES

Cyc. 3 ἐμμανής, 5 γηγενῆ, 6 ἐνδέξιος, 15 ἀμφῆρες, 19 ἀπηλιώτης, 21 μονῶπες, 22 ἀνδροκτόνοι, 26 ἀνοσίου, 30 δυσσεβεῖ, 31 ἀνοσίων, 44 |[72] ὑπήνεμος, 53 μηλοβότα, 54 ἀγροβάτα, 59 ἀμερόκοιτοι, 64 θυρσοφόροι, 66 ὑδροχύτοις, 72 λευκόποσιν, 79 μονοδέρκται, 82 πετρηρεφῆ, 89 ταλαίπωροι, 91 ἄξενον, 93 ἀνδροβρῶτα, 124 ἄχορον, 125 φιλόξενοι, 127 ἀνθρωποκτόνωι, 206 νεόγονα, 215 εὐτρεπής, 226 συμμιγῆ, 235 τριπήχει, 241 ἀληθές, 245 κρεανόμωι, 247 ὀρεσκόου, 289 δυσσεβῆ, 292 ἄθραυστος, 294 ὑπάργυρος, 296 δύσφρονα, 298 πυριστάκτωι, 302 βουπόροισι, 305 δοριπετῆ, 306 ἀνάνδρους, ἄπαιδας, 310 εὐσεβές, 318 ἐναλίας, 342 ἄμεμπτος, 344 διαφόρητον, 348 ἀνοσίου, 349 ἀλίμενον, 360 δασυμάλλωι, 365 ἀποβώμιος, 371 ἐφεστίους, 378 ἀνοσιωτάτους, 380 εὐτραφέστατον, 386 χαμαιπετῆ, 388 δεκάμφορον, 394 παλιούρου, 396 θεοστυγεῖ, 399 χαλκήλατον, 416 ἔκπλεως, ἀναισχύντου, 429 ἄμεικτον, 432 ἀσθενής, 436 προσφερῆ, 438 ἀνόσιον, 442 πανουργοῦ, 462 φαεσφόρωι, 493 ἀπαίδευτον, 501 μυρόχριστον, 526 εὐπετής, 560 ἄδικος, 574 ἄδιψον, 578 ἄκρατος, 590 εὐγενῆ, 592 ἀναιδοῦς, 596 ἀδάμαντος, 598 ἀπάλαμνον, εὐτρεπῆ, 602 ἄκρατος, θεοστυγεῖ, 610 ξενοδαιτυμόνος, 611 φωσφόρους, 616 ἄσπετον, 621 φιλοκισσοφόρον, 631 διάπυρος, 642 σύμμαχοι, 647 αὐτόματον, 658 ξενοδαίτης, 666 μηλονόμος, 680 ἐπήλυγα, 689 παγκάκιστε, 693 ἀνοσίου.

Total: 90 in 709 lines, i.e. 130 per 1000 lines

ARISTOPHANES

Ach. 1–400: 3 ψαμμακοσιογάργαρα, 40 μεσημβρινοί, 47, 53 ἀθάνατος, 74 ἄκρατον, 79 καταπύγονας, 83 πανσελήνωι, 88 τριπλάσιον, 95 ναύφαρκτον, 104 χαυνόπρωκτε, 105 κακοδαίμων, 119 θερμόβουλον, 142 φιλαθήναιος, 163 σωσίπολις, 181 ἀτεράμονες, Μαραθωνομάχαι, σφενδάμνινοι, 188 πεντέτεις,

193 τριακοντούτιδες, ἐπίκωπος, 242, 260 κανηφόρος, 252 τριακοντούτιδας, 254 θυμβροφάγον, 264 ξύγκωμε, νυκτοπεριπλάνητε, 265 παιδεραστά, 288 ἀναίσχυντος, 315 ταξικάρδιον, 390 σκοτοδασυπυκνότριχα, 400 τρισμακάριε
  (ca. three -φόρος nouns or adjectives?: 216 σπονδοφόρος, 242, 260 κανηφόρος)
  Total: 29 (32?) in 400 lines, i.e. ca. 75 per 1000 lines

Nu. 1–200: 2 ἀπέραντον, 44 ἀκόρητος, 76 ὑπερφυᾶ, 103 ἀνυποδήτους, 104 κακοδαίμων, 115 ἀδικώτερα, 116 ἄδικον, 125 ἄνιππον, 129 ἐπιλήσμων, 135 ἀμαθής, 166 τρισμακάριος.
  Total: 11 in 200 lines, i.e. 55 per 1000 lines

  Total for Aristophanes: 40 in 600 lines, i.e. ca. 66 per 1000 lines

CHAPTER 4

Satyr Play and Tragedy, Face to Face (and East to West?)

The Pronomos Vase

For all that this is the most important, most informative, and most discussed of all vase-paintings having to do with the performance of Athenian drama, the Pronomos Vase continues to be the object of more questions than answers. Whom, and what, does it depict? What is it for? Why was it painted? For whom was it originally intended, and for what occasion/place/function? What did it mean?

It is agreed that the vase was painted in Athens, ca. 400 BCE.[1] The fact that the names of the chorus members, musicians, and playwright inscribed on it seem likewise to be Athenian has encouraged many scholars to think that the vase was intended, maybe commissioned, to commemorate an actual, particular performance at an Athenian dramatic competition, or else that it is a reproduction of a celebratory monument (*pinax*) actually erected in Athens for such a commemorative purpose—presumably a victory monument, perhaps in honor of the aulete Pronomos.[2] Yet the vase was found in a tomb in Ruvo, in a region that (unlike the cities of Tarantum or Metapontum) was not even Greek-speaking, and where the local population, however theater-loving, can hardly have known which plays had been recently performed in Athens' Theater of Dionysos, nor cared which individual Athenian citizens performed in the chorus there.[3] A majority of scholars have therefore concluded that the vase must have reached Italy via the second-hand market, some time after it lost its immediate, topical appeal in Athens. Others have insisted, however, in light of the strong (and ever-growing) evidence of Metapontine and Tarentine (and also Sicilian and Paestan) interest in Athenian theater from ca. 400 BCE onwards—evidence that seems to establish beyond reasonable doubt the live performance of both Athenian tragedy |[48] (perhaps in

---

[1] Beazley *ARV*² 1336, 1. See Burn (2010), with further references. For helpful comments and criticisms of earlier drafts of this chapter, I am very grateful to David Jacobson, Leslie Kurke, and Andrew Stewart, as well as to the editors of Taplin and Wyles (2010).

[2] So e.g. *DFA*², Bieber (1961), Csapo and Slater (1995), and Csapo (2010).

[3] On the significance of the find-spot and the geopolitics of Taranto and the Metapontum region in the late fifth and early fourth centuries, see Buschor (1932), Carpenter (2005), Burn (2010).

"Satyr Play and Tragedy, Face to Face," *The Pronomos Vase and its Context*, eds. O. Taplin and R. Wyles (Oxford 2010) 47–63. © 2010 Oliver Taplin and Rosie Wyles. By permission of Oxford University Press. www.oup.com

modified form) and Old Comedy in those regions[4]—and in light of the many other early fourth-century theater-influenced vases that have been excavated from tombs in these regions (a high proportion of them produced not in Athens but in Italian and Sicilian workshops)—in light of all this we should not ignore the possibility, even likelihood, that the Pronomos Vase was indeed originally intended for precisely this audience and this market—that is to say, it was painted in Athens, but for a south Italian clientele.

Obviously it makes quite a big difference to the interpretation and meaning of the vase, whether we see it, on the one hand, as an essentially Athenian product, reflective of local interests and performance activities—perhaps even of a particular victory in the City Dionysia (as the choreuts' names, the garlands, and the choregic tripods painted below the handles seem to suggest), or, on the other, as a funerary monument destined from the outset to sit inside or next to an Italian tomb, perhaps with a view to facilitating a better afterlife for the deceased, in a context far removed from the Athenian Theater of Dionysos and among people who might never have actually seen or heard Pronomos pipe.[5] On balance, I am myself inclined towards the second hypothesis: that is to say, I agree with those who have argued that the scene(s) on the Vase, even if it is based on an actual celebratory *pinax*, represents not any one particular Athenian production, but an idealized synthesis of typical Dionysian moments and elements of Attic tragic-satyric performance, as conceived by or for a south Italian audience.[6]

In this chapter, I discuss the relationship between satyr play and *tragôidia* as represented on and by this Vase, and the overall effect and significance, or signification, that the vase conveys through the choice and arrangement of its figures— *all* of its figures, front and back, top and bottom. For even though, until recently, most of the studies of the iconography of the Pronomos Vase have focused almost exclusively on the identity and costuming of just those figures who are definitely concerned with performing a play (i.e., the actors, choreuts, musicians, and writer),[7] it is obvious even to a casual viewer that the painter is very much concerned

---

[4]Dearden (1999), Allan (2001); also Taplin (2007). See too Giuliani (2001), who suggests that Athenian tragedies—unlike comedies—were read as texts but not performed in Italy during the early fourth century. [For discussion of theater-construction in the west, especially Sicily, see Marconi (2012): large wooden theaters were apparently being constructed by the mid-fifth century, if not earlier; stone theaters began to take their place during the fourth century.]

[5]See e.g. Carpenter (2005), Giuliani (1995).

[6]So e.g. Junker (2003), and Junker, Osborne (2010). As for the Athenian-looking names, I discuss them briefly below (n. 44). Solving the riddle of origins of the Vase and its painter's intentions is not the chief purpose in this chapter. And even if the vase was in fact originally produced for Athenian consumption, some south Italian importer must at some point have thought these images appropriate to their new context (funerary? sympotic? perhaps even both at once, given the nature of Apulian banquets for the dead?). So we need to think about this set of meanings too, even if they were only secondary.

[7]These, and only these, are of course the figures who are conveniently captured in Furtwängler and

in the work as a whole to show how Dionysian celebration, both inside and outside |[49] the Theater, combines multifarious components and techniques so as to provide a unified—collective and individual—psycho-social effect. That is to say, every figure on this Vase is significant, even as we must also acknowledge that no viewer can ever look at all of them simultaneously: each viewer at any moment can only see part of the Vase and some of the figures. Only in retrospect, or conceptually (perhaps with the guidance of an expert interpreter, e.g. at a symposium or funeral feast?) can the totality of this scene, or montage of scenes, be adequately assessed.[8]

But before I try to "read" the Vase along these lines, four basic principles that underlie my reading need to be articulated. None of these principles is entirely novel; but none is universally agreed, either. So it is as well to lay them out explicitly from the outset.

(i) Satyr plays are part of the tragedy competition. Throughout the fifth century, when a playwright and choregos, together with their assigned team of actors, compete successfully at the City Dionysia, they win with a tetralogy of plays. So, for example, the "Didaskalic" inscriptions (*IG* ii² 2319–2323) have no separate listing of satyr plays, and the manuscripts' *hypotheses* routinely list all four plays (as e.g. for Aischylos' *Oresteia*, Theban saga, and *Danaids-Suppliants* sequence; likewise Euripides' *Medeia*).[9] Likewise the comprehensive lists of each tragedian's plays, eventually assembled and catalogued in Alexandria, and duly recorded in the author's *Life*, or appended to their Byzantine manuscripts, tend to mix the satyr dramas quite indiscriminately in with the tragedies. So tragedies and satyr plays were not thought of as separate repertoires—indeed, Euripides' *Alkestis*, performed fourth in its tetralogy, seems to have blurred the distinction between the two genres. And it has proved impossible to determine which of the many Sophoklean play fragments and play titles that we possess are tragic, which satyric: at least 30 of these plays ought (statistically) to be satyr plays, that is, one-quarter of the total of 120 titles preserved; but only a handful of them are definitely identified as such.[10] And not only the texts, but the production elements too show more similarity than difference, with the same two or three actors, same musician(s),

---

Reichhold's splendid facsimile reproduction, which forms the basis of most of the images reproduced in books and articles on Greek tragedy that refer to this Vase; see Fig. 5a and also Lissarrague (2010).

[8] Of course, to some degree the same problem exists even for interpreters of a performed drama, since there too the chronological evolution of the plot, scene by scene, renders all interpretation provisional and partial until the whole play is over—at which point there are no longer any performers actually present to be seen or heard. For this visual "problem," common to all vases with continuous decoration and/or two complementary scenes on different sides, see further Giuliani (1995), (2001), and Lissarrague (2010).

[9] Aischylos' *Oresteia* (*hypoth. Ag.* 21–3, cf. POxy 2178), Theban saga (POxy 2256 fr. 2), *Danaids-Suppliants* sequence (POxy 2256 fr. 3); Euripides' *Medeia* (*hypoth*). See *TrGF* 1 DID 1A, pp. 3–16, *DFA*² 104–9; also Hall (2010).

[10] See further Griffith (2006) [= Chapter 3], with further references and discussion.

and (as far as we know) same fifteen chorus-members performing all four plays.[11] So a representation of the performers of a successful |[50] set of plays must properly take into account their full range of costumes/identities/modalities in both genres.

This leads to our second basic principle:

(ii) Satyr plays are in any case very similar to—in many respects almost indistinguishable from—tragedies, especially in the costuming, behavior, and language of the main characters, who would of course be played by the same two or three lead actors as performed the speaking roles in the tragedies.[12] It is largely the chorus, plus the single figure of Papposilenos, that differentiate themselves markedly in looks, diction, music, and relationship to the action, and that give the genre its "playful" and less dignified reputation. If a modern reader opens up a passage of actor's rhesis or dialogue from a satyr play, s/he will often be unable to tell any difference between this and a piece of tragedy. The diction and the metrical behavior of the trimeters are more or less identical—far different from comedy.[13] And the actors' costumes are apparently identical too (to judge from the appearance of 4 and 9 on the Pronomos Vase). Even the choral satyrs' ithyphallic costumes are much less gross and ugly than those employed in Old Comedy (though modern productions, reconstructions, and discussions tend often to overdo the ithyphallism and comic elements, and thus turn the stage satyrs into grotesques and monsters, more similar to the cruder sixth-century black-figure representations of silenes).[14] To judge from the surviving fifth-century Attic red-figure representations of choreuts wearing satyr costumes, it seems that, in reality, stage satyrs were often rather "cute" and almost childlike, and their behavior and language in the surviving texts were experienced by the audience as being more appealing than repulsive; their energies, though disruptive and shameless, are harmless and often quite positive in their final outcome, and the audience's connection with them

---

[11] The numbers for the tragic chorus did not remain completely stable throughout the fifth century: we are told that they were originally twelve (Aischylos), later fifteen (Sophokles and Euripides). On the question, why there appear at first glance only to be eleven choreuts on the Pronomos Vase, and why only nine are named, see below (pp. 142–44). Bieber asserts that there were always only twelve chorus-members for satyr play; Seaford (1984) suggests that a different group performed as satyr-chorus from those in the preceding tragedies: but scarcely anybody has been persuaded by either suggestion. It is much more likely that either the artist does not feel compelled to be exactly accurate, or else—in my opinion, the most convincing explanation—we should include the scene on the reverse of the Vase, which contains another three satyrs, now in mythological rather than dramatic guise (12, 27, 31). This brings the number up to fourteen; and then perhaps Papposilenus is the fifteenth. (On the notorious problem, whether Papposilenos is to be regarded as the chorus-leader, or as a separate actor, see Seaford (1984), KPS (1999), 24–5, and below, n. 36.)

[12] See KPS (1999), 12–40, Seaford (1984), 26–48, Griffith (2002) [= Chapter 1].

[13] KPS (1999), 16–17, Kaimio (2001), Griffith (2006) [= Chapter 3].

[14] For further discussion of these issues, see Hedreen (1992), KPS (1999), 53–73, Voelke (2001), Kaimio (2001), Griffith (2002) [= Chapter 1], (2005) [= Chapter 2].

could be quite close and sympathetic.¹⁵ |[51]

(iii) Because every tragic performance (at least at the City Dionysia in Athens, during the fifth century) routinely ends with a satyr play, it would presumably be customary for a tragic troupe of performers to be seen, or imagined, as celebrating its victorious achievement with the chorus still dressed as half-naked, phallic satyrs—even as the main actors and aulete would retain their same ornate, long-sleeved "look" throughout all four plays.¹⁶ As both Jack Winkler and Edith Hall have pointed out, the immature-yet-hyper-masculine self-presentation of this standardized choral group in the fourth play thus also begins the process of reintegrating the citizen choreuts into the Athenian male body politic following their explorations of more varied (female, foreign, aged, or déclassé) identities in the tragic plays that have preceded. "Ithyphallic males behaving badly…" are a familiar sight for Athenian audiences, inside (and possibly outside) the theater, and this satyr chorus, for all its incongruity (if judged by normal, sober, adult, civic standards), presents quite a uniform and almost standardized group identity to the Athenian viewers. It might be said, indeed, that this *is* who "we (all)" are (or become) in the final stages of Dionysian celebration.¹⁷ A choregic monument, or a celebration of "musical" (auletic, choral, histrionic) accomplishment in the *tragôidia* competition of fifth-century Athens, should be expected to recognize the satyric component if it is to be fully inclusive—just as in Plato's *Symposium* the victorious young tragedian Agathon hosts a celebration that is itself more satyr play than *tragôidia*, focused as it is on honoring and enacting Eros, and dominated as it turns out to be by the snub-nosed, playful Sokrates and the shamelessly comastic and romantic Alkibiades (as well as by the benevolently daimonic spirit of the absent-but-present, erotically inspired Diotima).¹⁸

(iv) The fourth basic principle underpinning my reading of the Vase concerns the nature of the thematic relationship between tragedy and satyr drama. I do not belong to the populous school of criticism that sees satyr plays as constantly "subverting," "critiquing," or "parodying" tragedy in general, nor individual tragedies in particular. Too much critical attention, I think, has been directed at seeking in satyr plays possible echoes, allusions, and inversions of the (rather few) tragedies that we happen to possess.¹⁹ Granted that even many extant *tragedies* allude (at some level or another) to other tragedies, or to generic norms and conventions

---

¹⁵See further Kaimio (2001), Griffith (2002) [= Chapter 1], esp. Figs 6, 7, 8b; also (2005) [= Chapter 2]; from a different angle emphasizing male adolescent aggression, see too Hall (1998) and (2006).
¹⁶See Taplin (2010).
¹⁷Winkler (1990), Hall (2006); see too Easterling (1997b), Voelke (2001), Foley (2003).
¹⁸I shall return to this notion of satyr drama as a kind of "playful" and erotic tragedy below, in relation to the various female figures shown interacting with Dionysos on the Vase (i.e. those numbered 6, 8, 15; also 7 and 13).
¹⁹Thus for example Euripides' *Cyclops* is often read as a parody of *Hekabe*, or even of Sophokles' *Philoktetes*. For sensible reservations about this general approach, see KPS (1999), 36–7.

that govern audience expectation,[20] I see no good grounds for |[52] imputing to satyr drama a distinctive, constitutional tendency towards parody comparable to that of Aristophanic Old Comedy, nor a merely parasitic dependency on its more hefty, serious cousin/sister—as if satyr drama were nothing more than light relief, anti-tragedy, or burlesque tragedy, rather than a dramatic form with its own distinct and positive appeal. Instead, I propose that we should regard satyr plays and tragedies as coexisting side by side, face to face (or back to back), presenting alternative realities or parallel universes, within a single tetralogy played to the same audience in the same performance space in an uninterrupted sequence.[21]

Proceeding, then, from these four basic principles, I suggest that the Pronomos Vase should be viewed as a celebration of tragic-satyric drama as a unit, all at once: the poet, musicians, and chorus are represented in their final and (in a sense) most characteristic garb. We might even say that, if drama is a Dionysian ritual, this scene represents the "final stage" of those *teletai*.[22] And when my chapter-title proclaims that satyr play and tragedy are here "face to face," I do not mean to imply that satyr play is necessarily "confronting" (commenting on, challenging, or subverting) its more serious sister/cousin/colleague. Rather, the two forms are "playing together" with the satyr drama extending tragedy's range of action, and collaborating in the art of leading (transporting) the hearts and minds of the spectators into fantastic places and processes (*psychagôgia*), in accordance with the expectations of a theater festival designed to honor Dionysos and the Dionysian.

The well-known expression of Demetrios that "satyr play is tragedy at play" (*tragôidian paizousan*) is usually quoted in isolation.[23] But the larger context of

---

[20]This process is already well developed in the very oldest tragedy that we possess: for Aischylos' *Persians* in its first two lines directly adapts or parodies the opening of Phrynichos' *Phoinissai*. The *Oresteia* too is heavily indebted to (or intertextually engaged with) Stesichoros. It seems too that another (maybe dramatic) predecessor inspired the Dokimasia Painter to imagine his famous diptych of the deaths of Agamemnon and Aigisthos on the Boston calyx-krater (Boston 63. 1246, ARV^2 1652)—unless perhaps it was the vase painters who sometimes inspired the tragedians?

[21]See further Griffith (2002) [= Chapter 1], with particular discussion of the satyric *Proteus* as a component of the *Oresteia*. On all these scores, the contrast with Japanese theater is instructive: there, the texts, actors, and visual components of Nôh vs. Kyogen drama are all radically different, even though the Kyogen scenes are often played in alternation with Nôh dramas, and the two respective acting companies may sometimes collaborate. Kyogen actors may take minor (low-class) roles in the Nôh dramas, where their language and acting style are distinctly marked as coarser than those of the elite characters (*shite*, *waki*). But never in Kyogen plays do upper-class characters show up, masked and speaking and singing the high poetry of Nôh, as heroic characters in Greek satyr drama speak tragic diction and wear tragic costume. [See further p. 17 n. 7 and p. 29 n. 47 above.]

[22]And there is surely no need at all—despite Peter Wilson's (2000) anxieties, and Carpenter's (2005) too, with reference, e.g., to DFA^2 363—even to consider the possibility that the performers on the Vase constitute a dithyrambic group rather than a dramatic one.

[23]*De Int.* 169. Demetrios seems probably to belong to the third century BCE, and thus is writing quite a bit later than the heyday of Athenian tragic tetralogies. Nonetheless he seems to be a fairly orthodox Peripatetic; and he surely had much better access than we to satyr drama texts from the fifth

his remark is instructive. Demetrios is discussing the various sources of *charis* ("charm, grace, elegance, engagingness") in literary style. He sees *charis* as a |[53] particularly vital ingredient of the "smooth, middle style" of composition (*glaphyros charactêr*, 127–30), a style which every author should be able to employ on the right occasion. The description of this ingredient (127–28) sounds remarkably like a recipe for satyr drama: "gardens of the nymphs, wedding-songs, people falling in love (*nymphaioi kêpoi, hymenaioi, erôtes*)." Yet we may also note that his favorite source of quotations from this stylistic register is "all of Sappho's poetic output" (*holê hê Sapphous poiêsis*).[24] It is in this context, of mixing or tempering the high style with the "playful" and mildly comic—as Demetrios says Sappho does (163–69)—that the remark about *tragôidia paizousa* is made. We may be reminded of such passages as the end of Gorgias' *Defence of Helen*, where he remarks that the whole mini-speech has been a "piece of playfulness (*paignia*); or the ending of Longos' pastoral love-story of *Daphnis and Chloe* (4.40: again, *paignia*).[25] So Demetrios—whatever his date and whatever his knowledge of satyr plays of his own era or of the more or less distant past—seems to be thinking of satyr plays as an especially "charming" and "playful" kind of *tragôidia*, not as a wholly separate art-form.[26]

In light of this intimate association of the two forms of drama, we may recognize the two representations of the romantic, divine-heroic couple, Dionysos and Ariadne on the Pronomos-Vase (5 and 6, 14 and 15) as being eminently suitable, indeed integral, to the overall tragic occasion, as conceived by a typical Athenian (and/or south Italian) theater audience. For tragic tetralogies quite frequently—indeed, perhaps more often than not—did end with boy and girl (hero and princess, or god and nymph) getting married, in a celebration of social bonds reinforced, marital bliss reaffirmed, and plenty of satyric aulos-music.[27]

With these basic principles stated, how should we set about interpreting the Pronomos Vase and its detailed, yet fantasized, depiction of the interface between tragic and satyric performance? Leaving aside the question whether the scene (or pair of scenes) depicted on the Vase is meant to illustrate one actual, historical

---

century.

[24]*De Int.* 128; cf. too 163. One might have expected Theokritos, or from a later period, Longos; but no Peripatetic or Peripatetic-influenced critics ever seem to cite pastoral or the prose romances as any kind of literary model.

[25]Whichever we read as the preceding (penultimate) word—*poimenôn*? or *paidiôn*—either would do well for satyrs, who are both "rustics" and "children," or even "slaves."

[26]For further discussion and speculation concerning the connections between pastoral, "romance," and Athenian satyr drama, see further Griffith (2006) [= Chapter 3] and (2008) [= Chapter 5].

[27]KPS (1999), 28–32, Griffith (2006) [= Chapter 3]. Sophokles, the most successful of all fifth-century Athenian tragedians, was renowned as an inveterate playboy-*lover*, and also as a brilliantly beautiful performer in his youth, both as lyre-player and as naked dancer—not unlike our Pronomos Painter's "Demetrios" (19) and "Charinos" (22), or even Dionysos himself (5, 14). There is good reason to believe that most of Sophokles' love-scenes came in his satyr plays: see Griffith (2006) [= Chapter 3].

troupe of tragic-satyric performers—chorus plus actors, author, and |[54] musicians—at the moment just before or just after their victorious presentation of a particular sequence of plays,[28] or whether it comprises instead, as I am more inclined to believe, a more generalized representation of the cultural phenomenon *choros + tragôidoi + instrumentalists* (i.e., an idealized, typical tragic-satyric theater-making ensemble), let us begin instead by trying to read the Pronomos Vase in purely "formalistic" terms. What does the composition—the arrangement of figures in relation to one another and to the viewer—signify to that viewer (us) concerning the dynamics, values, and effects—the meaning—of Dionysian theatrical performance?

The main focus of the vase-painting on both sides is Dionysos + Ariadne with their attendants (or perhaps we should call them "accompanists"). Both the scenes represent the celebration of love and marriage—in theatrical terms, a "happy ending." On the reverse (scene B), the couple are surrounded by dancing satyrs and maenads: Dionysos (14) carries a tortoise-shell lyre (though he doesn't play it); one satyr (16) is vigorously blowing the auloi; a live panther is posed at the front (29), and two of the satyrs (27, 31) are, as is their wont, dancing with, and/or assaulting, two of the maenads (28, 30), who seem quite unfazed. Attendant on the bridal pair is a male winged figure (13), presumably Eros/Himeros (Desire). This is, then, in its own terms a "mythological" scene, not a theatrical one. But the presence of the lyre and auloi, and of the elements of dance, and the fact that this scene "bleeds" so easily into the activities of the groups depicted under the handles and on the Side A,[29] encourage the viewer to treat the whole vase as one composition—especially as both the main scenes focus on the same happy romantic couple.[30] Our interpretation of the Vase must take full account of the prominence and centrality of this reiterated bridal couple—divine and human, in motion and in repose, and of the ways in which the mythological scene is simultaneously separated from, and

---

[28] An objection to this notion, as e.g. Csapo (2010) notes, is the fact that we have no *chorêgos* depicted—the single most important member of the production team, to judge from all other available evidence (esp. Wilson 2000 *passim*). See, however, Wilson (2010) on Charinos as *chorêgos*. I shall return to this point at the end.

[29] See Lissarrague, Calame (2010). See *DFA*² 186–8 on the "bleeding" of masks and actors on the Pronomos Vase, whereby the actors and their characters seem to merge identities. The bleeding extends also across the boundary between the "wilderness" scene and the "urban-theater" scene, as is most strikingly exemplified by the drinking cup that dangles from the wild satyr's extended hand (12), splashing its contents onto the leg of the adjacent stage-satyr (11). See also Lissarrague (2010).

[30] It is notable that so many interpretations of the vase, and such a high proportion of references to it by theater historians, choose to ignore not only the reverse scene B, but even the whole Dionysos-Ariadne nexus—as if this loving pair were included by the painter merely out of obligation and some kind of conventional necessity. So, for example *DFA*² 186: "Dionysos and Ariadne... certainly divine and irrelevant to our purposes" (sc. of reconstructing the costumes of human actors in the Theater of Dionysos, and/or identifying the particular play that this troupe is rehearsing or reprising). For a valuable corrective, see Carpenter (2005) and Lissarrague (2010).

yet linked to, the |[55] theater-rehearsal scene, through the sequence of intervening figures, postures, and gestures of the various satyrs and satyr-choreuts.

That the two scenes are indeed separated and contrasted is obvious enough—and it is this fact that has led all too many critics to treat them in complete isolation from one another. For on Side B the "wild" satyr-group and bridal pair are entirely mythological and *au naturel*, apparently existing in the countryside, far from emblems of civilization. They have no furniture; plants are growing; two of the figures in the upper register there (12, 16) are not even given complete pairs of legs, as if rocks or hillocks obscure their lower extremities or they are hovering in the air, partly covered in mist; an animal (panther, 29) joins cheerfully in the thiasos; and both male and female celebrants are active together (dancing? sparring? "playing"?), as they often are in the imaginary maenad-satyr band that attends Dionysos on the mountain-side although probably not in actual ritual practice.[31] By contrast, in the scene on Side A, which takes place in an urban (*polis*) setting—perhaps imagined as a sanctuary of Dionysos—, we find a fairly naturalistic representation of a group of Athenian theater-makers *pretending* to be satyrs or mythological heroes, or rehearsing for such a staged pretense: all are complete (no missing legs) and they even have several pieces of furniture (an elaborate couch, a chair, a stone block, steps, columns and tripods)—and the panther has now been converted into a piece of costuming (worn by Papposilenos, 10)!

Several key elements (in addition to that panther-skin) do, however, recur in both scenes, connecting them together: not only "satyrs" and the pair of lovers, but also similar musical instruments (both strings and pipes) and a (non-realistic) winged figure symbolizing "Desire" (7, 13: about whom I shall have a little more to say below). In both scenes, too, the grouping of the figures presents similar patterns, as the happy couple presides over and is framed by (in theatrical terms, we might say, "spotlighted" within) a swirling group of dancers and musicians, with everyone energizing the bridal couple and at the same time drawing energy from them. At the fringes of the central scene of Side B, even as the two outer satyrs on the lower level (27, 31) are dancing inwards and directing the whole group's energy towards the loving couple, the two (slightly truncated) satyrs at the upper level (12, 16) are each reaching out and pointing more inclusively towards the other characters on Side A.[32] One of them (12) is offering his wine-cup in the direction of the human choreut to his left (11). The other (16) |[56] is energetically blowing his auloi to the right, in a posture strikingly parallel to that of Pronomos himself (21), though this satyr seems to be standing while Pronomos—unusually for an aulete—is sitting. The satyr appears to be blowing so hard and so loud that all those

---

[31]Recent scholars have mostly concluded that in real-life Dionysian rituals men and women were not usually found in the same celebratory groups and choruses: see Henrichs (1984); *contra* Dodds (1961), and see Seaford (1984), also Cole (2007).

[32]It is unfortunate, but telling, that these figures often are excluded from modern reproductions of the central scene and therefore ignored in discussions of the vase's meaning and purpose.

choreuts sitting and standing in that direction (1–3, 17–18) should surely hear his music-making. The musical spirit of the "wild" satyr(s) is thus shown circulating (again, "bleeding") into the midst of the mask-holding chorus that occupies the transitional area between the two focal scenes. This visual representation of the "circulation" of (musical) energy is a vital element in the Vase as a whole, and reminiscent in important ways of the dynamics of Dionysos' Theater, whether in Athens, or Syracuse, or anywhere.[33] For there too, the actors in center-stage (or, from the opposite perspective, the archon and Priest of Dionysos sitting on the center thrones in the auditorium's front row) are usually surrounded by choreuts and faced by a centrally located piper, while the sounds of the aulos and singers circulate round the theater, and the interfaces between actor and actor, and between actor and chorus, are all observed by the surrounding throng of spectators (*theatai*)—who in this respect resemble us, the viewers of the Vase.

With these preliminary ideas in mind about the relationship—and continuities—between the "wild" satyrs and the "theater" satyrs, let us turn at last to focus on Side A of the Vase. Particular attention should be paid to three formal features of the arrangement of the figures there, both "face to face" and "back to back": the direction of the satyr choreuts' gazes, antics, and gestures; the positions and postures of the two main actors (4, 9), standing between the different realms; and the prominence of the musical, choreographical, and textual elements in the central, spotlighted area(s)—showcasing the four stars of this tragic-satyric Dionysian performance (19, 20, 21, 22).

Starting at the upper level, all the satyr choreuts—and three of their masks—are looking inwards, towards Dionysos and Ariadne. Meanwhile, at the lower level, the choreuts are combined in more or less self-contained pairs (with one obvious exception, 20, who will be discussed separately), but with the main orientation again towards the center. Thus these stage satyrs are represented as mirroring and continuing the interactions of the mythological satyr-maenad group on the reverse Side B, but in a more restrained and deliberate manner, as they watch, chat, and perhaps wait to perform their singing and dancing roles, not (as yet) ecstatically possessed by the spirit of the music. But here on Side A, unlike the arrangement of Side B, the chorus members are also marked off |[57] distinctly, at both levels, from the central scene of divine repose above (5, 6, 7, 8) and of human poetic composition below (19, 21, 22), by the placement of those imposing, individual actor-figures (4, 9), elaborately dressed and dignified, whose gazes are directed the other way, outwards.[34] These imposing and "heroic" (i.e., tragic and

---

[33] Cf. Calame (2010). It is still, by the way, hotly disputed whether (and/or when) the Athenian Theater of Dionysos was rectangular (or roughly trapezoidal, as at Thorikos) or circular in the fifth century BCE (see, e.g., Bieber (1961), Csapo and Slater (1995)). The theaters in Akragas and Syracuse seem to have been circular. Even in a rectangular/trapezoidal orchestra choral movement can be said to "circulate," if only metaphorically.

[34] Further redirection of the flow of energy, away from the central figures, is provided by the

non-satyr-like) actor-figures thus form a kind of barrier between the other characters on the Vase (elite human, heroic, or divine) and the satyr-chorus.

What do I mean by a "barrier"? These two actors on the upper level (4, 9), wearing their ornate tragic costumes (as was normal, as far as we know, for the main characters in satyr drama also), seem to separate and segregate the semi-clad, youthful, satyr-ish choreuts from the reclining, privileged divine figures in the center (5, 6). The masks that these two actors are holding look straight out at the viewer, ignoring the figures around them; but the actors themselves are looking towards the satyrs, with their shoulders and backs turned towards the divine group. They are thus virtual "gate-keepers," guarding admission to that highest, divine level. The figure on the left (4)[35] gazes in parallel with the satyr mask of the choreut close to him (3), just as the actor playing Herakles on the right (9) gazes outwards the other way in parallel to Papposilenos' mask (10); and both these two mature, bearded actors stand considerably taller and look much more imposing than the unbearded choreuts who gaze towards them. In fact, none of the choreuts is really engaged, it seems, with either of these actors; the choreut-pairs are more self-absorbed and restricted in their gazes and interactions. Only the Papposilenos-actor (or *koryphaios*?)[36] is interacting with either of the actors (a point to which we shall return at the end). Access to the divine marriage-party thus proceeds through the heroic main characters; satyrs are relegated to the side, or lower down, to the ground-level register. Thus the relationship between these elite character-actors and satyr chorus, as portrayed on the Pronomos Vase, seems to mirror exactly the pattern of tragedy and—especially—of satyr drama itself as performed in the theater, a pattern in which both sets of persons—the heroic, iambic-speaking main characters and the satyric, singing-and-dancing chorus, each in their separate and unequal modes—combine to bring about the desired "happy ending," that is, an outcome that usually involves, for the human-divine elites, a marriage and/or social reintegration into the world of the polis (or at least of a properly ordered society), and, for the exuberant and apolitical, undomesticable satyrs, a return to |[58] their carefree, childish, and musical—yet sexually and maritally unfulfilled—"service to Dionysos" in the wild.[37]

But at the same time, as we contemplate Side A with its two-tiered central scene, even as we recognize the superior status and dignity of those bearded and costumed actors, we cannot mistake the fact that they are not the source nor main vehicle of the flow of energy, the spirit of divine play, that is shown transforming ordinary young (adolescent) men via choral performance into conveyors of Dio-

---

outward-facing satyr-masks held by those choreuts who stand closest to them (3, 23; even 10).

[35] Several scholars have suggested that this actor is playing Laomedon; but he might be just a generic king; see Osborne (2010).

[36] Debate over the status of Papposilenos in Athenian satyr drama continues to rage: is he an actor or leader of the Chorus? Or something in-between? See KPS (1999) 24–5; see below, pp. 143–44.

[37] Griffith (2002) [= Chapter 1], (2005) [= Chapter 2].

nysian bliss and spiritual elevation for themselves and for others too. This energy clearly comes, not from those costumed actors at the upper level (since they are standing still, calm, and inactive, at ease or perhaps somewhat "on guard"), but from the swirling poetic and musical activity of the inner group portrayed on the lower register (19, 20, 21, 22)—mirrored in certain respects, as we noted, by their "wild" equivalents (27, 28, 29, 30, 31) on Side B. It is they, it appears,—the dancing choreut, composer, and two musicians—who are the energized and energizing conduit of Dionysian spirit for all the other figures on the Vase. Of course it is the young piper who sits at the very center and commands the viewer's prime attention and recognition, and it is he whose name has traditionally been given to the Vase. And not only is he seated in the "spotlight," but he also wears an outfit of long-sleeved finery (as theatrical auletes actually did), in striking contrast to the nearly-nude figures on either side of him. Nonetheless, Pronomos the piper is in fact only one of four participants in the musical activity that fills center-stage, and I suggest that the visual arrangement of this entire foursome needs to be carefully assessed. Indeed, in tandem with the grouping of the figures immediately above it, this group might be said to comprise the key to the larger dynamic of the Vase as a whole.

As the viewer confronts Side A of the Pronomos Vase, looking square-on from the front, the two-tiered central cluster of figures (4, 5, 6, 7, 8, 9; 19, 20, 21, 22) is both sealed off to a large degree from the surrounding figures (since these mostly recede out of view by reason of the Vase's shape; and also, as we have noted, through the posture and gestures of the figures themselves, esp. 4 and 9), and at the same time tightly interconnected through the group's own internal arrangement. The cluster is flanked at the bottom level, left and right, by the young, nude poet-musicians: "Demetrios" (19) with his papyrus roll(s) and nearby lyre, and "Charinos" (22) with his silent-but-ready lyre and hand extended in encouragement of Pronomos (21).[38] To the left, Demetrios' head (19), together with his neglected lyre and the tragic mask held low by the actor above (4), combine to enclose the focal group on their right and establish their |[59] place in the spotlight ("center stage," as it were), while on the right Charinos' head (22) and dangling lyre on the right lead the eye up to the mask that the Herakles actor is holding (9), thus framing that central group symmetrically from the other side.

The two elite actor-characters (4, 9)—the "tragic" dignity of whose speaking roles even in satyr play seems rarely (to judge from the surviving texts) to be verbally or metrically/musically compromised[39]—comprise one vital component of

---

[38] Peter Wilson (2000) 353 n. 74, and again, more fully, Wilson (2010), has suggested that Charinos is the *choregôs*, "conducting" the aulete, and thus implicitly is in charge of the whole musical performance.

[39] This convention—that the main characters speak trimeters, and do not usually sing or dance—is symbolized here visually by the written text (papyrus roll, held by 19) and high-status lyres immediately below them (held by 22; also hanging next to 19), as well as by the actors' costuming, height, and erect

the tragic-satyric performance, a component that is echoed also in the youthful, heroically-nude, lyre-carrying figure of Dionysos on Side B (14). That is indeed one way (in Nietzschean terms, we might say the "Apollinian" way) to dramatize the heroic and the divine, and to earn a man's passage to marital and poetic bliss. But clearly the Dionysian energy of the auloi, and of choral song and dance, may achieve effects unattainable by the more restrained lyre(s) and the more pedestrian spoken/written word. Our gaze is thus led—as the painter evidently intends—to focus on the dancing satyr-choreut at the front center-left (20). He is the only person on the whole Vase actually wearing his mask (*prosôpon* on *prosôpon*, we might say, and thus "face-onto-face" in a different sense), rather than just looking at it or dangling it from his hand. And the result is that *he cannot keep still*. He jumps out of the frame towards the viewer/spectator, his feet extending below the decorative pattern at the base of the painting, even as his head extends into the upper register—and out of/into his very head sprouts the vine-shoot that also decorates the marriage-couch of Dionysos and Ariadne (5, 6). The combined inspirational power of wine, music, and *choreia* could not be more vividly represented. Dionysos' thyrsos likewise, to judge from its angle and direction, fuels this satyr-choreut's dance—as well as Pronomos' musical inspiration. The young man has been literally transformed, from a human choreut-with-mask into a Dionysos-possessed satyr, his gaze directed... where? (perhaps towards the "wilderness"-scene on the Side B, or even towards more distant spectators, somewhere behind us?), even as his *sikinnis* (dance)-gesturing hand acknowledges his interface with Pronomos' soulful pipe-blowing right next to him.[40]

We come now to the central figures that are "face-to-face" on the upper level of Side A (4, 5, 6, 7, 8, 9—and perhaps 10). The focus here is on Dionysos and |[60] Ariadne (5, 6), united in love and happiness, gazing blissfully into one another's faces as they recline on their couch; that much is obvious, and must inform any interpretation of the Vase as a whole. Much scholarly debate and disagreement, however, has revolved around the identity and function of the seated female figure to the right of them (8), attended by small winged "Himeros" (7). Who is she? A majority of scholars have seen this figure (8) as a member of the cast, that is, a young male actor dressed as a female character prominent in the Herakles-focused satyr play: so presumably Hesione, daughter of Laomedon (if this is the character played by the bearded actor to the top left, 4). The tiara has been thought to support this view; and scholars suppose that this (unbearded and especially youthful) actor has been allowed by the painter to "bleed" into his female role to

---

posture (no dancing or lounging for them!).

[40]Whether he is in fact dancing the *sikinnis*, or some other typical satyr-dance, cannot be determined for certain but it seems probable: see Seidensticker (2010). In any case, it is clear from the numerous other images of dancing satyrs employing this same hand-gesture that positive interaction, not rejection, is thus indicated.

the point that even without his mask he looks like a woman.[41] But there are serious objections to this view. Not only do we seem to have too many actors (if Papposilenos is an actor, rather than the Chorus-leader), but, more crucially perhaps, this female figure seems to belong much more closely with the divinities on the couch than with the actors (9, 10) standing behind her.[42] She completely ignores Herakles (9), and looks instead pointedly towards the amorous couple (5, 6).

Much more likely, then, this figure (8) is not an actor but a divinity, one who is so intimately connected to drama and the performance context that she is actually wearing a tragic actor's costume and holding a mask. Several scholars have therefore argued for a personification, such as *PAIDIA* ("play/entertainment") or *TRAGÔIDIA*, or even the spirit of *SATYR DRAMA*.[43] But all these suggestions, attractive and heuristically fruitful though they each may be, are in my view mistaken. The figure must, it seems to me, be Aphrodite. No other divinity is so automatically associated with "Himeros," or with a romantic scene like that taking place here between Dionysos and Ariadne (compare 13, 14, 15 on Side B). The reason why the figure is holding a mask and wearing theater costume must, in that case, be because Aphrodite (or Eros) exercises such a pervasive and determinative influence on the satyr dramas that conclude and finalize each tragic tetralogy. For when those tragic actors are joined in the fourth play by a chorus in satyr costumes, then the presiding deity of the concluding performance—in conjunction, of course, with Dionysos—will typically be the goddess of Desire herself.[44] |[61]

---

[41] See above, n. 29.

[42] This point is well brought out by Hall (2007) and (2010).

[43] Bieber (1961) argues pointedly, *contra* Buschor (1932), that "Satyr play," or "Play" in general, rather than "Tragedy" must be meant. As Edith Hall has recently pointed out, however, satyr drama does not really have a feminine noun-form that could be readily personified, as Comedy and Tragedy do; Hall (2007) with further references. Hall's arguments and supporting iconographical evidence (2007 and further 2010) in favor of "Tragedy" are more convincing: she points to comparable female figures, more clearly labeled as *"Tragôidia,"* who are behaving rather like Maenads and even in one case being assaulted by a satyr.

[44] See Griffith (2006) [= Chapter 3], (2008) [= Chapter 5]. In Syracuse during the third century BCE, there were "Artists of Laughing Aphrodite" (*hilaras Aphroditas technitai*), who seem to have been equivalent to "Artists of Dionysos" elsewhere (*Dionusou technitai*): Griffith (2008) [= Chapter 5]. With regard to the iconography of this figure on the Pronomos Vase, Andrew Stewart points out to me that she resembles the Aphrodite of the Meidian vases and of the later Praxitelean-Scopaic group at Megara.

At the conference in Oxford, I presented the very tentative suggestion that this figure might be understood as *CHARIS*. The close association between her and Himeros (7) might support this, since Himeros in literary and visual sources is in general rather closely identified with *charis* or *charites* and with scenes of poetic composition and performance (e.g., Hesiod's proem to the *Theogony*, 62–5). I noted too the presence nearby of "CHARINOS" (22), together with nine named dancers (as it were, an Athenianized, male set of "Muses," cf. *Theog.* 75–7). But I have come now to accept that we should not expect to see one single Charis sitting or reclining by herself; the Charites usually operate as a trio or group. I reiterate that she (8) should in the first place be regarded as Aphrodite.

The final face-to-face confrontations that we need to consider are those between Herakles (9) and Papposilenos (10), and between the other tragic actor (4) and the chorus-line (1, 2, 3). And at this point I need to return to the questions with which I began—that is, the questions that are provoked by a depiction of an Athenian theater scene that was painted in Athens but brought to south Italy, and that should perhaps (therefore) be interpreted as meaning something special for/in its eventual—presumably funerary—context. I offer a few observations and tentative suggestions.

First, we may acknowledge that the presence of Herakles is not only common enough in satyr plays in general, but also highly appropriate to scenes of romantic union and celebration such as we have been discussing. Even if Greek Herakles is not always especially musical (less so than the Roman Hercules, it seems), he is certainly a notoriously successful lover and victor. Here on our Vase, in addition to the conventional indication of heroic strength, upstandingness, and restraint conveyed by the figure (9) in his tragic Herakles costume (and the other actor too (4), to a slightly lesser degree)—as contrasted with the younger, more lightweight and "musical" satyr-choreuts in general—we also observe the interesting, direct confrontation of the imposing hero-actor (9) with the shaggy Papposilenos-actor (10).[45] Is there anything in particular that should be read into this confrontation?

Of course Herakles is always at home in the contexts of both satyr play and tragedy; perhaps no other hero can boast quite this same interchangeability. Satyr plays constantly pit the rascally and shameless Papposilenos against him and/or other noble characters in dialogue and in action.[46] So the portrait here may be simply generic—a (typical) "stage tragic-satyric moment." But it is worth bearing in mind too that Herakles, of all mythological heroes, is the one par excellence who can conquer, or mitigate, Death. In the prosatyric *Alkestis* it is he who brings Admetos' lost wife back from the dead; in Aristophanes' *Frogs* it is to him that Dionysos turns for help and whom he uses intermittently as a model in attempting to bring his favorite poet back to Athens from Hades. |[62] And of course in mythological tradition, Herakles himself succeeded ultimately in conquering Death and becoming immortal. This would make him a particularly suitable presence in a funerary context, if that was the purpose of this Vase. Possibly too this figure of Papposilenos (10)—a sober-looking, quite dignified actor holding his grotesque mask up for both himself and Herakles to contemplate—may carry some of the associations of "the wise Silenus" of mythological (and Nietzschean) tradition, and of Platonic-Socratic invention (in the *Symposium*). This figure's appearance (his exterior mask, his fleecy costume) may be gross and in some respects subhuman; but "underneath" these he possesses secret knowledge that can be of supreme val-

---

[45] It is not too important for my purposes whether this figure is an "actor" or "chorus-leader"; see above, n. 36. If he is an actor, then 25 is presumably the chorus-leader.

[46] See KPS (1999), 28–34.

ue.⁴⁷ It is true that, like Sisyphos in the so-called Kritias fragment, Papposilenos in satyr drama often tries to behave like a hero and fails, or seeks to get away with heroic aspirations for which he is completely unsuited and incapable: the satyr plays thus reinforce the distance between those manly heroic main characters (heroes, gods) and the slavish- or childish-incompetent others (satyrs). Accordingly, Papposilenos does not wear the dignified actors' costume; and for this reason too, doubtless, this figure does not stand so close as they to the divine couple on their couch. But he might be a reminder, nonetheless, that a satyr may have a kind of divine blessing, an animalistic yet daimonic passport to impunity and eternal life.

Certainly the satyr chorus in Athenian drama, fuelled and propelled by their aulete (sometimes by the string-player too), has the capacity to bring about miracles even without being physically or morally capable of performing noble, heroic, or courageous action of their own. A delightful scene from Euripides' *Cyclops* exemplifies this well (642–53). Here, even as one by one the satyrs ignominiously chicken out of their pact to assist Odysseus in manipulating the hot stick to put out Polyphemos' eye, they insist—correctly—that they can sing and dance in such a way that miracles will happen: the stick will be charmed by their incantation into putting out his eye of its own accord (*automaton*). This power of theirs comes from (consists of) song and dance, as they marshal the musical and magical strains of Orpheus himself (646 *epôiden Orpheôs*). And as the painter of our Vase has likewise shown, this musical, transformative power (whether Apollinian-Orphic or Dionysian-satyric) lies at the heart of the Greek theatrical experience. Perhaps it is a source of comfort for the afterlife as well?

Whether or not Athenian tragedies and satyr plays actually traveled to Tarentum or Metapontum to be presented in theaters during the late fifth century,⁴⁸ this Pronomos Vase scene certainly does not require that its viewers had seen |[63] any particular tragic and/or satyric performance. On the contrary, it proclaims its general and specific message very clearly, in the form of a moment just "outside" an actual performance (whether before or after, may not be relevant). Tragedy and satyr play are both present, face to face and in dialogue with one another. The heroic actors stand, speak, and gaze with dignity and distance, as befits the noble, upstanding individuals that they are, verging on the blissful, divine/mythical world symbolized by the marriage scene between them. The satyr choreuts—junior, smaller—are just chatting, casually; their Dionysian contributions are for the most part still latent or potential. Between the two groups (actors, choreuts), the relationship is close—yet reserved. Each of these two main actors is linked with circular/vertical flow from Charinos-lyrist and Demetrios-author, respec-

---

⁴⁷ On these aspects of wise Silenus, see now Sorabella (2007).

⁴⁸ See n. 4 above. Dearden (1999) suggests that plays, or parts of plays, were indeed performed there, though maybe whole choruses did not travel from Athens, only actors. See too Allan (2001), and also now Taplin (2007).

tively (framed by the two lyres), even as they are also performing their significant iconographic role of "facing"—and politely restraining?—the satyr chorus that surrounds them. But it seems to be Pronomos and the immortalizing power of Dionysos that the Vase is primarily celebrating.

The one participant who actually hears and responds directly to Pronomos' Dionysian music is the one who has seized the performative spotlight (20), and his transformation, as we saw, is a model for the response of all. The musical-erotic "charm" (*charis*) and "desire" (*himeros*) of the occasion jump out at us, the viewers, even as this dancing satyr looks at his author, Demetrios (19)[49] and gestures towards his musical accompanist-inspiration, Pronomos (21), the twin sources of his—and our—tragic-satyric rapture and (perhaps) salvation.

---

[49] Perhaps the playwright's name, "DEMETRIOS" (otherwise unknown, though of course a common name, as Osborne (2010) observes), is chosen here as being appropriate to an initiatory group honoring the Earth-Mother, who is a close associate in many Attic and south Italian ritual contexts with Dionysos.

CHAPTER 5

Greek Middlebrow Drama (Something to Do with Aphrodite?)

1. INTRODUCTION: TRAGEDY AND COMEDY (JUST THESE TWO?)

As Aristotle remarks early in the *Poetics* (4.1449a15), tragedy found "its own true nature" in the plays of Sophocles and Euripides, i.e., in Athens during the mid-fifth century BCE. He insists too that there has always been a sharp and inescapable distinction between tragedy and comedy, between "good, serious, high" subjects and objects of representation and "bad, shameful, low" ones (σπουδαῖοι vs. φαῦλοι, αἰσχροί: *Poet.* 2.1448a1-18, etc.). This distinction is rooted in the conviction that some people and actions just are lower-class and worse while others are higher-class and better;[1] and it can be traced back to the formal and ethical discrepancies that Greek critics noted between epic on the one hand, and iambus on the other (e.g., *Poet.* 4.1448b34-49a6). Likewise the reactions provoked in audiences and readers were supposed to be distinctly different: "pity and fear," "tears and sympathy" in the one case, "laughter" and "mockery" in the other; and they were not supposed to be mixed.[2] All Greek and Latin literary genres, indeed, like those of most of Renaissance Europe during its various classicizing phases, were based on this assumption of distinction between "high" and "low," and the different levels of seriousness expected of each.[3]

Nowhere was this distinction more consistently maintained, it is usually argued, than in the theater. Oliver Taplin has shown how closely and |[60] symbiotically Athenian tragedy and Old Comedy complemented and played off one an-

---

[1] On these notions in Aristotle, as well as the difficulties of reconstructing his general views on comedy, see Lucas (1968), ad locc., Halliwell (1986), 158–62, 266–76. [See further on this, and for further discussion of much of the material discussed in this chapter of mine, Shaw 2014.]

[2] As Cicero puts it: *Et in tragoedia comicum vitiosum est et in comoedia turpe tragicum* (*De opt. gen. orat.* 1). See below, pp. 162–63, on Demetrius and "playful tragedy."

[3] See e.g. Guthke (1966), 3–22, Hirst (1984), 7–17. For "tragicomedy," *kômôidotragôidia*, and *hilarotragôidia*, see p. 164 and n. 63 below.

"Greek Middlebrow Drama (Something to Do with Aphrodite?)," *Performance, Iconography, Reception: Studies in Honour of Oliver Taplin*, eds. M. Revermann and P. Wilson (Oxford 2008) 59–87. © 2008 Oxford University Press. By permission of Oxford University Press. www.oup.com

other throughout the fifth century, and how distinctively each of these two genres was received and appreciated in subsequent centuries.⁴ But it is worth pausing to consider just how arbitrary—and in some respects how inadequate—Aristotle's binary distinction really is, as an account of Greek drama and of the "natural" propensities of theatrical performance, whether ancient or modern, western or eastern. For while it is self-evidently true that the competitions in drama at the City Dionysia and other festivals were regularly divided into these two distinct categories, *tragôidia* and *kômôidia*, it is also apparent (as we shall see) that each of these categories was both quite capacious and also subject to changing definitions and conventions. Whatever the Athenian performance categories (and Aristotle) might suggest, there really were not just two types or "natures" of drama in existence during these centuries: the variety of formal and thematic possibilities seems to have been much greater, even if no separate labels for most of them were assigned.⁵

Tragôidia as such (we are told) was invented in Athens by Thespis ca. 535 BCE, under the regime of the Pisistratids (or else perhaps ca. 510 BCE to celebrate the new Cleisthenic democracy).⁶ It was thus a form of drama specifically designed to be a component of a particular festival and a specific social-political scene. Likewise "Old" *kômôidiai* first came into existence (at least, were first institutionalized) in Athens during the 480s for this same festival—and in some sense to complement the *tragôidiai*. But both of these dramatic forms, with their rather elaborate rules and conventions, had been preceded by other performance-modes, some of which apparently continued to offer alternative possibilities for the wider world of dramatic and literary production, from the Classical and Hellenistic eras into Roman and Byzantine times.

The best known of these "alternatives" of course is satyr play, a major dramatic form in its own right that was closely associated in Athens with tragedy, yet was quite distinct in its conventions and mood from either tragedy or comedy. Satyr drama flourished in Athens throughout the fifth and fourth century; but it had existed elsewhere before its introduction into Athens, and satyr plays continued to be popular in many parts of the Greek world for several centuries longer.⁷ Yet notoriously satyr drama is almost |[61] completely ignored by Aristotle,⁸ as it

---

⁴Taplin (1993); also (1983) and (1986), including reference to the end of Plato's *Symposium*. From a very different angle, see too Silk (2000), 42–97 (ch. 2 "Comedy and tragedy").

⁵For analysis of the wide range of plot types and levels of seriousness found within Athenian tragedy, even while the decorum of "high style" is consistently maintained, see Mastronarde (2000), to which this essay of mine is much indebted; also n. 63 below.

⁶For the latter theory, see Connor (1989).

⁷See below, pp. 159–65.

⁸Aristotle mentions satyr drama only briefly, in connection with the origins of tragedy (*Poet.* 4.1449a20); see pp. 159–61 below and Cozzoli (2003) 268–69. For modern discussion of satyr drama, see esp. Seaford (1984), KPS (1999), Kaimio et al. (2001), Voelke (2001), Griffith (2002) [= Chapter 1], Cozzoli (2003). Taplin (1986) reminds us of the existence of this third, "middle" form between tragedy

was until recently by most modern scholars of the ancient theater, so much more comfortable have they been with a simple binary opposition of "high" vs. "low," "serious" vs. "comic," with occasional focus on (mainly Euripidean) experiments with "tragicomedy" or "melodrama" or "drama of mixed reversal" or "ironic tragedy," as if these were a late and, as it were, slightly decadent development out of a purer and more naive original tradition.[9] But I think that a good case can be made that, even among the more "serious" (non-"comic") plays that were conventionally labeled "tragedies," quite a variety of mythologically- and historically-based plays existed (what I shall generally be calling "romantic dramas"), some of which may not have resembled at all closely the surviving plays of Aeschylus, Sophocles, or even Euripides. Likewise, "comedy" was hardly a single, uniform category of drama either. The comic performance traditions of (e.g.) Syracuse, Megara, and Tarentum all appear to have produced dramas that were significantly different from those of Athens (which itself was famous for at least two, and perhaps three, quite different kinds of *kômôidia*);[10] and several of these comic traditions apparently continued to be influential throughout the Greek world for centuries.

If, then, we remove from our eyes the critical blinkers (or Aristotelian bifocals) that have conditioned us to think that (i) tragedy and comedy exist naturally and essentially as the two basic, proper, and best forms of drama (even of "world view"), while other dramatic subforms function only as parodies, offshoots, degenerations, etc. of the two "original" masterforms, and (ii) that "drama" as such was really invented in Athens during the fifth century BCE, then we may come to appreciate better what a wide range of dramatic enactments and choral impersonations could be found all over Greece. Along with this modification in outlook may come a recognition that the proper audience response to theater was (is) not necessarily supposed to be EITHER "pity and fear" (for high, serious tragedy) OR "laughter and mockery" (for low, |[62] gross comedy, or burlesque).[11] Oth-

---

and comedy, though this is not emphasized in his *synkrisis*. Horace (*Art of Poetry*) and Demetrius (*On Style*), however, along with several other ancient critics, see satyr drama as a third genre of almost equal prominence; see 161–63 below.

[9]Many twentieth-century critics have focused on Euripides as a pioneer of a new kind of tragedy or "tragicomedy": e.g. Burnett (1971), Knox (1979), 250–74, Seidensticker (1982), Foley (1985), Gibert (2000).

[10]In the case of Athenian "Old, Middle, and New" Comedy, there is vigorous recent debate about the validity of thus separately and sequentially categorizing them. Many of the elements traditionally described as belonging to "Middle" Comedy are found already in several plays of the "Old" (fifth-century) period: see Csapo (2000), Nesselrath (2000), Sidwell (2000).

[11]For the sake of completeness, I should also specify another possibility: "tragicomedy," i.e. a subgenre combining tragic and comic elements in such a way as to produce a peculiar and distinctive mixture of these two sets of reactions. Tragicomedy has intermittently attracted intensive interest and discussion, but is not really my topic in this chapter. For good discussion of the term in relation to Euripides' plays, see Seidensticker (1982), Mastronarde (2000), 29–30, 35–36. The earliest occurrence of the term (*tragicomoedia*) is found in the Prologue to Plautus' *Amphitryo* (tongue-in-cheek, from

er responses and feelings may be legitimate too, such as local or patriotic pride, wonder, comfort, erotic desire, religious awe, and joy—to say nothing of pleasantly and confusingly "mixed feelings" too. That is to say, maintaining the sharp dichotomy and separation of "high" tragedy from "low" comedy, while it may sometimes be critically helpful as a way to think about different types of theatrical and aesthetic effects (and while it may have produced an interesting symbiosis of its own, especially through the works of Aristotle and his Renaissance followers)—just as it was a necessary practical mechanism by which the Athenians could organize their festival competitions—is often hopelessly reductive and constricting. As a pair these two "types" do not begin to exhaust, or even exemplify in any adequate way, the possibilities of dramatic experience; and certainly they do not do justice to the chronological, generic, and geographical variety of the ancient Greek theatrical traditions.

We might speculate for a moment. What if the Athenians had not instituted those two distinct festival competitions when and as they did? Perhaps the simplistic critical binary of high vs. low, tragedy vs. comedy, might never have taken over. Or if Athenian culture and *paideia* (abetted by the Artists of Dionysus) had not become so Panhellenically dominant from the late fifth century onward, perhaps Plato's and Aristotle's definitions and categories might not have prevailed so completely with posterity.[12] As we look around at other theater traditions worldwide, we can immediately observe that they |[63] have not generally divided their plays neatly into "high" and "low" forms; or if they have, they have allowed a wider range of subjects and emotions (especially romantic love) into their "high" forms than we normally assign to Greek tragedy. But the familiar model (and surviving manuscript texts) of the great Athenian tragic triumvirate and their great comic opposite numbers (Aristophanes and Menander) is hard to escape: they have for so long been the dominant paradigm. So I should like in this essay to take

---

Mercury), though fifth- and fourth-century plays by Alcaeus and Anaxandrides were apparently referred to as (entitled?) *komôidotragôidia* (see LSJ s.v., and *PCG* 2, pp. 9–10). On Giambattista Guarini's *Compendio della poesia Tragicomica* (1601) and the 17th century Italian and French fascination with (self-styled) tragicomedies, see e.g. Zardini Lana (1991); and in general Guthke (1966), Hirst (1984), Foster (2004). In the modern era, it is said: "Tragicomedy has established itself in the twentieth century as the dominant dramatic form" Hirst (1984), xi; or even, "The tragicomic is the basic pattern of human experience.... Controversial in the Renaissance, tragicomedy has in modern times replaced tragedy itself [sic] as the most serious and moving of all dramatic kinds": Foster (2004), 9, 10. But in the present essay, I am concerned with "middlebrow" or "romantic" drama, not with tragicomedy—nor with *hilarotragôidia*, a form of tragic burlesque supposedly invented by Rhinthon of Syracuse; see below, pp. 163–64.

[12] Another way of putting this: did the ubiquitous symbolic pair of theater masks, one tragic, one comic, along with the parallel opposition of the "laughing" philosopher (Democritus) vs. the "crying" philosopher (Heraclitus), come into existence as a result specifically of the dominance of Athenian theater culture and its attendant iconography? For discussion of a threefold division of dramatic types and scenes, see below, p. 163 (on the Boscoreale wall paintings).

a look at some of the other dimensions and constituents of the history of Greek drama—especially that nebulous area between tragedy and comedy that I am calling "middlebrow" drama.

2. NON-ATHENIAN PREDECESSORS (AND SUCCESSORS) TO ATHENIAN TRAGEDY AND COMEDY

While Homer (of course) was always to be regarded as the true origin of both tragedy and comedy, there were two quite different ways in which this derivation could be traced. Either (as Aristotle suggests) the *Iliad* and *Odyssey* represented the high, serious forerunners of tragedy, while the mock-heroic *Margites* set the tone for the lower, grosser forms that culminated in dramatic comedy;[13] or, on a different trajectory, the *Iliad* could be viewed as essentially "tragic," while the *Odyssey*, with its romance elements and—especially—its happy ending, could be seen as anticipating Euripides, New Comedy, and even the prose novel.[14] To add to the confusion, Aristotle's account of the post-Homeric development of tragic *mimêsis* posits at least two additional "beginnings" for Athenian *tragôidia*: one "from those leading off the dithyramb" (*Poet.* 4.1449a10) and another "from the satyric" (4.1449a20). Likewise in the case of *kômôidia* he acknowledges that Dorian accounts of its origins are at variance with Attic ones, while he also refers to the quite |[64] separate (and very early) contributions of the Sicilians Epicharmus and Phormis (4.1448a29-48b3, cf. 5.1449b5-7).

Nor is Aristotle alone in such muddle-headedness or over-schematization (combining too many theoretical and historical "origins"). Across the board, references in the ancient Greek tradition to "tragic choruses," "tragedies," and "tragedians" show up frequently in contexts that seem to have little to do with the Athenian-derived art-form that we are familiar with. It is small wonder that *tragoudô, tragoúdi* evolved in due course into the standard Modern Greek words for "sing" and "song"—while the term *drama* was often used as early as Late Antique and Byzantine times to refer to a verse or prose novel that had nothing to do with

---

[13] *Poet.* 4.1448b30; see Lucas (1968), ad loc.; also Cooper (1947), Janko (1984).

[14] On the *Iliad* as "tragedy," see e.g. Rutherford (1982); on the *Odyssey* as "comedy," see e.g. Longinus 9.15, where it is especially the elements of characterization and subheroic behavior (*êthikôs biologoumena*) that are noted; and on ancient and Byzantine scholiastic discussions of comic elements in the surviving tragedies, sometimes with reference to the *Odyssey*, and occasionally with confusing reference also to satyr drama, see Meijering (1987), 212–19. See too Richards (1900a). The plays that are described in the scholia as being "rather comic" (*kômikôteron*) or as containing inappropriately comic scenes or characters are Eur. *Andromache, Hecuba* (!), *Alcestis*, and *Orestes*, along with Soph. *Electra* (!—for its chariot race, recognition scene, and happy(?) ending). Ioannis Tzetzes was particularly interested in the problems of such mixing of genres.

Dionysus or theatrical performance at all.[15]

Several of the early poets who are described in the ancient sources as being "tragedians" have little or nothing to do with Athens.[16] In Bruno Snell's compilation of fragments from the "minor tragedians" (i.e. all the known writers of tragedies from Greek antiquity except the big three), fourteen of the first twenty-two listed (covering the period ca. 535–430 BCE) are definitely Athenians. Eight of these fourteen belong to the three great families: Aeschylus (5) and his two sons Euphorion (12) and Euaion (13); Sophocles (10) and his son Iophon (22); Euripides and his father and son, all named Euripides (16, 17, 18). Two more are the famous father-son pair Phrynichus (3) and Polyphrasmon (7).[17] The other four tragic poets of this early era whose names have survived and who certainly, or probably, were Athenian-born, are Thespis (1); Choerilus (2); Mesatus (11); and Carcinus (21).[18] Two more are of completely unknown origin: Euetes (6) and -ippus (8 = ?Nothippus?). From other cities we find: Pratinas (4) and his son Aristias (9) from Phleious; Aristarchus (14) from Tegea; Neophron (15) from Sicyon; Ion (19) of Chios; Achaeus (20) of Eretria—and maybe Carcinus (21), if he is from Acragas as |[65] the *Suda* states: a total of six or seven, most of them quite famous. But this is not the whole picture. Among the listings in *TrGF* vol. 1, mostly tucked away near the end, are several additional early poets and culture figures who were cited by one or more ancient authorities as being "tragedians," but whom Snell himself (like most modern historians of tragedy) regarded as not legitimately belonging in that category—hence listed as *poetae falsi vel maxime dubii*. The list is impressive and interesting: it includes Arion of Methymna/Corinth (227), who, mythical or fantastic though his status is (hardly more so, however, than Thespis), must loom large in any hypothetical history of dithyramb and tragedy; and we find also such names as Epigenes of Sicyon (239), Minos/Minon (247) and Auleas (231) of Crete, Simonides of Ceos (263), Pindar of Thebes (260), and Empedocles of

---

[15] For *tragoúdi*, see Sifakis (1967), 122 with further references. For the evolving use of the term *drama*, see Richards (1900b); and for application of this term to Byzantine novels (many of which in the 11th and 12th century were written in verse), see H. Gärtner art. "Roman" *Kleiner Pauly* (1972), 1451, Marini (1991), Beaton (2003), Roilos (2005), 38–39, 105, 199, with further references. The novel was variously referred to in the classical era as *logos, muthos, apologos, ainos, diêgêma, diêgêsis, historia, drama, plasma*. For self-reference within the Greek novels to their own "theatricality," see Walden (1894), Ruiz-Montero (2003), 35–36; also below.

[16] In what follows, I shall largely be following the references collected in Snell (1971): each tragedian's assigned *TrGF* number will be given in parentheses. For discussion of pre-tragic, proto-tragic, and early tragic poets, and remarks on the non-Athenian origins of several of them, see esp. Lesky (1983), Herington (1985).

[17] On the tendency for tragic playwrighting (like most forms of expertise) to run in families, see Sutton (1987), Easterling (1997c), 216, Scodel (2001). In the fourth century one of the most successful tragedians was Astydamas, another descendant of Aeschylus.

[18] The *Suda* states that Carcinus was from Acragas (see below); but most modern scholars regard him as Athenian.

Acragas (50).[19]

In each of these cases, it may readily be conceded that the poet in question probably never composed a drama which fifth-century Athenians, or Aristotle in the fourth century, if they ever saw or read it, would call a true *tragôidia*. An Athenian archon might not "grant a chorus" to any of them. On the other hand, it is quite likely that several of them did at one time or another compose and direct performances on mythical or historical/topical subjects at a festival or the court of a prominent elite, in a mode that involved a chorus and a "leader" (ἐξάρχων or χοραγός), and perhaps also an "actor/answerer/interpreter" (ὑποκριτής), whether or not any kind of mimetic acting out of scenes, dialogues, and actions took place. Surely none of these poems/dramas (what should we label such performances?) involved the requisite combination of regular alternations of spoken and sung passages, a costumed *aulêtês*, masks, entrances and exits, etc., that would qualify them as (true) *tragôidiai*. Perhaps we might call them "choral dramatic lyric" or "mimetic lyric"—but such terms did not exist in the Greek classificatory system: only "dithyramb," "tragedy," and "comedy."[20] To later authorities, however, such texts or performances apparently resembled "tragedy," at least in some broad sense, closely enough to be so classified.

Other "tragic poets" from outside Athens existed whose names are not recorded at all. We may wonder, for example, who were the authors of the "tragic choruses" that were being performed annually in Sicyon during the early sixth century (Hdt. 5. 67–68), first in honor of Adrastus and later |[66] for Dionysus. Epigenes of Sicyon is said by the *Suda* (s.v. Thespis) to have been "the first tragic poet" (*TrGF* 1. 1 [Thespis] T 1. 2–3; cf. T 18); but no verses of his survive and he is relegated by Snell to the obscurity of the *dubii* (239). The fragmentary remains of Stesichorus (e.g., *Geryoneis* frs. S7-87, or *Thebaid* fr. 222A, both containing vigorous dialogue, pathos, and violent action)[21] or Bacchylides' "dithyramb" about Theseus (18), with its alternating stanzas from chorus and solo character voice, may give us an idea of the possibilities of such a lyric medium. On a different front, what kinds of contemporary performance should we imagine that the Homeric bards and their audiences envisaged when they described (in hexameters) Demodocus singing the amusing, erotic—and by no means low-comic—story of Ares and Aphrodite, to the accompaniment of dancing boys and girls (*Od.* 8)? By fifth-century Athenian standards, none of these performances came close to providing the requisite com-

---

[19]Distinguished non-Athenian tragic poets from later eras include Theodectes of Phaleris, Callimachus of Cyrene (234), Aratus of Soli and Apollonius of Rhodes (224), along with others of the Pleiad tragedians.

[20]I will return below to further discussion of satyr play: but in any case there is no likelihood at all that any of the above-mentioned "dubious or false tragedians" were composing Athenian-style satyr dramas.

[21]See too pp. 166–67 below, for Stesichorus' poem about Daphnis (fr. 279 Campbell) as a possible precursor of both satyr drama and Theocritean pastoral.

bination of spoken actors' lines and sung choral interludes—so these too were, by definition, not *tragôidiai*. But some of them at least would fit quite comfortably into most modern definitions of "drama" (better than, e.g., several of the plays of Samuel Beckett or many medieval Mystery Plays).

The standard account of the "history" or "development" of Greek tragedy, based partly on Aristotle's *Poetics*, partly on the surviving texts of the three great tragedians, and partly on didascalic evidence concerning dates and conditions of performance—but also conditioned, perhaps, by modern assumptions about the organic rise, flowering, and decadence of artistic movements—describes the following sequence: first, several non-dramatic antecedents (choruses, narratives, improvisations); then Thespis ("small" plots, just one actor?); next Phrynichus (heavily choral? not much action, dialogue, or individual acting); and so to Aeschylus (introducer of the second actor; architect of the connected trilogy; "creator of tragedy" and father of Western drama); Sophocles then refines and perfects the form; Euripides begins to experiment with it (mixing forms—tragicomedy, romantic tragedy, tragedy substituting for satyr play; etc.),[22] and thus we enter the decadent period that persists throughout the rest of antiquity, until the glorious recuperation of true tragedy in the Elizabethan Age. It is this history of supposed evolution from original *naiveté* and simplicity into mature complexity and (over-ripe?) mixing of genres that has also led many modern scholars to conclude that Pratinas' celebrated lyrics (*TrGF* 1 4 F 3 = *PMG* |[67] 708), apparently sung by a satyr chorus dissatisfied with recent musical innovations, must have been composed, not by the famous early fifth-century satyr play expert Pratinas, but by someone else of the same name influenced by the New Music of Timotheus and Philoxenus.[23]

But even the Athenian tragedians during the fifth century could vary their style of drama considerably. Not all of their plays fit Aristotle's idea of what a tragedy should ideally be. Apart from Phrynichus' famous historical plays (*Capture of Miletus, Phoenician Women*) and Aeschylus' *Persians*,[24] we know of Aeschylus' *Aetna*, designed to celebrate the founding by Hieron of a new Sicilian city and—unlike standard Athenian plays performed in the Theater of Dionysus—involving several changes of scene.[25] Back in Athens, later in the fifth century, Agathon composed

---

[22] See above for references; but Mastronarde (2000) is rightly more circumspect about the "generic" fluidity of Greek tragedy.

[23] For recent discussion, see Zimmermann (1986), Csapo (2004), 213–14 (both favoring a late fifth-century date and a non-dramatic dithyrambic context), D'Alessio (2005) arguing for a satyr play (and presumably the original Pratinas as its author). For discussion of the Hellenistic revival of interest in Pratinas and the *lêma Pratineion* ("spirit of Pratinas"), see Nicolucci (2003), Fantuzzi (2007).

[24] On which see now Taplin (2006), suggesting that Aeschylus produced this play as part of a widespread burst of post-war celebratory performances that were being generated both in Athens and elsewhere. On the Gyges-tragedy (which most scholars now attribute to a post-fifth-century date), see below.

[25] *TrGF* 3 (ed. S. Radt) F 6–11 (pp. 126–30); also *Life of Aeschylus* 9.

at least one tragedy (*Antheus*) on a made-up subject with non-mythical names of characters;[26] and Chaeremon's *Centaur* was apparently composed in an unusual style of "mixed" meters.[27] Intriguing too is Philoxenus of Cytherea's *Cyclops or Galateia* (*PMG* 819 = *TrGF* 1 257 T): both its title and the surviving fragment are suggestive of satyr drama or pastoral romance. Philoxenus (late fifth century-early fourth century) was mainly known as a dithyrambic poet and expert in the New Music; but this |[68] was apparently a drama, not a dithyramb, and scholia to Aristophanes' *Wealth* describe him as a τραγικός and τραγῳδοδιδάσκαλος.[28]

Euripides, while visiting the royal court in Macedonia, produced a drama in honor of King Archelaus (*TrGF* 5 (13) F 228–64); and the biographical tradition reports that he and the king had some disagreement as to whether such a play, with a happy ending, should be called a "tragedy." (Euripides was determined that there should be a happy ending, in order to "please"—χαριζόμενος—his host.) Whatever the local and personal relevance of this play at the time, it was certainly reperformed in later centuries and locations.[29] In the mid-fourth century, Theodectes' play *Mausolus* was performed as part of the funeral commemoration for that great man (*TrGF* 1 72 T6, 7). Like Mausolus himself, Theodectes was a Lycian (from Phaselis), but he had become a successful tragedian and rhetorician in fourth-century Athens (admired by Aristotle, among others). Unfortunately, we know little about the play, other than that it was described both as a *tragoedia* and a *laus* ("encomium"), which was defeated by Theopompus' prose eulogy in a

---

[26] Ar. *Poet.* 9.1451b21 = *TrGF* 1. 39 F 2a. Aristotle remarks that this play "delights" (*euphrainei*) its audiences as much as any myth-based tragedy; see the next n.

[27] *TrGF* 1 71 F 9a-11. Aristotle describes this as a "mixed *rhapsôidia* made up from all kinds of meters" (*Poet.* 1.1447b21-23, 24.1460a2-3); but Athenaeus (13. 608E) calls it a "polymetric drama," and the *Suda* likewise lists it as a drama. For a full recent discussion and attempt at reconstruction of the play's contents, see Morelli (2003). Mixed-media dramas of this kind were said in antiquity (sometimes with disapproval) to contain especially "sweet, pleasurable" qualities, and they often seem also to involve pastoral themes. (Actually, the *Suda* states that Chaeremon was a "comic playwright" (*TrGF* 1 71 T 1): this may simply be a mistake, since the titles of the plays that are listed there (eight, including *Centaur*) all sound tragic or satyric. It is worth noting, however, that several other "tragedians" too are occasionally listed as comic poets, e.g. Aristias: maybe it was not always obvious what was a "comedy" and what was not? The term "comedy," like "tragedy," could be quite elastic, cf. Richards (1900a) and n. 11 above.) A didascalic inscription referring to a victorious actor, especially remarkable for his boxing skills, seems to suggest a more tragic mode for Chaeremon's dramas, however: "At Dodona, in Euripides' *Archelaus* and Chaeremon's *Achilles*" (*TrGF* DID B 1.12–13 = *IG* V 2, 118, ca. 275–220 BCE = Csapo and Slater # 163). See further Collard (1970), Morelli (2003).

[28] Schol. Ar. *Plutus* 290, and *Suda* s.v. (see Snell's Testimonia ad loc.); on Philoxenus, see too Csapo (2004), etc. We should recall that several breakthrough musical inventions were attributed by the Greeks to rustic contexts: e.g. the lyre (staged, e.g., in Sophocles' satyric *Trackers*), the syrinx, and the first reeds for the auloi. Satyric and pastoral themes seem in general to have been especially conducive to (new) musical experiments. [See further now Griffith 2013b.]

[29] See Kannicht *TrGF* 5 (13) iia = Diomedes, *Ars gramm.* 3, 9, 3; also Kovacs (1994) *Letters of Eur.* 5, and Hanink (2007). For the reperformance, see e.g., Csapo and Slater (1995), 200 # 163, Kannicht ad loc.

prize competition.³⁰ Theodectes' *Mausolus* must presumably have been one of the models for the Italian/Roman *fabula praetexta*, i.e. plays based on recent events and the careers of prominent local dignitaries: examples (mostly lost) are Naevius' *Clastidium*, celebrating the victory of Marcellus in 222 BCE, Ennius' *Ambracia* (ca. 189 BCE), and Pacuvius' *Paulus*, celebrating the battle of Pydna of 168 BCE; also, of course, from a later era we have ps.-Seneca's remarkable *Octavia*. There was nothing quite like this performed in Athens during the heyday of tragedy in the fifth century (though Phrynichus' *Phoenissae* and Aeschylus' *Persians* are in some respects comparable); but such historical-eulogistic plays appear nonetheless to have been a well-known component of the Greco-Roman tradition(s) of "tragic drama" in its broader configurations. |[69]

In the Hellenistic and Roman eras, the range of performance venues and styles expanded still further, even while simultaneously the normative effects of Athenian cultural dominance (including the Artists of Dionysus as performers, and the schoolrooms as Panhellenic purveyors of Attic "literature" and style) continued to maintain a strong habit of binary thinking concerning tragedy vs. comedy. This is not the place to attempt a thorough survey of all the later types of play composed during these eras, nor of all the different venues and conditions to suit which the "old" tragedies and comedies must often have been adapted when they were revived or recited by individuals or groups of actors. But a short sketch may be helpful, as a reminder that the competitions in tragedy and comedy at the Theater of Dionysus in fifth-century Athens represented just one of many places, and two of many occasions, at which "drama" was experienced in ancient Greece.³¹

Two of the longest samples of post-fifth-century Greek tragedy that survive are the so-called *Gyges drama* (*TrGF* 2 *Adespota* F 664) and Ezekiel's *Exagôgê* (*Exodus*). The former consists of some fifty lines of iambic trimeters (sixteen of them almost perfectly preserved), composed in correct and rather stylish tragic idiom and presenting a sequence of scenes that involve the wife of Candaules and Gyges.³² It thus covers the same famous episode that is narrated in Book One of Herodotus' *Histories,* though with important differences. Modern literary/cultural critics tend to fall into two camps when discussing Herodotus. Some empha-

---

³⁰Aulus Gellius says that there was a *"certamen laudibus eius dicundis..."* at which Theopompus (another former student of Isocrates) defeated Theodectes and other rivals; and he goes on to state: *exstat nunc quoque Theodecti tragoedia quae inscribitur Mausolus...* (10.18.5). Some scholars have interpreted his testimony to mean that Theodectes competed with a prose eulogy and only later composed this tragedy. In either case, the existence of a tragedy on the subject of the recently deceased king is not in question.

³¹In what follows, I am following for the most part the excellent discussions and presentation of evidence in Sifakis (1967), Jones (1991), Taplin (1993), Csapo and Slater (1995), Easterling (1997).

³²The papyrus (*POxy.* 2382) was first published in 1949. The play has been variously assigned to a wide range of dates, from the early fifth century (e.g., E. Lobel, D. L. Page, B. Snell) to the mid-Hellenistic era (e.g. K. Latte, A. Lesky, and most others); see Kannicht-Snell ad loc. On the dramatic technique and relation to Herodotus, see esp. Travis (2000), Porter (forthcoming).

size his "tragic" world-view (tyrants crashing to ruin, divine warnings, a moral purpose comparable to that of Sophocles and Aeschylus, etc.); others see him as a "comic," off-beat precursor of the novel (travel, exotic locations, adventures, miracles, sex, and incongruous mixtures of solemn and crudely down-to-earth behaviors): both currents seem to flow simultaneously, side by side and intermingled in his text.[33] The Gyges story, which may be based on a folk tale, clearly did not originated with Herodotus; it seems to have been already in the Greek world—as it became again in the Renaissance—common property to many narrators (and illustrators), representing several different genres. The trajectory of the |[70] story fits squarely into what we should call "romance," rather than tragedy, involving as it does sexual desire, deception, (re)marriage, even (in some versions) a ring of invisibility and return from the land of the dead. The link here between "drama" (theatrical tragedy) and "drama" (the novel) seems particularly close.[34]

As for Ezekiel's *Exagôgê* (*TrGF* 1. 128), these are by far the longest segments of post-fifth-century tragedy to have survived to us in quotation—almost 300 lines, in about a dozen separate but largely continuous passages.[35] This drama on the story of Moses and the Exodus does not contain much dialogue in the surviving quotations, as mostly individual characters are narrating what they have seen or heard, or God is enunciating instructions; but we do have short passages of verbal interaction between Sepphora and ?Moses (60–65), between Sepphora and her suitor Choum (or Chous) (66–67), between Raguel and Moses (83–89), and between God and Moses (112–31). No lyrics are included in the quotations, and it is unclear whether or not there was a chorus in the play: but the numerous changes in both temporal and geographical setting during the course of the play make it likely that there was not.[36]

Certainly it was a drama containing much "romance" material: exotic locations and descriptions, a courtship rivalry and marriage, a divinely sent dream and epiphany/voice, a miraculous rescue. There is nothing that is "tragic" in the Aristotelian or modern sense—no unity of action, no *peripeteia*, no *anagnôrisis*, little discernable interest in *êthos* or even *pathos* (apart from wonder and awe): no catastrophe for the main character. Clearly this is not a comedy, however, and the play's diction, meter, and tone stay generally close to those of classical tragedy and

[33] For a tragic Herodotus, see e.g. Stahl (1968), Chiasson (2003); for a comic or folkloric *histôr*, see Porter (forthcoming) with further references. For "mixed" interpretation, see e.g. Dewald (1987), Pelling (2006).

[34] On the Gyges theme in ancient and modern literature and art, see esp. van Zyl Smit (1998); Laird (2001); also Porter (forthcoming). On the first publication of the Gyges papyrus, one scholar even argued that it came, not from a tragedy, but from a novel: Cantarella (1952).

[35] The author is identified by Eusebius (presumably following his source, Alexander Polyhistor) as "Ezekiêlos in his tragedy..."; some of the lines are also quoted by Clement of Alexandria as coming from "Ezekiêlos, the composer of the Jewish tragedies, in the drama that is entitled *Exagôgê*..." See esp. Holladay (1983), Jacobson (1983), Gruen (2002), 124–25.

[36] Jacobson (1983), 31–33; cf. Sifakis (1967), 122–24, Taplin (1976).

satyr drama. Whether the play was intended to be performed, recited, or read, we should surely regard it as a "romance drama," akin in some respects to the (prose) *Alexander Romance* and *Life of Apollonius of Tyre*, and predecessor in turn to some of those Byzantine medieval verse narratives that we call "novels" but they themselves termed "dramas"—as well as the tragic-pastiche *Christus Patiens* and *Christus Gaudens*.[37]

In the case of plays that were originally composed for performance at Athens in the Theater of Dionysus during the sixth or fifth century BCE and |[71] subsequently reperformed (as "old tragedies") elsewhere, it is impossible to know how similar the musical and choreographical elements can have been to those of their first production. But it seems highly unlikely that (e.g.) the melodies and dance steps of Aeschylus or Pratinas were preserved into the fourth century—or that anyone would even have wished to perform or watch/listen to such songs had they been preserved.[38] The evidence from the Hellenistic era is scanty, but sufficient to show that sometimes quite small choruses (six or seven members, even three) might be employed in addition to one or more Artists of Dionysus (and sometimes a specified aulete too). In some contexts tragedies seem to have been performed with no chorus at all; but in others it appears that large and well-rewarded choruses were integral to the production.[39] The existence of a raised stage would obviously make a difference; and so would the availability (or not) of suitably skilled dancer-singers to work with the professional actors, with or without a designated *chorodidaskalos* to train them.

Standard accounts of the evolution of tragedy from the fourth century into the Hellenistic era and beyond[40] mention the rise of the actors, the practice of excerpting and adapting fifth-century originals (already "classics"), and the proliferation of venues for performance.

> Once actors had their own individual repertoires and did not have to rely on the poets chosen for a particular dramatic festival... there was plenty of scope for change and development.... By the time of Caligula... there is no doubt that "performing a tragedy" typically meant solo performance either by a singer (*cantor*) or by a danc-

[37] See above, pp. 154–55, and below, pp. 166–67. On Byzantine romances, see Beaton (2003), Roilos (2005), 67–68.

[38] The evidence of Aristophanes' *Frogs* suggests that Aeschylus' music and choreography were already regarded as quaint by then. The major, ongoing innovations in melodies, vocal techniques, and aulos-capabilities known as the New Music became quite mainstream by the fourth century, with the result that most earlier forms of musical performance probably became obsolete: see Barker (1986), West (1990), Csapo (2004). In any case, techniques for preserving melodies or choreography through textual annotation were still very primitive.

[39] Sifakis (1967), Csapo and Slater (1995), #165A, 165B; etc.; cf. too Stefanis (1988), Wilson (2000), Le Guen (2001), Aneziri (2001) for the activities of *chorēgoi* and Artists of Dionysus around the Mediterranean world.

[40] See esp. Sifakis (1967), Stefanis (1988), Easterling (1997), Dearden (1999), Revermann (1999–2000), Allan (2001), Easterling and Hall (2002), Martina (2003)[, Liapis and Petrides (forthcoming)].

er (*saltator, pantomimus*).... Once the performance of the pantomime could be described as "tragedy," a crucial artistic move had been made, since this was an essentially balletic and musical performance.... The common elements between this and traditional tragic drama might be no more than the mythological story and perhaps some features of verbal style.[41] |[72]

But spoken dialogue (e.g., Electra's grief over the urn containing her brother's supposed ashes, or Orestes' madness) and sensational visual effects produced by theater machinery were also much appreciated, and no less intimately associated with the notion of what "drama" and "theater" were all about. Thus one of Plutarch's convivial aesthetes remarks in passing (*Quaest. Conv.* 4.2.665E):

> It is time, as in a comedy (*kathaper en kômôidiai*), to hoist the stage-machinery (*mêchanas*) and introduce some thunderclaps (*brontas*)....

What kind of "comedy," in the strict sense, this might be is hard to imagine: New Comedy does not generally include thunderbolts or other sensational stage effects. Perhaps the term is used loosely for other kinds of drama in general (like the Comédie Française)?[42]

Not all of these departures from "traditional tragedy" were new, of course—indeed, the impulse to replicate Athenian practice through the organization of the Artists and their deployment of Athenian-style conventions in festivals elsewhere may in some respects have imposed greater uniformity of theatrical performance style and expectation than had previously existed. (That is to say, "traditional tragic drama" may have become "traditional" only in the late fifth century.) Long before the Hellenistic era, there had been other theaters outside Athens. Some dated back even to the sixth century—and some may even have been bigger and better than the Theater of Dionysus in Athens.[43] Performers from Sicyon and Phleious,

---

[41] Easterling (1997), 220–21, referring to Suetonius *Caligula* 57 and providing further references, including Jones (1991). Plutarch (*Quaest. Conv.* 9. 15.748) offers corroboration of Easterling's last sentence: "Dance (ὄρχησις) has suffered especially from bad public taste (κακομουσίας) ... and now rules over the stunned and mindless theaters (ἐμπλήκτων [or ἐμπληκτικῶν, MSS] καὶ ἀνοήτων κρατεῖ θεάτρων)." But elsewhere in the same dialogue (7.8.711E-712E), theatrical performances of rather different kinds are discussed in terms of their suitability for dinner parties: "Tragedy is not at all appropriate, as it is too solemn and elevated..." (711E); more acceptable is solo dancing such as the "Bathylleion... that presents a dance interpretation (ὑπόρχημα) of a Pan or Satyr revelling with Eros (σὺν Ἔρωτι κωμάζοντος)." Less desirable, because hard to stage, (δυσχορήγητον) are the "mimes they call *hypotheses*" (712E), which are clearly non-comic—though also quite untragic—dramatic performances that combine story, elaborate visual effects, and some kind of verbal enactment: middlebrow indeed.

[42] See Richards (1902a).

[43] On Syracuse (perhaps the first circular, rather than rectangular, theater of all) and its theatrical traditions, see Moretti (1993), Aneziri (2001), with further references on Artists of Dionysus and musical contests there and elsewhere; [also now Marconi (2012)]. Other large theaters existed from an early date e.g. at Argos and Acragas. Unfortunately we know nothing about the performance space(s) at Sicyon or Phleious; but see Nicolucci (2003), 327–28 on Sicyon's artistic traditions, and ibid. 336–39

or Syracuse and Acragas, might thus have had more, not less, to work with than their Athenian counterparts in the early fifth century. Certainly, Athenian music had small claim to distinction or originality: all the best modes and melodies (and probably dance steps too) were apparently imported, whether from other parts of Greece or from Anatolia and Thrace, to judge from the terms used to |[73] describe them by contemporary and near-contemporary music critics and from internal references within the surviving lyrics of tragedy and satyr drama themselves.[44]

3. SATYR DRAMA (AND ITS "CHARMS")—SEPARATE AND IN BETWEEN

Of course, by far our best-attested and most critically discussed form of "middle-brow" dramatic entertainment, neither tragedy nor comedy—though distinctly closer to tragedy in most of its elements—was satyr play.[45] This too was not an Athenian invention. Pratinas of Phleious (a town close to Sicyon and to Corinth) first introduced satyr dramas to Athens around 500 BCE, whereupon they were quickly instituted as an integral part of the annual festival. Pratinas himself was credited with thirty-two satyr dramas out of a total of fifty plays in all (yet only one Athenian victory in the tragedy competition); his son Aristias was also successful in the same idiom, as well as composing successful tragedies. Of the four other playwrights whose satyr plays were especially highly regarded in fifth-century Athens, two were Athenians (Aeschylus and Sophocles) while the two others were outsiders: Ion of Chios and Achaeus of Eretria. A remarkably large number of fairly substantial fragments of these four playwrights' satyr dramas have survived, both in quotation and in papyrus finds, compared with the fragments of their tragedies.[46] (The situation is very different for Euripides.)

Like tragedies, satyr dramas involved mythical-heroic subject matter and characters; and in the fifth-century Athenian festival competitions the same cast of actors and chorus performed the satyr drama to conclude each tragedian's tetralogy. (The conventions changed repeatedly in the fourth century.) The themes and mood of the plots often included several "romantic" elements eschewed by trage-

---

for Pratinas' Hellenistic *Nachleben*.

[44] The music of fifth-century Athenian drama (before the arrival of the New Music) was thus generally characterized as "Dorian," "Aeolian," "Lydian," "Phrygian," "Carian," "Ionian," etc.; there is no "Attic" strain ever mentioned; see Barker (1989), West (1990), Griffith (2013a). (Furthermore, the best auloi players performing in late fifth-century Athens were mostly Thebans.)

[45] See in general Seaford (1984), Seidensticker (1979), KPS (1999), Kaimio (2001), Voelke (2001), Griffith (2002) [= Chapter 1], (2005) [= Chapter 2], (2006) [= Chapter 3], Harrison (2005) [and now Lämmle (2013)].

[46] For the satyr dramas of Ion and Achaeus, see KPS (1999), 480–525; also *TrGF* 1, 95–128.

dy, however: pastoral settings, ogres, adventures and miraculous escapes, necromancy and resurrections from the dead, dinners, symposia, musical and athletic competitions, and successful erotic |[74] encounters (meetings, falling in love, courtship) often ending in matrimony.[47] The language and style (diction, meters, costumes) employed by the main characters were almost identical to those of tragedy—far removed from the gross linguistic and visual conventions of Old Comedy—and it is often hard to tell whether a passage of dialogue quoted out of context by an ancient source comes from a satyr play or tragedy. Of the several substantial quotations from Sophocles' satyr dramas that are preserved, quite a few contain erotic/sympotic content and descriptions of the positive effects of love;[48] and it is notable that Ion's and Achaeus' satyr dramas about Heracles' affair with Omphale were particularly favored for quotation.[49] Striking too is the large number of papyri containing satyr dramas that have emerged from Egypt over the last century or so: in addition to several substantial pieces of Aeschylean satyr drama (*Theoroi, Dikyoulkoi, Prometheus*) we have a very large chunk of Sophocles' *Trackers* (*Ichneutai*: based on the story narrated in the—archetypically middlebrow—Homeric *Hymn to Hermes*), little pieces of his *Inachus* (the story of Zeus' pursuit of Io and her transformation into a cow), and substantial (but badly damaged) fragments of at least six additional satyr dramas by unknown authors.[50]

Euripides was less acclaimed, it seems, for his satyr plays; but two medieval manuscripts contain the entire *Cyclops*, and other bits and pieces survive in quotation.[51] Especially tantalizing are the surviving quotations (and ? papyrus fragment) of *Sisyphus*, a satyr drama composed either by Euripides or by Critias, containing

---

[47] Seaford (1984), 33–44, KPS (1999), 28–32, Griffith (2002) [= Chapter 1], (2006) [= Chapter 3]. It is worth noting that many of these thematic elements seem also to have been present in the Sicilian comedies of Epicharmus—and perhaps also in some fifth-century Attic comedies closer to the spirit of so-called Middle Comedy than to that of the surviving plays of Aristophanes: see Csapo (2000), Sidwell (2000). In Epicharmus' case, the following titles (from *PCG* vol. 1) might suggest themes close to the spirit of satyr drama: *Bousiris, Hêbês Gamos, Heracles, Kyklops, Logos kai Logina, Mousai, Odysseus, Persai, Pyrrha and Prometheus, Sirens, Sphinx, Thearoi, Trôes, Choreutai, Cheiron.* See further Rodríguez-Noriega Guillén (1996), Kerkhof (2001); [also Shaw (2014)].

[48] See Griffith (2006) [= Chapter 3] for fuller discussion both of vocabulary and of romantic elements.

[49] Of the twenty plays by Achaeus whose titles are attested, eight are definitely or probably satyric: *Athla* (or *Athloi*), *Aithon, Alcmeon, Hephaestus, Iris, Linos, Moirai,* and *Omphale*. 53 lines (or part-lines) survive from *Omphale*, amounting to well over half the total number of lines preserved from all Achaeus' plays. From Ion, 23 lines survive from his satyric *Omphale*; another 15 survive from his *Phoenix*, which may also have been a satyr drama—or else some kind of "mixed" drama of the middling type. No other play of his is nearly so well represented. See further KPS (1999), 480–525.

[50] *TrGF* vol. 2 (*Adespota*) F 646a, 655, 656, 675, 679a and b, 681; cf. KPS (1999) 624–42. Titles of possible satyr plays by anonymous authors listed by Kannicht-Snell include: *Amymone, Argo, Atlas, Hermes, Helios, Heracles, Hephaestus, Iris, Io, Mathetai, Perseus, Persephone, Prometheus* (bis), *Sphinx, Telephus, Triptolemus, Philoctetes, Phorcides.*

[51] KPS (1999), 403–78, Pechstein (1998).

a remarkable account of the "invention" of religion as a |[75] system of social repression and law-enforcement (*TrGF* 1 43 F 19). Scraps of *Peirithous* (likewise ascribed both to Euripides and Critias) also survive in quotation and on papyrus, in which Heracles arrives at the Underworld to attempt the extrication of his friend's friend from imprisonment there (43 F 1–14). Euripides also experimented with at least one quasi-satyric composition in which many of the conventions of satyr play were observed, but no satyr-chorus appeared (*Alcestis*)—a rather different phenomenon from tragedies that end happily and/or include "comic" elements mixed into the tragic ones (though these are also present in *Alcestis*).[52]

The rules for the performance of satyr plays and tragedies at the Athenian City Dionysia did not remain hard and fast, but shifted repeatedly. Between 535 and ca. 500, only tragedies were performed there (and we know virtually nothing about their plot, style, or flavor). Then, from ca. 500 until some time in the (early?) fourth century, tragedians apparently competed with three tragedies (sometimes connected, as usually in Aeschylus' case; but more often not) and a satyr play. Thus every "tragedian" was also necessarily a satyr dramatist (though, as we have seen, not every major satyr dramatist necessarily competed often with tragedies—e.g. Pratinas and Aristias). During the fourth century a separate satyr play was performed first, and then the tragedies—perhaps by different authors. Later still, a boom in satyr play production occurred, and competitions involved sets of three satyr plays at once. Thus fashions changed, with interest in satyr plays waxing and waning.[53]

But in general, the popularity of satyr drama never died;[54] and during the Hellenistic period it clearly experienced quite a boom outside of Athens, including some innovative experiments in the genre.[55] This was doubtless the reason for the remarkable prominence assigned to this topic in Horace's |[76] *De Arte Poetica* (220–50): here the recommended style and diction are characterized as "midway" between those of tragedy and of comedy (243 *de medio*), avoiding crudity and colloquialism, and making careful use of "texture and combination" of words (242

---

[52] See Slater (2005), and above; further Meijering (1987), Gibert (2000), Mastronarde (2000); also below, on tragicomedy and on Euripides' "middling" style. For another approach to the intermingling of "high" and "low" literary and cultural elements, see e.g. Andreassi (1997).

[53] Sifakis (1967), 91–94, 116–18, 124–26, KPS (1999), 10–12, Martina (2003).

[54] In Greek schools, once the standardized curriculum of "classics" had been instituted (i.e. by the late fourth century, it appears), satyr plays as such do not seem to have been designated as required reading. But all the plays (or selected passages) seem usually to have been organized into one combined alphabetical order for each author, with satyr plays included among the tragedies; and, as is clear from the number of quotations that survive from anthologies, grammarians, Athenaeus, etc., satyr plays were still copied and read, at least by enthusiasts of the theater (especially, to judge from the papyri, in Ptolemaic and Roman Egypt: perhaps there was a liking there for the more "romantically" tinged plays, in an era when the novel was also becoming increasingly popular).

[55] See KPS (1999), 566–642, Di Marco (2003), Nicolucci (2003), and esp. Cozzoli (2003) on Sositheus' *Daphnis*, Pretagostini (2003) on Python's *Agên*.

series iuncturaque), such as are appropriate for one (Silenus) who is "a guardian and attendant of the god whom he raised and cared for" (239 *custos famulusque dei Silenus alumni*).⁵⁶ The genre as a whole, as Horace describes it, involves "modifying serious things with/into play(fulness)" (226 *vertere seria ludo*)—clearly not burlesque or outright mockery of the high characters and heroic stories,⁵⁷ but rather a light, playful shifting of mood and tone.

A similar commentary is supplied by Demetrius, a critic of (probably) the third century BCE, in his work *On Style* (*Peri Hermeneias*), which is designed primarily to advise orators how to modify their prose style for appropriate effect in different kinds of speeches and contexts. In his lengthy discussion (128–89) of the "elegant style" (γλαφυρὸς χαρακτήρ)—otherwise known as the "middle style," between the "grand" and the "plain"—he identifies "charm" (χάρις) as the quality most to be desired, while also going to some lengths to explore and explain the relationship between "humor" (τὸ γελοῖον) and "charm" (χάρις). It is in this context that his often quoted remarks occur on the inherent incompatibility between tragedy and laughter (168–69), including his statement that satyr drama is in effect "playful tragedy" (τραγῳδίαν παίζουσαν). This is often interpreted to mean that satyr plays are full of humor and ridiculous antics. But this is not Demetrius' point. Rather, he is pointing out that satyr dramas involve much of the same subject matter and style as tragedies, yet include larger amounts of both "charm" and "humor"—even while remaining quite different from the low and ridiculous manner of comedy. Satyr drama seems in fact to be in some respects among his favored representatives of the "elegant style" of poetry: for even though it is Sappho's poetry that he cites and quotes most frequently with approval (along with Xenophon and Homer's *Odyssey*) as exemplary of the "charm" of the elegant style (129–30, 132, 140–43, 146, 148, 162–63, 166), we may note that the features singled out by Demetrius include "gardens dedicated to the |[77] Nymphs, bridal songs, loves…" (132; again 163). It is only when he begins to try to distinguish between "the charming" (τὸ εὔχαρι) and "the ridiculous" (τὸ γελοῖον) that he cites, first, the contrasting lyric styles of Sappho in her higher and lower types of poetry, and then the differences of aim and tone between tragedy, comedy, and satyr drama.⁵⁸

---

⁵⁶Sifakis (1967); but KPS (1999), 11–12 cite with approval Seaford (1984) for his conclusion that satyr drama faded from prominence during the Roman period and that the Romans themselves lacked the appropriate religious spirit. See Brink (1971) ad locc., however, for extended discussion of Horace's knowledge of Greek satyr drama and his interest in a "middle" style of dramatic composition, distinct from tragedy and comedy; and see p. 163 below for the Boscoreale murals, which give satyr drama plenty of space. On Hellenistic trends in the appreciation of satyr play and its (real or imagined) history, see also Fantuzzi (2007).

⁵⁷Modern scholarship on satyr drama has tended to emphasize perhaps too strongly the notion of satyr drama as a burlesque inversion or parody of tragedy, and its general grossness and comic quality: see instead KPS (1999), Kaimio (2001), Griffith (2002), (2006) [= Chapters 1 and 3 above].

⁵⁸Demetrius seems to vacillate between identifying two or three distinct levels or types of expression: thus for Sappho he characterizes one major distinction, between "beautiful" and "laughable" subjects,

Demetrius' main distinction here is between tragedy (charming, serious, pleasurable) and comedy (mocking, laughable, gross), and on the inappropriateness of introducing mocking laughter into contexts where charm and pleasure are desired. But he phrases this as a distinction (169) between the "charming [speaker/writer]" (εὐχάριτος) and the "laughter-making [one]" (γελωτοποιῶν), even as he goes on to observe that some contexts do allow for laughter (but not "mockery") when it is combined with charm (γέλωτος καὶ χαρίτων)—mentioning here both satyr play and comedy as examples—whereas other contexts do not: so "tragedy welcomes charm (χάριτας) in many contexts, but laughter is an enemy of tragedy. For nobody could think of a tragedy that is being playful (τραγῳδίαν παίζουσαν), since he will be writing a satyr drama rather than a tragedy (σάτυρον γράψει ἀντὶ τραγῳδίας)." Apparently, then, a charm-filled drama that is close to tragedy, while being somewhat more playful and laughter-full—without being mocking or prosaic, like a comedy (or a boisterous wedding song)—is a satyr play; and this genre would thus seem to correspond quite well to Sappho's "love affairs, spring and halcyon." In any case, like Horace, Demetrius is explicit in indicating both that satyr drama represents an important *tertium quid* between tragedy and comedy, and that it is in its own right a prime representative of the "charming" middle style.[59]

The same point comes across in the visual realm. The famous Boscoreale wall paintings that show the backdrop for, respectively, tragedy, comedy, and satyr play, are only intelligible if all three forms of drama are recognized as having their own distinctive subject matter, iconography, and imagined settings;[60] and this is explicitly confirmed for us by Vitruvius: "there are three |[78] types of scene-decoration...."[61] We may therefore be confident that this tripartite distinction was mainstream—no less well established in the popular imagination than Aristotle's binary opposition of "high tragedy" and "low comedy."

From an earlier period, the Pronomos Vase provides a useful perspective on several of these issues. Painted in Athens in the late fifth century, and soon (perhaps expressly?) exported to South Italy for funerary display, this large and impressive volute crater contains scenes of Dionysian and theatrical celebration that combine elements of both tragic and satyric performance.[62] The central presence

but also implies a further minor distinction between (i) "beauty" itself (περὶ κάλλους) and (ii) love affairs, spring, and the halcyon (περὶ ἐρώτων καὶ ἔαρος καὶ περὶ ἀλκυόνος); both of these are contrasted with the style in which she "mocks" (σκώπτει) the bridegroom in a wedding song, a style that he even compares to that of prose (διαλέγεσθαι ... χορὸς διαλεκτικός).

[59] As Johanna Hanink reminds me, Euripides was credited by several ancient critics with a "middling" style as well: e.g. *Life #5* in Kovacs (1994).

[60] The paintings are in the Metropolitan Museum, New York (New York 1953); illustrated and discussed e.g. in Bieber (1961), 124–25 with figs. 471–74.

[61] Vitruvius *De Architectura* 5.6.9 *genera autem sunt scaenarum tria...* etc. This seems good enough evidence that the Romans were not impervious to satyrs and their associations.

[62] See Griffith (2010) [= Chapter 4 above], and other contributions to Taplin and Wyles (2010).

of Dionysus and Ariadne on both the front and the back of the Vase highlights the "romantic" flavor; and the blending of urban theatrical setting (on the obverse) with rural images of nymphs and satyrs playing in the wild (on the reverse) suggests the fluid and transformative power of Dionysian performance and spectatorship. Tragic-satyric celebration here is a source of joy, desire, union, blessedness, and even ecstasy, not "pity and fear" or "laughter, mockery."[63]

It is interesting too to speculate what exactly Plato intends in the *Laws*, when he has his Athenian Stranger recommend that "Bacchic choruses" should be available for his Cretan citizens to perform, even as these citizens are generally to be barred from participating in tragedy or comedy.[64] Tragic actors may, it is recommended, periodically visit Magnesia, and may occasionally be allowed to demonstrate their superb vocal and histrionic expertise in (carefully censored) plays there (*Laws* 7. 817a-c). Comedies, which are intrinsically demeaning and shameful to perform, will be assigned to slaves and foreigners: the citizens will merely watch and appreciate the grossness of the performers (816c-e). But the third category of Dionysus-oriented dance performances that is mentioned, rather vaguely and circumspectly (*bakkheia*, 815 c-d), apparently has to take place outside the city |[79] boundaries. These "Bacchic choruses," some of which represent "Nymphs and Pans and Silenes and Satyrs, drunk," while others are concerned with "purifications and initiations (περὶ καθαρμούς τε καὶ τελετάς)," are not banned but allowed by the rather reluctant-sounding Athenian to remain, since these activities are to be counted "neither as warlike nor as peaceful" (χωρὶς μὲν πολεμικοῦ, χωρὶς δὲ εἰρηνικοῦ θέντας), so that "this whole kind of dance indeed is not really political [music] at all" (οὐκ ἔστι πολιτικὸν τοῦτο τῆς ὀρχήσεως τὸ γένος...): consequently he is prepared to "leave it alone and let it lie there as it is."[65] The new city, to be founded on the very island on which Dionysus was first united with Ariadne and on which baby Zeus was entertained by the dancing Kouretes and nymphs, will apparently not be able to flourish without such pastoral-romantic forms of choral entertainment—not tragic, not comic, but "Bacchic"—and while no satyr choruses are mentioned as such or even implied, these performances would seem

---

The Vase is Naples, Musaeo Nazionale 3240 inv. no. 81673 (*ARV*² 1336, 1). For good illustrations of the entire Vase (rather than just the scene of Pronomos and choreuts), see Bieber (1961), 10–11, Taplin and Wyles (2010), and Figs. 5b and 5c in this volume.

[63] A winged figure labelled HIMEROS ("Desire") is depicted on the obverse in conjunction with a theatrically costumed figure of (probably) Aphrodite, sitting next to the couch on which Dionysus and Ariadne are reclining. It is interesting to note that at Syracuse there was (at least during the Hellenistic era) a guild of Artists for Cheerful Aphrodite (*Technitai peri tên Hilaran Aphroditên*), separate from the Artists of Dionysus: see Moretti (1963), 41–43, and Aneziri (2001), who suggests that they were performers of mimes, perhaps phlyax plays (or *hilarotragediae*) of the type developed by Rhinthon of Tarentum.

[64] Cf. Griffith (2013a), and other papers on musical performance in the *Laws*, in Peponi (2013).

[65] Some editors and interpreters have taken this sentence to mean that these Bacchic choruses will in fact be banned. But see Griffith (2013a).

to involve many of the elements of satyr drama.

Overall, in the restaging (or reading, or reciting at dinner parties) of "old" satyr plays in the fourth century and later, we may wonder whether the original choral songs and dances were retained, or whether new satyric "interludes" may often have been substituted. Likewise, we can only speculate as to how the satyr choruses (and/or characters—Silenus? Pan?) were costumed and conducted themselves in Hellenistic performances. In any case, it seems likely that the peculiarly Athenian type of satyr choreuts, with their distinctive childish-slavish relationship to that particular citizen audience, may have been merged into a more generic spirit of Dionysian and Aphrodisiac/Erotic enthusiasm.[66] But this can be no more than speculation.

4. MIDDLEBROW AND ROMANTIC DRAMA—FROM TRAGEDY TO THE NOVEL[67]

By the time of Plutarch, Chariton, and other Greek writers of the Imperial period, terms such as "tragic," "comic," "theatrical," and "dramatic" were |[80] routinely used in senses that had little to do with Aristotle's specialized definitions or fifth-century Athenian performance conventions. Thus, as we saw, Plutarch's after-dinner conversationalists may describe sensational stage effects as typical of "comedy," while Chariton's novel, whose action begins with an Assembly held in the Theater at Syracuse (1.1.11–12), includes an "actor of Love" (ὑποκριτὴν ἔρωτος, 1.4.1) who has been hired by the "producer of the drama" (δημιουργὸς τοῦ δράματος, 1.4.3) to tell Chaireas a false story about Callirhoe's infidelity; and the novel culminates in an emotional courtroom "scene" worthy of the finest playwright:

> What dramatist (ποιητὴς ἐπὶ σκηνῆς) ever brought on such an unexpected and sensational turnaround of the plot (παράδοξον μῦθον)? You would have thought you were present in a theater (ἐν θεάτρῳ) full of innumerable emotions (μυρίων

---

[66] For suggestions concerning the psychological engagement of the Athenian audience with the satyr chorus during the fifth century, see Hall (1998) and (2006), Griffith (2005) [= Chapter 2 above]. Of course in the Athenian theater satyrs could also make up the chorus of comedies as well as satyr plays: see Storey (2005).

[67] Foster (2004) states (rather arbitrarily, in my opinion) that "romantic tragedy" is a quite separate category both from "ironic tragicomedy" and (true) "tragicomedy," and she thus excludes plays like Eur. *IT, Ion, Helen* from her consideration of predecessors to Shakespearean and modern tragicomedy. (She also never mentions at all *The Merchant of Venice*.) Since I myself am arguing that no clear distinction was generally maintained in antiquity between all these different forms or modes of drama, I have no stake in arguing about these differences. But "romantic tragedy" will do pretty well for me as an alternative category to "middlebrow tragedy."

παθῶν)—everything: tears, joy, amazement, pity, disbelief, prayers!

(5.8.2-3)

Later we also find reference made to "this whole drama" (ὅλον τὸ δρᾶμα τοῦτο), referring to Callirhoe's action-packed life (6.3.6).[68]

Few of these episodes would seem at home in an Athenian tragedy. Nor are they really characteristic of Menandrian comedy either, since his plays do not usually contain death plots, kings falling in love, or divinities miraculously rescuing their favorites in the way that Chariton's novel does. (Still less do they put one in mind of farce, phlyax, mime, or Old Comedy, with their grotesque masks, padded costumes, phalli, slave beatings, cooks, and obscene language.) The "drama" seems rather to be that of an adventure romance,[69] full of (what Demetrius would call) "charm" and permeated with the spirit of Aphrodite/Eros. The same is equally true of Longus' *Daphnis and Chloe*, a pastoral love romance set on the island of Lesbos and full of allusions both to Sappho and to Theocritean bucolic. The presiding genii of the novel are Pan and the Nymphs (Prologue; 1.4; 1.7-8; 2.24-34; 4.39; etc.), and there is even a scene in which the hero and heroine act out the story of Pan and Syrinx in words and dance (2.37). The resemblances to satyr drama in overall tone and |[81] plot structure are obvious and pervasive.[70] Yet virtually no literary historians or critics of the prose romances ever seem to consider the possibility that satyr drama and other subtragic stage performances may have been prime sources of the Greek novel.

We possess only little bits of Sositheus' *Daphnis or Lityerses* (*TrGF* 1 99); but to judge from the remarks of scholiasts to Theocritus and Vergil[71] this satyr drama seems to have been exactly the kind of play that may have inspired the "theatrical" impulse in the Greek prose romances: a handsome young man travels to a remote country to find his beloved girlfriend (actually, a nymph) who has been abducted by pirates, and rescues her from a king, Lityerses, a cruel ogre who daily employs harvesters and then decapitates them (while singing!), until Heracles arrives to deal with him. Most critics have thought that the "bucolic" content (Daphnis, harvesters) of this play is the result of the influence of Theocritus' new pastoral *Idylls*, and perhaps of Callimachus too; but as we have seen, pastoral settings, travel, adventure, and devoted romantic love had long been staples of satyr drama. Indeed, earlier still (back in the sixth century) the South Italian poet Stesichorus

---

[68] For further discussion of "theatrical" terminology and metaphors in the Greek novelists, see above, and e.g. Woronoff (1990) and Couraud-Lalanne (1998), though the latter tends to focus mainly on the notion of ritual, esp. rites of passage.

[69] One might think possibly of a pantomime: but that would hardly present the same spectacle of several different "actors" exhibiting such different emotions on stage at the same moment.

[70] See Griffith (2006) [= Chapter 3 above]; also pp. 162-63 above on Demetrius and the "middle/charming style."

[71] Schol. Theocr. 8 *arg.*, 8. 93a; Servius on Virgil *Eclogues* 8. 68. On Sositheus' play, see now Cozzoli (2003).

was credited with "founding this type of lyric poetry": he had composed songs commemorating the seduction of Daphnis by the nymph Thaleia, their love-pact, Daphnis' breaking of the pact through marriage to someone else, and the resulting romantic torments of all concerned.[72] Greek audiences did not have to wait for Theocritus' Daphnis or Polyphemus to enjoy the dramatic "sweetness, desire, charm" and mixed, bittersweet emotions of such narratives (*Id.* 1.1–3, 7, 61, 133–35; 11.3–4, 80–81).[73] Nor did the prose novelists have far to look in seeking "theatrical" elements for their romantic narratives: they only had to glance at their walls and vases—and visit their theaters—to see innumerable representations of such dramatic and emotional adventures.[74] |[82]

5. CONCLUSION (BUT NOT *DENOUEMENT*)

Apart from the heated debates and fads surrounding the term "tragicomedy" in Western Europe during the seventeenth century, most working playwrights (and many composers of operas too) over the years have shown a cheerful disregard for the supposed distinctness of these two forms and for the purity and unmitigated seriousness of Aristotelian/Ciceronian tragedy. At the age of sixteen, in a Jansenist school at Versailles, Jean Racine was surreptitiously leant by a friend a copy of Amyot's translation of Heliodorus, and thus picked up some of the finer points of his tragic art—points that he would never have discovered by rereading Aristotle, or even Euripides and Seneca.[75] In an earlier generation (to pick examples almost at random, but with an eye to their classical Greek antecedents), John Pickering's

---

[72] Aelian *VH* 10.18 τῆς τοιαύτης μελοποιίας ὑπάρξασθαι = Stesichorus fr. 279 [fr. 102 in *PMGF*]; cf. Diodorus 4.84.2–4. We may note that Theocritus connects his Daphnis with Stesichorus' place of origin, Himera (*Id.* 7. 74–75).

[73] See further Carson (1986), 77–97, 111–16.

[74] In this context, one may mention also the later Byzantine regulations and performance practices concerning "religious" drama and representation. In contrast to the Latin/Frankish West, where enactments of sacred scenes were approved and much appreciated by congregations/audiences, Byzantium frowned on the idea of actors impersonating saints, let alone Jesus and God the Father. Yet their iconographic tradition already provided a commonly recognized mimetic realm in which the biblical stories could be represented, while verbal art was channeled, not into scripts for dramatic recital, but into rhetorical displays (sermons and readings) that could bring those pictures to life and tell their stories with true dramatic flavor. As Maguire (2003), 217 observes: "It can be said that the rhetoric of images in Byzantium took the place that liturgical plays occupied in the west; that is, both forms of narrative introduced visual drama into the liturgy." Likewise in the classical period, visual culture (wall-painting, vase-painting, relief sculpture, etc.) must have played just as significant a role in maintaining popular awareness of "tragedy" and myth-based "drama" as the reading of texts or recital of dramatic passages in a purely verbal medium.

[75] Hägg (1980), 246–52, citing the recollections published by Racine's son, Louis, *Mémoires sur la vie de Jean Racine* (1747).

1567 adaptation of the *Oresteia*, an "Interlude" entitled *Horestes*, combines cute love duets between Egistus and Clytemnestra (based on contemporary pop songs) and an ubiquitously interfering character of Vyce (a cross between a Fool and a Medieval moral personification) with all the ethical anxieties and political intrigue endemic to Orestes' mythic actions. The confidently "romantic" tone—as to the (guaranteed) eventual outcome—does not undercut the moments of extreme pathos and adventure.[76] In the world of opera, John Gay's and Frederic Handel's delightful and pathetic *Acis and Galatea* reminds its audience not only of Theocritean pastoral but also of the epic/tragic world of heroes and romantic adventure. Or in the modern era, the recent Bollywood movie, *Lagaan* combines an engaging and delicately presented love triangle (based ultimately on the story of Krishna, Radha, and Rukmini) with an imagined moment in the Indian anti-imperialist movement of the 1890s, and culminates in a highly dramatic contest on whose outcome everything depends—a village cricket match.[77]

Sudden surprises, twists of fortune, spectacle, humor, music and dance... and above all, heart-wrenching scenes of desire and mutually reciprocated |[83] (or thwarted) love: these are the ingredients that theatergoers the world over have generally expected and that playwrights and actors have usually provided. The Greeks did not eschew these elements of drama, despite the impression we might gather from Aristotle's sketch of the "nature" of tragedy and of comedy. Middlebrow dramas of this romantic kind existed, even if, like the novel, they were largely omitted from highbrow critical discourse. And here and there they have resurfaced among our surviving texts (especially the ones rescued from Egypt); or we can trace their presence behind other related romance-types, such as pastoral and the novel.

As Oliver Taplin has reminded us, we (like the ancient Greeks themselves) have long been accustomed to the two archetypes of theatrical mask—"one grimacing, one grinning..." so that "...any spectator waking up in mid-play would immediately have known from the masks alone whether it was tragedy or comedy." Yet there were in fact scores of different character types, ages, hairstyles, and other characteristics that maskmakers built and the actors performed. Furthermore, as Taplin also observes in that same context, "the tragic mask is, in fact, rather blank and expressionless... waiting to take its 'expression' from the events of the play."[78] Tragedy (like comedy) could indeed be a very capacious performance mode, and the spirit of Aphrodite and Eros (as well as Pan) could often combine with that

---

[76] The full title of the work (whose musical score survives) is *A Newe Enterlude of Vice conteyninge, the History of Horestes with the cruell reuengment of his Fathers death, vpon his one naturall Mother.* See further Brewer (1982).

[77] Full title: *Lagaan: Once upon a time in India*, directed by Ashutosh Gowariker (2001). It is listed in movie-categorizing guides as "drama; musical; romance; sport."

[78] Taplin (1996), 189. He goes on to observe that "the predominant characteristic of the earlier comic mask... is clearly not merriment, but *ugliness*."

of Dionysus to produce adventures and happy endings that did not have to reinforce the intrinsic difference between "high" and "low" human beings, but might instead promote the capacity of all to enjoy the inclusive "charms" of middlebrow entertainment.[79]

---

[79] My thanks to Johanna Hanink, Martin Revermann, and Peter Wilson for their helpful comments and corrections.

Bibliography

Adelman, J. 1992. *Suffocating Mothers: Fantasies of Maternal Origin in Shakespeare's Plays.* New York.
Akrigg, B., and R. Tordoff, eds. 2013. *Slaves and Slavery in Ancient Greek Comic Drama.* Cambridge.
Allan, W. 2001. "Euripides in *Megale Hellas.*" *G&R* 48: 67–86.
Allan, W., andA. Kelly. 2013. "Listening to Many Voices: Athenian Tragedy as Popular Art." In A. Marmodoro and J. Hill, eds., *The Author's Voice in Classical and Late Antiquity.* Oxford, 77–122.
Althusser, L. 1972. *Lenin and Philosophy.* Trans. B. Brewster. London.
Aly, W. 1923. "Satyrspiel." *RE* 2A: 235–47.
Ambrose, Z. P. 2005. "Family Loyalty and Betrayal in Euripides' *Cyclops* and *Alcestis*: A Recurrent Theme in Satyr Play." In Harrison 2005: 21–38.
Anderson, W. B. 1966. *Ethos and Education in Greek Music.* Cambridge, Mass.
Andreassi, M. 1997. "Osmosis and Contiguity between 'Low' and 'High' Literature: *Moicheutria* and Apuleius." *Groningen Colloquia on the Novel* 8: 1–22.
Aneziri, S. 2001. "A Different Guild of Artists." *Archaiognosia* 11: 47–55.
Appel, W., and R. Schechner, eds. 1990. *By Means of Performance.* Cambridge.
Bäbler, B. 1998. *Fleissige Thrakerinnen und wehrhafte Skythen: Nichtgriechen im klassischen Athens.* Stuttgart.
Bakhtin, M. M. 1981. *The Dialogic Imagination.* Trans. M. Holquist. Austin.
Bakola, E. 2010. *Cratinus and the Art of Comedy.* Oxford.
Barker, A. 1989. *Greek Musical Writings*, vol. 2. Oxford.
Bassi, K. 1998. *Acting Like Men: Gender, Drama, and Nostalgia in Ancient Greece.* Ann Arbor.
Beaton, R. 2003. "The Byzantine Revival of the Ancient Novel." In Schmeling 2003: 713–33.
Belsey, C. 1985. *The Subject of Tragedy: Identity and Difference in Renaissance Drama.* London.
Bérard, C. 1983. "Le corps bestial." In C. Reichler, ed., *Le corps et ses fictions*, 43–54. Paris.
— . 1990. "Le satyre casseur." *Métis* 5: 75–87.
Bers, V. 1982. *Greek Poetic Syntax in the Classical Age.* New Haven.
Bethe, M., and K. Brazell. 1978–1982. *No As Performance (Cornell U. East Asia Papers* 16). Ithaca.

Bieber, M. 1961. *The History of the Greek and Roman Theater*, 2nd ed. Princeton.
Biehl, W., ed. 1986. *Euripides Kyklops*. Heidelberg.
Bierl, A. F. H. 2001. *Der Chor in der Alten Komödie*. Munich.
Bourdieu, P. 1990. *The Logic of Practice*. Trans. R. Nice. Stanford.
Bradley, A. C. 1910. *Shakespearean Tragedy*. Oxford.
Brandon, J. R., ed. 1997. *Nô and Kyôgen in the Contemporary World*. Honolulu.
Bremmer, J. 1991. "Walking, Standing, and Sitting in Ancient Greek Culture." In J. Bremmer and H. Roodenberg, eds., *A Cultural History of Gesture*, 15–35. London.
Brewer, D. S., ed. 1982. *Three Tudor Classical Interludes*. Totowa, NJ.
Brink, C. O., ed. 1971. *Horace on Poetry*. vol. 2: *The Ars Poetica*. Cambridge.
———. 1983. *Horace on Poetry*, vol. 3. Cambridge.
Brommer, F. 1959. *Satyrspiele. Bilder griechischer Vasen*, 2nd ed. Berlin.
Brown, N. O. 1947. *Hermes the Thief*. Madison.
Budelmann, F. 2000. *The Language of Sophocles: Communality, Communication, and Involvement*. Cambridge.
Burkert, W. 1962. "ΓΟΗΣ. Zum griechischen 'Shamanismus.'" *RhM* 105: 36–55.
———. 1985. *Greek Religion*. Trans. J. Raffan. Cambridge, Mass.
Burnett, A. P. 1971. *Catastrophe Survived: Euripides' Plays of Mixed Reversal*. Oxford.
Burn, L. 2010. "The Contexts of the Production and Distribution of Athenian Painted Pottery around 400 BC." In Taplin and Wyles 2010: 15–32.
Buschor, E. 1937. *Feldmäuse* (*SBAW* 1). Munich.
———. 1943–45. *Satyrtänze und frühes Drama* (*SBAW* 5). Munich.
Butler, J. P. 1990. *Gender Trouble*. New York.
———. 1993. *Bodies That Matter*. New York.
Calame, C. 1999. "Performative Aspects of the Choral Voice in Greek Tragedy: Civic Identity in Performance." In Goldhill and Osborne 1999: 125–53.
———. 2010. "Aetiological Performance and Consecration in the Sanctuary of Dionysos." In Taplin and Wyles 2010: 65–78.
Calder, W. M. III, ed. 1991. *The Cambridge Ritualists Reconsidered*. ICS Supp. 2. Atlanta.
Campbell, D. A., ed. 1992. *Greek Lyric vol. 3* (Loeb Classical Library). Cambridge, Mass.
Cantarella, R. 1952. "Il Frammento di Ossirinco su Gige." *Dioniso* 15: 3–31.
Carlson, M. 1996. *Performance: A Critical Introduction*. New York.
Carpenter, T. H. 1997. *Dionysian Imagery in Fifth-Century Athens*. Oxford.
———. 2005. "Images of Satyr Plays in South Italy." In Harrison 2005: 219–36.
Carson, A. 1986. *Eros the Bittersweet*. Princeton.
Case, S.-E., ed. 1990. *Performing Feminisms*. Baltimore.
Ceccarelli, P. 1998. *La pirrica nell' antichità greco romana: Studi sulla danza armata*. Pisa.
Chiasson, C. C. 2003. "Herodotus' Use of Attic Tragedy in the Lydian Logos." *CA* 22: 5–36.
Chourmouziades, N. C. 1974. *Saturika*. Athens.
Clay, D. M. 1958–1960. *A Formal Analysis of the Vocabularies of Aeschylus, Sophocles, and Euripides*, 2 vols. Minneapolis and Athens.
Clover, C. 1992. *Men, Women, and Chainsaws*. Princeton.
Collard, C. 1970. "On the Tragedian Chaeremon." *JHS* 90: 22–34.
Collinge, A. 1989. "The Case of Satyrs." In M. M. Mackenzie and C. Roueché, eds., *Images of Authority*, 82–103. Cambridge.

Collinge, N. E. 1958. "Some Reflections on Satyr-Plays." *PCPS* 5: 28–35.
Conacher, D. J. 1967. *Euripidean Drama*. Toronto.
—, ed. 1988. *Euripides Alcestis*. Warminster.
Connor, W. R. 1989. "City Dionysia and Athenian Democracy." *C&M* 40: 7–32.
Cooper, L. 1947. *Aristotle on the Art of Poetry: An Amplified Version with Supplementary Illustrations*. Ithaca.
Couraud-Lalanne, S. 1998. "Théatricalité et dramatisation rituelle dans le roman grec." *Groningen Colloquia on the Novel* 9: 1–16.
Cozzoli, A.-T. 2003. "Sositeo e il nuovo dramma satiresco." In Martina 2003: 265–91.
Cropp, M., and G. Fick. 1985. *Resolution and Chronology in Euripides* (*BICS Supp.* 43). London.
Cropp, M., K. H. Lee, and D. Sansone, eds. 2000. *Euripides and Tragic Theatre in the Late Fifth Century* (*ICS* 24–25). Baltimore.
Csapo, E. 2000. "From Aristophanes to Menander? Genre Transformation in Greek Comedy." In Depew and Obbink 2000: 115–33.
— . 2002. "Kallipides on the Floor-Sweepings: The Limits of Realism in Classical Acting and Performance Styles." In Easterling and Hall 2002: 127–47.
— . 2004. "The Politics of the New Music." In Murray Wilson 2004: 207–48.
— . 2010. "The Context of Choregic Dedications." In Taplin and Wyles 2010: 79–130.
Csapo, E., and M. C. Miller, eds. 2007. *The Origins of Theater in Ancient Greece and Beyond: From Ritual to Drama*. Cambridge.
Csapo, E., and W. J. Slater, eds. 1995. *The Context of Ancient Drama*. Ann Arbor.
Cunningham, M. 1994. "Thoughts on Aeschylus: The Satyr-Play *Proteus*." *LCM* 19: 67–68.
Curtius, L. 1929. *Die Wandmalerei Pompejis*. Köln. (Repr. Hildesheim 1960.)
Dale, A. M. 1968. *The Lyric Metres of Greek Drama*, 2nd ed. Cambridge.
Davies, M. I. 1969. "Thoughts on the *Oresteia* before Aeschylus." *BCH* 93: 214–60.
De Jong, I. J. F. 1991. *Narrative in Drama: The Art of the Euripidean Messenger-Speech*. Mnemosyne Suppl. 116. Leiden.
De Lauretis, T. 1992. *Technologies of Gender*. Berkeley.
Dearden, C. 1999. "Plays for Export." *Phoenix* 53: 222–48.
Depew, M., and D. Obbink, eds. 2000. *Matrices of Genre: Authors, Canons, and Society*. Cambridge.
Dewald, C. 1987. "Narrative Surface and Authorial Voice in Herodotus' *Histories*." *Arethusa* 20: 147–70.
Di Marco, M. 2003. "Poetica e metateatro in un dramma satiresco d'età ellenistica." In Martina 2003: 41–74.
Dougherty, C., and L. V. Kurke, eds. 2003. *The Cultures within Ancient Greek Culture: Contact, Conflict, Collaboration*. Cambridge.
Dover, K. J., ed. 1971. *Theocritus. Select Poems*. London.
— . 1978. *Greek Homosexuality*. Cambridge, Mass.
Durkheim, E. 1912. *The Elementary Forms of Religious Life*. (5th ed.; Eng. tr. K. Fields, New York 1995).
Easterling, P. E., ed. 1997a. *The Cambridge Companion to Greek Tragedy*. Cambridge.
— . 1997b. "A Show for Dionysus." In Easterling 1997a: 36–53.
— . 1997c. "From Repertoire to Canon." In Easterling 1997a: 211–27.

Easterling, P. E., and E. Hall, eds. 2002. *Greek and Roman Actors*. Cambridge.
Ehrenberg, V. 1961. *The People of Aristophanes*, 3rd rev. ed. London.
Fantuzzi, M. 2007. "Hellenistic Epigram and the Theater." In P. Bing and P. Bruss, eds., *Brill's Companion to Hellenistic Epigram*, 477–96. Leiden.
Fehling, D. 1989. *Herodotus and his Sources*. Trans. J. G. Howie. Liverpool.
Festa, V. 1918. "Sikinnis." *Memorie della Reale Accademia di Archeologia* 3: 2–60.
Fischer, I. M. 1958. *Typische Motive im Satyrspiel*. Göttingen.
Flickinger, R. C. 1913. "Tragedy and the Satyric Drama." *CP* 8: 261–83.
Foley, H. P. 1985. *Ritual Irony: Poetry and Sacrifice in Euripides*. Ithaca.
— . 2003. "Choral Identity in Greek Tragedy." *CP* 98: 1–30.
Foster, V. A. 2004. *The Name and Nature of Tragicomedy. Studies in European Cultural Transition*, vol. 18. Aldershot.
Friedrich, R. 1993. "Drama and Ritual." In J. Redmond, ed., *Drama and Religion = Themes in Drama* 5: 159–223. Cambridge.
Friis Johansen, H., and E. W. Whittle, eds. 1980. *Aeschylus: The Suppliants*. Copenhagen.
Frye, N. 1957. *Anatomy of Criticism*. Princeton.
— . 1976. *The Secular Scripture: A Study of the Structure of Romance*. Cambridge, Mass.
Gärtner, T. 1972. "Roman." In *Der kleine Pauly*, 1451. Stuttgart.
Gantz, T. 1993. *Early Greek Myth*, 2 vols. Baltimore.
Garber, M. 1993. *Vested Interests: Cross-Dressing and Cultural Anxiety*. New York.
Garvie, A. F. 1969. *Aeschylus Supplices: Play and Trilogy*. Cambridge.
Gaster, T. 1961. *Thespis*. New York.
Gibert, J. 2000. "Falling in Love with Euripides (*Andromeda*)." In Cropp, Lee, and Sansone 2000: 1–17.
— . 2002. "Recent Work on Greek Satyr-Play." *CJ* 87: 79–88.
Giuliani, L. 1995. *Tragik, Trauer, und Trost: Bildervasen für eine apulische Totenfeier*. Berlin.
— . 2001. "Sleeping Furies: Allegory, Narration, and the Impact of Texts in Apulian Vase-Painting." *Scripta Classica Israelica* 20: 17–38.
Gleason, M. W. 1995. *Making Men: Sophists and Self-Presentation in Ancient Rome*. Princeton.
Goffman, E. 1959. *The Presentation of Self in Everyday Life*. New York.
Goldhill, S. 1984. *Language, Sexuality, Narrative: The Oresteia*. Cambridge.
— . 1990. "The Great Dionysia and Civic Ideology." In Winkler and Zeitlin 1990: 97–129.
— . 1997. "The Audience of Athenian Tragedy." In Easterling 1997a: 54–68.
Goldhill, S., and R. Osborne, eds. 1999. *Performance Culture and Athenian Democracy*. Cambridge.
Gould, J. 1996. "Tragedy and Collective Experience." In Silk 1996: 217–43.
Green, A. 1979. *The Tragic Effect*. Trans. A. Sheridan. Cambridge.
Green, J. R. 1991. "On Seeing and Depicting the Theatre in Classical Athens." *GRBS* 32: 15–50.
Green, J. R., and E. W. Handley. 1995. *Images of the Greek Theatre*. London.
Greenblatt, S. 1980. *Renaissance Self-Fashioning*. Chicago.
Griffin, J. 1998. "The Social Function of Attic Tragedy." *CQ* 48: 39–61.
Griffith, M. 1977. *The Authenticity of Prometheus Bound*. Cambridge.

— . 1990. "Contest and Contradiction in Early Greek Poetry." In M. Griffith and D. J. Mastronarde, eds., *Cabinet of the Muses*, 185–207. Atlanta.
— . 1995. "Brilliant Dynasts: Power and Politics in the *Oresteia*." *CA* 14: 62–129.
— . 1998. "The King and Eye: The Rule of the Father in Greek Tragedy." *PCPS* 44. 20–84.
— , ed. 1999. *Sophocles: Antigone*. Cambridge.
— . 2001. "Antigone and Her Sister(s)." In A. Lardinois and L. McClure, eds., *Women's Voices in Greek Literature and Society*, 117–36. Princeton.
— . 2002. "Slaves of Dionysos: Satyrs, Audience, and the Ends of the *Oresteia*." *CA* 21: 195–258.
— . 2005. "Satyrs, Citizens, and Self-Presentation." In Harrison 2005: 161–99.
— . 2005/2010. "The Subject of Desire in Sophocles' *Antigone*." In V. Pedrick and S. Oberhelman, eds., *The Soul of Tragedy: Essays on Athenian Drama*. Chicago, 91–135 [abridged and slightly revised version "Psychoanalysing Antigone," repr. in S. Wilmer and A. Zukauskaite, eds., *Interrogating Antigone* (Oxford 2010)].
— . 2006. "Sophocles' Satyr-Plays and the Language of Romance." In I. J. F. De Jong and A. Rijksbaron, eds., *Sophocles and the Greek Language*. Mnemosyne Suppl. 269, 51–72. Leiden.
— . 2008. "Greek Middlebrow Drama: (Something to Do with Aphrodite?)." In M. Revermann and P. Wilson, eds., *Performance, Iconography, Reception: Studies in Honour of Oliver Taplin*, 59–87. Oxford.
— . 2010. "Satyr Play and Tragedy, Face-to-Face." In Taplin and Wyles 2010: 47–64.
— . 2013a. "Cretan Harmonies and Universal Morals: Early Music and Migrations of Wisdom in Plato's *Laws*." In Peponi 2013: 2–66.
— . 2013b. "Satyr Play, Dithyramb, and the Geo-Politics of Dionysian Style in 5th Century Athens." In B. Kowalzig and P. Wilson, eds., *Dithyramb and its Contexts*, 257–81. Oxford.
Gruen, E. 2002. *Diaspora: Jews amidst Greeks*. Cambridge, Mass.
Guggisberg, P. 1947. *Das Satyrspiel*. Ph.D diss. Zürich.
Guthke, K. S. 1966. *Modern Tragicomedy*. New York.
Hägg, T. 1980. *Eros und Tyche: Der Roman in der antiken Welt*. Mainz.
— . 1983. *The Novel in Antiquity*. Oxford.
Hall, E. 1989. *Inventing the Barbarian*. Oxford.
— . 1997. "The Sociology of Athenian Tragedy." In Easterling 1997a: 93–126.
— . 1998. "Ithyphallic Males Behaving Badly, or, Satyr Drama as Gendered Tragic Ending." In M. Wyke, ed., *Parchments of Gender*, 13–37. Oxford.
— . 2006. "Horny Satyrs and Tragic Tetralogies." In *The Theatrical Cast of Athens: Interactions between Ancient Greek Drama and Society*, 142–69. Oxford.
— . 2007. "Tragedy Personified." In C. Kraus, S. Goldhill, H. P. Foley, and J. Elsner, eds., *Visualizing the Tragic: Drama, Myth, and Ritual in Greek Art and Literature*, 221–256. Oxford.
— . 2010. "Tragic Theatre: Demetrius' Rolls and Dionysos' Other Woman." In Taplin and Wyles 2010: 159–80.
Halliwell, S. 1986. *Aristotle's Poetics*. Chapel Hill.
Hamilton, R. 1979. "Euripides' Cyclopean Symposium." *Phoenix* 33: 287–92.
Hanink, J. 2007. "Classical Tragedians and the Hellenistic Imagination: From Athenian

Idols to Wandering Poets." M.Phil. Thesis, Cambridge.
Harrison, G. W. M., ed. 2005. *Satyr Drama: Tragedy at Play*. Swansea.
Harrison, Thomas. 2002. *Greeks and Barbarians*. New York.
Harrison, Tony. 1990. *The Trackers of Oxyrhynchus: The Delphi Text 1988*. London. (Reprinted in *Plays* 4, London 2004.)
Harvey, D., and J. Wilkins, eds. 2000. *The Rivals of Aristophanes: Studies in Athenian Old Comedy*. London.
Hedreen, G. 1992. *Silens in Attic Black-Figure Vase-Painting*. Ann Arbor.
— . 2007. "Myths of Ritual in Athenian Vase-Painting of Silens." In Csapo and Miller 2007: 150–95.
Henderson, J. 1975. *The Maculate Muse: Obscene Language in Attic Comedy*. New Haven. (2nd ed. 1991.)
Henrichs, A. 1982. "Changing Dionysiac Identities." In B. F. Meyer and E. P. Sanders, eds., *Jewish and Christian Self-Definition*, vol. 3, 137–60, 213–36. London.
— . 1995. "Why should I dance?" *Arion* 3. 56–111.
Herington, C. J. 1985. *Poetry into Drama: Early Tragedy and the Greek Poetic Tradition*. Berkeley.
Hirst, D. L. 1984. *Tragicomedy*. London.
Holladay, C. R., ed. 1983. *Fragments from Hellenistic Jewish Authors*, vol. 2. Chico.
Holmes, B. 2010. *The Symptom and the Subject: The Emergence of the Body in Ancient Greece*. Princeton.
Hunter, V. J. 1994. *Policing Athens*. Princeton.
Jacob, O. 1928. *Les esclaves publics à Athènes*. Liege.
Jacobson, H. 1983. *The Exagoge of Ezekiel*. Cambridge.
Jameson, F. 1981. *The Political Unconscious*. Ithaca.
Janko, R. 1984. *Aristotle On Comedy*. Berkeley.
Jauss, J. R. 1974. "Levels of Identification of Hero and Audience." *New Literary History* 5.2: 283–317.
Jens, W., ed. 1971. *Die Bauformen der griechischen Tragödie*. Munich.
Jones, C. P. 1991. "Dinner Theatre." In W. J. Slater, ed., *Dining in a Classical Context*, 185–98. Ann Arbor.
Jones, N. F. 1999. *The Associations of Classical Athens*. Oxford.
Jouanna, J., and F. Montanari, eds. 2009. *Eschyle á l'aube du théâtre occidental* (*Fondation Hardt Entretiens* 54), Geneva.
Junker, K. 2003. "Namen auf dem Pronomoskrater." *MDAI(A)* 118: 317–35.
— . 2010. "The Transformation of Athenian Theatre Culture around 400 BC." In Taplin and Wyles 2010: 131–48.
Kaimio, M., et al. 2001. "Metatheatricality in the Greek Satyr-Play." *Arctos* 35: 35–78.
Kannicht, R., ed. 1969. *Euripides: Helena*. Heidelberg.
Käppel, L. 1998. *Die Konstruktion der Handlung in der Orestie des Aischylos*. Zetemata 99. Munich.
Katz, M. A. 1994. "The Character of Tragedy: Women and the Greek Imagination." *Arethusa* 27: 81–103.
Keene, D. 1966. *Nô: The Classical Theatre of Japan*. Tokyo and Palo Alto.
Ker, J. 2001. "Solon's *Theôria* and the End of the City." *CA* 19: 304–29.

Kerkhof, R. 2001. *Dorische Posse*. Munich.
Kertzer, D. I. 1988. *Ritual, Power and Politics*. New Haven.
Keuls, E. 1985. *The Reign of the Phallus*, 2nd ed. Princeton.
Kinser, S. 1990. *Carnival, American Style*. Chicago.
Klein, M. 1948. *Contributions to Psycho-Analysis, 1921–1945*. London.
Knox, B. M. W. 1964. *The Heroic Temper: Studies in Sophoclean Tragedy*. Berkeley.
— . 1979. *Word and Action: Essays on the Ancient Theater*. Baltimore.
Konstan, D. 1990. "An Anthropology of Euripides' *Cyclops*." In Winkler and Zeitlin 1990: 207–27.
Kossatz-Deissmann, A. 1982. "Zur Herkunft des *Perizoma* im Satyrspiel." *JDAI* 97: 65–90.
Kovacs, D. 1994. *Euripidea. Mnemosyne Suppl.* 132. Leiden.
— , ed. 1994. *Euripides: Cyclops Alcestis Medea* (Loeb Classical Library). Cambridge, Mass.
Kowalzig, B. 2004. "Changing Choral Worlds: Song-Dance and Society in Athens and Beyond." In Murray and Wilson 2004: 39-65.
— . 2007. "And Now All the World Shall Dance: Dionysos' *Khoroi* between Drama and Ritual." In Csapo and Miller 2007: 221–51.
Kowalzig, B., and P. Wilson, eds. 2013. *Dithyramb in Context*. Oxford.
Krauskopf, I. 1990. S.v. "Himeros." *LIMC* 5.
Kristeva, J. 1980. *Desire in Language*. Trans. T. Gora et al. New York.
Krumeich, R., N. Pechstein, and B. Seidensticker, eds. 1999. *Das griechische Satyrspiel*. Darmstadt.
Kurke, L. V. 1992. "The Politics of ἁβροσύνη in Archaic Greece." *CA* 11: 92–120.
— . 2003. "Aesop and the Contestation of Delphic Authority." In Dougherty and Kurke 2003: 77–100.
— . 2010. *Aesopic Conversations: Popular Tradition, Cultural Dialogue, and the Invention of Greek Prose*. Princeton.
Labiano Ilundain, J. M. 2000. *Estudio de las interjecciones en las comedias de Aristófanes*. Amsterdam.
Lada, I. R. 1993. "'Empathic Understanding': Emotion and Cognition in Classical Dramatic Audience-Response." *PCPS* 39: 94–140.
Lämmle, R. 2013. *Poetik des Satyrspiels*. Heidelberg.
Laird, A. 2001. "Ringing the Changes on Gyges: Philosophy and the Formation of Fiction in Plato's *Republic*." *JHS* 121: 12–29.
Laplanche, J., and J.-B. Pontalis. 1973. *The Language of Psycho-Analysis*. Trans. D. Nicholson-Smith. New York.
Lasserre, F. 1973/1989. "Le drame satyrique." *RFIC* 101: 273–301 (repr. in Seidensticker 1989: 252–86).
Lausberg, H. 1990. *Handbuch der literarischen Rhetorik*, 3rd ed. Stuttgart.
Lawler, L. B. 1964. *The Dance of the Ancient Greek Theatre*. Iowa City.
Lawson, J. C. 1910. *Modern Greek Folklore and Ancient Greek Religion*. London.
Le Guen, B. 2001. *Les Associations des Technites dionysiaques à l'époque hellénistique*. Nancy.
Lesky, A. 1983. *Greek Tragic Poetry*. Trans. M. Dillon. New Haven.
Lhamon, W. T. 1998. *Raising Cain: Blackface Performance from Jim Crow to Hip Hop*. Cam-

bridge, Mass.
Lissarrague, F. 1990a. "Why Satyrs are Good to Represent." In Winkler and Zeitlin 1990: 228-36.
— . 1990b. "The Sexual Life of Satyrs." In D. Halperin, J. Winkler, and F. I. Zeitlin, eds., *Before Sexuality*, 53-82. Princeton.
— . 1993. "On the Wildness of Satyrs." In T. H. Carpenter and C. A. Faraone, eds., *The Masks of Dionysus*, 207-20. Ithaca.
— . 2010. "From Flat Page to the Volume of the Pot." In Taplin and Wyles 2010: 33-46.
— . 2013. *La cité des satyres*. Paris.
Lloyd-Jones, H., ed. 1963. *Aeschylus*, vol. 2, Appendix (Loeb Classical Library). Cambridge, Mass.
— , ed. 1996. *Sophocles III Fragments* (Loeb Classical Library). Cambridge, Mass.
Long, A. A. 1968. *Language and Thought in Sophocles*. London.
López-Eire, A. 2003. "Tragedy and Satyr-Drama: Linguistic Criteria." In Sommerstein 2003: 387-412.
Loraux, N. 1986. *The Invention of Athens: The Funeral Oration in the Classical City*. Trans. A. Sheridan. Cambridge, Mass.
— . 1991 [1987]. *Tragic Ways of Killing a Woman*. (Eng. tr. A. Foster) Cambridge, Mass.
— . 1998 [1990]. *Mothers in Mourning*. (Eng. tr. C. Pache). Ithaca.
Lott, E. 1993. *Love and Theft: Blackface Minstrelsy and the American Working Class*. Oxford.
Lucas, D. W., ed. 1968. *Aristotle: Poetics*. Oxford.
Ma, J. 2007. "A Horse from Teos: Epigraphical Notes on the Ionian-Hellespontine Association of Dionysiac Artists." In P. Wilson, ed., *Greek Theatre and Festivals: Documentary Studies*, 215-45. Oxford.
MacAloon, J. J., ed. 1984. *Rite, Drama, Festival, Spectacle: Rehearsals Towards a Theory of Cultural Performance*. Philadelphia.
Maltese, E. V. ed. 1982. *Sofocle: Ichneutae* (Papyrol. Florentiana X). Florence.
Marconi, C. 2012. "Between Performance and Identity: the Social Context of Stone Theaters in late Classical and Hellenistic Sicily." In K. Bosher, ed., *Theater Outside Athens*, 175-207. Cambridge.
Marini, N. 1991. "Drama: Possibile denominazione per il romanzo greco d'amore." *SIFC* (3) 9: 232-43.
Marshall, C. W. 1995. "Idol Speculation: The Protean Stage of Euripides' *Helen*." *Text & Representation* 16: 74-79.
— . 2000. "Alcestis and the Problem of Prosatyric Drama." *CJ* 95: 229-38.
— . 2005. "The Sophisticated *Cyclops*." In Harrison 2005: 103-118.
Martina, A., ed. 2003. *Teatro greco postclassico e teatro latino: Teorie e prassi drammatica*. Rome.
Mastronarde, D. J. 1998. "Il coro euripideo: Autorita e integrazione." *QUCC* 60: 55-80.
— . 1999. "Knowledge and Authority in the Choral Voice." *Syllecta Classica* 10: 87-104.
— . 2000. "Euripidean Tragedy and Genre: The Terminology and its Problems." In Cropp, Lee, and Sansone 2000: 23-39.
— . 2010. *The Art of Euripides: Dramatic Technique and Social Context*. Cambridge.
Mathews, G. 1997. "Aristophanes' 'High' Lyrics Reconsidered." *Maia* 49: 1-42.
Mayne, J. 1993. *Cinema and Spectatorship*. London.

McCarthy, K. 2000. *Slaves, Masters, and the Art of Authority in Plautine Comedy*. Princeton.
McDonald, M. 1992. *Ancient Sun, Modern Light: Greek Drama on the Modern Stage*. New York.
Meijering, R. 1987. *Literary and Rhetorical Theories in Greek Scholia*. Groningen.
Metz, C. 1979. *The Imaginary Signifier: Psychoanalysis and the Cinema*. Bloomington.
Michelini, A. N. 1987. *Euripides and the Tragic Tradition*. Madison.
Montrose, L. A. 1980. "The Purpose of Playing: Reflections on Shakespearean Anthropology." *Helios* 7: 51–74.
Moorhouse, A. C. 1982. *The Syntax of Sophocles*. Mnemosyne Suppl. 75. Leiden.
Morelli, G. 2003. "Per la ricostruzione del *Centauro* di Cheremone." In Martina 2003: 11–27.
Moretti, J.-Ch. 1993. "Les debuts de l'architecture théâtrale en Sicile et en Italie méridionale." *Topoi* 3: 72–100.
Moretti, L. 1963. "I technitai di Siracusa." *RFIC* 91: 38–45.
Most, G. W. 2000. "Generating Genres: The Idea of the Tragic." In Depew and Obbink 2000: 15–34. Cambridge, Mass.
Mostkoff, P. "Thinking the Theater: The Theatrical Spectator in Psychoanalytic and Critical Theory." Ph.D diss., in progress. Berkeley.
Mulvey, L. 1975. "Visual Pleasure and Narrative Cinema." *Screen* 16.1: 6–18.
Murray, P., and P. Wilson, eds. 2004. *Music and the Muses: The Culture of Mousike in the Classical Athenian City*. Oxford.
Nagy, G. 1990. *Pindar's Homer*. Baltimore.
Naerebout, F. G. 1997. *Attractive Performances: Ancient Greek Dances: Three Preliminary Studies*. Amsterdam.
Neale, S. 1983. "Masculinity as Spectacle: Reflections on Men and Mainstream Cinema." *Screen* 24.6: 2–17.
Nesselrath, H.-G. 2000. "Eupolis and the Periodization of Athenian Comedy." In Harvey and Wilkins 2000: 233–46.
Nicolucci, V. 2003. "Il dramma satiresco alla corte di Attalo I." In Martina 2003: 325–42.
Nogami Toyoichirô. 1930. *Nô: Kenyû to Hakken*. Tokyo.
O'Kell, E. 2003. "The 'Effeminacy' of the Clever Speaker and the 'Impotency' Jokes of *Ichneutai*." In Sommerstein 2003: 283–308.
Orgel, S. 1975. *The Illusion of Power*. Berkeley.
— . 1999. "Why did the English Stage Take Boys for Women?" In M. C. Riggio, ed., *Teaching Shakespeare through Performance*, 102–13. New York.
Osborne, R. 2010. "Who's Who on the Pronomos Vase?" In Taplin and Wyles 2010: 149–58.
O'Sullivan, N. 1992. *Alcidamas, Aristophanes, and Early Greek Stylistic Theory*. Hermes Einzelschriften 60. Stuttgart.
O'Sullivan, P., and C. Collard, eds. 2013. *Euripides* Cyclops *and Major Fragments of Greek Satyric Drama*. Oxford and Oakville, Conn.
Page, D. L., ed. 1959. *Poetae Melici Graeci*. Oxford.
—, ed. 1963. *The Oxyrhynchus Papyri. Part XXIX*. London.
—, ed. 1968. *Lyrica Graeca Selecta*. Oxford.
Parker, A., and E. K. Sedgwick, eds. 1995. *Performativity and Performance*. New York.
Parker, L. P. E. 1997. *The Songs of Aristophanes*. Oxford.

—, ed. 2007. *Euripides. Alcestis.* Oxford.
Pearson, A. C. 1917. *The Fragments of Sophocles*, 3 vols. Cambridge.
Pechstein, N. 1998. *Euripides Satyrographos.* Stuttgart.
Pelling, C. P. 2006. "Educating Croesus: Talking and Learning in Herodotus' Lydian *Logos.*" *CA* 25: 141–77.
Peponi, A. E., ed. 2013. *Performance and Culture in Plato's* Laws. Cambridge.
Pickard-Cambridge, A. W. 1927/1962. *Dithyramb Tragedy and Comedy*, 2nd ed. Revised by T. B. L. Webster. Oxford.
—. 1968/1989. *The Dramatic Festivals of Athens*, 2nd ed. Revised by J. Gould and D. M. Lewis. Oxford. (3rd ed. 1989.)
Porter, J. (forthcoming). "Gyges, or the Adulterer *malgré lui.*" *CA*.
Prag, A. J. N. W. 1985. *The Oresteia: Iconographic and Narrative Tradition.* Warminster.
Pretagostini, R. 2003. "La representazione dell' *Agên* e la nuova drammaturgia." In Martina 2003: 161–75.
Propp, V. I. 1958. *Morphology of the Folktale* (1929; Eng. tr., Publ. American Folklore Soc. V. 9). Bloomington.
Radt, S., ed. 1977, 1985. *Tragicorum Graecorum Fragmenta* (*TrGF*), vol. 3 (Aeschylus), vol. 4 (Sophocles). Berlin.
—. 1982. "Sophocles in seinen Fragmenten." *Fondation Hardt Entretiens* 29: 185–231.
Raglan, F. R. S. (Lord). 1936. *The Hero: A Study in Tradition, Myth, and Drama.* Oxford.
Rawson, E. 1969. *The Spartan Tradition in European Thought.* Oxford.
Redondo, J. 2003. "Satyric Diction in the Extant Sophoclean Fragments: A Reconsideration." In Sommerstein 2003: 413–31.
Richards, H. 1900a. "On the Use of the Words τραγῳδός and κωμῳδός." *CR* 14: 201–14.
—. 1900b. "On the Word *drama.*" *CR* 14: 388–93.
Roberts, W. Rhys, ed. 1902. *Demetrius On Style.* Cambridge.
Rode, J. 1971. "Das Chorlied." In Jens 1971: 85–115.
Rodríguez-Noriega Guillén, L., ed. 1996. *Epicarmo de Siracusa. Testimonios y Fragmentos.* Oviedo.
Rogin, M. 1996. *Blackface, White Noise.* Berkeley.
Roilos, P. 2005. *Amphoteroglossia: A Poetics of the Twelfth-century Medieval Greek Novel.* Washington, DC.
Rorty, A. 1992. "The Psychology of Aristotelian Tragedy." In A. Rorty, ed., *Essays on Aristotle's Poetics*, 1–22. Princeton.
Rose, P. W. 1992. *Sons of the Gods, Children of Earth.* Ithaca.
Roselli, D. 2002. *Gender and Class in Athenian Material and Theater Culture.* Ph.D. diss, U. Toronto.
—. 2011. *Theater of the People: Spectators and Society in Ancient Athens.* Austin.
Rosen, R. M. 1988. *Old Comedy and the Iambographic Tradition.* Atlanta.
Rossi, L. E. 1971. "Il *Ciclope* di Euripide come κῶμος 'mancato.'" *Maia* 23: 10–38.
—. 1972/1989. "Das Attische Satyrspiel." In Seidensticker 1989: 222–51. (Originally "Il dramma satiresco attico." In *Dialoghi di archeologia* 6 (1972): 248–301.)
Ruiz-Montero, C. 2003. "The Rise of the Greek Novel." In Schmeling 2003: 29–85.
Rutherford, R. B. 1982. "Tragic Form and Feeling in the *Iliad.*" *JHS* 102: 145–60.
Said, E. 1978. *Orientalism.* New York.

Sansone, D. 1978. "The *Bacchae* as Satyr-Play?" *ICS* 3: 40–46.
Schechner, R. 1977. *Essays in Performance Theory 1970–1976*. New York.
— . 1985. *Between Theater and Anthropology*. Philadelphia.
Schmeling, G., ed. 2003. *The Novel in the Ancient World*. [1996, rev.] Leiden.
Scodel, R. 2001. "The Poet's Career, the Rise of Tragedy, and Athenian Cultural Hegemony." In D. Papenfuss and V. Stocks, eds., *Gab es das griechische Wunder?*, 215–25. Mainz.
Scott, J. 1990. *Domination and the Arts of Resistance*. New Haven.
Seaford, R. 1976. "On the Origins of Satyric Drama." *Maia* 28: 209–21.
— . 1978. "The 'Hyporchema' of Pratinas." *Maia* 29/30:81–94.
— . 1981. "Dionysiac Drama and the Mysteries." *CQ* 31: 252–75.
— , ed. 1984. *Euripides. Cyclops*. Oxford.
— . 1994. *Reciprocity and Ritual*. Oxford.
— . 1996. "Something to Do with Dionysos—Tragedy and the Dionysiac." In Silk 1996: 284–94.
Sedgwick, E. K. 1985. *Between Men*. New York.
Segal, C. P. 1997. *Dionysiac Poetics*, 2nd ed. Princeton.
Seidensticker, B. 1979. "Das Satyrspiel." In G. A. Seeck, ed., *Das griechische Drama*, 204–57. Darmstadt.
— . 1982. *Palintonos harmonia: Studien zu komischen Elementen in der griechischen Tragödie*. Hypomnemata 72. Göttingen.
— , ed. 1989. *Das Satyrspiel*. Darmstadt.
— . 2003. "The Chorus of Greek Satyr-Play." In E. Csapo and M. C. Miller, eds., *Poetry, Theory, Praxis*, 100–21. Oxford.
— . 2010. "Dance in Satyr Play." In Taplin and Wyles 2010: 213–30.
Shaw, C. A. 2014. *Satyric Play: The Evolution of Greek Comedy and Satyr Drama*. Oxford.
Sidwell, K. 2000. "From Old to Middle to New: Aristotle's *Poetics* and the History of Athenian Comedy." In Harvey and Wilkins 2000: 247–58.
Siegmann, E. 1948. "Die neuen Aischylos-Bruchstücke." *Philologus* 97: 59–124.
Sifakis, G. M. 1967. *Studies in the History of Hellenistic Drama*. London.
Silk, M. S., ed. 1996. *Tragedy and the Tragic*. Oxford.
— . 2000. *Aristophanes and the Definition of Comedy*. Oxford.
— . 2014. "The Greek Dramatic Genres: Theoretical Perspectives." In E. Bakola, L. Prauscello, and M. Telò, eds., *Greek Comedy and the Discourse of Genres*, 15–39. Cambridge.
Silverman, K. 1983. *The Subject of Semiotics*. Oxford.
— . 1992. *Male Subjectivity at the Margins*. New York.
Simon, E. 1982. "Satyr-Plays on Vases in the Time of Aeschylus." In D. Kurtz and B. Sparkes, eds., *The Eye of Greece*, 123–48. Cambridge. Revised in Seidensticker 1989: 362–403.
Slater, N. W. 2005. "Nothing to Do with Satyrs? *Alcestis* and the Concept of Prosatyric Drama." In Harrison 2005: 83–101.
Slenders, W. 2005. "Λέξις ἐρωτική in Euripides' *Cyclops*." In Harrison 2005: 39–52.
Smethurst, M. J. 1989. *The Artistry of Aeschylus and Zeami*. Princeton.
Snell, B., ed. 1971. *Tragicorum Graecorum Fragmenta*, vol. 1. Göttingen.
Sommerstein, A. 2002. "Comic Elements in Tragic Language: The Case of Aeschylus' *Oresteia*." In Willi 2002: 151–68.
— , ed. 2003. *Shards from Kolonos: Studies in Sophoclean Fragments*. Bari.

Sorabella, J. 2007. "A Satyr for Midas: The Barberini Faun and Hellenistic Royal Patronage." *CA* 26: 219–48.
Stahl, H.-P. 1968. "Herodots Gyges-Tragödie." *Hermes* 96: 385–400.
Stallybrass, P., and A. White. 1986. *The Politics and Poetics of Transgression*. Ithaca.
Stanford, W. B. 1940. "Three-word Trimeters in Greek Tragedy." *CR* 54: 8–10.
Stefanis, I. E. 1988. Διονυσιακοί Τεχνίται. Heraclion.
Steffen V., ed. 1935. *Satyrographorum Graecorum Reliquiae*. Posen.
— . 1979. *De Aeschyli fabulis satyricis*. Posen.
Stehle, E. 1997. *Performance and Gender in Ancient Greece*. Princeton.
Stevens, P. T. 1945. "Colloquial Expressions in Aeschylus and Sophocles." *CR* 39: 95–105.
— . 1976. *Colloquial Expressions in Euripides*. Hermes Einzelschriften 38. Wiesbaden.
Stewart, A. F. 1997. *Art, Desire, and the Body in Ancient Greece*. Cambridge.
Storey, I. 2005. "But Comedy has Satyrs too." In Harrison 2005: 201–18.
Strauss, B. S. 1993. *Fathers and Sons in Athens*. Princeton.
Sutton, D. F. 1980. *The Greek Satyrplay*. Meisenheim.
— . 1984. "Aeschylus' *Proteus*." *Philologus* 128: 127–30.
— . 1987. "The Theatrical Families of Athens." *AJP* 108: 9–26.
Taplin, O. 1976. "*XOPOU* and the Structure of Post-Classical Tragedy." *LCM* 1: 47–50.
— . 1983. "Tragedy and Trugedy." *CQ* 33: 331–34.
— . 1986. "Fifth Century Tragedy and Comedy: A Synkrisis." *JHS* 106: 163–74.
— . 1992. *Comic Angels and Other Approaches to Greek Drama through Vase Paintings*. Oxford.
— . 1996. "Comedy and the Tragic." In Silk 1996: 188–202.
— . 2006. "Aeschylus' *Persai*: The Entry of Tragedy into the Celebratory Culture of the 470s?" In D. Cairns and V. Liapis, eds., *Dionysalexandros*, 1–10. Swansea.
— . 2007. *Pots and Plays*. Los Angeles.
Taplin, O., and R. Wyles, eds. 2010. *The Pronomos Vase and its Context*. Oxford.
Travis, R. M. 1996. *Allegory and the Tragic Chorus in Sophocles' Oedipus at Colonus*. New York.
— . 2000. "The Spectation of Gyges in P. Oxy. 2382 and Herodotus Book 1." *CA* 19: 330–59.
Trendall, A. D., and T. B .L. Webster. 1971. *Illustrations of Greek Drama*. London.
Turner, V. 1982. *From Ritual to Theatre*. New York.
Tyler, R., ed. 1992. *Japanese Nô Dramas*. Harmondsworth.
— . 1997. "The *Waki-Shite* Relationship in Nô." In Brandon 1997: 65–90.
Ussher, R. G. 1977. "The Other Aeschylus." *Phoenix* 31: 287–99.
— , ed. 1978. *Euripides Cyclops*. Rome.
van Zyl Smit, B. 1998. "The Story of Candaules, His Wife, and Gyges." *Groningen Colloquia on the Novel* 9: 205–28.
Vernant, J.-P., and P. Vidal-Naquet. 1981. *Myth and Tragedy in Ancient Greece*. Trans. J. Lloyd. Brighton.
Voelke, P. 2001. *Un théâtre de la marge: Aspects figuratifs et configurationnels du drame satyrique dans l'Athènes classique*. Bari.
— . 2003. "Drame satyrique et comédie: A propos de quelques fragments sophocléens." In Sommerstein 2003: 329–51.
Walden, J. W. H. 1894. "Stage-terms in Heliodorus' *Aithiopika*." *HSCP* 5: 1–43.

Walin, D. 2012. *Slaves, Sex, and Transgression in Greek Old Comedy*. PhD dissertation, UC Berkeley.
Wehrli, F. 1946. "Der erhabene und der schlichte Stil in der poetisch-rhetorischen Theorie der Antike." In O. Gigon et al., eds., *Phyllobolia für P. von der Mühll*, 9–34. Basel.
Werre-de Haas, M. 1961. *Aeschylus' Dictyulci: An Attempt at Reconstruction of a Satyric Drama* (diss. Leiden = Papyrologica Lugduno-Batava 10). Leiden.
West, M. L. 1982. *Greek Metre*. Oxford.
— . 1985. *The Hesiodic Catalogue of Women*. Oxford.
— . 1992. *Ancient Greek Music*. Oxford.
Whitman, C. H. 1951. *Sophocles: a Study of Heroic Humanism*. Cambridge, Mass.
— . 1974. *Euripides and the Full Circle of Myth*. Cambridge, Mass.
Wilamowitz, U. von. 1921. *Griechische Verskunst*. Berlin.
Willi, A., ed. 2002. *The Language of Greek Comedy*. Oxford.
Williams, L., ed. 1995. *Viewing Positions*. New Brunswick.
Williams, R. 1977. *Marxism and Literature*. Oxford.
Wilson, P. 1999. "The *aulos* in Athens." In Goldhill and Osborne 1999: 58–95.
— . 2003. "The Sound of Cultural Conflict: Kritias and the Culture of *Musike* in Athens." In Dougherty and Kurke 2003: 181–206.
— . 2010. "The Man and the Music (and the Choregos?)." In Taplin and Wyles 2010: 181–212.
Wilson, P. 2000. *The Athenian Institution of the Khoregia*. Cambridge.
Winkler, J. J. 1985. "The Ephebes' Song: *Tragôidia* and *Polis*." *Representations* 11: 26–62. (Repr., with abbreviations, in Winkler and Zeitlin 1990.)
Winkler, J. J., and F. Zeitlin, eds. 1990. *Nothing to Do with Dionysos?* Princeton.
Winnicott, D. W. 1971. *Playing and Reality*. London.
Winnington-Ingram, R. P. 1948. *Euripides and Dionysus*. Cambridge.
— . 1981. *Studies in Aeschylus*. Oxford.
— . 1985. "The Origins of Tragedy." *CHCL* 1. 258–63.
Wohl, V. J. 1998. *Intimate Commerce*. Austin.
— . 2002. *Love Among the Ruins: The Erotics of Democracy in Classical Athens*. Princeton.
Worman, N. 1997. "The Body as Argument: Helen in Four Greek Texts." *CA* 16: 151–203.
— . 2002. *The Cast of Character: Style in Greek Literature*. Austin.
Woronoff, M. 1990. "Theatrical Awareness as a Deliberate Technique in the *Aithiopika*." In J. Tatum and G. M. Vernazza, eds., *The Ancient Novel: Classical Paradigms and Modern Perspectives*, 33. Hanover.
Wright, E. 1998. *Psychoanalytic Criticism: A Reappraisal*, 2nd ed. New York.
Zagagi, N. 1999. "Comic Patterns in Sophocles' *Ichneutae*." In J. Griffin, ed., *Sophocles Revisited*, 177–218. Oxford.
Zanker, P. 1995. *The Masks of Socrates: The Image of the Intellectual in Antiquity*. Berkeley.
Zardini Lana, G. 1991. *La Tragicommedia*. Fasano di Puglia.
Zeitlin, F. I. 1995. *Playing the Other*. Chicago.
Zimmermann, B. 1984. *Untersuchungen zur Form und dramatischen Technik der Aristophanischen Komödien*, vol. 1. Königstein.
— . 1986. "Überlegungen zum sogenannten Pratinas-fragment." *MH* 43: 145–54.

INDEX OF AUTHORS AND WORKS DISCUSSED

Achaeus, 15, 159, 160
  F4 (*Athla*), 35n.65
  Omphale, 160n.49
Aeschylus
  Amymone, 54–55, 107n.98
  Dictyulci (*Net-Fishers*), 19n.14, 31n.52, 34n.61, 40, 44n.103, 79–81, 85, 93n.73, 103–108, 110, 118n.38, 160
  Isthmiastai or *Theoroi*, 31n.52, 80, 82–85, 160
  Prometheus Pyrkaeus, 19n.14, 80, 85, 160
  Proteus, 57–74, 134n.21
  F 281 (*Dikê*-drama), 80, 83, 110
  F 301, 70
  Agam., 62–63, 66–69, 73n.187, 112–115
  Cho., 112–115, 117
  Eum., 69, 72–73, 112–115
  Oresteia, 57–74, 131
  Pers., 112–115, 134n.20, 155
  Supp., 84n.44, 112–115, 131n.9
  Th., 84n.44, 112–115
  Myrmidons, 50n.117, 121n.45
  [Aesch.], *Prom.*, 112–115
Agathon, *Antheus*, 153–54
Anacreon, 43nn.96 and 100, 84, 85, 124
Animal House, 96n.80
Aphthonius, 85n.48, 86n.50
Arion, 151
Aristias, 15, 56n.135, 151, 154n.27, 159, 161
Aristophanes
  Acharnians, 19n.14, 112–116, 125n.54
  Clouds, 112–115
  Frogs, 18n.12, 19n.14, 41n.87, 78n.17, 112n.12, 117n.36, 143, 157n.38
  Thesm., 18n.12, 50n.116, 97n.81
  Wasps, 19n.14, 43n.96
Aristotle
  Poetics, 2–3, 16n.6, 23n.27, 26n.38, 56n.134, 77, 78n.16, 88n.60, 90, 112n.12, 146–48, 150, 153, 154, 168
  Rhetoric, 36n.36, 78n.16
Athenaeus, *Deipn.*, 57, 87n.56, 121n.45, 154n.27

Bacchylides, 152

Carcinus, 151

Chaeremon
  Achilles, 154n.27
  Centaur, 154
Chariton, *Chaereas and Callirrhoe*, 165–66
Christus Patiens and *Gaudens*, 157
Cicero, *De opt. gen. orat.*, 146n.2
Clement, 155n.35
Cratinus, *Dionysalexandros*, 12, 17n.8, 84
Critias(?)
  Peirithous, 161
  Sisyphus, 23n.29, 80, 110, 160–61

Demetrius, *On Style*, 16n.6, 110n.5, 111n.7, 112n.12, 124n.50, 134–35, 146n.2, 148n.8, 162–63, 166
Dissoi Logoi, 70n.176

Ennius, *Ambracia*, 155
Epicharmus, 17n.8, 150, 160n.47
Epigenes, 152
Euripides
  Cyclops, 18n.12, 19n.14, 22n.23, 23n.28, 25n.36, 26–27, 31–33, 36n.68, 39n.82, 40, 41n.87, 43, 77n.13, 80, 81, 82–86, 91, 93n.73, 96–97, 107n.98, 110, 112–115, 133n.19, 144, 160
  Peirithous (?), 161
  Sisyphus (?), 160–61
  Alcestis, 2, 15n.5, 22n.23, 25n.34, 51n.122, 55, 76n.8, 81n.23, 131, 143, 161
  Helen, 15n5, 50n.117, 55, 59–60, 64n.160, 66n.167
  IT, 72–74, 120n.43, 165n.67
  Orestes, 15n.5, 59, 109
  Andromeda, 50n.117, 55, 125
  Archelaus, 154
Eusebius, 155n.35
Ezekiel, *Exagôgê* 155–56

Gay, John (*see* Handel, George Frideric)
Gorgias
  Defense of Helen, 64n.160, 70, 135
  (on deception) 70
Gyges-drama, 153n.24, 155–56

Handel, George Frideric, *Acis and Galatea*, 168
Hecataeus, 59n.146
Heliodorus, *Aethiopica*, 167
Herodotus, 58–60, 64n.160, 67n.171, 117n.36, 118, 152, 155–56
Hesiod, 18n.10, 59, 64
   Theogony, 142n.44
   Works and Days, 18n.13, 36n.66
   Catalog of Women (Ehoiai) 18nn.10, 13, 59–62, 68n.173
Hesychius, 42n.95
Homer
   Iliad, 57n.139, 68n.172
   Odyssey, 57–58, 61n.152, 109, 150, 152
   Cyclic Epics, 68n.173, 71–72
   Margites, 150
   Homeric Hymn to Hermes, 18n.10, 41n.89, 82, 117, 160
Horace, *Ars Poetica*, 16n.6, 78n.16, 110n.5, 161–62

Ion of Chios, 151, 159, 160
   Omphale, 160n.49
   Phoenix, 160n.49

Lagaan, 168
Longus, *Daphnis and Chloe*, 17, 43n.100, 44n.104, 82, 109, 124, 135, 152, 166

Naevius, *Clastidium*, 155

"Old Oligarch" (ps.-Xenophon), 97n.81
Ovid, *Metamorphoses*, 107n.99

Pacuvius, *Paulus*, 155
Philoxenus, *Cyclops* or *Galatea*, 154
Phrynichus
   Phoenissae, 134n.20, 151, 153, 155
   Capture of Miletus, 153
Pickering (Pikeryng), John, *Horestes*, 167–68
Plato
   Laws, 23n.28, 35n.65, 75, 87, 94, 164
   Phaedrus, 60, 64
   Republic, 23n.27, 75, 94, 124–25
   Symposium, 21n.21, 77n.10, 133, 143, 147
Plutarch
   Quaest. Conv., 158
   Symp., 20n.18
Porky, 96n.80
Pratinas, 1, 15, 20n.18, 56n.135, 151, 158n.43, 159, 161
   F 3, 42n.94, 84n.42, 86, 153, 157

Racine, Jean, 167

Sappho, 124n.50, 135, 162–63, 166
Semonides, 43n.96
[Seneca], *Octavia*, 155
Shakespeare, William, *Hamlet*, 29n.47, 33n.60
Shane, 52n.123
Sophocles
   Achilleôs Erastai (Lovers of Achilles), 120–22
   Colchides, 120n.45, 123
   Dionysiscus, 117–118
   Helenês Gamos (Marriage of Helen), 19n.14, 51n.120, 114n.22, 118, 127
   Ichneutai (Trackers), 4, 5, 19n.14, 22n.23, 31n.52, 40, 43nn.95 and 99, 44, 45n.105, 77n.13, 80, 81, 82–84, 86, 93n.73, 110, 113–114, 116–118, 160
   Inachus, 84n.42, 86, 160
   Krisis, 119
   Manteis, 119
   Niobe, 121n.45, 123
   Oeneus, 22n.23, 118–119, 123
   Oenomaus, 122, 123
   Salmoneus, 119, 121n.46
   Tyro, 119
   F 769, 119
   F 772, 43n.97
   F 841, 121n.45, 123
   F 941, 123, 125n.53
   F 1130, 116, 119, 123
   Adesp. F 656, 119
   Ajax, 112–115
   Antigone, 112–115
   Electra, 112–115
   OC, 112–115
   OT, 112–115
   Phil., 112–115
   Trach., 112–115
Sositheus, *Daphnis or Lityerses*, 161, 166–67
Stesichorus, 18n.10, 152, 167n.72
   Oresteia, 64–74, 134n.20
   Palinode, 59–74
Suetonius, *Caligula*, 158n.41

The Man Who Shot Liberty Valance, 52n.123
Theocritus, *Idylls*, 82, 124, 135n.24, 166, 167
Theodectes, *Mausolus*, 154–55
Thespis, 151–53
Thucydides, 78n.17, 89n.62, 95n.77

Vergil, *Eclogue* 6, 21n.21, 40n.86
Vitruvius, *De Arch.*, 163

GENERAL INDEX

Actors, 15, 17, 25, 46–47, 51, 54, 102, 108, 131–34, 138, 139–44, 152–59, 165, 166–68
  in satyr drama, 25, 32, 39–40, 51, 54, 77, 86–87, 92–93, 102, 108, 110, 131, 132–34, 136, 138, 139–44
  comic, 77, 87
  tragic, 25, 34–35, 51, 54, 76, 152–59
  Japanese, 17, 29, 134
  (*see also* Costume)
Afterlife, 130, 144
Amazons, 88
Amymone, 19, 24, 27, 36, 51, 54–55, 107, 160
  (*see also* Poseidon, *and see* Figs. 8a and 8b)
Anaphora, 116, 117, 119, 123–24
Animals
  satyrs as wild animals, 10, 14, 18, 23, 24, 34, 40, 42–45, 48, 50, 81–82, 86–87, 93, 103, 110, 111, 117, 144
  animals and comedy, 18–19, 39
  animals in Dionysian contexts, 12, 22–23, 81–82, 106, 137
  (*see also* Goat, Horses, Pastoral)
Apollo, 19, 24, 26, 27, 36, 64, 81
Aphrodite, 37, 41, 51, 67, 88, 107, 119, 142, 146–69 *passim*
Apulia, *see* Italy
Ariadne, 12, 37, 51, 135–38, 141–42, 164
auloi (pipes), *aulêtês* (piper), 12, 32, 38–39, 42–43, 86, 97, 129, 133, 135–38, 140–41, 144, 152, 154, 157, 159 (*see also* Pronomos)

Babies, baby, 22, 24, 26, 33, 40, 41, 44, 86, 104–108, 111, 117–118, 164
Blackface minstrelsy, 11, 37, 48, 97–101, 107
  (*and see* Figs. 11 and 12)
Bollywood, 168

Centaurs, 18, 19, 36, 49, 55, 88, 154
Choregic monuments, 130, 133
chorêgos, 57, 131, 136, 140
Chorus
  and the origins of Athenian drama, 1–2, 14–15, 19, 150–53
  audience's relation to, 6–10, 14–16, 22–57, 69, 76–79, 87–88, 91–96, 102–103, 108, 118, 137–38, 141–43, 165
  of satyrs, *passim*
  characteristics of lyric utterances of satyr chorus, 31, 33, 70, 84–87, 96, 144
  number of choreuts, 15, 32, 69, 132, 139, 143, 144, 157 (*and see* Fig. 5; *see also* Papposilenos)
  (*see also* Costume, Dance, Nôh drama, Pronomos Vase, Tragicomedy)
City Dionysia, 2, 6, 14, 15, 20–21, 23, 35, 38, 133, 147, 161
Class and status distinctions, 7–9, 11, 21, 24, 55, 75, 88–91, 96, 102, 139–40 (*see also* Heroes)
Colometry of lyric meters, 28, 31, 78, 80, 83–86, 114, 152, 153, 159, 162, 166–67
Comedy
  and satyr play, differences between, 6, 11–12, 15–25, 36, 39–51 *passim*, 77–78, 81–88, 110–117, 121, 125, 132–34, 146–69 *passim* (*and see* Figs. 2 and 3)
  Sicilian, 12, 129–30, 150, 160
  (*see also* Actors, Costume, Obscenity, Phlyax plays)
Compound adjectives, *see* Diction
Costume, 17–18, 38–43, 47–48, 76–81, 86–87, 110, 132, 139–43, 165–66
  of satyr-choreuts, 32, 38–43, 86–87, 110, 165 (*and see* Figs. 4–9)
  of actors and Papposilenus, 40–41, 49, 81, 86, 132, 136, 143–44, 164 (*and see* Fig. 5)
  of satyr play vs. comedy, 41–42, 77, 109, 132, 166 (*and see* Figs. 2, 3)
  of Nôh and Kyôgen drama, 17
Cyllene (Kyllene), 19, 24, 42, 81

Danae, 33, 81, 104, 107, 108
Dance, 10, 17, 19, 29, 31–32, 35, 38, 42–45, 54, 55, 86–87, 93, 96–100, 103, 111, 119, 124, 135, 136–42, 144, 152, 157–59, 164–65, 166, 168
  pyrrhichê, 87
  sikinnis, 42–43, 52, 87, 141
Daphnis, 17, 43, 44, 82, 109, 124, 135, 152, 161, 166–67
Deer (*or* fawn), 43, 45, 61–63, 87, 106

185

186 GENERAL INDEX

Demeter, 72, 145
Diction
  frequency of compound adjectives as mark of "higher" style, 82, 112–114
  obscene vs. informal/indecent language, 81–82, 110, 117–119, 166
  (see also Sympotic language)
Didascalic inscriptions, 2, 55, 131, 153, 154
Dionysus, *passim*
  Dionysiac ritual, 1, 3–7, 15–16, 19–21, 34–35, 52–53, 109, 134, 137, 145
  (see also City Dionysia)
Dithyramb, 3, 12, 20, 35, 76, 112, 134, 150, 151–54
Drama, changing meanings of term, 3, 11–12, 147–58, 165–69

Eido (and Eidothea), 58–60, 63, 73
eidôlon, see Phantom
Ephebes, 35, 87
Eros, 50–52, 116–25, 133, 136, 142, 158, 166, 168
  homoerotic relations, 40, 120–21
  Sophocles' reputation as lover, 124–25
  (see also Aphrodite, Himeros, Romance, Sex)
Exclamations and interjections, 31, 45, 81, 96, 111–112, 117

Film criticism, 8–9, 52, 75, 92–93, 98–99, 168
  (see also Psychoanalytic criticism)
François Vase, 41–42, 46 (*and see* Fig. 1)
Funerary ritual and monuments, 130, 143, 145, 163

Goat (*tragos*), 20, 35, 43, 44, 45, 62
Gods (in satyr drama), 19, 21–22, 26, 36, 48–49, 75, 81, 87–96, 121, 125, 144

Helen, 15, 19, 39, 50, 55, 57–60, 63–74, 107, 125, 135 (*and see* Fig. 3; *see also* Phantom)
Hephaestus, 19, 37, 40, 41, 46, 49, 51 (*and see* Fig. 1)
Heracles, as hero of romance/adventure stories and/or satyr play, 17, 21, 22, 24, 26, 32, 42, 49, 50, 51, 54, 62, 86, 122, 139–43, 160, 161, 166 (*and see* Fig. 5)
Hermes, 18–19, 26, 27, 33, 60, 82, 86, 117, 160
Heroes (= elite characters in drama), 8–10, 16–17, 19, 21–29 *passim*, 87–96, 102, 107–108, 116, 125, 134, 135, 137–39, 141, 143–44, 150, 162, 168
hilarotragedia, see Tragicomedy
Himeros, 12, 37, 43, 136, 141, 142, 145, 164
Horses (and colts), 10, 20, 35, 37–43, 86–87, 101

Iphigenia, 50, 59–66, 73–74, 120 (*and see* Figs. 9, 10)
Italy, South (Apulia, Tarentum, Paestum, Ruvo, etc.), 12, 87, 129, 130, 143, 163

kisses, 119
Klein, Melanie, 6, 48–49, 92, 94, 97–100
kottabos-game, 119 (*see also* Symposium)
kômos, 19, 20, 36, 46, 51, 93, 94, 96, 103 (*and see* Fig. 1)
Kyogen drama, 17, 134

Lott, Eric, 11, 28, 37, 48–49, 52
Love, *see* Aphrodite, Eros, Himeros, Romance
Lyre, 22, 33, 38, 44, 86, 135, 136, 140–41, 144, 154 (*and see* Fig. 5)
  invention of, 22, 33, 44

Maenads (or Bacchants), 12, 36, 37, 39, 45, 51, 136–38 (*see also* Nymphs; *and see* Fig. 5)
Marriage, weddings, courtship (in satyr dramas), 11, 20, 22–23, 44, 51, 55, 91–92, 102, 107–109, 109–111, 116–25, 135–36, 139–41, 156, 160, 161, 163 (*see also* Romance)
Masks, *see* Costume
Masturbation, 36, 45, 111, 117
Meidias Painter, 142
Meter
  iambic trimeter, resolutions in, 23–24, 70, 83, 110, 112, 132
  Porson's Bridge, 83, 112
  three-word trimeters, 114–15
  trochaic tetrameter, 82
  lyric meters, 28, 31, 53, 80, 83–84
  use of astrophic lyrics, 84–85
  anapaests, 83–86
  proceleusmatics, 86
"Middle style", 12, 111, 114, 116, 123–24, 135, 146–50, 162–63 (*see also* Index of Authors and Works Discussed *s.vv.* Demetrius, Sappho)
Music, *see auloi*, Dance

Nôh drama, 17, 29, 32, 134
Novels (Greek), theatrical elements in, 17–18, 120, 122–24, 150–51, 156–57, 161, 165–68
  (*see also* Romance)
Nymphs, 12, 24, 32, 36, 37, 45, 51, 91, 120, 135, 162, 164, 166 (*see also* Maenads)

Obscenity, 20, 42, 82–83, 109, 111–112, 117–118, 166 (*see also* Diction, Sexual language

and behavior)
Orpheus, incantation of, 22, 33, 144
outidanoi ("nobodies"), satyrs considered as, 18, 30

pais, paides
  satyrs as children and/or slaves, 10, 18, 22, 31, 34–35, 45–46, 51, 86–88, 91–93, 96, 101–102, 135
  (*see also* Babies, Play, Silver Age)
Panther, 136–37 (*see also* Animals; *and see* Figs. 4, 5)
Papposilenos (Silenus), 21, 26, 32, 40, 42, 45, 49, 77–78, 81, 104–108, 110, 132, 137, 139, 142–44, 161–62, 165
Parallel universe, satyr play as, 88, 91–95, 133–36, 149
Pastoral, 11–12, 17, 22, 82, 111, 135, 152, 154, 159, 166, 168 (*see also* Daphnis, Polyphemus)
Penis, *see* Phallus
perizôma, see Costume
Perseus, 17, 26, 33, 50, 104–107, 118
phalakron, 105, 108, 118 (*see also* Phallus)
Phallus, 16, 18, 19, 38–40, 51, 86–87, 92, 105, 116, 118 (*see also* Costume)
Phantom (*eidôlon*), 57, 59–72
Phleious (Phlius), 15, 20, 151, 158, 159
Phlyax plays, 39, 164, 166 (*and see* Fig. 3)
Play, playing (*paizô, paidiá, paignion*), 15, 36, 41, 46, 49, 76–80, 107, 118, 119, 134, 135, 137, 142, 164 (*see also* Dance)
Polyphemus, 19, 22, 23, 26, 27, 32, 33, 36, 39, 40, 42, 44, 82, 85–86, 144, 147 (*see also* Index of Authors and Works Discussed s.v. Eur. *Cyclops*)
Porson's Bridge, *see* Meter
Poseidon, 21, 24, 26, 42, 51, 54–55, 81, 107 (*and see* Figs. 8a and 8b)
posthê, 108, 118 (*see also* Phallus, Sexual language and behavior)
Pronomos, 12, 42, 86, 129, 130, 137, 140–41, 145, 164 (*and see* Fig. 5)
Pronomos Vase 12, 32, 35, 37, 38, 42, 43, 77, 81, 86, 110, 129–45, 163–64 (*and see* Fig. 5)
Psychoanalytic interpretation of drama, 1, 6–7, 11, 25, 45–49, 75, 79, 91–95, 131
Psycho-social effects of drama, 1, 6, 7, 49, 131 and *passim*
pyrrhichê, see Dance

Rape, 36, 41, 103, 107

Romance
  definition of vs. comedy and tragedy, or tragicomedy, 17–18, 55–56, 82, 91, 109–111, 135, 150, 164, 167
  erotic/"romantic" themes and language, 11–12, 17, 21–24, 55–56, 82, 91, 102, 116–25, 154–63, 166–68 (*see also* Aphrodite, Eros, Marriage)
Ruvo, *see* Italy

Scatological language, *see* Obscenity
Sciron (Skeiron), 40, 42
Self-presentation, 45–47, 75, 78–80, 88–85, 103–104, 133
Sentence-length, 115–116
Sex, sexual language and behavior, 2, 6, 11, 16, 20, 32, 36–39, 41–47, 49–52, 54, 68, 82, 92, 94, 96–108 *passim*, 109, 111, 116–25 *passim*, 156 (*see also* Aphrodite, Eros, Obscenity, Romance)
Shakespeare, William, 21, 33, 37
  minor characters in, 29, 33
  romance elements in, 37, 165
  (*see also* Index of Authors and Works Discussed *s.v.*)
Sicily (including Acragas, Syracuse), 130, 138, 142, 148, 149, 158, 159, 164, 165 (*see also* Index of Authors and Works Discussed *s.vv.* Epicharmus, Stesichorus)
Sicyon, 151, 152, 158, 159
sikinnis (satyr dance), *see* Dance
Silen(e)s, 5, 20–21, 32, 37–39, 41–42, 101, 132
Silenus, *see* Papposilenos
Silver Age (Hesiodic), 18, 36
Slaves, slavery, *see pais, paides*
Stallybrass, P., and A. White, 9–11, 37, 47–49
Style, *see* Diction, Meter, "Middle style"
Symposium
  sympotic language, 22, 32, 116–20, 160
  sympotic behavior, 26, 32, 38, 45–46, 52, 85, 96, 101, 116–20, 130

Tarentum, *see* Italy
Tetralogy, 2, 11, 15, 16, 54, 56, 57, 69, 103, 131, 134, 135, 142, 159
Three-word trimeters, *see* Meter
Tragedy, Greek, *passim*
  trends in modern criticism of, 5–9
  split/shifting dynamics of audience responses to, *see* Chorus, Class distinctions, Heroes
  function(s) of chorus in, *see* Chorus

relationship to satyr play, *passim*
Tragicomedy
  ancient and Renaissance theories of, 142, 149, 164, 167
  modern definitions of, 2, 146, 148–49, 161, 165 (*see also* Romance)
tragoudi, 150–51

Wine, 19, 26, 36, 41, 45–46, 94, 96–97, 105, 116, 137, 141 (*see also* Symposium)
Winnicott, D. W., 6, 92

www.ingramcontent.com/pod-product-compliance
Lightning Source LLC
Chambersburg PA
CBHW021757230426
43669CB00006B/107